About this Book

Living Silence is particularly valuable for its study of the psycho-logical effects of military rule on the people of Burma. The real struggle in Burma is the struggle between the desire to opt for the easy option of submitting to the demands of the powers that be and the commitment that leads to the hard road of resisting the threats and blandishments of a ruthless regime. By exploring the impact of military rule on the lives of ordinary people against a broad historical and social backdrop, Christina Fink makes an important contribution towards an understanding of the root causes of the problems and choices that the people of Burma are facing today.

Aung San Suu Kyi

The Burmese students have found their Boswell. Christina Fink has carefully recorded their statements and thoughts. Now, no one can dismiss the tragedy of Burma as the fiction of outsiders.

Professor Josef Silverstein, Rutgers University

Christina Fink's *Living Silence* is a meticulous study of the surreal horror imposed upon the people of Burma by its illegitimate rulers. Read this book and never forget them.

John Pilger, author

About the Author

Dr Christina Fink trained as an anthropologist at the University of California, Berkeley. She served as the editor of the *BurmaNet News* from mid-1995 to 1997. During the writing of *Living Silence* she was supported by an Open Society Institute fellowship. This is her first book.

. . . .

Living Silence: Burma under Military Rule

Christina Fink
. . . .

White Lotus
BANGKOK

University Press Ltd
DHAKA

Zed Books
LONDON • NEW YORK

Living Silence: Burma under Military Rule was first published by Zed Books Ltd, 7 Cynthia Street, London N1 9JF, UK and Room 400, 175 Fifth Avenue, New York NY 10010, USA in 2001.

Published in Thailand by White Lotus Company Ltd, GPO Box 1141, Bangkok, 100501.

Published in Bangladesh by the University Press Ltd, Red Crescent Building, 114 Motijheel C/A, PO Box 2611, Dhaka 1000.

Distributed in the USA exclusively by Palgrave, a division of St Martin's Press, LLC, 175 Fifth Avenue, New York, NY 10010, USA.

This book was supported by a grant from the Open Society Institute's Individual Project Fellowships Program.

Photographs are reproduced by courtesy of Nic Dunlop.

Second impression, 2001

Cover designed by Andrew Corbett
Typeset in Monotype Dante by Ewan Smith, London
Printed and bound by Biddles Ltd, *www.biddles.co.uk*

A catalogue record for this book is available from the British Library.

Library of Congress Cataloging-in-Publication Data: available

ISBN 1 85649 925 1 cased
ISBN 1 85649 926 X limp

In Thailand ISBN 974 7534 68 1

Contents

List of Illustrations /vii   Acknowledgements /viii
Author's Note /ix   Glossary /x   Acronyms /xii
Maps /xiv, xv

Introduction   1

1 *Historical Legacies*   13

Pre-colonial principalities and kingdoms /14   British rule /17
Independence /21   Beginnings of militarization /26

2 *The Ne Win Years, 1962–88*   31

The Revolutionary Council, 1962–74 /31   The BSPP era,
1974–88 /36   Resistance in the cities /42
Outside the 'legal fold' /46

3 *Breaking the Silence, 1988–90*   50

Six weeks of nationwide protests /55   Civil society re-emerges /58
The need for leadership /60   The election campaign /63
Post-election struggles /69

4 *Military Rule Continues*   77

Military ascendancy /78   The National Convention /82
The release of Daw Aung San Suu Kyi /86   Student
demonstrations, 1996 /91   The regime changes its name /94

5 *Families: Fostering Conformity*   100

Collective amnesia /101   Activist families /105   Shifting
values /112   Split families /114   Ethnic minority families /117

6 *Communities: Going with the Flow*   120

Obedience is a habit /121   A nation of prisoners /123
A climate of fear /127   The threat of independent groups /133
Corruption /135

7   *The Military: A Life Sentence*   143

Reasons for joining /145   The danger of expressing an
opinion /148   1988–90 /151   Brutality and desertion /154
The rise of the military intelligence /156

8   *Prison: 'Life University'*   159

Torture and maintaining morale /162   Life university /163
Feelings of guilt /166   Female prisoners /167   Covert
assistance /169   Release /172

9   *Education: Floating Books and Bathroom Tracts*   174

The curriculum /175   Buying good grades /178
University life /179   Study groups and floating books /183
Teashops and bathrooms /186   Radio and other educational
sources /190

10   *The Artistic Community: In the Dark, Every Cat is Black*   197

Censorship /197   The power of music /202
'Mad' art /207   Public talks /209

11   *Religion and Magic: Disappearing Jewels and Poltergeists*   213

Buddhism and politics /213   The disappearing jewels /218
Monks and the NLD /220   Repression of Christians /222
Exploitation of Muslims /225   Fortune-telling and sympathetic
magic /227   Spirits of the dead /230

12   *The Internationalization of Burma's Politics*   232

Foreign governments' relations with Burma /232
Corporations, the media and international campaigns /242
Political and humanitarian assistance /245

13   *Conclusion: A Different Burma*   250

Where is Burma's Ramos? /251   The restoration of civil
society /253

Notes   257
Bibliography   270
Index   276

Illustrations

Pages 9–12

1. Patrolling in front of the Secretariat Building, Rangoon
2. Farmers transplanting rice, near Mandalay
3. A Tatmadaw soldier overseeing forced labour, Kachin State
4. Even monasteries are not free of soldiers, Kachin State

Pages 73–6

5. Daw Aung San Suu Kyi speaking from her gate, surrounded by bodyguards
6. Crowd attending one of Daw Aung San Suu Kyi's weekend talks
7. Daw Aung San Suu Kyi holding a list of questions to be answered
8. Intelligence agent and students, Mandalay University (the agent told the photographer to leave the campus immediately)

Pages 139–142

9. Praying at a pagoda, Mandalay
10. Tatmadaw soldiers being trucked through Rangoon
11. Eking out a living in rural Burma, near Mandalay Hill
12. A Tatmadaw signboard, central Mandalay

Pages 193–96

13. A Rangoon teashop, a favourite hangout for students and intelligence agents
14. Remnants of free expression: secondhand books on sale, Rangoon
15. Remembering the good old days, Mandalay
16. Karen villagers fleeing a Tatmadaw offensive and seeking refuge in Thailand, 1997

Acknowledgements

§ First and foremost, I would like to thank those who shared their stories with me. I know that for some it was a painful experience, bringing up feelings of suffering and loss. For others it was risky, because to speak against the government is a crime in Burma. Unfortunately I was not able to include everyone's stories here, but each and every one helped me to understand Burma better. I would also like to express my gratitude to all who helped to arrange interviews for me, to those who interpreted and translated interviews, often at short notice and late hours, and to those who have answered so many questions for me over the past several years. Although I would like to name everyone here, in the interests of their safety, I think it best not to.

I am grateful to Nic Dunlop for working with me to create the photo essay, to Ko Sitt Nyein Aye for allowing me to use the title of one of his articles, 'In the Dark, Every Cat is Black' as a chapter title, and to Ko Maing Kyaw Khin for agreeing to let me use one of his cartoons. Also to Ko Mun Awng for his song of defiance, and to the former political prisoner who shared his song of sadness with me. Thanks to Darin Jensen for his assistance in making the maps and to Ko Zaw Oo and U Aung Saw Oo for their help reconstructing a list of student protests and school closures from 1962 to 1999.

The book has benefited greatly from the comments and suggestions made by several people who read earlier drafts; most especially, Hadley Arnold, Nancy Chen, MZ, Josef Silverstein, Martin Smith and WM, as well as CT, Mathea Falco, KK and UTZ. Needless to say, any mistakes are my responsibility alone.

I am deeply grateful to the Open Society Institute for providing me with a fellowship to research and write this book. Robert Molteno, my editor at Zed Books, was also wonderfully supportive. And Chris Beyrer and Edith Mirante gave me much helpful advice throughout the writing process.

I am indebted to Maureen Aung-Thwin, who first stimulated my interest in Burma with her infectious enthusiasm. And I will never forget the Burmese residents of the two houses where I was based while conducting much of my research. Their generosity, good humour and fantastic cooking deepened an already great love for Burma.

Author's Note

Burmese Prefixes

In Burma it is polite to put a prefix in front of the name of the person to whom one is talking. The speaker chooses the prefix according to the age of the other person, relative to one's own age. Thus if a woman's name were Mee Mee, and she were about forty years old, a girl would call her 'Daw Mee Mee', but someone in his or her thirties would call that same woman 'Ma Mee Mee'.

Daw – for aunts, older women
U – for uncles, older men
Ma – for older sisters, women slightly older than oneself
Ko – for older brothers, men slightly older than oneself
Nyi ma – for younger sisters, girls
Maung – for younger brothers, boys

There are also specialized terms for military officers, teachers, doctors and abbots which are put in front of individuals' respective names.

A Note on Pronunciation

'ky' is pronounced 'ch', thus 'kyi' is pronounced 'chee'.
'gy' is pronounced 'j', thus 'gyi' is pronounced 'jee'.

Glossary

ah nah day	a feeling of obligation to others that makes one act in a restrained way
awza	influence, the ability to command others
Bogyoke	General
Coco Island	a penal colony where political prisoners were sent under the Ne Win regime
Dobama Asiayone	'We Burmans' association, emerged in the colonial period
Four Cuts	military strategy of cutting enemy access to food, money, recruits and intelligence
gahta	a magical incantation
haw byo bwe	a public lecture
jinglee	a sharpened bicycle or umbrella spoke used as a weapon
kamauk	a wide-brimmed farmer's hat, used by the NLD as its symbol
kaung ma	derogatory term for a woman akin to 'bitch'
kyat	Burmese currency
Lanzin Youth	the youth wing of the Burma Socialist Programme Party
longyi	a sarong, or piece of cloth sewn into a tube, worn by women and men
lu ye gyun	award for outstanding students at high school and university level
nat	a spirit in nature or of a dead person
pinni	a traditional cotton jacket
Pyu Saw Hti	a paramilitary force named after a legendary hero
sangha	the Buddhist monkhood
sawbwa	the title for hereditary Shan princes
tat	militia
Tatmadaw	the Burmese government's armed forces
thakin	master
thanaka	a yellowish facial powder made of ground sandalwood
thangyat	chorus songs mocking authorities, sung at Burmese new year
thingyan	Burmese new year, which takes place in mid-April

Thirty Comrades	thirty young men who went to Japan for military training before World War II
yadaya chae	cheating fate by the use of magic to ward off undesirable occurrences
Zaw Gyi	a legendary wizard who lives in the forest

Acronyms

ABFSU	All Burma Federation of Students' Unions
ABSDF	All Burma Students' Democratic Front
AFPFL	Anti-Fascist People's Freedom League
ASEAN	Association of South East Asian Nations
BBC	British Broadcasting Corporation
BSPP	Burma Socialist Programme Party
CNF	Chin National Front
CNLD	Chin National League for Democracy
CPB	Communist Party of Burma
CRPP	Committee Representing the People's Parliament
DDSI	Directorate of the Defence Services Intelligence
DKBA	Democratic Karen Buddhist Army
DPNS	Democratic Party for a New Society
DVB	Democratic Voice of Burma
ICRC	International Committee of the Red Cross
KIO	Kachin Independence Organization (armed wing: Kachin Independence Army)
KMT	Kuomintang (anti-communist Chinese force)
KNPLF	Karenni State Nationalities People's Liberation Front
KNPP	Karenni National Progressive Party
KNU	Karen National Union (armed wing: Karen National Liberation Army)
MI	military intelligence
MMCWA	Myanmar Maternal and Child Welfare Association
MWEA	Myanmar Women's Entrepreneurial Association
NCGUB	National Coalition Government of the Union of Burma
NCUB	National Council of the Union of Burma
NGO	non-governmental organization
NLD	National League for Democracy
NMSP	New Mon State Party (armed wing: Mon National Liberation Army)
NUP	National Unity Party

PVO	People's Volunteer Organization
RFA	Radio Free Asia
RIT	Rangoon Institute of Technology
SLORC	State Law and Order Restoration Council
SNLD	Shan Nationalities League for Democracy
SNPLO	Shan State Nationalities People's Liberation Organization
SPDC	State Peace and Development Council
SSA	Shan State Army
UNDP	United Nations Development Programme
UNICEF	United Nations International Children's Emergency Fund
UNLD	United Nationalities League for Democracy
USDA	Union Solidarity and Development Association
UWSA	United Wa State Army
VOA	Voice of America

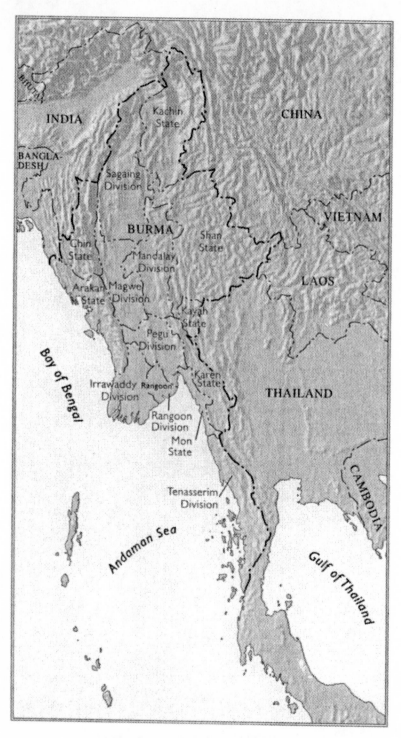

Map of Burma's States and Divisions

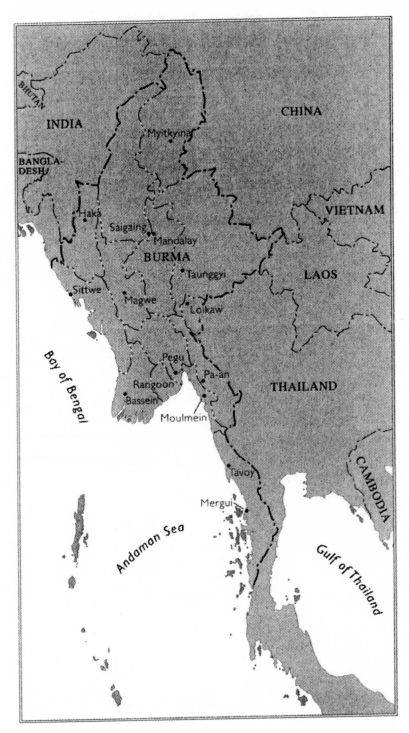

Map of cities and towns in Burma

To Friends in Burma

Introduction

§ Burma is a surprising country. Boasting emerald-green rice fields, a multi-tude of tropical flowers and fruits, and brilliantly painted temples and shops, it is awash with colour. Most Burmese, men and women, continue to wear *longyis* (sarongs) decorated in striking patterns, and children run around with sweet-smelling sandalwood paste smeared on their faces. A carefree cheer-fulness seems to characterize the people, but if you mention 'democracy' or Daw Aung San Suu Kyi, people freeze.[1]

The majority of the country's 50 million inhabitants are farmers. In the rural areas, oxcarts are still the primary mode of transportation, and television sets remain a luxury. Rangoon, the capital, is dominated by the shimmering golden Shwedagon Pagoda, although new high-rise hotels and office buildings have begun to clutter the view. The capital's markets and teashops bustle with activity, but the universities are often quiet. They are shut down for months or years at a time whenever student protests occur.

Burma has been under military rule since 1962. In 1988, pro-democracy demonstrations broke out nationwide, shattering the silence that had char-acterized political life for so many years. Students, professionals, civil servants and even some soldiers took to the streets to celebrate their new-found freedom. But after six weeks, the military was able to re-establish control, in part by promising multi-party elections for a new government. In 1990, the National League for Democracy, led by Daw Aung San Suu Kyi (pronounced chee), won a landslide victory, and change seemed imminent. But the regime refused to transfer power and instead began arresting some of those who had been elected. Daw Aung San Suu Kyi herself had been put under house arrest in 1989.

Twice military rule had been on the verge of ending, but both times the military managed to reassert control. The Burmese people were exhausted and the international community appeared largely uninterested. Overcome with frustration, two Burmese students decided to take drastic measures. One of the two, Soe Myint, recalls: 'There was nothing in the media about Burma. We needed to do something. I found hijacking the best way to get inter-national attention.'

Innocent-faced, with an irrepressible grin, he hardly looked the part. He had been a final-year International Relations student in 1988, and he hoped to enter the Foreign Service and eventually become a military attaché. But when the demonstrations broke out, he joined in and began working as a reporter for a hastily-formed student magazine. When the military retook power on 18 September 1988, he was arrested with his camera and hauled around the capital in a military van for the day while soldiers periodically jumped out to fire at demonstrators who refused to disperse. Seeing people being shot and hearing the soldiers label demonstrators on the streets as communists, he was profoundly shaken. He fled to the Thai–Burma border and began military training with several thousand other students who had come to believe that armed resistance was a necessary part of the struggle for democracy in Burma.

Calling themselves the Justice and Liberation Warriors, Soe Myint and his colleague arrived at Bangkok's Don Muang airport on 10 November 1990, and boarded a flight to Rangoon. Halfway into the flight, Soe Myint got up from his seat and headed towards the front. Having never been on a plane before, he wandered into the bathroom by mistake before finding his way to the cockpit. He told the pilot that his friend had a bomb and if the pilot didn't take them to Calcutta, they would blow everyone up.

The pilot complied as Soe Myint explained to him about Burma's democracy movement and his own frightening encounters with the military during the 1988 demonstrations. Back in the main cabin, Soe Myint's partner threatened the passengers with a Chinese doll attached to what appeared to be C-4, a plastic explosive. It was actually a bar of Lux soap.

After the plane landed in Calcutta, the hijackers insisted that the Thai ambassador, the Burmese ambassador, and a representative of the Indian government come to the airport. Soe Myint and his partner released some of the older women and children, sending their press statements along with them. The plane sat on the runway for eight hours while the hijackers waited for the diplomats and the press to arrive. The hijackers passed out the snacks and drinks they had brought along for the passengers and talked to them about Burma's problems. One passenger suggested they ask for asylum. Some of the Burmese passengers slept.

Soe Myint said that after the Indian government agreed to some of their demands, including a press conference at the airport, the hijackers apologized to the passengers. He recalled: 'We said we were sorry. I also cried because we had had to do this. Some of them began to cry too.' Everyone was released, and the hijackers met with the waiting journalists. The story was picked up around the world. Soe Myint and his partner spent a few months in prison in India but were soon freed. Yet inside Burma, nothing changed.

Ten years later, Burma was still under military rule. Daw Aung San Suu Kyi had been released from house arrest in 1995, but when she continued to demand a transfer of power, or at least a dialogue about it, the military regime began restricting her movements and harassing members of her party who refused to resign. Most universities had been shut since 1996 because of student protests. More than one thousand political prisoners were languishing in prison. In the meantime, the regime had built up its army from 180,000 troops in 1988 to as many as 400,000 in 1999.[2] Overwhelmed, several armed ethnic nationalist groups agreed to ceasefires with the regime, although one of the largest groups, the Karen National Union, still refused to give in.

Some Burmese students in exile felt more and more distressed. It seemed that neither the peaceful activities of Daw Aung San Suu Kyi and pro-democracy supporters inside the country nor the armed struggles of groups based in the border areas were having any effect in dislodging the military regime. At the same time, they believed that the international community was not doing enough to put pressure on the junta.

On 1 October 1999, five young men, calling themselves the Vigorous Burmese Student Warriors, seized the Burmese embassy in Bangkok. Carrying their M-16s (real ones this time) in guitar cases, they entered the visa section and took everyone hostage. After demanding that the Burmese military regime release all political prisoners and begin a dialogue with Daw Aung San Suu Kyi and the pro-democracy movement, they asked for safe passage to the Thai–Burma border. Twenty-five hours later, the Thai government produced a helicopter and the Deputy Foreign Minister, M. R. Sukhumbhand Paribatra, offered himself in exchange for the hostages. Ordering the pilot to fly them to the Thai–Burma border, the five hostage-takers slipped into the jungle on the Burmese side, finding refuge with a small splinter group of Karen soldiers known as God's Army.[3]

Many Thai officials and members of the Thai public expressed sympathy towards the embassy raiders. Having gone through periods of military rule themselves, they understood the frustration of the young Burmese. However, when ten gunmen seized a hospital in Thailand a few months later, the Thai public and many Burmese activists in exile were furious. The former students and their Karen partners had gone too far. Daw Aung San Suu Kyi, opposed to the use of violence, agreed.[4]

Inside the country, Daw Aung San Suu Kyi continued to advocate peaceful resistance. Focusing on the legitimacy of her party's election victory, she sought to rebuild the National League for Democracy. In 1998, she and her colleagues set up a Committee Representing the People's Parliament to carry out what tasks it could until the full Parliament could meet. She also asked Burmese citizens to join her in a non-violent movement for political change, at the very least by refusing to participate in government-sponsored propaganda activities.

Many Burmese citizens readily admit their dissatisfaction with military rule.

They are tired of the political repression, the widespread use of forced labour in the countryside, and the inability of the regime to manage the economy. But they hesitate to take action, for even reading an opposition newspaper can land them in prison for years. Instead, they attempt to get on with their lives, indulging in the dream that perhaps one day the United States, NATO, or the United Nations will swoop in and remove the regime for them.

Such a scenario is extremely unlikely. While international interest in Burma has increased in recent years, no government or international body has proposed any kind of military action. Instead, foreign governments have tried both sanctions and offers of financial aid to encourage the regime to take a more conciliatory approach to its opposition. But the regime has bristled at what it sees as outside interference in its internal affairs, despite its severe economic problems. As the Foreign Minister in 1998, U Win Aung, put it, 'Giving a banana to a monkey and asking it to dance is not the way. We are not monkeys.'5

Despite the regime's tenacity, it has to be asked how the military has managed to stay in power for so many years. Many factors have combined to keep Burma under military rule, including fear, a tradition of political passivity, and successful propaganda by the regime, particularly with regard to ethnic minority political demands. In the 1990s, international players also contributed to the regime's staying power, with China providing massive military support to Burma's armed forces and foreign companies investing significant amounts of money in joint ventures with military-owned businesses.

Still, resistance has periodically emerged. In the cities and towns of central Burma, expressions of discontent have taken the form of street demonstrations, opposition parties, underground organizing, anti-government literature, and many other small measures. Over the years, some disaffected Burmese from the plains also headed to the hills to form pro-communist or pro-democracy armies bent on establishing a new political order. They joined ethnic nationalist armies fighting primarily to extricate themselves from centralized control. But cooperation was often limited because of different political agendas and a legacy of mistrust.

The struggles of the resistance armies in Burma's mountains have been well documented by other authors (Martin Smith in *Burma: Insurgency and the Politics of Ethnicity*; Bertil Lintner, *Burma in Revolt* and *Land of Jade*; and Edith Mirante in her travelogue, *Burmese Looking Glass*) and Daw Aung San Suu Kyi has put forth her ideas in *Freedom from Fear, Letters from Burma* and *The Voice of Hope*. But little has been written about the experiences of Burmans and ethnic minorities in central Burma and how military rule has affected them. This is because since the military took power in 1962, so few social scientists have been allowed to conduct research in Burma and journalists are limited in how long they can stay and where they can go. At the same time, Burmese scholars and authors inside the country have not been able to write openly about such matters because of strict censorship rules.

This book offers an overview of Burma's recent history, and considers how people in government-controlled areas of Burma have felt compelled to live their lives in ways that help perpetuate military rule and how, at times, they have resisted. How has the military regime created techniques of control that lead people to act in ways that foster continued military rule? What kinds of resistance have emerged and in what spaces? By looking into households and communities, prisons, schools, barracks and religious centres, the penetration of military rule into all facets of people's lives becomes clear. But in all of these settings, there are also people who have tried to live by different rules and, in doing so, reaffirm their commitment to bringing about political change. The book concludes with a discussion of the role of the international community in Burma's political struggle and asks how Burma's political conflicts might be resolved in the future.

Before going any further, it should be made clear that while it is possible to talk about 'the military' and 'the people' as separate categories, in fact the reality is much more complicated. Many families have members in both the military and the pro-democracy movement. A significant percentage of soldiers do not approve of military rule even though they continue to carry out their superiors' commands. And a number of students who became pro-democracy activists in 1988 originally intended to become military officers. At a deeper level, the military's propaganda and ways of operating have profoundly shaped even those opposed to military rule.

It is not without irony that I have selected *Living Silence* as the title of this book. Burma is such a vibrant and lively place, yet so many subjects are off-limits, or only talked about in whispers, behind closed doors. People in Burma are reluctant to speak up because they are living under the seemingly omni-present surveillance of military intelligence personnel and informers. Those who act against the regime risk torture, long-term imprisonment and being treated as outcasts for life. To protect themselves and their families, Burmese participate in creating the silence that constrains many aspects of their lives.

Moreover, although the regime now allows foreign investment and tourism, it denies outsiders access to areas where human rights abuses are rampant and insists that what damaging information does get out is unsubstantiated. The regime has tried to muffle Daw Aung San Suu Kyi, the most prominent critic of the regime, by frequently cutting her phone line, restricting others' access to her house, and blocking her from travelling outside Rangoon.

To recognize other voices besides that of the military regime, I have followed the pro-democracy movement in using Burma rather than Myanmar. Although in Burmese 'Bama' and 'Myanma' are used interchangeably for the name of the country, the choice of names in English has political connotations.

The military regime unilaterally changed the English name of the country to Myanmar without consulting the country's citizens.

Despite the regime's stifling of its citizens' creative potential for so long, Burma is not the same place today that it was in the early years of military rule. Because of their liberating experiences during the 1988 pro-democracy movement and their increasing awareness of far better living conditions in other countries, Burmese today are less willing to accept the regime's claims that military rule is necessary. Daw Aung San Suu Kyi has provided focus and leadership while a vocal opposition movement in exile has helped make Burma much more of an international issue than it ever was in the past.

At the same time, Burma has drawn international concern because of its status as one of the world's top two heroin producers, along with Afghanistan. Burma is also rapidly becoming a key amphetamines producer, with the drugs flowing out of Burma and leading to rising addiction rates in neighbouring countries. Along with the expansion of the drug trade has come a worsening HIV/AIDS epidemic, with high infection rates not only in Burma but also in other countries in the region. Many governments have sought to work with Burma's military regime on these issues, but with limited success.

As international engagement with Burma increases but political change continues to remain elusive, it is important to consider the interactions between the military regime, the pro-democracy movement, international actors and ordinary citizens. However, Burma's problems are complex, and there are significant variations in the experiences of Burmans versus ethnic minorities and people in the cities versus people in remote areas. This book attempts to reveal some of the dynamics and tensions that exist in Burma today without pretending to explain them all.

I first came to know about Burma's political struggles through meeting members of the resistance movement on the Thai–Burma border. While conducting anthropological research with the Karen ethnic minority group in Thailand in 1992–93, I visited Manerplaw, the headquarters of the Karen National Union's resistance army which had been fighting for political autonomy since 1948. This was also a coordinating centre for other ethnic nationalist groups as well as the Burmese students and elected politicians who had fled central Burma between 1988 and 1991. I was struck by the fact that they were risking their lives for demands that I took for granted: democracy, human rights and freedom of expression. But why had the struggle gone on for so long and what kind of a role should the international community be playing? I looked for a job that would help me learn more.

From mid-1995 until 1997, I worked for the Open Society Institute's Burma Project running an online newspaper called *The BurmaNet News* and meeting with the Burma Project's grantees. Spending much of my time on the Thai–Burma border, I also made six trips into Burma and travelled to the China–

Burma border and the India–Burma border. I left my job at the end of 1997 to devote a year to carrying out more extensive interviews with Burmese from all walks of life. Most of my interviews were conducted outside Burma.

While the military regime carefully watches foreigners' activities in Burma, at any one time there are more than one million Burmese abroad, including undocumented migrant workers, traders and businessmen who regularly go back and forth. Civil servants' wages are so low in Burma and decent-paying jobs so hard to find that former teachers, soldiers and university students can be found along with many Burmese farmers and day-labourers working in the factories, shops and fields of Burma's neighbouring countries. There are also students and members of religious orders who travel outside the country, political activists living on Burma's borders, and thousands of Burmese who have settled abroad to escape military repression or simply to live a more comfortable life.

In 1998, I followed up on contacts from Burmese friends and other interviewees, and again travelled to China and India as well as Thailand, Singapore, Australia, Europe and different parts of the United States to meet with a variety of people from Burma. In all, between 1995 and 1999, I interviewed over 150 people, including students, farmers, soldiers, teachers, doctors, lawyers, politicians, civil servants, writers, artists, musicians, monks and priests. The interview dates are not footnoted in the text although other references are. The names of all except prominent public figures have been changed in order to protect their identities.

I found it much easier to conduct interviews outside Burma, even with some of the people I had previously met inside the country, because in general neither of us was worried that the conversation was being overheard by an informer. Many were eager to tell their stories, to revel in moments of triumph, and to pour out feelings that had been held inside for so long. But for some, the telling was painful, as it brought up difficult moral questions and feelings of despair.

What is a life well lived under military rule? Survival depends on submitting to those in power. Truth is often irrelevant. And people have to face choices that are hardly imaginable in a free society. Should you take the high road and be honest or engage in corruption so your family can make ends meet? Should you raise your children to accept military rule as normal or should you encourage them to resist and risk years of imprisonment? Is hijacking a plane or seizing an embassy justified if the world is ignoring your people's call for help?

While this book deals with the specifics of life under military rule in Burma, it raises questions about the human condition in general. Repression is not unique to Burma. And at various times, people everywhere have participated in uncomfortable silences with regard to political and social issues, when speaking up was a very difficult thing to do. Yet momentous changes do occur, often catching us by surprise. Burma then has a place in a broader history of people's struggles for political systems that can guarantee both prosperity and justice.

1. Patrolling in front of the Secretariat Building, Rangoon

2. Farmers transplanting rice, near Mandalay

3. A Tatmadaw soldier overseeing forced labour, Kachin State

4. Even monasteries are not free of soldiers, Kachin State

CHAPTER I
. . . .
Historical Legacies

'The problems in Burma have not been brought on by the military alone. Everyone is responsible.' (A Burmese professor)

§ There are two key political issues in Burma today: the restoration of democracy and the resolution of the political rights of ethnic nationalities. Despite domestic and international pressure for a return to democracy, the military regime has insisted that such a change must come gradually. At the same time, the regime has remained committed to the concentration of political power at the centre so as to prevent what it calls 'the disintegration of the union'. Resistance to military rule has come from both pro-democracy supporters and ethnic minority groups who value greater independence. However, these struggles have overlapped only partially. Many ethnic nationalist leaders are more concerned with autonomy in their areas and wonder whether a democratic government would really safeguard minority rights. At the same time, many Burman pro-democracy activists are not particularly sympathetic to the ethnic nationalists' demands for autonomy, which they perceive as potentially leading to the break-up of the country.

That said, there are numerous ethnic minority politicians, students and others who have worked actively in the democracy movement as well as ethnic Burmans, including Daw Aung San Suu Kyi, who understand the need to take the ethnic nationalists' demands seriously. In recent years, the different opposition groups have come closer together, but they are still often hampered by the lack of a shared vision for Burma's future.

Burma today is a country divided ethnically, religiously and politically. While the military regime has insisted that it is working to unify the country, its promotion of the majority Burman population and Buddhism at the expense of other ethnic groups and religions has in many ways exacerbated pre-existing divisions. The regime has sought to bring all the ethnic areas, which make up half the country, under centralized control and to limit the use of ethnic minority languages. Resentment towards these policies, coupled with brutal military campaigns in the areas where ethnic nationalist armies operate, drove members of the ethnic minorities to join nationalist armies bent on maintaining territory under their own control.

Burma is inhabited by a mix of people whose past historical relations were often contentious. In the pre-colonial days, Burman kings routinely conquered other peoples, and in three periods consolidated their rule over a number of neighbouring kingdoms and principalities. The successes of such expansionist campaigns brought pride to the Burmans, but in some cases involved terrible massacres. Under British colonial rule ethnic groups were pitted against each other and minority groups were privileged politically and economically. Later, Burma's military regimes attempted to erase the humiliation of colonialism and shore up their own legitimacy by linking their political and religious activities to the accomplishments of great Burmese kings in the past.

To understand the dynamics of Burma's contemporary politics, it is necessary, first, to consider briefly Burma's geography and history, focusing particularly on ethnic relations and aspects of political culture. The legacies of both the pre-colonial and colonial periods have partially shaped the way that politics and ethnic relations are understood by people in Burma today.

Pre-colonial Principalities and Kingdoms

Burma consists of a flat heartland encircled by mountain ranges to the north, east and west. The country is dissected by the Irrawaddy, Salween and Chindwin rivers, and the Irrawaddy delta in the lower part of Burma offers particularly rich soil and bountiful rice harvests. To the south lies the sea. The largest population groups on the plains are the Burmans, Karens, Mons and Arakanese (or Rakhines). It should be noted that 'Burman' refers to the ethnic group, while 'Burmese' refers to the language that Burman people speak as well as to all citizens of Burma. However, 'Burmese' is often used inter-changeably by outsiders and native speakers to refer to ethnic Burmans and all people living in Burma.

Burma's great kingdoms evolved in the lowlands, where much wealth was put into the construction of great Buddhist monasteries and pagodas, many of which are still standing. Most people survived as farmers and fishermen, and Buddhism, mixed with spirit worship, was the dominant religion. The Shans, living primarily in the north-eastern hills, are also predominantly Buddhist and developed principalities centred around prosperous rice-growing valleys. They were often linked in tributary relations to Burman rulers on the plains, but Burman officials never directly administered their territory.

A number of different peoples also live in the mountains, including the Chins, Kachins, Karennis (also known as Kayah), Nagas, Pa'os, Palaungs and Was, as well as many smaller groups. Hundreds of thousands of Karens can also be found in the eastern mountains along the Thai–Burma border. Members of many of these minority groups converted to Christianity although others became Buddhists or continued to worship ancestral and territorial spirits. Because of the difficulties of communication and transportation, the people in the hills have tended to live in small communities, and in the pre-colonial period developed more limited political organizations.

In pre-colonial times, there were numerous kingdoms in the territory now known as Burma. Burman kings were periodically able to build empires stretching across much of modern-day Burma, but at other times, Mon and Arakanese rulers presided over flourishing kingdoms of their own in what is now lower Burma. The size of the kingdoms fluctuated dramatically, depending on the number of tributary relations kings could establish and maintain. When kings were weak, appointed princes, pretenders and tributaries often revolted and sought the throne for themselves or looked for alliances with other rising powers.

One of the primary strategic concerns for rulers throughout mainland South East Asia was acquiring more manpower to till the land, expand the army, and build temples, palaces and irrigation works.[1] In many war campaigns, the victorious army returned not only with loot but also with thousands of captives who were compelled to join the local workforce.[2] As a result, there was a tremendous mixing of people, particularly around the capitals.

Unlike neighbouring India, Burma never had a fixed class structure. However, social and political relationships were ordered by status considerations. Older people were considered higher in status to younger people, monks to lay people, and kings' appointees to commoners. In each case, the senior person in the relationship expected to be heeded by the junior person. Much of political life operated according to a patron–client model with inferiors providing goods and services to superiors in return for protection.

Rulers of lowland kingdoms often claimed suzerainty over surrounding mountainous regions, and in some cases patron–client relationships were established, with local chiefs and princes sending tribute to the kings. But kings typically exerted little effort in trying to bring these sparsely inhabited areas under their control. The mountainous areas were mainly seen as buffer zones between lowland kingdoms and were generally traversed only in times of war.[3]

Burmese kingdoms were characterized by great social mobility, permitting people of ability to move from humble origins to high positions without much difficulty. However, downward mobility was also common, because there was no permanent bureaucracy. The power of kings was absolute, and they could remove or even execute their officials at any time, for the slightest offence.[4] Upon the death or dethronement of a king, his officials often lost their jobs too. In such a fluid political environment, elites at every level watched carefully for the emergence of rivals who could threaten their precarious control.

Resulting feelings of fear, jealousy and suspicion come across vividly in the legends of the thirty-seven *nats*, spirits who were propitiated in the pre-colonial period and continue to be cultivated by many Burmese today. Most of the *nats* were talented individuals who were killed by kings because they or one of their relatives had slighted the king or appeared to be a potential threat. After becoming *nats*, they were understood to be powerful but capricious beings who could influence human affairs.

To give just one example, the legend of the Mahagiri (King of the Mountain) spirit claims he was originally a handsome and strong blacksmith with a growing reputation for his might. The king worried that the blacksmith might eventually try to usurp the throne, so he devised a plan to get rid of him. The king married the blacksmith's sister, and after some time asked the blacksmith to come to the palace so that he could confer an official title on him. The poor blacksmith arrived suspecting nothing, and was immediately hurled into a fire and burned to death. Hearing his anguished cries, his sister was overcome with grief and threw herself in the flames and died too. The brother and sister spirits were so angry at the king's betrayal that they killed anyone who came near the tree in which they had taken up residence. The king had the tree cut down and discarded in the river. The trunk floated downstream to the territory of another king, who decided to give the spirits a proper home. He built them a shrine on Mount Popa and had images of the pair carved, covered in gold and attired in courtly robes.[5]

Mount Popa is an old volcano which juts straight out of the plains behind the ancient capital of Pagan, and the two *nats* became known as the protector spirits for Pagan and all who came to worship them. Eventually, the Mahagiri *nat* became the household guardian spirit, with many rural Burmese even today presenting coconut offerings for him in their homes.

The cultivation of the *nats*, which represented separate and uncontrollable sources of power, marked a symbolic challenge to the kings who were trying to unify power under their own rule. Burma's first empire-building king, Anawrahta, went so far as to chain up a set of the thirty-seven *nat* images in a cave to signify that their power had been contained. Beginning with Anawrahta, Burmese kings promoted Theravada Buddhism, which emphasized the need for each individual to focus on his or her own spiritual path in order to achieve a higher rebirth and, eventually, freedom from the cycle of birth and death altogether. Kings served as the patrons of the Buddhist religion, supporting the Buddhist clergy and commissioning the construction of pagodas and monasteries.

Although Burman kings ultimately depended on the threat of force to maintain their rule, they were still believed to have obtained such high positions because of meritorious deeds in their past lives. They did little to improve the material welfare of their subjects but, through their support of the monkhood and pagoda-building projects, they were seen as providing spiritual benefits.

Burman kings often waged war in the name of Buddhism, and Anawrahta invaded the Mon kingdom in lower Burma in 1057 with the justification that the Mon king had refused to give him a copy of the Theravada Buddhist scriptures. After sacking the Mon capital, he moved large numbers of Mon scholars and monks back to his capital in Pagan to disseminate Theravada Buddhist teaching and culture. The Burmese script and Burmese literature were subsequently developed from Mon, which had its origins in the Pali and Sanskrit languages of India. As Theravada Buddhism spread throughout the plains, monks began teaching boys in the villages to read and write so they could deepen their knowledge of Buddhist teachings. As a result, literacy in pre-colonial Burma was widespread.

Like the predominantly Buddhist Mons and Arakanese, Burmans later associated the rule of their kings with the glorification of the Buddhist faith. After the British conquered Burma, some of the most prominent resisters were monks who felt that their religion was being slighted.

British Rule

British merchants first entered Burmese waters in the 1600s, and they soon began to exchange weapons in return for trading concessions. In 1824, the British seized the Tenasserim and Arakan regions (now southern and western Burma), after Burman forces entered into British-controlled territory in pursuit of fleeing political opponents. The British sought to protect their Indian empire and to counterbalance the French, who were busy colonizing modern-day Vietnam, Cambodia and Laos. The French hoped to expand their trade with China and to obtain freer access to resources in Burma. The British wanted these advantages for themselves and went on to annex lower Burma in 1852–53 and central and northern Burma in 1885–86.[6]

The British originally ruled Burma as an appendage of India, but they also brought with them western notions of states as fixed and bounded, and they immediately set about delineating their territory. Parts of the mountainous 'frontier areas', which had never been under any lowland kingdom's direct rule, were mapped into Burma and many hill populations ended up split between Burma and neighbouring countries.[7] This was of little concern to the colonial officials who relied on existing princes, chiefs and headmen to collect taxes, but otherwise rarely interfered in local affairs. In the plains, however, the British ruled directly, banishing the king and his immediate family to exile in India.

In the mountainous areas, after initial resistance to British rule had been quelled, acceptance of the colonial government was surprisingly widespread. In part, this was because the British froze local rulers' power, rather than eliminating them. While most Burmans bitterly resented colonial domination, some Karens and other upland minorities considered the period of British rule as a golden age, because lowland armies no longer came through on war campaigns against neighbouring realms.[8] Moreover, the colonial regime allowed missionaries to establish schools and hospitals throughout the country, including in the hill areas, providing hill peoples with much appreciated access to education and health care. Many Karens, Karennis, Kachins and Chins converted to Christianity.[9] The British also promoted ambitious ethnic minorities to posts in the civil service and the colonial defence force. The people of the hills felt that for once they had a chance to catch up with the people in the plains.

Nevertheless, the main concern of the British was to make money. By keeping the ethnic minorities in the hills and the people in the plains divided, it was easier to maintain control. Besides exporting great quantities of rice, the colonial government and the British East India Company focused their energies on extractive industries such as teak, petroleum, tin and gems. To move these goods, they established a network of roads, railroads and river transport. Eager for more manpower, they encouraged the immigration of Chinese and Indians, particularly men. Indian peasants flocked to newly opened cultivation areas in lower Burma, while Indian clerks were brought in to staff the civil service and to serve in the defence force. Many Indians and Chinese also found niches for themselves in the commercial sector, transporting goods and setting up their own shops and businesses.

In the plains, the British government introduced a civil service and legal codes so that administration and justice would operate efficiently and uniformly. Although determined to maintain law and order so business could flourish, the British also believed that the new system offered the Burmese an improvement over the arbitrary exercise of power by kings and their officials in the past. Nevertheless, most Burmese were not happy to be under foreign rule, and the colonial government faced opposition from several quarters. During the first years of British occupation, guerrilla forces sprang up throughout the countryside and attacked British troops and their garrisons. Even after the rural revolts had been quelled, resentment simmered.

Monks and lay people were particularly incensed by what they perceived as British disrespect towards Buddhism. The British refused to take off their shoes in monasteries, as was required by local custom. Many Burmese were also upset that the colonial administration would not install a new religious patron to replace the banished king. In 1906, the Young Men's Buddhist Association, modelled on the Young Men's Christian Association (YMCA), was formed to address religious and social issues. In 1917, it was folded into the more political General Council of Burmese Associations (GCBA). This association set up chapters around the country and provided gathering places for monks, intellectuals and others committed to nationalist causes.

U Ottama and U Wisara, two monks who had travelled abroad, took up politics to promote the protection of Buddhism. The colonial government arrested them for making seditious speeches against the British, but the arrests served only to increase their support. To protest the colonial government's regulation forbidding the wearing of monks' robes in prison, U Wisara engaged in a hunger strike which lasted 166 days, until his death.[10] This ultimate sacrifice profoundly moved many Burmese who had not concerned themselves with politics before.

Resistance to the British in the early days tended to look to the past for inspiration, recalling the days when Burmese kings had promoted Buddhism for the benefit of all. However, as students began to return from studies in the West, they brought back new ideas about representative government and democratic practices. Lending libraries opened with wide assortments of books. Those with a thirst for knowledge could plunge into western philosophy, history and economics. Over time, Burmese demands shifted from seeking the restoration of the monarchy to calling for the establishment of an independent Burmese state with a modern form of government.

University and high school students played an instrumental role in developing a new political consciousness which combined a commitment to Buddhism with a desire for independence and a progressive form of government. In 1920, students organized a strike when the colonial government proposed to establish Rangoon University, but limit entrance to an elite few who would be trained as bureaucrats for the colonial regime. The students demanded wider access and a more comprehensive curriculum. On 5 December 1920, they gathered at the symbolic centre of Rangoon, the Shwedagon Pagoda, where relics of the Buddha were believed to be enshrined. Refusing to go back to school until their demands were met, they camped out at the pagoda and set up their own classes. Finally, the administration relented, but the strike served as the impetus for the development of National Schools, Burmese-run institutions which were independent of the British educational system.

Resentment about being treated as second-class citizens in their own country led a group of students to begin calling themselves *thakin*, or 'master', to emphasize that they were the rightful masters of Burma. The *thakin* movement, which also encouraged wearing traditional homespun clothing rather than western apparel, was formalized through the establishment of the Dobama Asiayone, or 'We Burmans Association', in the early 1930s. As local chapters formed throughout the country, they became hubs of political activity.[11]

In 1936, student demonstrations broke out again after two university students, both of whom later became prominent political figures, were expelled. Nu, the head of the student union, publicly called for an overhaul of the university's teaching staff and curriculum. Aung San, the editor of the student magazine, refused to divulge the identity of the author of an article entitled 'Hellhound at Large', which defamed one of the university adminis- trators. Demanding their reinstatement, fellow students refused to return to classes and again headed to the Shwedagon Pagoda. The strike continued for several months and spread to colleges and high schools in other parts of the country.

In 1938, university student union members and Dobama Asiayone chapters joined with industrial workers to organize a march from the oil fields in central Burma to the capital in Rangoon. Such strikes, boycotts and demonstrations reflected the growing organizational strength of the Burmese nationalists. The newspapers, magazines and independent associations which emerged helped to spread their message.

Peasants also took action after the worldwide depression hit Burma in 1929. Burmese farmers suffered tremendously as rice prices dropped and taxes became harder to pay. They lost much of their land to Indian money-lenders. A charismatic former monk named Saya San spearheaded a mass revolt against British rule which lasted from 1930 to 1932. Thousands of armed peasants attacked colonial offices throughout rural Burma. The British brutally re- pressed the rebellion and publicly displayed the severed heads of some of their captives. Saya San was captured and hanged, while many more peasants died in battle, some because they had believed their magical tattoos and charms would make them invulnerable to bullets. Although the revolt was unsuccessful, Saya San and his followers' audacity further stimulated nationalist feelings.

Nationalist passions were also aroused because of the way in which the British had privileged ethnic minority groups over the dominant population. Many Indians and Chinese were prospering through their association with the British, often at the expense of the Burmese. In addition, large numbers of foreign men were taking Burmese women as their wives and mistresses. Burmese anger and resentment periodically exploded in the form of anti- Indian and anti-Chinese riots.[12]

The British introduced new ethnic tensions to Burma and through their exploitative economic practices turned many against capitalism. However, the British did eventually introduce limited representative government, permitting elected politicians to participate in governance. In 1923, the British handed over some minor decision-making powers to an elected domestic assembly, with the provision that the British governor could veto any decision he did not like. Burmese politicians heatedly debated whether there was any point in participating in such an administration. Conflicts were also sparked by the fact that a number of the domestic assembly seats were reserved for British commercial interests, Indians, and Karens living in the plains. Later, when the issue of separating Burma from India came up, some Burmese opposed it fearing that the Burmese would be granted fewer political rights than the Indians. Nevertheless, the two countries were separated in 1937, and the British put into effect a new constitution which provided for an elected House of Representatives and an Upper House, half of whose members were elected. Although a number of Burmese politicians enthusiastically contested the elections, the British government's continued refusal to grant full self-government infuriated many others.

By the late 1930s, young urban nationalists began looking to Asian powers for military training and assistance in establishing an armed resistance movement. In early 1941, student-leader Aung San and twenty-nine colleagues secretly left for Hainan Island where they were given military training by the Japanese. These men, later known as the Thirty Comrades, re-entered Burma with Japanese troops in late 1941.

When the Japanese invaded Burma, the British colonial forces beat a hasty retreat to India. Although the Burmese originally viewed the Japanese as their liberators, the Japanese ruled Burma like a conquered territory and their secret police terrorized the local population. Aung San, by then a general, and other nationalists became increasingly disillusioned. On 27 March 1945, they began a coordinated resistance movement in cooperation with Allied troops who marched back into northern Burma from India. Burmese from many different political backgrounds joined together under the Anti-Fascist People's Freedom League (AFPFL) to help drive the Japanese out.

Once the war was over, the British tried to reinstate colonial rule. But the Burmese nationalists were insistent on independence and organized widespread strikes to make their point. Without Indian troops or the financial resources to maintain a large British force, the colonial government could not easily enforce submission and finally relented.

Thus British colonial rule ended with a mixed legacy for Burma. An extensive transportation infrastructure in the form of roads, railways and steamships had been built, laying the foundation for the development of the economy. A civil service had been created and the idea of representative government introduced. Many Burmese had obtained university degrees and had been abroad for further study, allowing them to broaden their ideas about political and economic development. However, bitter feelings had developed between Burmans and the Indian and Chinese immigrants as well as between Burmans and some of the indigenous ethnic nationalities.

Independence

Before the British government handed over power, it insisted that the political status of the peoples in the frontier areas be resolved. Burman politicians wanted the frontier areas to join the new union of Burma, but some ethnic leaders were reluctant. During World War II, some of the ethnic nationalities, such as the Karens and the Kachins, had fought with the British against the Japanese. After the British had fled, there were incidences of Burman soldiers massacring Karen villagers, and Karens retaliating by killing Burmans. By the end of the war, the Burmans had shifted their support to the Allies, but animosity remained between Burmans and Karens in particular. Moreover, some ethnic leaders had hoped that the British would support their demands for independent statehood.

The British had set up a serious problem by governing the frontier areas differently from the plains. The fact that ethnic minority soldiers in the colonial defence force had participated in putting down Burman rebellions against colonial rule had also increased Burman resentment towards the ethnic nationalities. At the same time, many Burman leaders saw themselves as superior to the minorities and did not want to give in to their demands.

The one person who seemed to have the vision and diplomatic skills to resolve this problem was General Aung San. Leading the pre-independence executive council in 1947, General Aung San reached out to non-Burmans. He folded the ethnic troops who had fought under the British into the new Burma Army and appointed a Karen as commander-in-chief. He selected non-Burmans for several other high-ranking posts in the government, made trips to ethnic nationality areas to meet with ethnic leaders, and organized a multi-ethnic conference at the Shan town of Panglong to come up with a political structure which both Burmans and the ethnic nationalities in the frontier areas could accept. Although the Karens attended only as observers and several other minorities were not invited, Kachin, Shan and Chin representatives participated. The concept of a federal union was agreed upon, and ethnic states were to be created with full autonomy over their internal affairs.

Burmese leaders were worried that the British would renege on their promise to grant independence, so the constitution for the new union was hurriedly written by an elected constituent assembly dominated by the AFPFL under General Aung San. The constitution stipulated that the new Union of Burma would be ruled by a democratically elected parliament and prime minister. The ethnic states would have their own state councils, whose members would also serve in the union government's parliament, and the head of each state would automatically be a member of the union government's cabinet.

Originally, four ethnic states were to be created. The Karenni and Shan states were accorded the right to secede after ten years if they were not happy with their status in the union.[13] The Kachin State was not allowed to secede because it consisted partly of territory which had been under Burman control in the past. The Karen State was to be established but, at the time of drafting the constitution, there were still serious disagreements over its boundaries.

The Karen population was scattered across much of lower Burma, and many Karen leaders were dissatisfied with a proposal that would give them control only over the portion of the eastern hills and no political representation in the Irrawaddy delta area. The Chins did not ask for a state, and the Mons and Arakanese were not offered states. However, a provision was included for the possible formation of new states in the future.[14]

Within most of the ethnic groups, there were people who were willing to join the new union as well as people who were adamantly opposed to it. Thus, as the constitution drafting took place, groups of Karens, Karennis, Mons, Buddhist Arakanese and Muslims in Arakan territory began preparing for armed struggle, while the leading Burmese politicians looked for more moderate ethnic representatives with whom they could forge agreements. The failure to resolve adequately the ethnic nationalities' demands through the constitutional drafting process set the conditions for outbreaks of violence later.

Had General Aung San lived, perhaps Burma's history would have been different. On 19 July 1947, U Saw, an ambitious senior politician, had his gunmen assassinate the thirty-two-year-old general and most of his cabinet. Apparently expecting the British to ask him to form a new government, U Saw was instead immediately arrested. He was executed the following year. Whether other individuals or organizations were also involved in the plot remains a mystery.[15]

Despite the loss of some of its foremost leaders, Burma became independent on 4 January 1948, at 4.20 a.m. This early hour was selected by Burmese astrologers as the most propitious for the country's new beginning. The AFPFL took power with the devoutly Buddhist statesman, U Nu, as the country's first prime minister.

The decade from 1948 to 1958 was Burma's first experiment with full democracy. Citizens were able to elect their own representatives, and policies were widely debated in the Parliament as well as in independent newspapers and teashops. People could speak freely, and hopes were high that Burma would prosper. Nevertheless, Burma's new political leaders faced enormous problems. There were not enough trained Burmese professionals, because most government posts had been held by foreigners. Many Indian civil servants had fled during World War II, afraid of what the Burmans might do to them once the British were gone. The country was still recovering from the massive destruction and displacement caused during the war, guns were readily available, and banditry was wreaking havoc in much of the countryside.[16]

Of even greater concern, several groups sought to bypass the electoral process and wrest power by force, challenging the stability of the new government. The Communist Party, originally a member of the AFPFL, split into two factions and both went underground. The Red Flag branch had decided to take up arms even before independence, and the much larger White Flag branch followed suit in March 1948. Determined to institute a communist state through an armed revolution, both groups relocated to jungle strongholds and sought to mobilize local populations around issues of land reform. The armed People's Volunteer Organization (PVO), which had been set up by General Aung San for World War II veterans, also turned into an insurgent group.

Meanwhile, on 31 January 1949, Karen forces turned on the struggling government. Karen and Burman leaders had been unable to agree on the boundaries of a new Karen State and communal tensions had been growing, leading many Karens in the Burma Army to mutiny and join local Karen defence forces in an armed rebellion. At one point in 1949, the central government controlled little more than the capital city of Rangoon. However, General Ne Win, who replaced a Karen as commander-in-chief of the army, led government troops in slowly pushing the various anti-government forces away from the towns in the plains. Many of the government troops were actually ethnic minorities who were committed to the new federal union. Local militias, or *tats*, working with the socialist faction of the AFPFL, also helped retake control of some of the districts. By 1952, much of the countryside was back in the government's hands, although it was still too dangerous for trains to run after dark. Passengers had to get off at sunset and were able to continue their journey only when the sun rose the next morning.

During this period, the Burma Army had to contend with Chinese troops as well. After Mao Zedong took power in 1949, anti-communist Kuomintang troops fled to northern Burma. Hoping to regroup and launch counter-offensives into China, they operated in Burmese territory with the covert support of the United States' military but without the Burmese government's permission. Meanwhile, the Chinese government was printing maps showing large parts of northern Burma as belonging to China, and Mao Zedong's troops were making incursions to chase down the Kuomintang. The government in Rangoon tried to use diplomacy to settle its problems with China, while also sending Burmese troops on operations to root out the Kuomintang in Shan State. However, the Burmese troops acted like a conquering force, mistreating Shan villagers and causing many Shans to question whether joining the union had been the right decision.[17] Similar violence and disaffection broke out in Karenni State, and Mon and Arakanese nationalists had also taken up arms.

In central Burma, the government set about trying to rebuild the economy and introducing development projects. Committed to the idea of a welfare state, the government initiated a mass education programme in the rural areas and made public education free. Land reform programmes redistributed some of the land which had ended up in the hands of foreigners and absentee landlords during the colonial period. Low-interest loans were issued to farmers, and money was allocated for communities to build wells, roads, schools and reading rooms.

Despite the government's good intentions, many of the social welfare programmes had little impact because of problems of implementation. The national leaders saw the need to help communities, but they did not incorporate people at the community level in the design of the programmes. Thus, the projects did not always fit with community needs, and villagers felt little commitment to the programmes. At the same time, some politicians tied the provision of welfare programmes to political allegiance. If local leaders could bring in the vote for a certain politician, he would reward them with government projects.[18]

The concept of a legal opposition was still new and often resisted. The political parties of the day sought to monopolize power and eliminate their opposition altogether. The idea that the opposition could play a constructive role in offering different points of view had no roots in Burma. Opposition in the past had always been understood as insubordination, and politicians in the 1950s found it difficult to negotiate, compromise or work together with political representatives from other factions and parties.

Too often, politicians undermined democratic principles in order to maintain their positions. Political debates in Parliament often degenerated into mudslinging and name-calling, and some politicians even resorted to underhanded techniques to disempower their rivals. Members of the ruling party sometimes accused more left-leaning rivals of being communists and had them imprisoned. Although the courts would release them if there were a lack of evidence, such goings-on damaged the credibility of the ruling party. Politicians even tried to use student organizations as proxies in their struggles against rival political parties. In the 1950s, there were two university student unions: the Democratic Students' Organization, which strongly supported the government, and the Students' United Front, which was more leftist-leaning and had some associations with communists. The activities of university students became absurdly politicized, with even a demand for the extension of a university holiday becoming a 'leftist–rightist' issue.

Meanwhile, in towns and rural areas, private armies under the pay of politicians were sometimes used to intimidate and even murder opposition party members and their supporters. Villagers found that the best way to survive the violence and political rivalries was to stay as neutral as possible, and to demonstrate political allegiance only to the party that was clearly going to win. Rarely venturing far beyond their own districts, they continued to spend their days farming, raising their families and engaging in religious rituals.

Given Burma's geographical position between two powerful neighbours,

India and China, U Nu's government wisely adopted a neutralist foreign policy. Widely respected in the developing world, the government was outward-looking in its trade policies and participated actively in international affairs.[19] At the same time, U Nu often intertwined his deeply Burmese religious and cultural sensibilities with the country's politics. He devoted much energy to promoting Buddhism through sponsoring meditation programmes for lay people and organizing a Buddhist synod which brought together monks from all over Burma and other Buddhist countries. Although the state was officially secular, U Nu was establishing himself as the patron of Buddhism in much the same way that Burmese kings had in the past.

U Nu's willingness to place religious concerns above ongoing political crises irritated more educated, urban politicians and intellectuals but did not bother less worldly villagers. At one point, U Nu took a forty-five-day leave of absence from his job as prime minister to meditate at Mount Popa, the home of the Mahagiri *nat* discussed earlier. Despite the fact that the country was facing urgent problems, villagers in upper Burma reportedly supported his decision. Because U Nu's horoscope indicated that this period was inauspicious for him, the villagers believed U Nu was doing the country a favour by temporarily removing himself from national politics.[20]

Thus, although Burma was nominally a democracy, earlier authoritarian traditions informed the way that politics operated in post-independence Burma. The establishment of a freer society had permitted the proliferation of newspapers, independent associations and political parties. Still, a winner-takes-all mentality remained the norm, and frequent instances of political violence and abuse of power hampered the development of a democratic culture.

Beginnings of Militarization

Most Burmese citizens in the 1950s viewed the Burmese armed forces, or the Tatmadaw, with respect. Along with the AFPFL, the Tatmadaw was credited with playing a significant role in bringing about independence and in rescuing the country from dismemberment by insurgent forces. The Burmese population in the lowlands was eager to see peace restored in their towns and villages, and most were relieved when the various forces were pushed back by the Tatmadaw.

The Tatmadaw had begun as a small, disorganized army, but it was quickly professionalized through intensive battle experience and institutional development initiated by military men who had trained at military academies abroad. Seeking a certain degree of financial independence, the military set up its own profit-making corporation in order to guarantee that the battalions would always be sufficiently supplied. The corporation originally ran shops selling bulk goods, but it soon expanded into the import–export business and became a major player in the domestic economy.[21] Boosted by its military and economic successes, the Tatmadaw increasingly identified itself as playing an essential role in the country's internal affairs.

Meanwhile, as 1958 approached, hereditary Shan *sawbwas*, or princes, and young Shan leaders began debating the status of the Shan states in public meetings. According to the 1947 constitution, the Shan *sawbwas* could continue to govern their territories as principalities, with representatives to one of the two houses in the state council elected from the people and representatives to the other selected among the princes. They also had the right to leave the union in 1958 if political integration wasn't working out. The central government wanted them to stay in the union, but among the Shans, feelings were mixed. Some princes close to the government supported the union, while many Shan students and farmers favoured independence. Many Karennis felt the same. This concerned Tatmadaw leaders, who did not want any of the ethnic states to secede.

At the same time, some military officers were openly voicing discontent with parliamentary rule. They disliked the government's willingness to rehabilitate insurgent left-wing politicians and resented civilian interference in their affairs. They were also disturbed by the disorderliness of the parliamentary system, in which politicians were constantly attacking each other and seemingly doing little to resolve the country's problems. The AFPFL continued to dominate the Parliament, but it split into two antagonistic groups, the Clean and the Stable AFPFL, in April 1958. Each group tried to outmanoeuvre the other by wooing army leaders and ethnic representatives in the government. Rumours spread that a group of military officers were plotting a coup.[22]

In September 1958, General Ne Win and two other senior officers, Maung Maung and Aung Gyi, took power. Prime Minister U Nu tried to limit the damage to the constitutional government by inviting General Ne Win to form a caretaker government. U Nu announced that the handover had been voluntary, but it became clear later that he had had little choice in the matter.[23]

The public did not initially oppose the caretaker government, because the elected parliament was in such disarray. Rangoon was filled with squatters who had fled the dangers of life outside the capital. Huts lined many of the city's thoroughfares and covered vacant lots, and the drains were like open latrines. If a military government could do a bit to clean up the cities and restore order, it was welcome.

Under the caretaker government, known in Burmese as the *Bogyoke* (General's) government, General Ne Win achieved several successes. He concluded a significant border demarcation agreement with China which led to better relations between the two governments. He also convinced the Shan and Karenni hereditary leaders to give up their powers and allow for the election of all political representatives in their states. Most importantly to those in the cities, he kept food prices low and moved the squatter communities to newly established satellite towns.[24]

However, thoughtful individuals viewed the government's handling of the squatters with concern. The squatters were given only twelve to twenty-four hours' notice before military trucks picked them up, and many were unable to bring all their things with them. The new sites were not adequately prepared as residential areas, and the new residents had to make do as best they could. In this and other projects, the army showed little respect for the people it was supposedly helping.

The caretaker government was sensitive to criticism and imprisoned numerous journalists for daring to challenge it. And much to civil servants' annoyance, battlefield commanders were brought in to replace or work alongside bureaucrats. After the general's government extended its term twice beyond the original six-month period, pressure increased for an election to restore democracy.

General Ne Win complied, and the election date was set for February 1960. Nevertheless, some military leaders hoped to influence the outcome, and some Stable AFPFL politicians flaunted their connections with high-ranking officers, thinking this would win them the support of the people. But they miscalculated, for the voters wanted the military to return to the barracks and were annoyed by the military's attempts to manipulate the election. At the same time, many Burmese Buddhist voters were drawn by U Nu's pledge to make Buddhism the state religion. They gave a landslide victory to his 'Clean' faction of the AFPFL, which had been reorganized as the *Pyidaungsu*, or Union, Party.

Among the ethnic nationalities, however, discontent with U Nu and other senior Burmese politicians was growing. Despite their promises, the parliamentary governments of the 1950s had done very little to develop the minority regions. Moreover, the central government had relinquished few powers to the ethnic states, and the Tatmadaw's presence in areas of insurgency had often resulted in the suspension of the rule of law. Most upsetting to Christian minorities, U Nu pushed a law through Parliament making Buddhism the state religion. In doing so, he went against General Aung San's insistence on keeping the state secular. With majority rule, it seemed that the ethnic minorities could do little to stop measures supported by the far more numerous Burman representatives. Frustrated Kachins began talking about armed resistance.

In the meantime, U Nu continued to meet with ethnic leaders to discuss their demands, and he did agree to the idea of setting up separate Mon and Arakanese states. He offered amnesties to ethnic fighters who surrendered, but he was finding it difficult to work out a settlement with the Shans and Karennis, who were considering seceding. Most Burman politicians continued to oppose increased political autonomy for the ethnic minorities. As Dr Ba Maw, a Burman who served as prime minister during the Japanese occupation, put it: 'The Burmese as a rule show a big-race mentality in their dealings with the smaller native races; they find it hard to forget their long historical domination over those races.'[25] Some of the ethnic areas had never been under Burman domination, but most Burmans still very much wanted the minority areas to remain part of modern Burma.

By 1961, Shan and Kachin nationalists were organizing resistance armies along the lines of the Karen. They increasingly felt that negotiating with the government was pointless. Still, older and more prominent minority leaders remained committed to working out a solution with the elected government. It was on 2 March 1962, during a high-level seminar on federal issues attended by Prime Minister U Nu and senior Shan representatives, that General Ne Win again seized power. This time, U Nu, members of his government, and many Shan leaders were arrested.

General Ne Win's colleague, Brigadier Aung Gyi, justified the coup by insisting that the union was in danger of disintegrating. A month after the coup, General Ne Win declared that parliamentary democracy, as practised so far, had not worked. The new military government, it was implied, could manage the country's affairs more effectively.

Even though most people had voted against the military-backed Stable AFPFL in 1960, two years later they were willing to give the military another chance. In part, people were disappointed with how democratic rule had functioned, and there was hope that General Ne Win would act in the nation's best interest. Others were cynical about government in general. Burmese have traditionally identified the government as one of the five enemies, the others being fire, water (floods and storms), thieves and malevolent people. Ordinary people had never had much control over the political process and felt it was best just to get on with life regardless of who was in power.

The major political parties stayed quiet, but some student groups did make statements against the coup. Within the military itself, particularly among those who had worked with the British before independence, there was also some opposition. One man who was a high-ranking naval officer at the time later said: 'Some of us worried that now Ne Win was here to stay. We did get from the British the idea of the separation of politics and the military.' Bo Let Ya, a popular member of the Thirty Comrades, sent out word that all former military comrades should state as a group that the military should not stay in power. He was arrested.

General Ne Win had already eliminated many of his rivals within the military the year before. Telling U Nu that they had been involved in election irregularities in 1960, he had eleven senior officers expelled from the army and others transferred to inactive posts. Although General Ne Win had started life with little promise, having dropped out of university and worked as a postal clerk, he had come a long way. He was admired for being a man of action and, as one of the Thirty Comrades, he was viewed as untouchable. He had expanded the army from a few thousand men in 1948 to 100,000 in 1962, and with his close rivals removed, the lower ranks were willing to follow him obediently, whether out of respect or fear.

In retrospect, one can ask how things might have been different if General Aung San had lived. Perhaps democratic norms would have gradually developed, and the ethnic political demands would have been resolved at the negotiating table. But growing ethnic political tensions and a legacy of authoritarianism had inhibited the development of a stable, open society. Having rid themselves of the British, the Burmans had found a renewed pride in their numerical dominance and their heritage as a conquering race, and this hindered their ability to understand and resolve the ethnic nationalities' demands. In addition, a smoothly functioning democratic system had yet to develop. Because of the civil war, the military often ignored due process in areas where it operated, and politicians were able to use pocket armies not only to go after bandits but also to intimidate their opposition. Although the government did seek to develop the country, there was little substantive dialogue between politicians and the people in their constituencies, and too many politicians were consumed with their own personal interests. As a result, democracy was only superficially rooted in Burma, and the military was able to take over with little resistance.

. . . .

CHAPTER 2

The Ne Win Years, 1962–88

'One Energy Minister said, "To spare the wood, use charcoal." But you see charcoal is made from wood. Those kind of people were governing.' (U Po Khin)

The Revolutionary Council, 1962–74

After the 1962 coup, General Ne Win and his Revolutionary Council immediately set about imposing order, and the universities were one of the first targets. The military regime announced stricter regulations for university students, one particularly irksome rule being that dormitories were locked at 8 p.m. to prevent students from going out to visit friends or chat in teashops. Angry students broke through the locked doors to shout in protest for three successive nights. As the protests continued, the students' union took over the leadership.

On the afternoon of 7 July, students held a mass meeting in the assembly hall of the Rangoon University student union building. Then, they went out to demonstrate for about an hour. Just as they were dispersing, riot police stormed the campus and took over the student union. According to witnesses, a riot began, with the police firing tear-gas and students throwing stones. Some students also lit fireworks, increasing the chaos. Students shouted insulting slogans against General Ne Win, while soldiers entered the campus with their guns ready. When the protest did not immediately break up, they began shooting. Over one hundred students were killed, although the government admitted to only fifteen deaths.[1] In the early hours of the next morning, the military blew up the student union building, the centre of student activism since colonial days.

While General Ne Win succeeded in stopping the student protests, his recourse to such extreme measures provoked bitterness against the regime. U Pyone Cho, a university student at the time, recalled: 'You didn't find a lot of students that were really political at that stage. But because of the killing and all, that really made students start thinking. And from then on, every month there would be a book of poems. And every 7th [July], people would wear black [in commemoration of the killings]. I won't say all the students, but quite a few.'

The university was closed for four months, and as students travelled back to their home towns, they brought with them news of what had happened. The event was kept alive through the memorial song 'Old Union', set to the tune of a popular song, 'Old City of Pagan'. But the crackdown on students was just a taste of what was to come.

Through his Revolutionary Council, General Ne Win sought to remake Burmese politics and society. Land and wealth were to be redistributed, foreigners stripped of their assets, and self-serving politicians and capitalists replaced with loyal army men dedicated to serving the nation. General Ne Win started by replacing approximately 2,000 civilian members of the country's administration with military personnel.[2] Security and administrative councils were also set up at the divisional, township and village levels. These new military-guided councils served as the primary structure through which the Revolutionary Council interacted with society. The ethnic states lost what autonomy they had had, with security and administrative councils established there as well.

The Revolutionary Council instituted what it called 'the Burmese Way to Socialism', a programme which was supported by some intellectuals and politicians who felt that the AFPFL's watered-down socialist policies had not gone far enough. Many still linked capitalism with foreign exploitation and supported the regime's decision to seal the country off from foreign investment. Between 1963 and 1965, all banks, industries and large shops were nationalized. Most of the businesses were run by Indians and Chinese; by taking state control, the government intended to return the profits to indigenous Burmese. In March 1964, the Revolutionary Council demonetized 50-kyat and 100-kyat notes also with the intention of removing wealth from foreign hands. As a result, hundreds of thousands of Indian and Chinese business people lost everything and left the country. Those businesses that did not collapse came under state ownership.

Military men were brought in to run the businesses, but had little education or relevant experience and found it difficult to handle their new jobs. In cases where skilled civilians remained on staff, the new bosses often felt threatened by them. With no other opportunities available, many experienced professionals and bright young people emigrated, starting the brain drain which has continued ever since. The Revolutionary Council appeared to be unconcerned by the departure of so many of its most talented people, but the effect on industry was devastating. Burma had been ahead of both Malaysia and Thailand in industrial production in the 1950s, but declined steadily from 1964 onwards.

Agricultural production was also profoundly affected. While land reform programmes carried through by the regime gave agricultural plots to many landless farmers, farmers were told that from now on they had to sell all their rice to the government, at below market prices. Frustrated with the new system, some farmers put less effort into their cultivation while others hoarded as much rice as possible and sold or bartered it surreptitiously on the black market. Because rice exports were one of Burma's primary sources of foreign exchange, the dramatic fall in rice exports, from 1.8 million tons in 1963 to 0.3 million tons in 1968, made it impossible for the government to pay for necessary imports.[3] Both industrial and agricultural production suffered. The regime responded not by liberalizing the sale of rice but by cutting imports, including machinery and spare parts. This further hindered agricultural development.

With the nationalization of shops also came the establishment of co-operatives, where people could buy their daily necessities at subsidized prices. At first the shops were well-stocked and the government prided itself on taking care of the people. But soon stocks of even the most basic goods were insufficient, and waiting in line for rations became a part of daily life. To make up for the inadequacies of the cooperatives, a thriving black market emerged, with goods coming from Thailand and other neighbouring countries.[4]

In what at first seemed a positive development, the military regime announced that it would hold peace talks in Rangoon for all groups willing to participate. Safe passage to and from the talks was guaranteed. In 1963, many representatives of armed ethnic groups as well as communist leaders came to Rangoon, but the regime took a hard line with all of them. The communists were told to give up their armed struggle, and the regime refused to consider various ethnic nationalist demands for increased autonomy. When the talks broke down in November, students and others staged demonstrations. The universities were closed again, and a number of students were arrested and sent to a penal colony on Coco Island.[5] When the schools opened a year later, a new system was introduced. One of the most significant changes was that teachers were made more responsible for the conduct of the students. The regime hoped to use the teachers as their eyes and ears to reduce the likelihood of more protests.

In the meantime, independent associations also started to come under pressure. Even library clubs, such as U Pyone Cho's in Rangoon, were forced to shut down. U Pyone Cho and his university friends had established their library club in U Pyone Cho's father's garage on 141st Street shortly before the coup. The club had begun by having its members sweep the street and clear the drains every weekend. Members took turns volunteering for night shifts to watch out for fire, a frequent problem in those days. When people in the neighbourhood saw that the club was working for the good of the community, they began giving monthly contributions. The club boasted over one hundred members and rented out all kinds of books, including the anti-government poetry books and other literature written in commemoration of the 7 July killings. The club also staged citywide essay-writing competitions, sending announcements to all the schools and publicizing the winning essays in newspapers.

With police permission, the club held public lectures on big stages in the streets. People from all over Rangoon would come to listen. The club was so popular that many debate teams and writers' clubs wanted to join, so they were taken on as affiliate members. Gradually, though, it became more difficult to acquire permits for public talks. When the library club committee decided to hold a debate between several famous writers at Gandhi Hall with the provocative title 'Man is Worse than a Dog', they were originally denied permission by the police. The permit was granted only when a higher-ranking military officer over-ruled the police chief, thinking the club was planning to attack the deposed Prime Minister U Nu. Instead, the speakers discussed the dangers of military rule. Not long after, the regime announced that private associations had to register with the government or close down. After a visit from a government official in which they were told their club did not meet the new regulations, U Pyone Cho and his friends had to shut the library and stop their activities.

As the Revolutionary Council expanded its control, most independent associations and newspapers were either absorbed by the government or forced out of existence. All publications had to pass through a newly formed censorship board. Private schools were nationalized, and a government-controlled Burmese language curriculum was imposed throughout the country. Meanwhile most foreign missionaries, scholars and western foundations were forced to leave and foreigners' access to Burma was tightly restricted.

Independent trade unions were outlawed, and existing political parties were also compelled to disband, with the only legal political party being the government's Burma Socialist Programme Party (BSPP). Originally, membership in the BSPP was restricted to the military and the administration; however, the regime later expanded membership and established other mass organizations under state control. As time went on, people's only avenues for participation in civic life were through regime-sponsored organizations which were primarily dedicated to maintaining military rule. In these associations, there was little room for personal initiative or creative thought. The regime was looking for passive supporters, not free-thinkers. This was the beginning of the end of civil society in Burma for many years to come.

Meanwhile, the effects of the government's mismanagement of the economy became clear in 1967 when the scarcity of rice in Rangoon became a severe problem. Civil servants would sign in at their offices in the morning and then leave to spend the day searching for rice in villages outside the city. Although the government's inappropriate procurement and distribution policies were largely to blame for the shortage, people's anger turned against Chinese merchants who controlled much of the black market rice trade. Merchants were stockpiling rice, knowing they could sell it for a higher price as the crisis worsened. Some Burmese had also been irritated by the fact that the Chinese embassy was encouraging support for the Cultural Revolution among Sino-Burmese, including the wearing of Mao badges. Riots broke out, and the Chinese embassy and many Chinese-owned shops and homes were attacked. The military regime declared martial law and solved the problem by ordering all the warehouses to be opened and the surplus rice to be distributed. Dissidents have argued that this was an early example of how General Ne Win was able to deflect the people's anger away from the regime and channel it into communal riots.[6]

The military regime sought to demonstrate its commitment to ensuring public safety by announcing projects to rid the streets of crime. The police were ordered to round up a certain number of criminals during each project period, and in order to meet their quotas they often arrested people against whom they had no evidence. The detainees' families were not informed, and they were usually not tried. The prisoners could only hope that for one reason or another they would eventually be released.

U Tint Zaw, a Rangoon University professor who was imprisoned for his connections with student activists and for his refusal to join the regime's Burma Socialist Programme Party, met many such hapless prisoners during his years in prison. He remembered one bizarre case where the wife of a man who was arrested assumed that her husband had gone off with another woman. She put an announcement in the newspaper stating that he was her legal husband and anyone keeping him would be sued. In those days, prisoners were still allowed to read the newspaper, and the man saw the announcement about himself and showed it to the prison officer. An intelligence officer was sent to question him and only then was he released. U Tint Zaw himself was never charged for his 'crimes', but when he was arrested he was invited 'to stay for some time' in prison. That 'some time' turned out to be nine years.

Although General Ne Win had hoped to win popular support with his nationalization and land reform programmes, they led to economic disaster. In order to establish a more legitimate administration, he decided to re-organize his government. He and nineteen other senior officers resigned from the military in 1972 and assumed civilian titles. He also announced that the regime planned to draw up a new constitution and institute a one-party system, with elections for a People's Assembly (*pyithu hluttaw*) and local councils. In theory, the one-party system would give people a voice in managing the country's affairs, but that was to prove illusory from the start.

The BSPP Era, 1974–88

While the new constitution was being drafted, government authorities announced that citizens were welcome to send in their suggestions. But when several Chins wrote in recommending the adoption of federalism and a multi-party system, they were arrested. Perhaps because the Chins had always been loyal to the government and there were no Tatmadaw troops in Chin State, the authorities felt they had to act particularly harshly to stifle such demands. As a result, a member of a Chin youth group who signed his name on a letter calling for a federal union spent ten months in solitary confinement, a Chin major in the Tatmadaw served a two-year prison sentence, and a Chin public health assistant was imprisoned for several months, with his family having no idea what had happened to him.[7] When the public health assistant was re-leased, he was given a letter stating that he would never be permitted to work in Chin State again.

In December 1973 there was a national referendum in which people had to vote for or against the new constitution which called for a unitary state under one-party rule. It received 90 per cent support with an astounding 95 per cent of eligible voters voting.[8] Were people that delighted with the idea of one-party rule? Did so many ethnic minority voters support a unitary state? Many Burmese say that few understood the new system, but at least it offered the possibility of popular participation. Certainly some people hoped that greater civilian involvement would result in improvements. However, there were also instances of intimidation and ballot-box tampering which appear to have helped to produce such resoundingly positive results.

Saw Tu, a high school headmaster and a member of the election commission in Karen State, explained how the results were obtained in the remote area of the country where he worked. Saw Tu was the first from his township in Karen State ever to attend university. After graduating, he came back and taught in a district high school and was later promoted to headmaster. In 1973, he was appointed to the district commission responsible for overseeing the referendum.

He explained that, starting in the mid-1960s, the regime conducted a population survey of the distant hill villages through the cooperative shop in town. All the mountain villagers had to buy their goods at their designated cooperative shop (which carried no coffee, milk or sugar, because the authorities said mountain people didn't need these luxuries). Whenever a villager came to the shop, the clerk asked him or her the names of all the residents in that person's village. Because the villages were small, with only twenty or thirty families, the villager could easily name everyone. After some time, the authorities were able to obtain almost all the names of the villagers and villages, without ever having to travel there themselves. When the referendum was held, the government was able to use the name lists to their advantage. Everyone eighteen years old and over was supposed to vote in the referendum, but ballot boxes never reached the hill people in Saw Tu's district. Yet when the results came out, he was astounded to see that they had all apparently voted for the constitution.

Saw Tu also spoke of a case in one village where everyone put their votes in the black box, meaning they were against the constitution. Military authorities went to the village and asked the residents, 'Are you for us or against us?' Then they made the villagers vote again. That time, they all put their votes in the white box.

In town, the military authorities could not easily order people to vote again, but they made it clear that there could be consequences for those who dared to vote against the constitution. In Saw Tu's district, how people voted was obvious to the officials on duty because of the way the ballot boxes were arranged. The curtain around the voting area reached only to about knee-length and the two boxes were placed far apart. It was not possible to stand next to the box for 'yes' votes and reach the box for 'no' votes. Saw Tu remembered that some town people who voted against the constitution were put under watch, but the clerks were able to protect some 'no' voters by pretending not to know who they were. The clerks were reluctant to turn in their friends, particularly since many of them were not all that hopeful about the new constitution themselves. Bertil Lintner reported a similar occurrence in Shan State, where some of the student vote-counters took it upon themselves to move ballots put in the 'no' box to the 'yes' box, because they didn't want anybody to get in trouble.[9]

With the development of a one-party system, General Ne Win sought to use the BSPP to cement the allegiance of civil servants and others to his military-backed regime. In the 1970s, party membership was open to all and not joining carried negative consequences. Party members took over many of the administrative posts at all levels of government, and civil servants were expected to become members.

Saw Tu said he had no interest in joining the party and just wanted to put his energies into teaching. But the officials kept after him, and he finally gave in. He said he was pressured more than most, because the officials hoped that if they could win him over, they could use him to bring in more Karen members. Although he didn't even bother to fill out the entire application form, he was soon presented with his party membership card. Following that, on many ceremonial occasions, such as Independence Day and Union Day, he and other civil servants were ordered to give speeches praising the BSPP and denouncing the Karen National Union (KNU), which had been fighting for autonomy since 1949. Many Karen in his district had sons or relatives who had joined the KNU.

I asked him if he didn't feel as if he was promoting the regime by making such speeches. He replied that the speeches were meaningless, because everyone knew they had been written by the party. Even if you wrote the speech yourself, he said, you had to give it to the BSPP for editing. Still, I wanted to know, didn't he feel anything when he read those speeches? He replied, 'Actually, internally I didn't feel quite right. In 1962, on the 7th of July, I was there.' He had been a university student in Rangoon then and had joined his friends at the demonstration. He had also seen his fellow students shot down. But he felt that he had to go along with the regime now that he was a headmaster. He explained, 'You had to act in a certain way so that they would trust you. Only then could you work safely for your people.'

Saw Tu travelled to mountain villages encouraging young Karen to get an education. But the authorities suspected he was trying to link up with the rebels. Finally he did just that. He and his family joined the KNU.

There were civil servants who refused to join the BSPP, but they often suffered as a consequence. Because health care was nationalized, all doctors and nurses belonged to the civil service and were expected to become party members. Dr Aye Win, who did not join, talked about having to attend monthly indoctrination sessions for the first two years of his service. But Dr Aye Win felt that medicine, not politics, was his business. He knew that if he didn't join, he might not get a promotion or he might get transferred to a remote area, but he decided that wasn't important. His first supervisor didn't mind, but he warned Dr Aye Win, 'It may be hard for you in your next posting.'

His next assignment was at a hospital in a Karen town in a 'brown' area. The military refers to districts where both government and anti-government forces operate as 'brown' areas. 'White' areas are totally under government control and 'black' areas under opposition control. Dr Aye Win remembered that, at first, the BSPP members there thought he was a member and treated him well. But once they found out he wasn't a member, they began pressuring him. They reported that he wasn't doing his job properly and criticized him for treating all patients without asking whether they belonged to an insurgent organization. The local party authorities told him that as a township medical officer, he was expected to be a role model for the community.

One day the BSPP authorities announced that there should be a hospital clean-up with community participation the following Sunday. Dr Aye Win said that was not necessary because the staff were already taking care of the cleaning. But the party members told him that the people should feel that they are helping others. Dr Aye Win asked, 'Why are you forcing people to volunteer? I'll take any real volunteers, but not people who are forced to do this work.' This only exacerbated his problems with the party authorities. Eventually, he had to leave the district.

As much as the Ne Win regime encouraged people to join the BSPP in most areas of the country, in the predominantly Chin town of Kalaymyo, Chin citizens were often prevented from joining. At that time, there was no anti-government insurgency movement among the Chins, and relations between the Christian Chins and Buddhist Burmans in Kalaymyo were good, with frequent cases of intermarriage. 'But,' said Salai Zal Seng, a Chin church leader living in Kalaymyo, 'the administrative body wanted to split us.' Chin citizens found it difficult to become BSPP members, with the result that less than a quarter of the 900 BSPP members in the township were Chins. The township committee was also dominated by Burmans, with only an occasional Chin member. Frustrated by this, Salai Zal Seng's father, a civil servant, asked the township military commander, Captain Soe Win, why the distribution of power was so uneven. Captain Soe Win replied, 'Do you think that power is given by the sharing method?' Salai Zal Seng's father insisted that he saw no reason why power couldn't be shared since everyone was living together without any problems. The captain didn't say anything but had Salai Zal Seng's father transferred to a remote district on the Indian border.

In central Burma, many people who became party members also had high ideals and were committed to working for their country, but they found they could do little. Ohn Myint was a third-generation BSPP member who lived in a large town in central Burma. Both his parents and his grandfather were members of the party. He himself attended many of the training courses given by the party's youth organization. But, by the time he was in high school, he realized the BSPP wasn't really working for the people. He recalled, 'My grandpa was one of the leaders of our BSPP unit, and they had to hold meetings every month. First when they had the meetings, they would discuss what was happening in the public, and what the problems were, and they wrote reports to the upper levels, but there was never any response. So as time went on, they usually didn't hold meetings anymore. At that time, I helped to write the reports for my grandpa. I could just copy the old one to the new one and change the date and time.'

The judicial system also offered little hope of a fair hearing. Under the Revolutionary Council, courts were run by a panel of three judges, at least one of whom had to have some legal training. During the BSPP period, the three judges were elected, but had to be party members. The chairman of the three judges was generally a military officer, while the other two judges came 'from the people' and frequently included individuals with little education. From the government's perspective, a lack of education was not a problem because 'goodness', mainly characterized by loyalty, was more important. This was captured in the often repeated propaganda phrase '*lu gaung, lu daw*', which one Burmese writer has translated as 'good man first, smart man second'.[10]

Daw Mi Mi, a female lawyer during this period, explained that a lawyer would usually be there to act as an adviser to the people's judges, but they generally took their advice from the BSPP township council instead. Besides the political influence of the council, corruption was a constant problem. In non-political cases, rich men could often pay off everyone involved: doctors doing autopsies, police and judges. At a minimum, they could get their sentences reduced, if not thrown out. Sometimes the police took bribes from both sides, and tried to confuse the case by bringing in fake evidence or destroying real evidence. With civil servants' salaries too low to cover monthly living expenses, corrupt practices soon permeated many interactions between the public and the administration.

Although many civil servants did attempt to perform their jobs well, the system favoured those who did not challenge their superiors. Corruption was a far smaller crime than insubordination. General Ne Win had originally governed with the promise of efficiency and improving the national welfare, but things were falling apart. Lower-level officials realized it was safer to report only what their superiors wanted to hear, often masking the severity of problems under their jurisdiction. At the same time, no one wanted to take responsibility for making decisions, for fear of being punished. Thus, civil servants and party functionaries tended to send even small issues up to higher levels, with the result that little effective work was actually carried out.

The increasing presence of military intelligence agents, or MI, who functioned like a secret police in other countries, also dampened people's desire to speak out about problems. Besides plain-clothes intelligence agents, there were also informers in neighbourhoods and many workplaces. As a result, most people appeared to be obedient even if they didn't have faith in the regime's policies.

General Ne Win had originally shunned bringing religion into state affairs, both because of his government's socialist ideology and because he wanted to rein in the influence of the monks. In 1962, monks were ordered to register with the government, a stipulation which was rejected on religious grounds as monks are perceived to be above the realm of worldly affairs. When some monks protested in Mandalay, the demonstration was broken up by troops who shot several of the protesters.[11] In 1965, the regime organized a *sangha* (monks) conference which established an official monks' organization, and began registering all monks. Protesting monks were arrested, and several monasteries, where dissent was most fervent, were closed down.

By the late 1960s, however, General Ne Win began to demonstrate a more public interest in Buddhism, in order to gain some legitimacy with the majority Burman Buddhist population, for whom religious practice was central to their identity.[12] General Ne Win also began looking to Buddhist merit-making, astrology and sympathetic magic in support of his political ambitions. This was not particularly surprising to most Burmese, who frequently turn to such practices themselves. As much as Buddhism might ask people to recognize that all attachment is suffering, most people are still concerned with their daily affairs; in particular, job security, health, and the well-being of loved ones. They are looking for meaning and control over their lives, and by building pagodas and making merit in other ways, they hope to maintain or improve their current status.

At the same time, a belief in spirits, astrology and fortune-telling helps people make sense of why they get sick, why they get in trouble, and how to get out of these situations or prevent them altogether. Burmese parents have the astrological charts of their children calculated and written out soon after their birth. These charts indicate the general course of the child's life, but mothers continue to have readings done at significant times for more specific predictions. Astrologers are consulted about the appropriate date for weddings, shop-openings and Buddhist ordination ceremonies. People also seek out the services of other types of fortune-tellers who make their predictions based on palm reading, intuition or other signs. Unlike in the West where fortune-tellers and astrologers almost exclusively emphasize the positive, fortune-tellers in Burma often predict life-threatening dangers, illness and other serious problems. Luckily, they also suggest measures that individuals can take to ward off these troubles, called *yadaya chae*.

General Ne Win frequently appealed to fortune-tellers for advice on how to prolong his rule. On one occasion, he reportedly shot his image in the mirror so that he himself wouldn't be killed. Similarly, he had the lovely *go go* trees which provided shade along the road to his birthplace near Prome cut down, because the expression *go go that*, 'cut down the *go go* trees', also means to kill yourself. By removing the trees he believed that he could prevent his own political death. Most dramatically, in the mid-1970s he suddenly ordered cars to be driven on the right instead of the left. This was reportedly meant to stop the threat of a political attack from the right. Even today a number of old cars in Burma sport steering wheels on the wrong side because of this sudden decree.

For many people, such actions, no matter how bizarre, suggested that General Ne Win had special powers on his side. This only reinforced a feeling of the futility of resisting. And despite dissatisfaction with many aspects of BSPP rule, some of the regime's propaganda did appeal to Burmese citizens. In particular, the regime was successful in convincing most people that a strong unitary state was necessary and the ethnic nationalist armies had to be defeated. In the press, the ethnic nationalist armies were portrayed as rapists and murderers, and, having never visited the remote areas themselves, many readers believed the accounts.

Also, General Aung San's name still carried tremendous meaning for

Burmese people, and General Ne Win claimed to represent Aung San's legacy. Both members of the Thirty Comrades, they had fought for independence together, and General Ne Win sought to play up this connection. General Ne Win presented his regime as carrying out the socialist policies General Aung San would have wanted to implement, and portrayed the army, founded by General Aung San, as continuing to sacrifice for the people in order to maintain the country's integrity.

In the meantime, few Burmese could travel outside the country, and foreign journalists could not easily come in. Even tourists could only obtain seven-day visas to Burma. Lacking information about how other countries were developing, most Burmese took military-backed, one-party rule as a given and tried to make the best of their situation. In many cases this meant joining the party or at least trying to benefit from connections to government officials.

Resistance in the Cities

Despite the general population's overall passivity, the BSPP regime under General Ne Win did face occasional resistance from monks, students and urban workers. However, it was generally only the most idealistic and brave members of each of these groups who initiated such activities, for they risked torture and imprisonment if they were caught. Each demonstration started with a specific grievance, and although the protests sometimes widened into calls for the end of the Ne Win government, there was little consensus on what kind of system should replace military rule.

University students in Rangoon, Mandalay and Moulmein took to the streets on several occasions between 1962 and the late 1970s. Inspired by the role students had played in leading resistance protests against the colonial regime and also because they were young and generally free of financial responsibilities, many of the students saw themselves as having a moral duty to speak out. Most students were motivated by anger at the injustices they witnessed around them. Once a demonstration started, the military feared, it could spread quickly. Thus, the military and riot police usually responded immediately to isolate and arrest the protesters. In the 1960s and 1970s, each spate of demonstrations was easily contained but, not long after, another crop of students volunteered to put themselves at risk again.

In 1969, a riot broke out at the South East Asian Peninsular Games held at a newly constructed university campus in Rangoon. Students who couldn't get tickets to see the boxing matches pushed their way in. Soldiers shot into the crowd to disperse them, leading to more protests and university closures. In 1970, some university students organized a fiftieth anniversary commemoration of the founding of Rangoon University. The regime ordered teachers to prevent students from politicizing the event, but a history of the

July 1962 killings was distributed and students at some other universities also handed out anti-government pamphlets. Students and teachers were punished, and universities around the country were shut for a month.[13]

In 1974, much larger demonstrations broke out in May and June, this time led by workers in state-owned factories demanding better pay and more subsidized rice. Rations had been cut in half because the authorities were not able to obtain enough rice to meet all their employees' needs. The numbers of workers taking to the streets increased in early June, and the military responded on 6 June by firing into the crowds. The government reported twenty-two deaths, although other witnesses cited much higher figures. The military sentenced more than one hundred workers to lengthy imprisonment and immediately closed the universities, fearing escalating protests.

In December 1974, university student protests broke out over the dictatorship's handling of U Thant's funeral. This time the protesters' anger was clearly directed towards General Ne Win, and speech-makers called for his removal. General Ne Win had been jealous of U Thant, a Burmese diplomat who became Secretary General of the United Nations in the 1960s. While General Ne Win was leading his country into isolation and economic ruin, U Thant was receiving international accolades for his level-headed handling of numerous crises during the escalating Cold War period. After U Thant died in New York, his body was flown back to Rangoon, but General Ne Win ordered that no state official should meet the body, and he would be buried like any other ordinary person. But when his body was unceremoniously laid out at Kyaikkasan grounds, the old race track, thousands of Burmese came to place wreaths and pay their last respects.[14]

Incensed at the regime's disregard for the senior statesman, a group of university students decided to take matters into their own hands. Amassing a large number of students from various campuses in Rangoon, they marched to Kyaikkasan grounds on 5 December. Once there, they persuaded the officiating monks to give them the body, which they took on a decorated truck to Rangoon University and then placed on a platform in the Convocation Hall.

One participant, Thein San, explained what happened next. The students began building a mausoleum for U Thant on the site of the old student union. Supporters outside the university donated money and food packets to the students inside, and thousands of people, including monks, came into the university compound in the evenings to pay their respects and to listen to the students' speeches. Many of the speeches dealt with the economic crisis, while others had a more explicit anti-government theme. Thein San said: 'I don't know whether it was out of love and respect for U Thant or to do anything against Ne Win and the way things were, but the ordinary people were just taking off their pieces of gold jewellery and donating them. People were giving money, jewellery, everything.' The value of the donations was estimated to be as high as $42,000.[15]

Meanwhile, the military brought in troops to prepare for an assault on the university. The government announced the closure of all universities and ordered all students from outside Rangoon to return home. As the numbers of people on campus diminished, troops cordoned off the area and, in the middle of the night, soldiers and riot police stormed the campus. They arrested almost 3,000 people, including a number of monks who were forced to take off their outer robes and sit like criminals before being taken to the interrogation centre. The regime reported that eighteen people were killed, but student estimates were as high as one hundred.[16] Outrage at way the monks in particular were treated led to riots in Rangoon, with people targeting police stations, BSPP offices, and especially the hated Ministry of Cooperatives. The regime was able to put a stop to this in a day, but had to declare martial law and nightly curfews to restore order.

Then in June 1975, students and workers held a joint demonstration marking the anniversary of the 1974 workers' strike. As they marched down a main thoroughfare in Rangoon, more and more people began to join in. The authorities quickly crushed the protest and shut the universities again.

In March 1976, students in Rangoon, Mandalay, Taunggyi, Moulmein and Bassein honoured the centenary of Thakin Kodaw Hmaing's birth. Thakin Kodaw Hmaing was a famous writer, nationalist and key supporter of the 1963 peace talks between the government and armed resistance groups. The commemoration turned into a demonstration and the universities were closed, with over one hundred students in Rangoon alone arrested and sentenced from five to fifteen years' imprisonment. Tin Maung Oo, a prominent student leader of Chin ethnicity, was hanged.

One student group tried to launch a '7-7-77 movement' to begin on 7 July 1977. Besides being a lucky number, 7/7/77 was also the anniversary of the military crackdown on the 1962 student demonstrations. Students handed out pamphlets in Rangoon, but the campaign did not take off and the organizers were arrested. There were more arrests at the Rangoon Institute of Technology in August and September 1978 after students were caught distributing an underground history of the student movement in Burma.

Despite all these protests in Rangoon, Mandalay and other towns, the activists did not succeed in creating an organization or leadership that could maintain momentum. While the military intelligence could not prevent small protests from breaking out, they were adept at identifying emergent student leaders and getting them quickly into prison. Even in the planning stages, activists found it difficult to link up with each other because of fears that intelligence agents had penetrated their circles. Once activists were released from prison, they were always under surveillance, making it nearly impossible for them to resume political organizing. Thus, individuals became known for their heroic speeches or actions during strikes, but they were never able to translate these into sustainable movements.

The BSPP regime tried to stamp out resistance by increasing surveillance and limiting contact between students. First, professors were held responsible for the political activities of their students. Thus, professors could not just look the other way but, in order to protect their jobs, had to try to stop students from engaging in anti-government activities. Second, they increased the number of MI among the students. And third, in the mid-1970s, the regime sought to separate university students by setting up regional colleges. University students from rural areas would spend their first two years at a regional college and come to campuses in Rangoon or Mandalay only for their final two years, when they were thinking more about their future careers and were less likely to be politically active. Political ideology classes were also made required subjects for all majors, and students were encouraged to join the BSPP.

The often spontaneous and uncoordinated actions of students, monks and workers can be compared with those of General Ne Win, who was in a position to implement long-range plans for maintaining power. One story that circulated among the writers' community at the time was that Ne Win, who loved horse-racing and gambling, once bought a horse and sent it to the best trainer. At every race, he told the jockey to hold the horse back, so that no one would think it had much potential. One day, he bet his entire fortune on that horse, and to everyone else's utter amazement, it beat all the other horses. Even in horse-racing, the story concluded, General Ne Win planned for the long run.

More worrying to General Ne Win than the student and monk-led protests was the uncovering of a coup plot by some junior officers in 1976. Within the military, some officers were also dissatisfied with the regime's failed economic policies and the increasing corruption among party members, and a small group sought to remove General Ne Win from power. Lt General Tin Oo (sometimes spelled Tin U), who later became a senior leader in the National League for Democracy, was serving as General Ne Win's chief of staff at the time, and he was widely respected for having urged restraint in dealing with the demonstrators in 1974 and 1975. The junior officers plotting the coup were reportedly considering asking Lt General Tin Oo to take over. When their plot was uncovered, both they and Lt General Tin Oo were imprisoned, although there was no evidence that he had prior knowledge of the plot. Nevertheless, many of Lt General Tin Oo's supporters were questioned and a number of the better-educated army officers were transferred or retired. General Ne Win also sought to reconsolidate his hold over the BSPP by dismissing more than 50,000 party members.

Outside the 'Legal Fold'

Besides occasional political challenges in urban areas, General Ne Win and his regime also had to contend with the armed groups headquartered in the mountainous areas ringing the plains. In Burma, armed groups who fight against the government are referred to as living outside the legal fold. When these groups or their members surrender, they are said to have returned to the legal fold or 're-entered the light'. In the Revolutionary Council and BSPP periods, the Communist Party of Burma (CPB) was the largest ideologically oriented organization outside the legal fold.

Some students who became politicized through campus protests, prison experiences or rough treatment from the authorities and wanted to continue their political work headed for the Communist Party. Nevertheless, it should be understood that those who joined the Communist Party did not necessarily have a firm grasp of communist theory. Rather, they believed that the communists were committed to a struggle for justice. As Aung Zeya, who grew up in Rangoon and joined the CPB at their headquarters on the China border in the mid-1970s, put it: 'What sent me to the border was not an admiration of communist ideology but the inspiration I got from communists who sacrificed for the country.'

In some intellectual circles, capitalism and democracy had been thoroughly discredited by the colonial experience and the actions of certain pro-West politicians in the 1950s who were seen as manipulative and self-serving. Aung Zeya, who now supports the democracy movement, says: 'We believed that democrats were traitors. There was only one way to sacrifice for the people, and the way was to become a communist.' As in other colonized countries in Asia, communism had been popular with Burmese intellectuals. General Aung San had even helped to found the Communist Party in Burma, although he later moved away from it. After independence, communism continued to have an appeal, in part because of communist-led victories against the West in countries like Vietnam and the apparent relevance of Mao Zedong's theories about protracted guerrilla warfare in peasant-based societies.

In the late 1940s, members of the two armed branches of the Communist Party occupied territory in lower and central Burma, but by 1975 the Tatmadaw had driven them out of these areas. However, the White Flag branch regained strength after establishing its headquarters in a mountainous region on the Chinese border. There the CPB recruited thousands of local Was and other minority peoples as soldiers, and until the mid-1980s they received support in the form of money, advisers, soldiers, weapons and other equipment from the Chinese government.[17] The Tatmadaw lost thousands of soldiers fighting the CPB and blamed the communists for every political protest that broke out in central Burma. In fact, the Communist Party devoted little energy to the political struggles in the cities and was unable to rally support in the lowland rural areas. While it continued to hold its ground in northern Burma, it could not reoccupy territory in the heartland of the country. Eventually, the Chinese government realized that the CPB was never going to capture Rangoon. It stopped supplying the CPB and gradually improved its relations with General Ne Win. Ultimately the Chinese leadership was not so concerned about whether the government of Burma was communist as long as it was willing to cooperate with Beijing.

In the 1970s, there were also pro-democracy supporters who turned to armed resistance. After U Nu was released from prison in 1966, he realized that he could do little to change the country from within. In 1969, he agreed to join with Edward Law Yone, a former newspaper editor who had also been imprisoned, and four members of the Thirty Comrades in setting up the Parliamentary Democracy Party (later renamed the People's Patriotic Party) based on the Thai–Burma border. Their plan was to launch joint attacks into Burma with the KNU and the New Mon State Party's army, while also encouraging monks to lead demonstrations inside the country. Although the force was openly tolerated by the Thai government and had some early successes, it was unable to maintain its momentum. Besides financial problems, the leaders had difficulties working closely with the Karens because of continued differences of opinion over the political rights of the ethnic nationalities in a post-Ne Win Burma.[18]

In addition to the Burman-led opposition forces, numerous ethnic armies seeking autonomy were continuing to battle against the regime during this period. The largest groups were the Karen National Union (KNU), the Kachin Independence Organization (KIO), the New Mon State Party (NMSP) and the Shan State Army (SSA), each with armies of several thousand members. Led by a mix of university-educated men and soldiers who had fought with the British, they were able to support themselves by logging, mining and maintaining toll-gates along Burma's borders. With a constant stream of black market traders going to and from neighbouring countries, those who controlled the toll-gates reaped huge profits. Some of the armies operating in the hills of northern Burma, including the CPB, also raised money through taxing the opium and heroin trade.

Most of the larger ethnic nationalist armies were anti-communist, but some of the smaller multi-ethnic groups, such as the Karenni State Nationalities People's Liberation Front (KNPLF) and the Shan State Nationalities People's Liberation Organization (SNPLO), trained with the CPB and adopted a communist-inspired organizational structure. Some factions in the KNU and the NMSP were also more left-leaning. At the same time, small armed groups of Muslims generally known as Rohingya were operating in Arakan State, and Pa'o and Palaung forces were fighting for autonomy within Shan State.

Much of the mountainous territory controlled by the ethnic armies had never been under direct Burman rule, and the villagers considered Burman troops to be foreign invaders. The larger ethnic nationalist armies set up administrative structures as well as clinics and schools, where students were taught in their native tongues with Burmese and English introduced as second and third languages. Most of the ethnic nationalist armies adopted defensive postures, trying to prevent Tatmadaw troops from entering their areas but not organizing strikes deep into central Burma.

While most recruits came from villages in the ethnic areas affected by the civil war, young people of various ethnicities continued to make their way out from the plains to join these armies. Saw Luther, an irrepressible Karen who comes from the Delta region and has worked with the KNU for over twenty years, explained why he joined in the 1970s. Even though he lived far from the fighting, he had heard about how Karen people in Karen State were suffering and wanted to do what he could to protect them. Moreover, as a young man, he was inspired by the heroism of the guerrilla fighters willing to risk their lives for the establishment of a Karen homeland.

Although alliances were formed between the various anti-government armies, many were in name only. Most of the ethnic nationalist armies distrusted the Burman-dominated groups, and their relations with other ethnic armies were also strained. Neighbouring ethnic armies sometimes fought each other over territory, and differences in ideologies also kept them apart. Thus each army generally fought on its own, neither making any headway nor being forced to surrender.

Civil war was the normal state of affairs for large portions of the country. The war affected not only the soldiers on both sides, but also all the civilians who lived in the military operation areas. Starting in the mid-1960s, the military regime ruthlessly implemented a policy known as the Four Cuts. The objective was to eliminate all forms of support to resistance forces by cutting their access to food, money, intelligence and recruits. Many villagers were forced to leave their villages and were often brutally treated and even killed, whether they had anything to do with the opposition forces or not. As Martin Smith has written in *Burma: Insurgency and the Politics of Ethnicity*: 'For the Tatmadaw in the Four Cuts campaign, there is no such thing as an innocent or neutral villager. Every community must fight, flee, or join the Tatmadaw.'[19] As a result of Tatmadaw campaigns in the Karen, Kachin and other areas, tens of thousands of people lost family members, their land and their homes.

Civilians in towns controlled by the government were also affected, because they could be rounded up as porters for military campaigns at any time. Young men were grabbed coming out of cinema halls or getting off ferries, and sent off to the frontlines with no guarantee they would ever return.

Given the regime's lack of interest in resolving the country's political problems through dialogue, it is not surprising that some Burmans and ethnic minorities joined armed resistance movements in an attempt to achieve their objectives by force. However, with none of these armies appearing to be making much headway, most Burmese became cynical about their abilities to effect change. Most ordinary citizens, whether farmers or lower-level civil servants, focused on just being able to get enough food on the table for the next meal. As a Burman teacher who taught primary school in Karen State in the 1970s and 1980s put it: 'If we had spare time, we wanted to do some work to earn money. People were only thinking about survival.'

. . . .

CHAPTER 3

Breaking the Silence, 1988–90

'If somebody is against the government, we have to follow. We have to show that we also don't like this way.' (Son of a military engineer)

§ From the late 1970s until 1987, fighting continued in the ethnic minority states but there were no large protests against the BSPP regime in central Burma. Farmers continued farming, suffering arrests when they could not pay their paddy quotas. Smugglers continued smuggling, as legal imports continued to be restricted and domestic industry languished. In 1987, the United Nations designated Burma a 'Least Developed Country', grouping it together with the poorest African nations. No one said anything, but a few students and intellectuals, gathering in teashops and friends' houses, hatched plans and wrote articles intended to shake people out of their passivity.

One person involved in underground organizing since the mid-1980s was Moe Thee Zun. He had purposely failed his third-year university exams so that he could stay on campus longer. Like many other activists, he believed that the best place to cultivate anti-government activities was in the university, where there are a large number of single people more willing to take risks.

When the military regime announced the demonetization of 25, 35 and 75-kyat notes on Friday, 5 September 1987, Moe Thee Zun and his colleagues thought their chance had finally come. Many people's savings were wiped out in an instant, and the activists believed people would surely take to the streets. But after a small protest organized by university students, the regime announced the closure of the universities. As a result, nothing could be done on campus, and no protests coalesced on the streets. Families stayed quiet, hoping the regime would eventually offer partial reimbursement, as it had after two previous demonetizations.

The universities reopened two months later, and exams were held immediately. Moe Thee Zun and some of his friends tried to stir up activity, but other students did not respond. Moe Thee Zun graduated, but he continued to frequent teashops near campus, meeting with friends to discuss why Russia was transforming and the Philippines had already changed but Burma hadn't. They shared books and formed study groups while continuing to recruit new members for their underground student union. Then in March 1988, they got another chance.

A teashop brawl broke out between university students and local youth on 12 March. Because the young man who started the brawl was the son of a BSPP official, he was quickly released. Students gathered in front of the police station to protest, and riot police stormed them, killing a student named Phone Maw. Phone Maw's fellow students were outraged. They demanded that the government announce the truth about what had happened in the government-controlled media. Instead, the regime's spokesmen blamed the students for inciting unrest.

The next day demonstrations broke out at Rangoon Institute of Technology and Rangoon University. Students gave impromptu speeches about the need for a student union to represent their interests. Soon they also began demanding the end of one-party rule. On 16 March, students from Rangoon University decided to march towards the Institute of Technology campus a couple of miles away. When they reached Inya Lake on Prome Road, they found themselves squeezed between soldiers in front of them and riot police behind them. To their left were large homes surrounded by high walls. To their right was the lake.

Min Ko Naing, a student activist who later became famous, tried to convince the soldiers to let the students pass. But the riot police attacked from behind, the soldiers followed suit, and the students were trapped in between. Some fleeing students made it down alleys and over walls into people's yards. Others ran into the lake with soldiers following them. Some students drowned because they couldn't swim or because they were beaten unconscious by soldiers. Witnesses recalled being horrified to hear the soldiers shouting 'Don't let them escape!' and 'Kill them!' as they beat the unarmed students. Several students were arrested and taken away. Forty-one suffocated to death in an over-crowded prison van. Later, word got out that some of the arrested female students were gang-raped. People were shocked. The event came to be known as the Red Bridge incident, because the site of the attack was a bridge that became splattered with blood.[1]

The next day, further demonstrations occurred at Rangoon University where students gathered for Phone Maw's funeral. It turned out that his body had already been secretly cremated by the military, but students gave fiery speeches throughout the day, while military men surrounded the area and cut the electricity and water. No one could enter or pass food in, although students were allowed to escape through a small back gate.

Ye Min, a medical student from a rural town who had never witnessed a demonstration before, came with a few friends to see what was happening. By the afternoon, he was hungry and thirsty and felt worn down by the military pressure outside the gates. He was preparing to slip out the back when he saw a female student going up on to the makeshift stage. He decided that if a female student had enough courage to make a speech in these conditions, he shouldn't leave. Later he was arrested with others and questioned at length, because the military was worried to see that the protests which had started in two universities the day before, now appeared to be spreading to the medical institutes. Approximately one thousand students were arrested that evening, while others were beaten and left, because there were not enough prison vans to take everyone.

The next day, a huge demonstration of over ten thousand people took place in central Rangoon, and many more were arrested. The regime closed the universities for two months. When they reopened on 1 June, Ye Min and three others learned they were to be expelled for attending the March demonstrations. That sparked a movement within the medical institutes to boycott classes until the four students were reinstated.

At Rangoon University, political organizing was also continuing, and Moe Thee Zun prepared to make his first public speech. Like Min Ko Naing (Conqueror of Kings), Moe Thee Zun was not his real name; to protect themselves from identification and arrest, and in imitation of the Thirty Comrades, many student leaders took on 'noms de guerre'. Moe Thee means 'hailstorm', a pen name he had used for his poetry in underground publications. He added Zun, Burmese for 'June'.

Moe Thee Zun recalled that, the night before, he wrote a good-bye letter to his parents, gave his younger brother a final hug, telling him they would meet again 'when victory had been won', and headed for the door. To his chagrin, his mother had suspected that he was up to something, so she had padlocked all the doors. He remembered, laughing: 'She thought she had caught the fish, so she was satisfied and went to sleep. But there was a big tamarind tree, and one branch went to the second floor window. My mother forgot that!'

He climbed down the tree, hopped on the back of his friend's bicycle, and they pedalled off into the night. After working until dawn making pamphlets announcing his speech, they went to Rangoon University to set up chairs, microphones and speakers. Soldiers had surrounded the university but students approached the stage, curious to hear what he had to say. Moe Thee Zun remembers how nervous he was, having never given a speech in front of a large audience before. But once he got started, he went on for almost three hours.

After explaining the history of the students' movement since 1962, he stressed his belief that students should fight for all the people, not just for students' rights. Specifically he urged the audience to denounce the demonetization and demand reimbursement. He insisted that because one-party rule was responsible for the country's decline, students should demand that multiparty democracy be reinstated.

Min Zaw remembers the abbot of his temple giving a religious speech to the community in which he told people that if they needed to do something, they should follow through and do it. Min Zaw said it was his way of encouraging the people to organize. The abbot also gave Min Zaw a *gahta*, or incantation, telling him, 'You have to practise saying it. It will protect you from arrest.'

When some local teachers organized a rally in early August, Min Zaw insisted on attending. A layman who had come to know Min Zaw at the temple and often gave him extra meals, encouraged Min Zaw to give a speech. After shouting nervously at the audience, 'Do you think I am a monk?', Min Zaw told them that he was actually a student from Rangoon University and explained everything he had witnessed during the demonstrations in March and June. The community had planned a protest for the next day, and Min Zaw decided he could no longer be a monk.[4] The next morning, he changed into street clothes, and walked out of the monastery. When the abbot saw him, he smiled and said nothing.

Six Weeks of Nationwide Protests

In Rangoon, following the walkout of the dock workers at 8.08 a.m. on 8 August, thousands of people took to the streets. Surprisingly, the soldiers just watched. Late that night, however, the killing began. Violence incited more anger, and people continued to come out on to the streets over the next few days. With the fearlessness of youth, high school students led numerous demonstrations in their school uniforms of white shirts and green *longyis*. Many provocatively bared their chests in front of the troops, daring the soldiers to shoot or bayonet them. Although a number of soldiers refused, others obeyed orders to kill the young students. Many soldiers had been brought into the city from remote areas, having been told that the students were communists bent on destroying the country. Between 8 and 12 August, several hundred people were killed in Rangoon alone.[5]

In Rangoon students played the central role in organizing demonstrations and handling local security. In Mandalay students and monks led together. Kyaw Tint, a student activist in Mandalay, remembers: 'We started on the morning of 8/8/88, but the monks had to eat their morning meal, so they asked us to please wait until after 11. But some students couldn't wait so they started. At that time one youth was shot and died. At 11.30 the monks' group started marching. And the next day, we started the boycott camps in monasteries and pagodas and some schools.'

In medical student Ye Min's township in the Delta, students began their demonstration at the local high school. As they marched, they called for the release of two locally arrested students as well as for the end of one-party rule. As in many rural areas where there were no soldiers, only local police, the atmosphere was not as frightening as it was in Rangoon or Mandalay. When the crowds poured into the police station, the police had no choice but to release the two students. In the following days, the students organized a strike committee camp at one of the monasteries with the full support of the monks. They formed a township student union including high school and university students, and encouraged teachers to become involved. Later, teachers' unions, workers' unions, a health workers' union, and a lawyers' union were also set up. Then the various unions joined together to select a township general strike committee. Other towns followed a similar pattern, with professional groups organizing themselves into impromptu unions and their leaders forming strike committees to coordinate demonstrations and later administrative affairs.

Back in Rangoon, Moe Thee Zun had become one of the leading speakers and strategists. He urged students to move their demonstrations out of the universities and into the markets and other centres of activity, such as in front of Rangoon General Hospital. When the students arrived and began speaking, troops followed. Unable to tell who was a student and who was a bystander, the soldiers beat everyone, and sometimes even shot people. As a result, everyone automatically became involved. Moe Thee Zun also encouraged activists to hold demonstrations in the evenings, when workers, farmers and others were on their way home. Such protests didn't interrupt their work, and the protesters could more easily escape if soldiers came after them.

In every demonstration, students carried fighting-peacock student union flags, banned since 1962, and portraits of General Aung San. In doing so, they sought to convey that they, not General Ne Win and the ruling government, represented General Aung San's true legacy. Moreover, the protesters sought to remind the army that General Aung San's vision had been of an army that defended the people's interests rather than killed its fellow citizens.

Nevertheless, during the demonstrations perhaps as many as 3,000 people in Rangoon and other towns were killed, most shot by the military while marching.[6] There were also incidents when civilians surrounded and killed suspected military intelligence personnel and others. Some civilians also came out with swords, daggers and *jinglee*, sharpened arrows fashioned out of bicycle and umbrella spokes. After years of feeling frustrated and powerless, the desire for revenge was overwhelming.

The ABFSU in Rangoon set up a security department early on to manage the crowds during demonstrations. Ko Doe, a serious-looking young man who was a member of the security department, remembers how difficult it was to stop some of the violence. He said: 'You have heard that many people cut heads. They didn't have any information, they just suspected or hated that person, so they killed him. I think some people had no reason. They knew that some of the people were MI, but some I don't think were MI.' Sometimes

Ko Doe and his team received telephone calls telling them to rush to a scene where violence was breaking out, but by the time they arrived, it would be too late. Ko Doe said: 'We students didn't want this kind of thing.'

Ko Doe explained that he and other student activists suspected two kinds of people were behind the killings: ordinary people who were angry and lost control and military people in plain clothes trying to create a chaotic situation so that the military would have a justification for clamping down. Although the students understood these problems, Ko Doe said they were too inexperienced to know how to prevent them. He admitted: 'When we ourselves caught military intelligence agents, sometimes we beat them and punched them. This is normal. But we didn't kill them.' Usually the students tried to get information out of them and then left them in a monastery under the protection of monks.

Ko Doe came from a military family, so his primary duty was to collect information about the military's activities. Through sympathetic military people, he was given information about what kind of guns and other equipment they had and, on some occasions, whether or not the soldiers had been given orders to shoot. Some of the military people he talked to told him they had to fire on the people because they were ordered to, but they didn't want to. He said: 'They felt really confused and found it difficult to understand. So they gave us all the information.'

Not only in Rangoon, but also in some rural towns and villages, there were soldiers, though rarely intelligence officers or higher ranking army officers, who helped the demonstrators. One longtime activist, U Myat Hla, who was in a town in central Burma at the time, said: 'Some of the local army men defected to the demonstrators and even told me they would give training to the villagers when the time came.'

U Myat Hla was helping villagers establish local strike committees, but he said that the situation in his area was chaotic. Mobs of villagers captured weapons from police stations, and it was very close to armed struggle. Although he told the villagers that they should use non-violent methods, they laughed at him and said he was naïve. U Myat Hla said: 'Ordinary people do not believe in non-violent methods. They were surprised that they shouldn't do anything when the soldiers shot at them. At least they wanted to use swords.' In U Myat Hla's area, local authorities apparently tried to stir up trouble by provoking clashes between Muslims and Burmese and allowing soldiers to steal rice and take all the money out of the local bank.

With demonstrations taking place all over the country, on 12 August 1988, General Sein Lwin was removed as president. On 19 August, Dr Maung Maung, a legal scholar with a senior position in the BSPP regime, was appointed as Sein Lwin's successor. Five days later, troops were called back to their bases and the shooting stopped.

With no fear of being killed, numerous people who had originally hesitated to come out now took to the streets. Even in the distant ethnic states, the demonstrations drew huge crowds. In Shan State over a two-week period, tens of thousands of villagers descended on a small market town which usually contained only a few thousand residents. These villagers had suffered more under military rule than farmers in the plains. Shan nationalist armies operated in the region, and villagers were frequently forced to accompany the Tatmadaw during their anti-insurgent operations, portering ammunition and supplies. Forced labour and the confiscation of their property were routine experiences.

In Pa-an, the sleepy capital of Karen State, Karens, Burmans and others also came in from miles away to march around the central area for days. Like villagers in Shan State, they had been the victims of military campaigns and faced far greater difficulties than people living near or in the urban centres of Rangoon and Mandalay.

Civil Society Re-emerges

During this chaotic, often violent but also exciting time, the first beginnings of a civil society re-emerged. After the soldiers retreated, independent organizations sprang up everywhere. Artists, actors, civil servants and housewives organized unions and marched in the streets. Large groups of people resigned from the BSPP and other military-controlled organizations, holding 'burn-ins' where membership cards were thrown into fires in front of local BSPP offices. Several dozen newspapers, magazines and pamphlets appeared overnight.[7] The budding free press provided information about what was going on as well as fresh ideas, while comedians critiqued the dictatorship in the streets. Zagana, a dentist and comedian, became a famous regular at Rangoon demonstrations, ridiculing General Ne Win's rule through savage mimes and satires.

As more and more professionals joined the movement, even the foreign service members began organizing. Many had found representing Burma's policies abroad humiliating. Maung Maung Nyo, a Canberra-based senior diplomat who eventually defected, talked about how he had usually taken what he called a 'minimalist approach' to dealing with foreign journalists and critics. He tried to avoid them, but if he absolutely had to meet with them, he would answer all their sensitive questions with 'no comment'. In August, the staff at his embassy in Canberra became consumed with discussions about what to do. They busily cabled back and forth to other Burmese embassies to see what steps they were taking. One staff member who had witnessed the killings in Rangoon insisted that they should do something, but many said that it would be better to minimize the risk to themselves by letting others take the lead.

Then, on 30 August, at the Foreign Ministry personnel in Rangoon put out a statement saying that the BSPP policy had 'tarnished Burma's pride and prestige in international fora. We've lost face implementing policies which lack essence.' They also called for free and fair elections under a multi-party system. Following this statement, letters of support were issued by staff members at many embassies, including the embassy in Canberra.

Not surprisingly, given the lack of respect for the law under the BSPP regime, lawyers were also active. The Bar Council drafted a statement critiquing the BSPP's disastrous monetary policies and abuse of the legal system. Selected lawyers simultaneously read out the statement all over the country.

Although groups were organizing everywhere to denounce the government, maintaining law and order was a more difficult problem. The student unions had called for a nationwide strike on 26 August but, in what appears to have been an effort to disrupt the strike, the authorities opened most of the country's prisons that morning. Daw Mi Mi, a lawyer living in a town in the Delta, remembered how terrified people were that anarchy would break out. Her township strike committee was able to resolve the problem by meeting with the prison authorities and the prisoners, convincing the latter to stay in prison under the protection of Buddhist monks. Each case would be reviewed by the town's lawyers and anyone who had been unjustly imprisoned or convicted of a minor crime would be released. Both the prisoners and the townspeople accepted the arrangement.

In Rangoon, the YMCA stepped in to take care of young people who had been released from juvenile prison. They also joined with other religious leaders to set up an inter-faith council of Buddhists, Christians, Hindus and Muslims which provided rice to some of the most needy in the city. In other areas, though, tensions began to rise because of the food shortages and widespread looting of government property. The strikes had caused a total breakdown in the transportation infrastructure, all work stopped, and getting food became increasingly difficult for many people. Many families feared that the mobs would not stop at the government warehouses but would raid their shops and houses too.

In most towns, local committees were set up to handle daily affairs; in particular, security and food distribution. These committees were usually run by teachers, lawyers, doctors and intellectuals, but in many places monks played the leading role. They provided shelter at their monasteries for those who could not return home, they restrained protesters who wanted to kill captured military men, and they settled disputes. At night, young monks armed themselves with sticks and patrolled the streets, watching not only for soldiers but also for criminals hoping to take advantage of the breakdown of order.

While the monks often tried to prevent killings, in many places they encouraged people to demonstrate their disapproval of BSPP rule. Linking the struggle against the regime to a need for spiritual purification, in Mandalay a group of monks led Burmese residents in evening rituals usually reserved for the last day of the new year celebrations. Gathering on street corners, monks asked the crowds three times, 'Do you want evil spirits, which make people suffer in all kinds of ways, to stay around here?' The people responded, 'No, we don't want that!', beating gongs and pots and pans to drive the bad spirits away. In this case, the spirits were not ghosts of the deceased but living members of the regime.

Monks also indirectly supported popular participation by giving demonstrators protective charms and tattoos. As in the days of the Saya San rebellion in the 1930s, many people still believed such charms could protect them and thus were emboldened to take to the streets. The deaths of those who had such protections were explained by the assumption that they must have broken one of the rules that drains the charm's efficacy, such as drinking alcohol. Some monks themselves were believed to have supernatural powers which allowed them to see the future and travel from place to place invisibly. Many demonstrators drew strength from the presence of the monks in the demonstrations.

The Need for Leadership

In the early days of the demonstrations, General Aung San's daughter, Daw Aung San Suu Kyi, played no role. Her father had died when she was two, and she had lived outside Burma since she was a teenager. Her mother was appointed ambassador to India, so the family moved to Delhi. Then she attended university in England and married Michael Aris, a British scholar of Tibet. Although she often returned to Burma for visits, she was settled in England where she and her husband were raising their two sons. She had written to Michael Aris before their marriage saying that if her country ever needed her, she would have to go, but such a scenario had appeared unlikely.

In 1988, Daw Aung San Suu Kyi happened to be in Rangoon taking care of her ailing mother when the demonstrations broke out. At first she stayed at home but, at the urging of others, she put out a statement calling for the establishment of an independent committee to oversee multi-party elections. Then she decided to make a speech on the field beneath Shwedagon Pagoda on 26 August, the day student organizers had called for a nationwide strike. That morning, the area filled with over half a million people, curious to see the daughter of their beloved national leader. Her eloquence and poise captivated the audience as she urged people not to turn on the army but to seek democracy in a peaceful and unified way.[8] She immediately became a key figure in the movement, although she was not affiliated with any particular group.

While the demonstrations drew widespread participation, the lack of a unified leadership became a problem. Block, neighbourhood and village organizations emerged to handle local affairs, but there was still no recognized national organization. Student groups took the lead in organizing demonstrations, but they were not capable of establishing a new administration. Veteran politicians and retired military leaders were out making speeches but none had total support. In September, rumours started to spread that the army was going to stage a coup. Pressure was increasing on the leading activists and politicians to try to establish an interim government.

On 9 September, former Prime Minister U Nu, who had returned to Burma under amnesty in 1980, released a press statement announcing that he had formed a government himself. Most people had lost faith in him and were dismayed by his cabinet appointees, many of whom were old cronies or his relatives.

Two days later, BSPP leaders announced that they would hold an election for a new multi-party parliament. Although they had dropped their original plan to hold a referendum to see whether people supported one-party or multi-party rule, many people still doubted whether the BSPP could be trusted to hold multi-party elections. As a result, the demonstrations continued.

Meanwhile, student representatives and veteran politicians went to a number of embassies to inquire if they would support an interim government. After receiving positive feedback from a few of the embassies, they held meetings on 13 and 14 September. Daw Aung San Suu Kyi, U Nu, Bo Yan Naing (one of the Thirty Comrades), U Tin Oo (the army chief of staff sacked in 1976), and Brigadier Aung Gyi (who had written the open letters to General Ne Win) participated. Moe Thee Zun was selected to represent the 100 leading student activists who attended, and he urged the five politicians to agree with the students' plan to form an interim government within forty-eight hours.

The meeting was held inside Medical Institute No. 1 in Rangoon, and loudspeakers had been set up on the street so that the thousands of people outside could listen. Moe The Zun remembered: 'We told the politicians, "Please forget your problems and form the interim government".' But U Nu insisted that everyone should support his government, and the others were unwilling to do so. The meeting ended without the leaders being able to come to any immediate agreement on how to proceed.

There were still many unresolved differences of opinion between the politicians, and some of the senior leaders felt that it was better to wait and see if the BSPP would follow through on its election promise. Meanwhile, student activists continued to try to build support for an interim government, meeting with representatives of the various professional unions and compiling a list of nominees, including Daw Aung San Suu Kyi. But the next day the military staged a coup, and their opportunity had gone.

The afternoon of the coup, on 18 September 1988, troops appeared on the streets all over the country and began clearing out strike centres and breaking down the protective barriers that residents had erected at so many crossroads. Anyone who resisted was shot. After two days and several hundred killings, especially of young students, the military re-established control.

General Ne Win's name did not appear in the new ruling junta, which called itself the State Law and Order Restoration Council (SLORC). But General Saw Maung, the chairman, and the other top leaders in the SLORC were known to be loyal to him. Meanwhile, General Ne Win was widely believed to be calling the shots from behind the scenes.

At that time, rumours began circulating of guns and ammunition at the Thai–Burma border. Students who were determined to continue the fight, and felt that armed struggle was their only alternative, streamed out of the cities. Others left to escape arrest. Moe Thee Zun recalled that he and some other students still believed in the need for a continued mass movement inside the country and they urged students not to leave, insisting, 'This is not a Rambo movie.' Nevertheless, as many as 10,000 students made their way to the Thai, Chinese, Indian and Bangladesh borders. While it was a frightening journey for the students who had never been in the jungle, in many cases they were not chased by Tatmadaw troops. The military regime was eager for the students to move out of the cities, recognizing that as successful as the students had been in organizing people in urban areas, they were no match for the battle-hardened Tatmadaw troops in the jungle.

Why did the 1988 demonstrations not succeed? The demonstrations had broken out spontaneously and while there was a fair amount of quick coordinating at the local level, there was no national leadership which could unite the strike committees. As the strikes continued, food shortages worsened, public services stopped and people grew tired, giving the military an opportunity to retake control.

Another factor was the marked lack of participation of the armed ethnic organizations. None of their armies came into the towns, although small groups ventured in to see what was happening and handed over a few weapons to individual contacts. The KNU and NMSP were actually fighting each other over contested territory at the time. While many of the ethnic minorities living in the cities and towns in the heartland of Burma participated, the leaders of the armed ethnic organizations felt this was not their struggle. They saw it as a battle between Burmans, so they remained on the sidelines. As General Mya, the head of the KNU, was quoted as saying in *Asiaweek*: 'The recent uprisings were good for the people, but we cannot yet say it will be directly beneficial to the revolutionaries.'[9]

Another group which did not send its army into the cities was the Communist Party of Burma.[10] As U Myat Hla, who had contacts in the CPB, put it, 'Many slogans were introduced by the CPB's underground movement members, but sometimes these UGs [underground operatives] did not consult the party. The SLORC scapegoated them, but they played only a limited role. Even one of the senior leaders in the CPB admitted that.'

Finally, the regime was able to regain control because the generals could command the obedience of enough of their soldiers. Although some soldiers did join the movement, or refused to shoot, there were plenty who did not desert but stayed to pull the trigger as they were told.

Still, the movement had a profound psychological influence on its participants. Before 1988, the police and intelligence agents had been widely disliked, but after the troops' killings of students and monks, the military itself became hated. People who had grown up assuming authoritarian rule would continue indefinitely now believed that the country's politics could be different. Activists from different generations had been able to link up and present a new vision for the country. As a result, people's hopes were raised that democracy would be restored, and the coup organizers were forced to offer the promise of change.

The Election Campaign

Just days after the coup, General Saw Maung, the chairman of the SLORC, announced that political parties could begin registering. The National League for Democracy (NLD), led by Daw Aung San Suu Kyi, U Tin Oo and U Aung Gyi, was one of the first to do so, on 27 September 1988. The day before, the National Unity Party (NUP) announced its formation. Former military men and BSPP loyalists made up the bulk of the NUP, which was quickly characterized as representing a continuation of the old order. The party had a distinct financial advantage because it was able to take over many of the BSPP offices and equipment for free. It soon became clear that the regime hoped to engineer the election so that the NUP would win an outright victory or at least become the leading member of a coalition government.

How did the SLORC think the NUP could win when people had participated in the democracy movement just a few weeks before? First, the regime, like most military dictatorships, tended to see and hear only what it wanted to believe. Thus, it over-estimated its support, particularly among soldiers and former active BSPP members. Second, it encouraged the formation of a plethora of parties which would divide pro-democracy voters. Third, as the campaign went on, it tried to weaken the other parties by arresting particularly popular and capable challengers. And fourth, it severely limited campaigning opportunities in direct and indirect ways.

Political parties were allowed to open offices and given telephone lines and extra rations of petrol at the subsidized government price. Most people believe that at least one of the reasons the SLORC provided these incentives was so that a large number of parties would form, people would feel utterly confused, and the vote would be split in a thousand directions. Indeed, over 200 parties were established in all, set up by former politicians, intellectuals, ethnic minority representatives and students. However, some of these so-called parties were nothing more than groups of friends who wanted a place to meet and access to the perks that were being offered. Others were formed by students who did not want to compete in the elections but needed a cover for continuing their political activities.

Before the SLORC's coup, both Daw Aung San Suu Kyi and U Tin Oo had called for the formation of an interim government. After the coup, they had asked civil servants to continue to stay home, but people were hungry and in desperate need of money. The junta ordered civil servants to go back to work by 3 October or lose their jobs. The offer was sweetened by the promise that they would receive back pay for September, when no one had gone to work. On 3 October almost everyone went back to their offices.[11] As a result, Daw Aung San Suu Kyi and other NLD leaders decided the best course was to push ahead with election campaigning, hoping to bring about change through the ballot box.

Student activists initially continued to press for an interim government which would write a new constitution and take responsibility for holding elections. To carry out their work, they too formed political parties. ABFSU members in Rangoon organized the Democratic Party for a New Society (DPNS), which held political education sessions at its offices and investigated and publicized the problems of farmers and relocated urban residents. In Mandalay, many high school and university students also wanted to continue the movement through underground organizing or armed struggle, both illegal. Recognizing that their activities could tarnish the image of the NLD, they too formed a separate political party, the Organization of Students and Youth for National Politics.

During this period, as many as sixteen student fronts appeared, including groups led by ethnic minority students. While they tried to unite, differences in ideology, mistrust between rural people and city people, and tensions between ethnic minorities and Burmans made it difficult for them to work together. Also, some of the larger student groups could not easily accept that they did not have the right to speak for everyone.

Senior politicians also often broke with each other over personal differences and contentious power dynamics. The difficulties that many of the political organizations faced with factionalism related to the fact that most were organized in the pattern of patron–client relations. When conflicts emerged, leaders were reluctant to compromise, and many thought the better option was to leave and form a new group.

Ethnic minorities who supported participation in the elections faced difficult decisions of their own. Some thought it was best to join the NLD, because the NLD had a chance of winning the election and effecting change nation-wide. Others chose to support ethnic-based parties which might succeed only in minority regions, but offered more space for voicing demands for ethnic cultural and political rights.

The NLD was the most successful in bringing diverse people together under a common platform, but it too had to struggle to maintain internal unity. It was composed of two different groups: ex-military men on the one hand, and intellectuals and students on the other. Nevertheless, the NLD quickly attracted widespread support, primarily because the public was so taken with Daw Aung San Suu Kyi. Almost three million people joined the party and large crowds attended her rallies. She and U Tin Oo campaigned extensively, including in the ethnic minority states. Wherever she arrived, excited crowds waited to greet her. The ethnic nationalities were particularly touched by Daw Aung San Suu Kyi's visits to their areas, which echoed her father's visits four decades earlier. Many hoped that she too would be sym-pathetic to their concerns.

Daw Aung San Suu Kyi and her party members stood out because when-ever they appeared in public they wore traditional clothes and often *kamauk*, the wide-brimmed farmers' hats which became the symbol of the party. Many men in the NLD wore dark-coloured Kachin *longyis* which had been favoured by student demonstrators in 1988. Daw Aung San Suu Kyi donned the clothes of the various ethnic groups in each region and, like Burmese women in the past, always pinned a sprig of flowers in her hair.

Daw Aung San Suu Kyi's words also resonated with the feelings of the people. Drawing on both western democratic practice and Buddhist ideology, she articulated what was wrong with authoritarian rule. She often talked about the ten ethical rules for kings, which are based on Buddhist concepts of loving kindness, tolerance and self-control.[12] Derived from Buddhist scriptures, the rules were widely applied to pre-colonial kings in Burma. It was believed that kings who strayed would see their kingdoms disintegrate, and they themselves would lose the right to hold power.

The SLORC realized that, despite the proliferation of parties, Daw Aung San Suu Kyi had the power to unite people and posed a serious challenge to their own party. Something had to be done. First the authorities threatened supporters with serious consequences if they attended her rallies, but people still came. The regime's propaganda wing circulated vulgar cartoon images of her and repeatedly argued that her long years abroad and marriage to a westerner made her unfit to be a leader.[13] Because of lingering memories of foreigners taking Burmese wives in the colonial period, this did bother some citizens, but her status as the daughter of a great national hero carried more weight.

In April 1989, when she arrived in the town of Danubyu in the Irrawaddy Delta and was about to address the crowd, an army captain gave six soldiers the order to shoot her. Just before they did, a major stepped forward and stopped the soldiers.[14] Daw Aung San Suu Kyi continued walking toward the stage, but the pressure had clearly escalated.

Although Daw Aung San Suu Kyi and the NLD focused on the election campaign rather than resuscitating a mass movement, they joined with student groups in commemorating the anniversaries of significant days from the 1988 demonstrations. The military saw such events as provocative and sent in troops. At a commemoration she attended for students killed at Myinegone the year before, soldiers shot and killed one of the student participants. Daw Aung San Suu Kyi herself was briefly arrested.[15]

What really upset the military top brass, however, was that Daw Aung San Suu Kyi dared to criticize General Ne Win by name. Furthermore, she urged the army to be loyal to the country and the people rather than to General Ne Win. The government-controlled press attacked her for sowing discord between the Tatmadaw and the people, and within the Tatmadaw itself.[16]

On 19 July, Daw Aung San Suu Kyi had planned to march with thousands of students to the tomb of her father to honour Martyr's Day, the day that General Aung San and his cabinet were assassinated in 1947. The SLORC responded by filling the streets with troops. Fearing that the military would storm the marchers, she called off the march at the last minute.[17] Rumours were already spreading that she would be arrested. It happened the next day. The military surrounded her compound on 20 July 1989 and put her under house arrest while sending thirty supporters who were there off to prison. On the same day, U Tin Oo was arrested at his house, although neither he nor Daw Aung San Suu Kyi was formally charged.[18]

The military intelligence had no legal justification for arresting Daw Aung San Suu Kyi, but they searched her compound thoroughly for anything that could be used against her. They had found out that General Kyaw Zaw, a leading member of the CPB and one of General Aung San's close associates in the Thirty Comrades, had sent a letter for Daw Aung San Suu Kyi through his daughter. Although the CPB had collapsed in April 1989 and the letter was apparently of a personal nature, the MI hoped to use it to show a connection between the NLD and the outlawed CPB.[19]

Daw San Kyaw Zaw, General Kyaw Zaw's daughter, was arrested. She had been a lecturer at Rangoon Institute of Economics but was never promoted to full professor because her father and other family members had joined the CPB. She insisted that she had not been able to meet with Daw Aung San Suu

Kyi and had destroyed the letter, but she was still ordered to sign a confession saying that she had delivered it. She refused. She was held at an interrogation centre for forty-five days, during which she was at first denied the right to sleep or bathe. Suffering from gynaecological problems, she was taken to a military hospital at one point, but not allowed to stay for treatment. Instead she was taken back to the interrogation centre where she says a drunk captain tried to rape her.

When they were not intimidating her, Daw San Kyaw Zaw's interrogators sought to break her resolve through flattery. They told her that she was much better than Daw Aung San Suu Kyi, because she had never left the country or married a foreigner. Still she held firm. When she started a hunger strike, they finally released her without having obtained the false confession. Nevertheless, the regime justified its arrest of Daw Aung San Suu Kyi with the charge that she was being manipulated by the CPB while also involved in a rightist conspiracy involving Burmese exiles and foreign embassies. The faulty logic implicit in the contradictory accusations did not seem to bother the SLORC, and they never produced any hard evidence.[20]

Numerous NLD members throughout the country were also arrested in July, and Daw Aung San Suu Kyi and U Tin Oo were both later disqualified from running in the election. U Nu was arrested in December 1989 for refusing to withdraw his claim that his party represented a parallel government. Some other active parties were banned for their supposed CPB connections. Arrests of leading student activists had begun even earlier. The students' commemorations of the bloody days of one year before were drawing large crowds. To prevent them from spreading any further, the SLORC decided to quash the organizers.

Min Ko Naing was taken in March 1989, and when the DPNS held its first conference in Rangoon, several central executive committee members were arrested and imprisoned. Moe Thee Zun managed to escape to the Thai–Burma border where he joined the All Burma Students' Democratic Front (ABSDF), which had formed in late 1988.

In addition, the SLORC imposed numerous restrictions which limited the parties' ability to campaign. First, martial law was still in effect and anyone who said anything considered to be an attempt to split or defame the Tatmadaw could be arrested. Moreover, meetings of more than five people were prohibited. Parties could not distribute party literature unless it had been cleared by the Home Ministry. The regime controlled all forms of media, and often used the media to attack the NLD and student organizations. Parties were promised the right to hold rallies and to have access to media airtime only during the last three months of the election campaign, but the election was not until May 1990, giving the regime over a year to try to manipulate the situation in its favour. Perhaps most worrying, when the election rules came out there was no mention of how or when a new constitution would be written or when power would actually be transferred.

Despite the political arrests, which totalled an estimated 6,000 by November 1989, members of the NLD continued to campaign throughout the country.[21] University students who had joined the NLD's youth wing were particularly active campaigners, finding the work both challenging and exhilarating. Even those who were not NLD members began to campaign for the NLD, realizing that only by uniting behind one party could they achieve a decisive election victory.

In the villages, those campaigning for the NLD often came into conflict with NUP organizers. Village heads who supported or were afraid of local military authorities sometimes let the NUP hold public speeches but not the NLD. To get around this obstacle, student activists sometimes pretended they were visiting friends and went quietly from house to house promoting the NLD. In some cases, the monks stood up for the NLD campaigners, giving them a chance to campaign more freely. But villagers were often afraid to be seen talking to NLD party members and publicly feigned indifference. They worried that if the NLD lost, they would be punished by the authorities and their livelihoods would be affected.

Another problem for the campaigners was that they often could not obtain the support of an entire village because of pre-existing social divisions. For instance, if there were two monasteries in the village, each abbot would have his own supporters. If one abbot came out in favour of the NLD, his supporters would follow suit. But the other abbot might refuse to support the NLD as a result. The same could happen if there were influential families in the village with long-standing rivalries.

Much of the campaigners' time was spent instructing illiterate villagers how to mark the ballot properly and how to recognize the parties' symbols. The campaigners also explained what they thought democracy would mean for the villagers. Economic issues were a key concern, and Dr Tint Swe, an NLD candidate, often emphasized in his speeches how Burma had once been the richest country in South East Asia, but was now one of the poorest. Putting it in terms the villagers could understand, he said that 5-ton trucks full of gold had disappeared because of General Ne Win's rule. Some campaigners told farmers that if the NLD won, they would be able to grow whatever they wanted without government interference, and they would no longer be locked in stocks in front of the police station if they could not meet their rice quotas.

Despite the authorities' harassment of political parties during the campaigning, the voting on election day itself was relatively free. Out of the 20.8 million people who had the right to vote, 72.5 per cent cast ballots.[22] Party representatives were allowed to be present at the polling stations, and the vote counting appears to have been fair. In the rural areas there were reports of intimidation, and some villagers could not reach polling stations because they were over a day's walk from their villages. Rangoon residents who had been moved to satellite towns because of their vigorous support for the pro-democracy demonstrations in 1988 also could not vote.[23] These problems, though, were relatively minor. It seems that the regime believed that, with the top NLD leaders under arrest and many of the leading student activists in prison or exile, the NUP could pull off an election victory.

When the results came out, both the military and the people were astonished by the NLD's overwhelming victory. Many who had not dared to admit they were planning to vote for the NLD had actually done so. Most significantly, the NLD won seats in military-dominated districts in Rangoon and elsewhere, indicating that a number of their votes came from army personnel. Although Daw Aung San Suu Kyi was still under house arrest at the time of the election, the votes that the NLD received were largely because people strongly desired a return to democracy and had faith in her ability to lead. In some districts the NLD candidates were not inspiring leaders, and some did almost no campaigning, but they were voted into office on the strength of the people's conviction that the NLD needed a decisive victory.

Out of the 234 registered parties, ninety-three ended up fielding candidates and there were eighty-eight independent candidates. The NLD won 392 of the 485 parliamentary seats, including all fifty-nine seats in Rangoon Division. The military-backed National Unity Party won only ten seats. Twenty-five other parties, nineteen of which were ethnic minority parties, and six independents captured the remaining eighty-three seats.[24] Out of those, the Shan Nationalities League for Democracy won twenty-three seats, and the Arakan League for Democracy took eleven seats.

Post-election Struggles

Before the election, the military had not mentioned when power would be handed over to the winning party, and General Saw Maung had said only that the winners would be able to form a provisional government and write a constitution. Once the regime realized it had lost, and badly, the generals began announcing delaying tactics. By early September, General Saw Maung was saying that first a National Convention would have to be created to draw up the ground rules for the new constitution. Then, the elected representatives could meet to write the constitution, which would have to be approved by the people in a referendum. In the meantime, military rule would continue.[25]

After the 1988 coup, the SLORC had tried to distinguish itself from the BSPP regime. This was symbolically represented by the Burmanization of place names, which was intended to instil pride in being Burmese. The long-used colonial transliterations were discarded and Rangoon became 'Yangon' and Burma, 'Myanmar'. However, the most significant change was the decision to open up the country to foreign investment. Many people had participated in the 1988 demonstrations as much for economic reasons as for political rights. Although the regime was stalling, Burmese citizens were at least left with the hope that the new economic policies might bring some measure of prosperity to the country.

Meanwhile, the NLD began planning how to transform their election victory into an actual transfer of power. NLD officials organized a party meeting at Gandhi Hall from 27 to 29 July to come to a consensus about how to proceed. Some members advocated negotiating with the regime, not wanting to do anything that might result in the disqualification of the party. Other members and many in the crowds outside the hall believed that the NLD should simply announce the formation of the government then and there. The meeting ended up calling for the convening of the parliament by 30 September, a move which was seen as too assertive by some and not assertive enough by others.

In the following weeks, some MPs-elect held a number of secret meetings to discuss the formation of a parallel government if the regime did not transfer power. After the SLORC generals found out about the plans, they tried to arrest all involved, including Dr Sein Win, Daw Aung San Suu Kyi's cousin. However, he and some of his colleagues escaped to the KNU's headquarters on the Thai–Burma border. There he and eleven other elected members of parliament in exile formed the National Coalition Government of the Union of Burma (NCGUB), an organization which could take the democracy movement's case to the international community.

Inside the country, monks and students, particularly in Mandalay, engaged in various forms of civil disobedience to put pressure on the regime. The monks in Mandalay had been active throughout the election campaign, often openly supporting the NLD and using religious rituals to express their discontent with the junta. On 8 August 1990, student activists organized a commemoration of the second anniversary of the 1988 uprising. Monks gathered on 84th Street, and Mandalay residents brought alms in remembrance of those who had died. The student unions also came with their flags coloured black as a sign of mourning. The situation turned ugly after the military insisted that the students lower the flag, and a high school student leader talked back to them. Soldiers started beating him in front of the crowd, and a monk came forward to plead with the soldiers to resolve the problem peacefully. Then the soldiers started beating monks, and people began throwing rocks at the soldiers. The soldiers shot into the crowd, reportedly killing two monks and injuring many others. Several people were arrested.

In the meantime, the monks in Mandalay were so upset about the killings and arrests that they decided to start a religious boycott (*patta ni kozana kan*) against the regime. The organizers contacted monks in Sagaing, Monywa, Pegu and elsewhere, encouraging them to join the boycott. Thus, starting on 27 August 1990, participating monks rejected alms from soldiers and their families. Monks also refused to attend merit-making ceremonies at the houses of army families. Many army members and their families were visibly upset. Merit-making was an essential part of their lives. If monks were not present at funerals, for instance, it was believed that merit could not be made for the dead, and they would become ghosts rather than moving on to a higher form of existence.

Tensions between soldiers camped out near or beside many of the larger monasteries in Mandalay and the inhabitants of the monasteries also increased. Many student activists were still based in the monasteries and traded insults with the soldiers. Finally, anger on both sides erupted into, of all things, slingshot battles. Apparently, the soldiers had been ordered not to fire their guns, but slingshots were permitted. In general, the soldiers fared much better in the battles at various monasteries than the untrained students and young monks. The soldiers knew how to coordinate their attacks and their ammunition was better. On one occasion the students beat a hasty retreat after it began raining. Their clay balls dissolved, while the military continued shooting steel balls.

Although it might seem strange that monks were participating in such violent activities, many people supported them, feeling that only the monks could continue the struggle for democracy. Older monks stayed away from the slingshot fights but did not punish the teenaged monks for breaking the monastic code of conduct.

After the religious boycott had continued for almost two months, spreading to other cities, without showing any signs of abating, the regime ordered it stopped. On 20 October 1990, military authorities in Mandalay were told to disrobe and arrest recalcitrant monks and to disband Buddhist organizations participating in anti-government activities. A few days later, the military raided over one hundred monasteries in Mandalay.[26] The boycott ended, and the remaining monks began accepting alms again. By forcing the monks into submission and chasing down and arresting elected members of parliament, the regime made it clear that protecting its own interests was its primary concern. A transfer of power appeared increasingly unlikely.

Although the elected MPs were unable to assume power, the NLD's election victory greatly enhanced the legitimacy of the pro-democracy movement both domestically and abroad. Clearly, the majority of the people in Burma favoured a democratic government under the leadership of Daw Aung San Suu Kyi and her party. The pro-democracy movement had also benefited from being able to set up a nationwide organizational structure which reached into nearly every district and township. In the following years, members of the pro-democracy movement tried to keep the political focus on honouring the election results while the military regime sought to de-legitimize the results and dismantle the NLD and other political organizations outside its control.

5. Daw Aung San Suu Kyi speaking from her gate, surrounded by bodyguards

6. Crowd attending one of Daw Aung San Suu Kyi's weekend talks

7. Daw Aung San Suu Kyi holding a list of questions to be answered

8. Intelligence agent and students, Mandalay University (the agent told the photographer to leave the campus immediately)

CHAPTER 4

. . . .

Military Rule Continues

'People might have had strong determination about '88, but in reality, the stomach also plays an important part. So, many people retreated.' (NLD member from Upper Burma)

§ In the years following the 1990 election, Burma's generals focused on four objectives. First, they sought to expand greatly the size of the armed forces in order to be in a stronger position against their armed and unarmed opponents. As a result, the number of soldiers was increased from 180,000 in 1988 to over 400,000 by 1999 and new bases were constructed throughout the country. Second, the ruling generals worked to break up the organizational structure of the pro-democracy movement and particularly the NLD. Third, they attempted to neutralize the ethnic nationalities by making ceasefire agreements with almost all of the armed groups. And fourth, they tried to improve the economy by opening up the country to trade and foreign investment.

Even as the regime refused to honour the election results, many of its members still apparently believed they were working for the good of the country. From the military perspective, the National League for Democracy would not be able to hold the country together. While some of the regime's early ceasefire deals gave de facto autonomy to the ceasefire groups, in other cases the ceasefires resulted in a weakening of the strength of the armed ethnic organizations and increased access into ethnic nationality areas for the Tatmadaw. Whereas in the 1970s and 1980s the Tatmadaw was facing numerous armed opponents along most of its northern and eastern borders, by 2000 only pockets of resistance remained.

Recognizing that the socialist economic policies had been disastrous, the regime attempted to resuscitate the economy by encouraging private business and foreign investment. However, the regime had no expertise in economic planning, and the generals were unwilling to delegate responsibility to trained economists. After an initial growth spurt in the early 1990s, the country suffered from declining investment, a severe depletion of foreign reserves and rampant inflation.

It should be noted that conditions throughout the country were not the same, but could be broadly divided into four categories. In the cities and towns there was some economic growth and new job opportunities. In many rural areas, there was less economic development, most villagers continued to farm, and they were periodically called for forced labour. In the ceasefire areas, fighting stopped, travel became much easier, and some economic development began, although the Tatmadaw also used villagers in ceasefire areas with relatively weak leaders for forced labour. In remote areas where fighting between the Tatmadaw and ethnic nationalist armies continued, villagers were subject to forced relocations, forced portering, rape, torture, and the confiscation of their property. Civilians generally had to pay taxes both to the Tatmadaw soldiers and to the ethnic nationalist armies, and many fled to neighbouring countries as refugees and migrant workers.

Military Ascendancy

The period following the May 1990 elections until Aung San Suu Kyi's release from house arrest in July 1995 was one of ascendancy for the military regime. The high energy of the 1988 demonstrations and 1989–90 campaign period had dissipated. Non-violent means of bringing about change seemed to have proven unsuccessful. The international community had not intervened. People felt demoralized.

With Daw Aung San Suu Kyi under house arrest and other prominent politicians and student activists in prison, in hiding or in the jungle, the democratic movement's momentum collapsed. Those who were still free had no clear plan of action for how to continue the struggle, and the military regime was taking steps systematically to eliminate its opposition.

Over the next two years, the military weeded out civil servants and military personnel who had been active in the 1988 demonstrations or showed clear anti-military attitudes. One way they determined who posed a threat was by administering a questionnaire to all civil servants in 1991.[1] This questionnaire had two functions: first, to identify those openly disloyal to the regime and, second, to intimidate others into submission. Those who answered 'yes' to the question, 'Is it appropriate to elect as the Head of State somebody who is married to a foreigner?' soon found themselves out of a job or transferred to a remote or inactive post. The question clearly referred to Daw Aung San Suu Kyi.

The SLORC's questionnaire for civil servants, 1991

1. Do you prefer insurgent organizations like the KIA, the KNU, the ABSDF and the NMSP to hold power ?
2. Do you prefer the insurgent CPB underground organization? Do you support it?
3. Can you accept having Myanmar ruled by a foreign country?
4. Do you prefer the CIA's intervention inside Myanmar?

5. Do you support Sein Win and others governing Myanmar at this critical time?

6. Do you support U Nu's so-called parallel government?

7. Do you support the broadcasts of foreign radio stations, such as BBC and VOA?

8. Do you want Myanmar to lose its independence?

9. Do you support NLD leaders U Tin U, Daw Suu Kyi, U Kyi Maung and U Chit Khaing?

10. Do you support absconders Sein Win, Peter Limbin, Maung Aung and U Sein Mya?

11. Do you want the situation to return to what it was in 1988?

12. Do you want the military to safeguard the country prior to the existence of a concrete constitution?

13. Do you accept that all citizens have their respective responsibilities for the existence of a concrete constitution?

14. Can you accept that all civil servants must stay out of party politics?

15. If not, explain why.

16. Were you a party member during the BSPP time?

17. If so, reveal your party membership number.

18. Reveal your position in the party.

19. As the government has already instructed civil servants to be free from party politics, do you know that disciplinary actions will be taken in case of violating these instructions?

20. Do you know that violating civil servants' rules and regulations can lead to being dismissed?

21. What is your main responsibility?

22. Did the military take sides in the last elections?

23. For long-lasting benefit to the country, how long should a systematic transitional period last?

24. Which organization has brought peace and stability to the country?

25. Which is the most suitable system for Myanmar?

26. How should the head of state (president) be chosen?

    (a) Direct election by the people

    (b) Step by step: Township, Division, National

    (c) Elected from among members of parliament

    (d) A qualified non-MP elected by parliament.

27. Is it appropriate to elect as the Head of State somebody who is married to a foreigner?

28. If so, what will happen to the country?

29. What punishment should be given to persons who threaten and cut off the heads of many people, who destroy the country's properties, and who cause splits in the military?

30. Which should be given preference – the country or an individual?
31. For the benefit of whom is the military working and what is it doing today?
32. How should the military, which is shouldering the country's welfare, regard those who view it as their enemy?
33. Is it right to have a head-on confrontation with the military?

In the meantime, there was no constitution in effect, and the SLORC ruled by decree, citing whichever laws from previous political eras proved useful. However, the SLORC initially appeared to follow through on its pledge to open the economy. Many people consoled themselves with the hope that at least their standard of living might improve and perhaps gradual political changes would result.

The SLORC legalized private enterprise and welcomed foreign investment, particularly in joint-ventures with military-owned companies. A number of foreign businesses came into the country to invest in oil, gas, lumber and mining, to set up labour-intensive manufacturing industries and to import consumer goods. New jobs became available to Burmese working with these foreign companies and in the service sectors that supported them. With the regime's promotion of tourism, several new hotels were constructed in Rangoon, Mandalay and Pagan, also providing employment. Opportunities for trade grew, and some Burmese were able to travel out of the country for business or pleasure.

To facilitate economic development, the SLORC initiated infrastructure projects such as roads, bridges and irrigation canals throughout Burma, although in many cases they were completed by forced labourers working under duress. Fertilizers were imported and efforts were made to make the agricultural sector more productive. In comparison to the BSPP period, when no private industry was allowed and there was almost no thought given to the country's infrastructural development, it seemed to be the beginning of a new era.

At the same time, the military regime was scoring victories in its long-standing battles with armed groups. In 1989, the Communist Party of Burma collapsed. The ethnic minority factions within the CPB broke off and agreed to ceasefires with the regime in return for minimal Tatmadaw interference in their internal affairs. In practice, this meant that the newly formed United Wa State Army and the Kokang-led Myanmar National Democratic Alliance Army could produce and traffic drugs with impunity. Between 1989 and 1991, twenty-three new heroin refineries opened in Kokang territory in the hills of northern Burma.[2]

In the early and mid-1990s, the SLORC was successful in splitting the armed Democratic Alliance of Burma, which included many of the ethnic nationalist armies who had previously agreed to negotiate with the regime only as an alliance. The Pa'o National Organization was the first to break with its allies and made a ceasefire deal with the SLORC in March 1991. Others, including the powerful Kachin Independence Organization, soon followed, leaving only a few diehard groups to battle on by themselves. Most of the groups felt that they could not compete with the increasingly powerful Tatmadaw, and they were better off signing a deal that would give them continued control over some territory as well as the chance to bring development to the civilians in their areas.

With the military firmly in control and taking some seemingly positive steps, many of the people who had participated so actively in the 1988 demonstrations and election campaign decided to forget about politics for a while. Instead they focused on finding good jobs and taking advantage of the new opportunities.

For student activists committed to continuing the struggle for democracy, it was a depressing period. At least three female students, including Tin Tin Nyo, a prominent activist in 1988, committed suicide after being released from prison in the mid-1990s, in part because they felt so alienated from their relatives and peers who had seemingly forsaken their ideals.

At the same time, the regime's new policies also made it more difficult for students to congregate. Because of the backlog of students who had graduated from high school but not been able to proceed on to the universities, when universities were finally reopened, one-year courses were reduced to three or four months. Thus, students had little chance to get to know each other before they found themselves taking exams and sent home on vacation again.

There were a few small protests, but these led only to more arrests. In December 1991, when Daw Aung San Suu Kyi was awarded the Nobel Peace Prize, there was a brief resurgence of hope and calls for her release by university students in Rangoon and Mandalay. The regime responded by closing the universities for several months. In February 1995, when former Prime Minister U Nu died, some students daringly unfurled party banners and sang pro-democracy songs as they marched in his funeral procession. Those who did not manage to run away in time were all arrested and sent to prison.

Still, some student activists, such as Min Zin, who spent from 1989 to 1997 in hiding, sought to keep the struggle alive. His father was a 1962-generation activist and private tuition teacher, and his whole family had been involved in the 1988 demonstrations. At the age of sixteen, Min Zin became the leader of a nationwide high school student union which worked closely with the university student unions and greatly expanded its membership during the election campaign. In early 1989, he gave speeches with Daw Aung San Suu Kyi in the Rangoon area. Soon he too was wanted for arrest. Not wanting to flee to the border, he decided to try to stay inside the country so that he could secretly continue his political activities. For the next eight years, he doggedly refused to give in. He moved from house to house and monastery to monastery, evading arrest, all the while continuing to write political pamphlets and articles for underground student magazines. He also helped lesser-known activists plan how to rebuild their networks and continue underground political work.

While few activists were in hiding as long as Min Zin, several spent considerable time closeted in safe houses or taking on new identities in far-away towns and villages. This type of student was by far the exception, but they continued to hope for another spark to set off a mass movement like that of 1988, despite people's still vivid memories of the widespread killings and destruction.

Most other professionals and students who had been active in 1988 felt that the odds were against them and increasingly looked for hope in the new economy. One former student activist, Zaw Zaw Oo, talked about how his feelings changed over the years. After the regime suppressed the NLD following the 1990 elections, he said: 'The NLD became less and less active, so I had to find something else.' He finished his university education and found a job with a foreign investment firm with interests in Burma. His job gave him not only a good salary but also a chance to travel and to meet with high-powered foreign businessmen and senior government officials. Zaw Zaw Oo said democracy is still a priority, but not his top priority. He believes that developing the country is more important. He sees his change in ideas as very much related to his experiences in the business world in which, he said, 'you look for possible things, not ideal things'. Particularly in the early and mid-1990s when the economy seemed to be turning around, many people agreed with Zaw Zaw Oo.

The National Convention

After sacking the increasingly erratic General Saw Maung in 1992, the remaining top junta members sought to institute a legitimate role for the military in public life by holding a National Convention to write a new constitution. The SLORC was nominally headed by Senior General Than Shwe, but Lt General Khin Nyunt and General Maung Aye appear to have been the two leading policy-makers, with General Ne Win still exerting influence behind the scenes. Lt General Khin Nyunt, known as Secretary-1 of the SLORC and the head of Directorate of Defence Services Intelligence, made his career in military intelligence. General Maung Aye, the vice-chairman of the SLORC and the Commander-in-Chief of the Army, rose through battlefield command positions. In general, the field commanders in Burma have looked down on the intelligence personnel, because they do not risk their lives for their country, but General Ne Win always nurtured the leading intelligence men in order to check the power of the field commanders. The intelligence officers gathered as much information on the commanders as they did on political dissidents.

Despite tension between the two branches, the leading generals seem to have agreed that holding the National Convention would help them all stay in power. Besides ensuring their own key role in the country's political life, the generals hoped to use the National Convention to marginalize the 1990 election winners and resolve the ethnic nationalities' demands without giving much ground. The first meeting was convened in January 1993. Of the 702 delegates whom the regime invited, only ninety-nine were elected members of parliament, out of which eighty-one were from the NLD. The other 603 delegates were all appointed by the SLORC. Some came from ceasefire groups, with a few being suspected drug-traffickers.[3]

With the announcement of the National Convention, the NLD had to decide whether it should participate or not. Some members believed it was important to keep the party legal, and by attending the convention they could have a forum for voicing their views. Others thought the NLD should boycott the National Convention because it was a sham and the entire process de-legitimated the 1990 election results. Finally, the NLD decided to attend.

Representatives of ethnic minority political parties who had won seats in the election also participated. Some were initially optimistic that the drafting process would allow them to create a political structure that would provide for greater ethnic autonomy. Once the convention began, however, their hopes were dashed. While many outsiders believed that the convention provided a viable arena for resolving Burma's political future, in fact the delegates never had a chance. The military regime did not allow the delegates to discuss the convention procedures outside the convention, but one delegate, Daniel Aung, later fled the country and explained how the convention actually worked.

An elected Lahu representative from the Lahu National Progressive Party, Daniel Aung was impressed with his invitation to participate in the National Convention. The letter stated that, because he was a political leader, he was responsible for drafting the constitution. He remembered: 'I thought they really meant it.' He had previously worked as an editor in the foreign department of the government-controlled Burma News Agency, but he had resigned in 1988 and run for election in 1990. Still eager to participate in the political process, he looked forward to the convention.

When he arrived at the first session of the National Convention, he was surprised when the meeting lasted only two days. Some delegates from distant towns hadn't even arrived, but that didn't seem to matter to the generals in charge. Lt General Myo Nyunt gave the opening speech, most of which, Daniel Aung recalled, consisted of praise for the military. Lt General Myo

Nyunt informed the delegates that the Burmese military was different from those in other countries. Because the Burmese military had saved the country from collapse so many times, it must take the leading role in political affairs.

Daniel Aung and the other delegates soon found out that the six main objectives of the constitution had already been written by the SLORC. Although no one had any arguments with the first five, the sixth objective stated that 25 per cent of the parliament's seats must be held by military members chosen by the chief of staff.

When the convention next convened, the delegates were divided into eight groups and ordered to come up with points to be included in the constitution. The SLORC had provided the delegates with a list of points drawn from other countries' constitutions, with many calling for military involvement in political affairs. Still, the delegates were told they could draft their own suggestions, and they were given access to a library with many constitutional books.

The working groups were told that they could discuss freely, but each group was assigned government clerks to take notes. The clerks became nervous when the delegates spoke against the institutionalization of the military's role in politics. Daniel Aung remembers a clerk passing him a note asking him to tell one of the delegates to stop talking. As the chairman of his working group, Daniel Aung wrote back, 'You are not responsible, I am,' and allowed the man to continue. Daniel Aung said that some of the clerks privately asked the delegates to forgive them, but they had to intervene in the meetings because of their bosses' orders.

Although the delegates were allowed to write their own suggestions, the SLORC took no notice of them. The delegates were not even allowed to read their drafts in front of the entire assembly. The authorities would rewrite their papers first and insist that the delegates read the corrected versions, without adding as much as a word. Daniel Aung remembers the authorities who handed them the revised papers saying, 'Feel pity on us and read it.' In one instance, a representative from the Shan State prefaced his paper by reminding the delegates how important it was that they not leave the country with a shameful legacy. At once, a general stood up and shouted to the chairman to silence him.

The authorities also maintained surveillance over the delegates in the barracks where they had to stay. Although the delegates were treated well by the various military people assigned to assist them, their primary function was to keep an eye on the delegates. If three or four delegates sat together talking, military agents would approach, turn their backs, and listen intently. The regime also tried to prevent delegates from the political parties from developing close relations with the non-elected delegates. The delegates who had been elected in the 1990 election were housed separately from the appointed delegates. They were also assigned separate tables in the dining hall and told not to mix. If the elected delegates tried to engage the appointed delegates in conversation, the appointed delegates became nervous. Among the appointed delegates were several of Daniel Aung's old friends and classmates, but they did not dare to talk to him

Like many of the other ethnic minority representatives, Daniel Aung was frustrated in his attempts to obtain political rights for his people. He hoped to create an autonomous region for the Lahus, most of whom live in four townships in Shan State. However, the regime rejected his proposal saying that the Lahu population did not constitute a majority in all four of the townships. Moreover, the regime was opposed to the word 'autonomy'. Only 'national area' was allowed, a term which did not convey any power or rights. The Wa representatives were also upset because no significant political rights were being accorded to them, although the United Wa State Army controlled significant portions of Shan State. But some of the other appointed ethnic representatives said little. They could not speak Burmese well, and there were no official translators.

Eventually, Daniel Aung and others realized that the principles they were supposedly drafting were already written. But still they had to participate in the charade. Attendance at the general assembly sessions was required. Many delegates simply read books or slept. Even Lt General Myo Nyunt, the chairman of the convention, could often be found dozing. Daniel Aung and many other delegates spent much of their time in the bathroom, the only place where they could talk freely.

When the military came out with the final draft of 104 basic principles, it bore little resemblance to what the committees had put together. What bothered Daniel Aung the most was that the generals thanked the delegates for doing such a good job. He told U Aung Shwe, the head of the NLD delegation, 'We have to protest.' Another delegate said that since the delegates were forced to attend, they didn't bear any responsibility for the constitution, but Daniel Aung insisted, 'We'll be blacklisted in history.'

U Aung Shwe suggested that each of the six elected parties attending write their own protest letters to the chairman of the Convening Committee. The letters all requested the military authorities to reconsider what they had done. Although Daniel Aung said he encouraged some of the non-elected delegates to join them in protesting, they were too afraid. For writing letters of protest, the NLD and the SNLD leaders were called in by Lt General Myo Nyunt, the head of the Convening Committee, and scolded for their insolence. Daniel Aung decided he had had enough. During the next break, he and his family went back to their home town in the north, rode motorbikes into the mountains, and continued on foot for four days to the Thai border. They have been living in exile ever since.

With the subsequent walkout of the NLD and the serious disgruntlement of some of the ethnic representatives, convention meetings were postponed indefinitely, although the generals sitting on the Convening Committee continued to meet periodically. The fact that the process was still on-going provided a convenient justification for why power could not yet be transferred.

The Release of Daw Aung San Suu Kyi

Daw Aung San Suu Kyi's release came as a surprise to almost everyone. On 10 July 1995 she was informed that her period of house arrest had ended. She did not rush out of her compound, and no announcement was made in the official media, but as the rumour of her release spread, people ventured near her house to find out if it was true. Soon she appeared from behind her gate, standing on a table, assuring her well-wishers that she was indeed free and in good health. That week she went to her gate every afternoon to greet the groups of people who continued to gather there. Finally she announced that she would come to the gate only on weekends because she had to get back to the party's political work, as if the almost six years of house arrest had been nothing more than a brief irritation.

Stories began emerging about the hardships she had faced during her house arrest. She had run out of money and refused donations of food from the military authorities. When her poor diet led to illness, she finally agreed to sell her furniture to the regime to obtain cash. On a few occasions her husband and sons had been permitted to visit, but most of her time was spent alone, reading, listening to the radio and meditating. Military intelligence lived just inside her front gate, preventing all except a few relatives from entering or leaving. Although she tried to befriend the intelligence agents, the personnel were changed regularly to prevent friendships from developing.

Upon her release, foreign journalists poured into the country to interview her. When they expressed sympathy with her plight she insisted that others had suffered much more than she had. Two other senior party members, U Tin Oo and U Kyi Maung, for instance, had been sent to Insein prison. But they had recently been freed and, when they learned of Daw Aung San Suu Kyi's release, they headed to her compound and agreed to work with her to rebuild the party.

It seems that the SLORC let Daw Aung San Suu Kyi go in order to improve relations with Japan. Japan was promising to resume full-scale development aid if the regime restored greater political and economic openness in Burma.[4] The SLORC felt confident that with the economy picking up, people would soon lose interest in Daw Aung San Suu Kyi, and she would fade from the political scene. Moreover, Daw Aung San Suu Kyi's party was in shambles, she and U Tin Oo had been removed from their positions on the Central Executive

Committee in 1991 to keep the party legal. Many NLD members were still in prison or had given up political work.

Daw Aung San Suu Kyi didn't appear to be much of a threat, but the regime under-estimated her power to revitalize the party and to draw international attention. Foreign journalists were captivated, NLD party members from the various townships and divisions came to Rangoon for instructions, and the NLD Central Executive Committee started holding daily meetings, with Daw Aung San Suu Kyi and U Tin Oo back in their former positions. Although a posse of military intelligence officers continued to live just inside the compound registering everyone who entered, at first they did not hinder anyone. Soon the compound was in full swing, with meetings, study groups and press conferences taking place. The National Convention was still holding sessions, but the NLD members who had attended the convention felt as frustrated as Daniel Aung did. When the convention reconvened at the end of November 1995, the NLD delegates decided to walk out, saying they would not return until a real political dialogue began. The SLORC dismissed their demand and announced their expulsion from the convention a few days later.

A new political centre emerged at Daw Aung San Suu Kyi's compound, with foreign governments, ethnic political leaders, and the domestic population carefully watching her every move. Many hoped that a dialogue between the NLD and the regime could take place, but the generals thought it was unnecessary. They believed they could limit Daw Aung San Suu Kyi's influence and maintain control without having to make any concessions.

With the regime seemingly unwilling to talk, the NLD felt compelled to raise its public profile. In January 1996, the NLD held an Independence Day celebration at Daw Aung San Suu Kyi's compound and invited a famous troupe of comedians and dancers from Mandalay to perform. Exhilarated by the NLD's resurgence, U Par Par Lay and U Lu Zaw used mime to parody the regime indirectly. In one skit, one of the comedians sat on a chair beaming. There was only a single chair, so when the second man came on to the stage, he gestured that he would like a turn. The first comedian refused to yield to him, despite the pleas for fairness and attempts at persuasion by the second one. Watching this, the audience was doubled over in laughter, for the chair obviously represented the government, the person sitting on the chair was the military regime, and the person asking politely for his turn symbolized the elected MPs.[5]

Because they dared to make these kinds of jokes, the two comedians were arrested. Daw Aung San Suu Kyi and several other members tried to go to Mandalay to attend the trial, but when they arrived at the train station in Rangoon, they were informed that their assigned carriage happened to have mechanical problems, so they wouldn't be able to travel. Meanwhile, the comedians were sentenced to seven years' imprisonment.[6] They were sent to a hard labour camp in Kachin State where they were originally set to work breaking rocks. The health of both declined rapidly, and they were later moved to a prison in Myitkyina, the capital of Kachin State.

Still, the NLD went on to hold large meetings in May 1996 to commemorate the 1990 election victory and in September 1996 to mark the eighth anniversary of the party's founding. Each time, military intelligence prevented large numbers of invitees from leaving their home towns, or put them under detention in military barracks until the meetings were over. In one case, delegates who made it to Daw Aung San Suu Kyi's street were simply put into a truck and driven to a rural area several miles out of Rangoon where they were dumped and had to make their own way back. By the time they arrived back in the city, the meeting was over.

In the meantime, Daw Aung San Suu Kyi had been giving public talks from her gate every weekend. On Saturdays, she would speak for an hour, and on Sundays, she, U Tin Oo and U Kyi Maung would each speak for twenty minutes. These talks, which came to be known as 'People's Forums', were an attempt by the NLD leadership to communicate their ideas to the people and to inspire them to take part in the political movement. Daw Aung San Suu Kyi had a mailbox attached to the front of her gate so that people could drop off questions during the week. Her staff selected the most pressing questions for her to address. The reading and answering of the letters gave the talks a give-and-take feeling, and the audience frequently chimed in with laughter and applause.

Two hours before the talk was scheduled to begin, people would begin arriving in front of her house, bringing pieces of newspaper to sit on and umbrellas to block the sun or rain. Soon hawkers would arrive peddling betel nut, cold water and snacks. Friends would gathered at appointed locations, chatting happily in the festive atmosphere. By 3 p.m., the areas in front of her gate, on the pavement and lawn across the street, and up the lane facing the gate would be packed with people. At 3.45, the crowd would begin chanting, 'Long live Daw Aung San Suu Kyi! Long live U Kyi Maung! Long live U Tin Oo!' By 3.55, the chanting would have reached fever pitch and when the NLD leaders arrived at the gate, everyone would leap up, shouting and clapping ecstatically.

On the several occasions that I attended, I found all kinds of people in the crowd, including students, retired businessmen, young couples, market vendors and monks. Once I made the mistake of sitting next to a wizened old man, long past seventy and missing most of his teeth. When Daw Aung San Suu Kyi appeared, he was so eager to signal his approval that he jumped to his feet and proceeded to twirl his umbrella over his head faster and faster, endangering the lives of all sitting around him. He had to be gently restrained by the students behind him.

Each week, Daw Aung San Suu Kyi urged her listeners to consider ways in which they could participate in the movement. Despite many people's hopes that she would effect political change for them, she realized that she and the remaining NLD members could do little without popular participation. On 16 March 1996, she urged her audience to recognize the power that they had but were not tapping into. She read out a question which had been sent to her. 'Why don't we have democracy yet in our country? Why is it delayed?' She answered, 'Some people [the generals] don't really want to give democracy. And people aren't really working for it. Democracy activists need to put in more effort ... The reason for the delay in getting democracy is that we Burmese people lack confidence in ourselves. People think they are not able to do it.'

She then brought up Vaclav Havel's essay, 'The Power of the Powerless'. Written about Czechoslovakia under Soviet rule, Havel's words had relevance for the struggle in Burma as well. She said, 'We need to understand that people who are not in power have their own power. Don't think you don't have any power just because you are not part of the power structure.' She talked about how the regime made great efforts to demonstrate they had the support of the people, for instance by staging pro-government rallies which people were forced to attend. The regime, she said, was using the power of the people to prop up their own power structure. If people didn't have power, the regime would not bother with them. She declared, 'That is why we rely on the people. Because you have power. For that reason, we are openly requesting people-power from the people.'

On Sundays, U Tin Oo talked mostly about legal issues and the application of Buddhist principles. After being expelled from the military and imprisoned in the mid-1970s, he studied law and also spent a period of time as a monk. On 18 February 1996, he related the words of the Buddha to the current political situation, explaining how the Buddha had said that you must do exactly as you say and you must be honest in reporting what you have done. The regime, he said, was always talking about restoring democracy but doing nothing to make it happen.

U Kyi Maung, also a former senior military officer who had retired in the 1960s, often used the format of his young grandson asking him simple questions. On 5 May 1996, he said that his grandson had asked him what kind of newspaper he wanted to see in Burma. Because all the newspapers in the country were under state control and the regime sought to turn public opinion against the NLD through scathing editorials, freedom of expression was naturally an important issue for the NLD. U Kyi Maung said that he told his grandson he wanted a newspaper which was 'not slanted, not weighted to one side, not expressing a personal point of view as if it's everyone's view'. He concluded by pointing out that in democratic countries there are no government-controlled newspapers.

The celebratory feeling at the talks was infectious. Here were people announcing over loudspeakers what other people only dared to whisper. Still, the talks never attracted more than 10,000 people, and usually only around 3,000 or so. The SLORC assumed people would soon become bored, but the crowds, while not growing, held steady. So the regime began intimidating the audience by having military intelligence personnel walk slowly through the crowds videotaping each and every face. This brought the size of the audiences down somewhat, but didn't eliminate them. Some people resorted to driving slowly back and forth in front of the house or taking the bus that passed the compound so that they could get a taste of the event without being identified. Others listened to the audio tapes or even watched videotapes of the talks, made and copied by pro-democracy supporters. The video and audio tapes found their way to Mandalay and other towns around the country, where NLD members set up free lending libraries. The regime began arresting people caught distributing these tapes outside Rangoon.[7]

The battle was also played out in the entertainment industry. The military-sponsored TV station ran a programme mocking Daw Aung San Suu Kyi. A dishevelled old hag missing her front teeth stood behind a rickety gate haranguing a group of sorry-looking children. Some people stoned the house of the actress who played Daw Aung San Suu Kyi. Around the same time, Leh Pyu, a popular rock singer, released a cassette entitled 'Power 54'. At first the censorship board passed it, but they later recalled all the cassettes when they realized that the 54 intentionally referred to, or would be interpreted as referring to, Daw Aung San Suu Kyi's home address, 54 University Avenue. Daw Aung San Suu Kyi made a joke about this in one of her speeches. She said, 'I have heard about the recently-released tape called "Power". The authorities said don't use "Power 54", so the band will just have to use Power 56!'[8]

Unwilling to tolerate continued public challenges to their authority, the generals decided to end the talks once and for all. Starting in late September 1996, the military simply placed barbed wire barricades at either end of the block every weekend and refused to allow people through. Daw Aung San Suu Kyi and U Tin Oo managed to get around the barricades to meet the crowds at another junction a few times, but on one occasion in November they were attacked by a mob of 200 people who pelted their car with stones and smashed it with iron bars. Daw Aung San Suu Kyi was not hurt, although U Tin Oo suffered minor injuries. Witnesses reported seeing the young attackers arriving on military trucks, and the attack took place in the lane in front of U Kyi Maung's house, where ordinary people had no access because it was cordoned off by government security personnel. Still, the regime denied its involvement and in a commentary in the government-controlled *New Light of Myanmar* wrote: 'As Suu Kyi is becoming more and more apparent as the one trying to destroy all prospects for stability of the state with her fangs, it is rather difficult to definitely indicate what sort of people do not want her.'[9]

During this period, the regime tried to split the NLD by focusing its attacks on Daw Aung San Suu Kyi and stressing her links to the West. Newspaper editorials often referred to her as 'Suu Kyi', dropping the first part of her name which links her to her father, the national hero. Alternatively, they called her 'Mrs Michael Aris', using her husband's name, which emphasized her marriage to a foreigner. This goes against Burmese norms in which women keep their own name after marriage and are not referred to by their husbands' names.

In the meantime, Daw Aung San Suu Kyi's political activities in 1995 and 1996 had spurred some old and new activists to take action. Many former student activists who had had little contact since 1988 found each other again at Daw Aung San Suu Kyi's compound. And as in the mid-1980s, a new generation of student activists began looking for activities they could undertake to spark a movement.

Student Demonstrations, 1996

The anniversary of the death of the student Phone Maw in 1988 was turned into an important occasion. In 1995, and more so in 1996, numbers of university students came to classes dressed in black. Some of the male students were particularly happy to see fashionable female models wearing black hats and black jean shirts with red roses attached, because the modelling industry had become extremely popular after the country had begun to allow foreign investment. Young activists also found inspiration in the Free Burma groups that began forming in the United States and elsewhere. The Free Burma Coalition was particularly active on American university campuses where students began boycotting Pepsi because of its investment in Burma. Some students quietly took up the Pepsi boycott in Rangoon as well. Although the students' activities were limited, they tried to work parallel to Daw Aung San Suu Kyi and the NLD by raising people's awareness and encouraging them to participate in simple acts of political defiance.

Student activism spread after a brawl in October 1996 similar to the March 1988 incident that sparked the demonstrations. Some students from Rangoon Institute of Technology got into an altercation at a restaurant with a few auxiliary police who beat them up. The students were detained, and the news quickly spread around campus. Students organized an on-campus demonstration protesting against police brutality and calling for the punishment of the auxiliary policemen and an accurate news report of the event in the official media. The beaten students were quickly released, but students involved in organizing the demonstration were later detained, prompting more demonstrations in early December. This time, the students took the demonstrations into the city centre. On the night of 2 December, students marched from the busy Hledan junction past the Shwedagon Pagoda and on to the American embassy. Then on the night of 6 December, they held another demonstration at Hledan junction, which I happened to witness.

When a friend and I arrived at around 7 p.m., the junction, usually full of traffic, was blocked off by military barricades in all five directions. We could hear people making speeches and the audience shouting its approval as we made our way through the wide circle of perhaps 2,000 standing people. In the centre about a thousand students were seated on the ground surrounding a student holding a fighting peacock flag on a makeshift bamboo pole. Other students held framed photographs of General Aung San, and some had hand-made posters with slogans in Burmese and English. Students took turns coming to the flagpole to give short speeches. One shouted: 'University courses are supposed to last a year, but we get only a few months. How can we learn anything like this?' Another countered: 'It will be OK if all of us are uneducated. The degree is not useful. So we have to sacrifice here to form the student union.'

Soon the speeches became more heated, with speakers calling on the audience to remember the country's long history of student activism. When-ever there was a lull in the speech-making, the students sang revolutionary songs and shouted in a call-and-response form: 'Do we have unity? Yes, we do!' and 'To set up student unions: our cause!'

I and the other dozen westerners present were approached by students eager to tell us why they were protesting. Many also wanted to inform us about the situation in their home towns. One student told me that he was from an island where his family and others routinely had to turn over their boats to the military authorities for their use, and they were recently pressed into forced labour to build a bridge to another island. Another one complained that all the houses in his village, including his own, were torn down without compensation to make way for a new prison. A third announced how fed up he was with the FOC system. When I asked what FOC meant, he said, '"Free of charge", the military just takes everything it wants without paying.'

A group of students circulated around the area distributing water and sweets donated by local shopkeepers, while others picked up rubbish. As students from different universities arrived and announced their presence, cheers broke out. But as the night wore on, and armed soldiers and riot police began moving closer, the atmosphere changed. Many students and onlookers became afraid and silently slipped away. Professors sent by the military came several times to ask the students to disperse, but they refused to leave until Lt General Khin Nyunt, Secretary-1 of the SLORC and also the chairman of the Myanmar Education Committee, came to meet with them. He did not. Instead, the troops and riot police began inching towards the students, clearly hoping to intimidate them into leaving without having to use force.

By 2 a.m., there were only 100 students left sitting in a tight triangle, praying as they faced the Shwedagon Pagoda. On the pavement, there were about 150 students and locals armed with chair legs, determined to fight back even while the students in the centre had called for non-violent resistance. The remaining onlookers, including myself and the other westerners, had moved up to balconies overlooking the junction. After giving a final warning, the troops trained water-cannons on the silent students and stormed the area. Everywhere shattering glass, screams and wails could be heard as people were injured and arrested. We made our way into people's apartments, where we sat out the rest of the night in utter silence and darkness, though some of the Burmese girls in the room could barely stifle their sobs. In the early morning hours, we were able to slip out, although the apartment owners were later interrogated and the leaders of the demonstration imprisoned.

Over the next week, several smaller 'lightning' demonstrations occurred in front of various universities in Rangoon and other towns, but the universities were soon closed down and barricades erected on all the main thoroughfares, making it impossible for the students to network. The demonstrations ceased, but the military was clearly troubled to see that many Rangoon residents had been quick to provide food and money for the students, even if they had not joined in themselves. Moreover, the demonstrators had included a number of ethnic minority students from all the different ethnic states.

From December 1996 until mid-1998, the main universities in Rangoon and Mandalay were closed. When universities in Rangoon were briefly re-opened in August 1998 so that registered students could take exams, protests broke out and the universities were shut again. One of the students involved in organizing the protests, Thet Win Aung, was sentenced to fifty-three years in prison, with the sentence later increased to fifty-nine years. Other student activists were also given long sentences in what was clearly an attempt by the regime to intimidate students from participating in political activities.

The regime eventually reopened some of the smaller institutes and colleges, but began preparations to move most of the student body out of the central campuses in Rangoon and Mandalay. Rangoon Institute of Technology and Mandalay Institute of Technology were folded into a new government technical college system with thirty small campuses around the country. The level of education offered at these colleges was lower than at the former institutes of technology, with six-year programmes being reduced to four years. When some of the new government technical college campuses opened in mid-December 1999, students protested because of the poor facilities and the downgrading of the educational level. Classes were cancelled indefinitely. Many students gave up on obtaining a university degree and enrolled in short-term diploma courses or went abroad as migrant workers.

The Regime Changes its Name

The regime continued to face challenges in the late 1990s, as it struggled with a weakening economy and sustained opposition from domestic political groups and foreign organizations and governments. Foreign investment began declining in the mid-1990s due to poor economic management and constantly changing regulations. The Asian economic crisis in 1997 and Daw Aung San Suu Kyi's repeated calls for foreign businesses to stay out also resulted in reduced investment. Throughout the late 1990s, inflation was running in double-digit numbers, eroding the value of fixed salaries and leading hundreds of thousands of Burmese to seek work outside the country.

In November 1997, the SLORC renamed itself the State Peace and Development Council (SPDC). The switch was meant to project a softer image, because the regime had been ridiculed for years for calling itself by such a monstrous-sounding name. At the same time, some of the most blatantly corrupt SLORC members, such as Lt Generals Tun Kyi, the Minister of Trade, Myint Aung, the Minister of Agriculture, and Kyaw Ba, the Minister of Tourism, were removed. All three had been prominent regional commanders in the past and were viewed as potential rivals to other senior SLORC members. Lt General Khin Nyunt and General Maung Aye used the occasion to strengthen their own positions by promoting younger, more loyal men to second-line leadership positions.

At the time of the name change, rumours were rife about possible splits in the military and whether these might not possibly lead to one side negotiating with the NLD. However, the differences appear to be ones of tactics rather than goals. Lt General Khin Nyunt was trying to destroy the NLD by having local authorities intimidate party members, harass their families, and incarcerate those who refused to resign. The intention was to isolate Daw Aung San Suu Kyi and reduce her party's legitimacy. Some of the field commanders, on the other hand, have apparently favoured more heavy-handed tactics such as mob attacks against her.

Likewise, while Lt General Khin Nyunt tried to break up and buy off armed ethnic nationalist groups with promises of lucrative economic concessions, General Maung Aye undertook military offensives and massive depopulations of the areas where the ethnic nationalist armies operated. The field commanders might resent the fact that their former enemies were being bought off, but the mixed tactics succeeded as a kind of good cop, bad cop strategy, in which many of the ethnic armies came to realize they were better off negotiating with Lt General Khin Nyunt than facing further military offensives in their areas.

Nevertheless, as an intelligence officer with no support base among the infantry, Lt General Khin Nyunt's position within the regime was contingent on General Ne Win's support. In an effort to make himself indispensable, he asserted his personal authority over many aspects of national policy. By the late 1990s, he still led the Directorate of Defence Services Intelligence and was also the chairman of over a dozen policy-making committees including the Office of Strategic Studies, the Information Policy Committee, the ASEAN steering committee, the National Health Committee, the Myanmar Education Committee, the Work Committee for the Development of Border Areas and National Races, and the Leading Committee for Perpetual All-round Renovation of Shwedagon Pagoda.[10]

The generals in the SLORC and the SPDC have relied on an expansion of the military, the staffing of administrative offices with loyal servicemen, and the creation of a new mass organization to widen and deepen their control over the general population. The regime dramatically increased the Tatmadaw's presence in cities and towns throughout the country, building dozens of new military compounds. If mass protests were to break out again, there would be troops everywhere ready to take action. The number of military intelligence agents was also increased, infiltrating opposition organizations and monitoring soldiers as well. The regime appointed a number of military men to ward, township and regional administrative positions, but it also tried to woo the masses through the establishment of the Union Solidarity and Development Association (USDA).

Although purportedly a social organization, the USDA was headed by Senior General Than Shwe and was often used to defend the interests of the regime.[11] Founded on 15 September 1993, membership in the USDA quickly rose to several million people. In rural areas, many farmers joined because they were informed that USDA members would not have to do forced labour building roads and bridges. Others became members so that they could travel without police harassment and receive other perks. The USDA also held occasional courses in computers, English and other subjects for its members.

Less-educated people in particular were drawn to the USDA, believing it was really working for the country. However, in several districts, people's names were simply added to membership lists without their ever being consulted. In some schools, teachers of eighth-standard students (age fourteen) and up were ordered to give the names of their students to the USDA for automatic membership. And it was virtually impossible to become a civil servant without first joining the USDA.

Beginning in 1996, the regime sought to turn the USDA into a counterforce against the NLD and student activists working for the restoration of democracy. This was reflected in many of the USDA leaders' speeches. On 11 December 1996, at the time of the student demonstrations in Rangoon, General Than Shwe gave a speech to a USDA management course, which ran as the lead story in the *New Light of Myanmar*. He said:

The trainees should notice the point that success is being achieved in building a modern nation. At the time of achieving success, it is necessary to keep revolutionary vigil on account of the fact that there are wont to appear various kinds of destructive acts inside and outside the country ... Parents, teachers and students must all keep vigil and prevent those with negative views, destructive elements and those subservient to colonialists from intruding into the education world and using students in their bids to gain political power.[12]

The authorities also gave military training to some USDA youth and used them to intimidate and attack Daw Aung San Suu Kyi and her supporters. The aim was to make it appear that the people, and not just the regime, were opposed to her and the NLD. Periodically, the USDA organized mass rallies throughout the country to demonstrate support for military rule and to denounce the NLD. As in the pre-1988 period, respected individuals were handed speeches which they were ordered to read with sufficient passion. While few people enjoyed attending these rallies, except in cases when they were happy for a break from work, almost nobody refused to go. Names were checked at the gate and those who did not turn up were threatened with fines and other unpleasant consequences.

Frustrated that the regime was refusing to engage in a political dialogue with Daw Aung San Suu Kyi, the NLD began taking more aggressive steps. After the NLD party congress held on 27 May 1998, the NLD urged the regime to recognize the 1990 election results and convene the parliament within sixty days. In August, the NLD announced that if the regime refused to convene the parliament, the NLD would do so itself. The regime responded by arresting hundreds of NLD members to prevent them from meeting. In September 1998, the NLD formed a Committee Representing the People's Parliament (CRPP), consisting of NLD and other political party members.

Determined to crush the NLD, the regime stepped up its efforts to shut down remaining party offices and force not only elected MPs but also party members to resign. In late 1998 and 1999, almost every day the state-controlled newspapers featured articles about the latest mass resignations from the NLD in various townships. Not reported in the newspapers was the fact that USDA members in some districts were going house to house threatening NLD members that, if they did not resign, they would suffer serious consequences. Afraid of losing their jobs or having their businesses closed down, many members did resign. In some cases, USDA members came by a few days later telling them they should now join the USDA.

One statement issued by the CRPP in February 1999 indicates the range of techniques the regime used to intimidate NLD members into resigning. According to the statement, the wife of an NLD MP-elect from Mandalay Division was called to the township chairman's office where she was told:

The NLD would inevitably be destroyed; that family members would be removed from public service and the children would be expelled from school; that every means would be used to cause loss in any business undertaking; that action would be taken against them for any [current] bank loans and future bank loans would be refused; that the NLD is an organisation that is in opposition to the government; and that these measures formed part of a special campaign.[13]

According to the CRPP statement, the family of another NLD MP-elect from the same township was told the same thing, and the next day both men were arrested and pressured to resign, but they refused. They were released after about nine hours but, soon after, the secretary of the local USDA chapter went house to house copying the names of all the people on the household registrations and asking the head of each household to sign. These names were then put into petitions which stated that the signees and their families had no confidence in the NLD MPs-elect, and the petition results were reported in the government-controlled media. By October 1999, only 183 of the original 485 representatives who were elected in 1990 remained valid, with many of the MPs-elect having resigned, been arrested or had their elections declared invalid.[14]

The regime sought to break down the NLD in other ways as well. The most talented thinkers in the party such as U Win Tin, an intellectual, and U Win Htein, a former military officer, were kept in prison along with many other committed party members. Because of the poor living conditions and lack of adequate medical care, many became ill and a few even died. Meanwhile, party members unhappy with some of Daw Aung San Suu Kyi's policies were cultivated by the regime, and their views were given prominence in the government's publications.

Communications between NLD party offices were limited, because the NLD was not legally permitted to print or reproduce party literature or to use a fax machine. The party had minimal funds for travel and communication expenses anyway, so keeping everyone informed of the central committee's policies was difficult. Whenever Daw Aung San Suu Kyi tried to travel outside Rangoon to meet party members, she was stopped and ordered to return home. In distant districts, NLD members usually learned about what was going on at the party headquarters through foreign radio broadcasts or informally from the occasional member who made a trip to Rangoon.

At the same time, the regime tried to destroy Daw Aung San Suu Kyi's morale by forcing her to choose between her family and her political activities. When her husband, Michael Aris, was dying in England in early 1999, the regime refused to give him a visa to come to Burma. The state-controlled media insisted that since she was the healthy one, she should be visiting him.

She made the painful decision not to leave, knowing that the regime would never allow her back in. But the generals punished her by cutting the line on every phone conversation she tried to have with her husband in the days before his death.[15] Michael Aris died on 27 March 1999, Burma's Resistance Day, and his fifty-third birthday.

Some of the remaining Thirty Comrades, particularly Bohmu Aung, repeatedly called for the military regime to engage in a dialogue with Daw Aung San Suu Kyi, but the regime ignored them. The regime also tried to prevent the formation of links between the NLD and the ethnic nationalities' organizations. The NLD members inside the country could not correspond directly with the armed ethnic groups, because the party could be declared illegal for having contact with insurgent organizations. But NLD members who fled to the border areas tried to develop good working relations with the leaders of the armed ethnic groups, as did students who went out to the ethnic-controlled areas in 1988.

On several occasions, the leaders of armed ethnic organizations wrote individual and joint statements declaring their support for Daw Aung San Suu Kyi and the democratic struggle. In January 1997, a number of ethnic minority leaders met in Mae Tha Raw Hta on the Thai–Burma border and signed an agreement calling for tripartite dialogue (the military regime, pro-democracy forces and ethnic leaders), a federal union and a democratic political system. The agreement stated: 'We agree also to join hands with the pro-democracy forces led by Daw Aung San Suu Kyi, and act unitedly and simultaneously for the achievement of rights of the nationalities as well as democratic rights.' While many of the attendees represented small organizations, the generals were upset that the United Wa State Army and the New Mon State Party, two large ceasefire groups, also signed. The SLORC later punished the NMSP for its attendance by cutting its monthly logging quota. A number of ceasefire groups who subsequently issued joint statements supporting the CRPP and calling for a tripartite dialogue were later ordered to rescind their statements, while the military regime urged other ceasefire groups to make statements against the CRPP.[16]

Inside the country, NLD members tried to build more cohesive relations with the ethnic political parties. In the period just after the 1990 election, the NLD and the UNLD, the alliance of ethnic minority political parties affiliated with the NLD, met regularly to discuss federalism and other issues. In the Bo Aung Gyaw Street Agreement No. 1, they promised to build a real democratic union of Burma, with the agreement that 'real democratic' meant in practice more autonomy for the ethnic states. At the National Convention, the elected ethnic and NLD party members were housed in the same barracks and had a chance to deepen their relationships.

In the late 1990s, the NLD tried to arrange meetings and informal get-togethers with ethnic political leaders, although the regime often blocked such efforts. Even Daw Aung San Suu Kyi's attempts to attend Karen New Year celebrations in Insein township, just outside Rangoon, were prevented. The CRPP included one ethnic representative, U Aye Tha Aung, a central executive committee member of the Arakan League for Democracy and a senior member of the United Nationalities League for Democracy. However, he was arrested in April 2000 on unspecified charges.

Despite the NLD's efforts to develop closer relations with ethnic nationality leaders, the regime continued to drive wedges between them. The armed ethnic groups were often reluctant to do anything that might jeopardize their ceasefire agreements. While the ceasefires had not resulted in the granting of ethnic rights and political autonomy, they did mean the end of decades-long civil wars and far less suffering for the civilian population. Thus, as long as the Tatmadaw was in control, most of the leaders of the armed ethnic organizations felt it necessary to cooperate with the regime. At the same time, some of the ethnic leaders, particularly in the remote areas, wondered whether any Burman-dominated government would honour their demands for greater political autonomy. Although perhaps less so than in the past, many Burmans continued to be suspicious of federalism, including some in the pro-democracy movement.

By 2000, the regime had not been able to raise the standard of living of the majority of the domestic population, however. While military generals' families and their friends managed to amass fortunes through virtual monopolies over many of the most lucrative businesses, ordinary Burmese businessmen found that without the necessary bribes and connections, they were not able to participate in the new market economy.

Water and electricity shortages became acute in 1998 and 1999, with frequent blackouts in Rangoon, and some rural towns receiving electricity only once every three to five days. Businesses and homes suffered alike. One joke circulating in Rangoon was: it's fortunate that the military government only takes responsibility for water and electricity, not air. Another joke suggested that Burma should be renamed 'Ye-mi-sia', which sounds like Indonesia and Malaysia. But the meaning of *ye-mi-sia* in Burmese is 'water-electricity-shortage'.

Thus, fifty years after independence Burma was still struggling to resolve its political and economic problems. The regime continued to cling to the idea of a unitary state with centralized powers, while the ethnic nationalities continued to insist on greater political freedoms. The military regime managed to severely damage the organizational capacity of the pro-democracy movement, but it was not able to build a prosperous nation. Because the regime devoted so much of the country's resources to repressing its citizens, everyone suffered.

CHAPTER 5

. . . .

Families: Fostering Conformity

'We're always acting, saying what we think the authorities want to hear. It's so exhausting.' (A pastor)

§ Individuals in Burma often talk and act in seemingly contradictory ways. When they sense that the political atmosphere is more relaxed, they are willing to complain in public about aspects of military rule or to voice quietly their support for Daw Aung San Suu Kyi and the pro-democracy movement. However, during periods of greater repression, they tend to stay silent or even criticize democracy activists as ineffective. At moments when the democracy struggle seems to have no chance of success, some people even dismiss its validity, as they seek to make peace with their lives under military rule.

Similarly, the public may enjoy reading critiques of the regime or watching movies that indirectly parody military rule, but when family members or neighbours are the ones acting against the government, they may find they have little support. This is because the authorities have been known to harass and arrest those who live with or even just casually associate with anti-government activists, even if they have done nothing against the regime themselves. By punishing those who surround activists, the authorities can isolate the activists and discourage activism from spreading. Thus, as much as friends and neighbours might admire those who are courageous enough to act for change, they can be reluctant to offer any direct support.

The following chapters look more closely at how families, communities and professional groups are torn between protecting themselves and standing up for what they believe. Under military rule in Burma, it seems that doing what is right is often directly opposed to doing what is necessary to survive. As the military's influence has seeped into virtually every aspect of people's lives, resistance becomes difficult to imagine. Yet, there are dynamic individuals who have tried to reclaim certain activities, such as education, social work, art and religious practice, from military control or to fend off military involvement.

Collective Amnesia

Despite their own dislike of the military regime, most parents are raising their children to conform with military domination, and even to become part of the system. When they were younger, a number of parents themselves participated in anti-government rallies, but as they aged and nothing changed, many began to see resistance as futile. Like parents everywhere, Burmese parents want their children to be successful and financially secure. Yet in Burma today, there are few possibilities for a 'successful' life outside the military's extensive sphere of influence.

In order to protect their children, many parents discourage them from critically examining military rule. One man, who was a university student in 1988, talked about his mother's reaction to his realization that the government's policies were not benefiting the people. After the March 1988 demonstrations, his university was closed and he came back to his home town, where he struck up conversations with local businessmen and people around the market. One day he said to his mother, 'I have some weird feelings which I've never had before. There is something wrong with this system.' She told him, 'Don't take it seriously. This is life.'

In Burma, most families are close-knit, and parents are very involved in their children's decisions about education and work. Not surprisingly, those who can afford their children's university fees strongly encourage them to major in subjects leading to secure and high-paying jobs after they graduate. Entering the Defence Services Academy, a university-level programme that trains military officers, is one option which many parents favour. Other prized careers include becoming doctors, engineers or administrators in the civil service. Although their salaries may be low, they will have a guaranteed job and will be provided with perks such as housing and the opportunity to make money on the side, often through corruption.

But with the civilian ministries generally headed by military men, non-conformists are quickly weeded out. To enter any of these professions, a high school or university graduate must have no history of anti-government political activities. Thus the need to foster conformity begins early. Parents encourage their children to join government-sponsored youth organizations, because those who don't are viewed with suspicion. In the Burma Socialist Programme Party period, students were urged to participate in such organizations even at the primary school level. And in many high schools, students were given extra points on their final exams as a reward for maintaining membership in the youth organization. Following the formation of the Union Solidarity and Development Association in 1993, high school students came under similar pressures, with educational advancement often linked to membership.

Throughout the period of military rule, successive regimes have held annual, nationwide *Lu Ye Chun*, or 'Outstanding Student' competitions. Just over 300 students are chosen each year. While the primary qualification is top grades, one aspect of the contests has been to demonstrate the ability to regurgitate party propaganda. The high school and university students who are selected as outstanding are sent on three-week trips to beautiful places by the ocean or in the mountains. The trips also include a state dinner in Rangoon where the winners are lauded by senior officials. The students are told that they will be the next leaders of Burma, and that the future of the country depends on them. A government publication from the BSPP days stated that one of the seven aims of cultivating the outstanding students was 'to create hardcores for socialist construction'.[1] Although the post-1988 military regimes rejected socialism, the authorities continued to hope that those honoured by the state would be imbued with a sense of loyalty to the regime's goals.

With many middle- and upper-class mothers so involved in their children's education that they regularly go through their school work with them, the greatest pride for parents is to have their child selected as an outstanding student. However, no matter how smart their children are, if they are caught writing anti-government pamphlets or drawing cartoons, they will not be honoured for their academic achievements.

Students who are arrested for participation in a local demonstration or for the distribution of political pamphlets are marked for life. They might not be able to finish their schooling, they won't be able to obtain a job in the civil service, and even finding a marriage partner becomes complicated, as parents worry that former political activists will bring nothing but trouble to their families. Thus, in order to ensure their children's well-being, most parents encourage them to go along with the regime, or at the very least to keep any negative thoughts to themselves.

Moe Thee Zun, the student leader, explained the attitude of parents when he was growing up in Rangoon in the 1970s and 1980s. He said: 'One type of parents strongly supported the BSPP and thought the BSPP could develop the country. Some parents hated the BSPP but said to their children, "Don't play with fire. If you want to do anything against the government, pack your bags." They really thought it was useless. Even my parents said, "Son, don't make any problem. Get your education. Make your life better. You can go abroad."'

The relatives of Ma Pyu, a university student who campaigned for the NLD in the 1990 election, expressed similar sentiments. They told Ma Pyu's parents: 'Ma Pyu doesn't know anything. Why are you letting her do this political work, fighting the government? Our government is very big and your daughter is so small and has no knowledge. It's useless.'

The attitude of Ma Pyu's relatives is exactly what successive military regimes have tried to cultivate. The relatives took it for granted that the people in power knew everything and ordinary people did not have the capacity to change the situation, so they should stay quiet. Not only did her relatives see themselves as powerless, but they sought to disempower Ma Pyu as well.

Despite the tremendous value placed on education in Burma, most parents have done little to make up for the regime's silence on much of the country's recent history. In particular, parents do not bring up past incidents of resistance, such as the 7 July protests at Rangoon University in 1962 or the anti-government demonstrations that erupted in the mid-1970s. They know that the authorities are not teaching these events in school or through the media, but they do not discuss such subjects at home. Some parents' silence can be attributed in part to a belief that it is not their duty to explain politics, but often it is due to a feeling that it is better if their children don't know. Indeed, some parents discourage their children from reading serious books for fear this will lead them into politics. Thus, children in Burma grow up thinking that the situation in their country is normal. They and their family might be suffering as a result of government policies, but these problems are accepted as routine problems. No one has given the youth a frame of reference for critiquing their country's current situation.

When children obtain positions in government, their parents are relieved. One diplomat with several dissident uncles but conformist parents told me that he had joined the foreign service to please his parents. Initially, he unquestioningly accepted the government's line that human rights should be considered only after there was economic progress. Without having ever studied how political rights were understood in other countries, he bought the 'Asian Values' argument that collective security was more important than individual rights. It wasn't until he had lived abroad that he began to see things differently. Finally, his ideas changed so radically that he ended up defecting.

The children of military families in particular grow up believing that the country is being run as it should. Military officers' families are given special privileges such as access to better equipped hospitals, sports facilities and housing. They are taught that they deserve these benefits because they are the ones who are sacrificing for the country. Few question this logic unless they spend time living on their own abroad. For instance, Kyaw Kyaw, a young man whose father was a high-ranking officer, has lived in a western country since the late 1980s, and his views have been completely reshaped by his experiences outside the sheltered environment in which he grew up. He said when he was young, he appreciated that his family's status was higher than that of ordinary people because his father was a military officer. Knowing that he would immediately be released whenever he was stopped by the police, he would brazenly drive over the speed limit and commit other traffic violations.

Kyaw Kyaw explained he understood the inequities that existed in Burma only after living abroad and experiencing an open society. He was surprised that, in the West, even top political leaders' sons had to obey the law and work for success. Now, he says, he is ashamed of his past. He thinks people should have to earn their cars and their houses, rather than receive them as gifts because of who their fathers are. Going back to Burma after ten years, he was shocked by the lives of some of his former friends from military families who think nothing of spending 30,000 kyat per day (the equivalent of ten months' salary in 1999) on food, drink and women. He found them to be totally unconcerned with the problems that ordinary people were facing. After expressing his dismay to his family, his parents became worried that he might air his views publicly. They urged him to continue to live abroad.

Having gone through the crackdown on the pro-democracy uprising in 1988 and the regime's refusal to honour the 1990 election results, few people outside the military talk about the current regime with enthusiasm, but they also have no idea about how to effect a change. While parents might reminisce about the past when their salaries went further and goods were cheaper, they rarely link their complaints to a political programme of action. As much as Daw Aung San Suu Kyi has called on people to resist unreasonable demands by the authorities, such as the extortion of supplementary school fees, parents tend to feel that they can best serve their children by going along with the regime. While they may believe that ultimately their children would be better off under a democratic government, they see that anyone who works for change is soon arrested.

As Ne Myo, a farmer and part-time carpenter from Mon State explained, even if the government-imposed rice quota is too onerous, farmers cannot protest because they have to think about their families' survival. He said: 'Let's say I get arrested and go to prison because the farmers gathered at my house and demonstrated. My family will starve. Since I'm afraid my family will starve if I go to prison, I won't dare to participate in demonstrations. Since I don't have food to eat and I'm struggling for food, I have to be afraid of everyone and I have to keep my head low, whether they are doing the right thing or not.'

The rural population of Burma is affected by military rule more than the urban population because, in many areas, villagers must perform forced labour on infrastructure projects and act as porters on military operations, unless they can pay bribes. Few have enough money to do so regularly. In addition, farmers who cannot provide the annual rice quota, which must be sold to the government at a price well below the market rate, must buy rice at the market price and sell it back to the authorities at the government price. As a result, farmers often have trouble providing for their families, and family members have increasingly migrated to neighbouring countries so that they can earn money to send home.

Unable to afford their children's school fees, Ne Myo and his wife joined several hundred thousand illegal Burmese migrant workers in Thailand, leaving their four young children with their maternal grandparents. Although their salaries at a garment factory were far below the Thai minimum wage and police raids left them without a penny some months, they managed to send money home regularly for school fees, food and clothing. Ne Myo explained: 'Now that I'm working in Thailand, I can send my children at least four outfits each a year. I can tell my parents to buy good quality rice. They can eat good curries. I am happy.'

Ne Myo's own father was able to pass on only his carpentry skills to Ne Myo, but Ne Myo wants to do more for his children. He thinks that if his children are well educated, they will live an easier life than he has. But the price he and his wife have had to pay is high. In order to provide for their children, they cannot live with them. When he sees Thai children on their way to school, he is reminded of his own children. 'I become really sad and tears well up in my eyes,' he said. 'I miss them very much.'

Ne Myo and his wife are admirable parents, doing all they can to take care of their children. Moreover, the grandparents don't have to suffer unduly because they now have enough money to pay off the military men who come to the house to extort fees for porters and forced labour. But by feeding money into the system that has put them in this untenable position, they are inadvertently helping to prop it up. I say this not to criticize families trying their best to survive but to demonstrate how a military regime becomes self-sustaining even when most of its citizens are opposed to it. The collective effect of almost every family protecting its own members is that challenges to military rule are generally not promoted or valorized except in rare situations, like 1988, when it looks as if real change is imminent.

Activist Families

There are some notable exceptions. Parents who are devoted activists do raise their children to be aware of the country's political problems. These parents try to live outside the government's reach, and often consign their families to poverty as a result. Such parents don't allow their children to attend government-organized activities, which is often hard on their children when they see all their friends participating. As they get older, though, many of these children follow in their parents' footsteps. Here I want to tell the story of two such families in detail, because I think it is easier to understand why people go along with the regime by looking at the experiences of those who don't.

Than Dai grew up with a father who was strongly determined to have the family live their lives untainted by involvement with the military regime. Total avoidance was impossible, because the children had to attend government-run schools. But Than Dai's father made tremendous efforts to ensure that his children were instilled with the moral and political ideas which he considered important. However, when Than Dai was young, he found it difficult to understand his father's extreme behaviour.

Than Dai's father had participated in anti-military demonstrations after General Ne Win seized power in 1962. A university student at the time, he was arrested and kept in custody at the police station. There he tutored the daughter of one of the policemen, and she later became his wife. Than Dai's father went on to become a private school teacher, but when his school was nationalized in the mid-1960s he automatically became a government school teacher. He loved teaching, and his students and their parents loved him but, from the authorities' perspective, this was a problem. He had a political record and could easily organize students, so, to keep bonds of attachment from forming, he was transferred again and again. Finally, he decided to leave the government service and start a private tuition class in his home. Than Dai's father was known by everyone in the town and respected for his intellect and moral convictions.

However, Than Dai's father was not appreciated by his wife's family. Than Dai's grandmother was ashamed to see Than Dai and his siblings dressed in old clothes, while her other children had prospered by cooperating with the authorities. Than Dai too found it difficult to put up with his family's poverty. Once he suggested that his father start an illegal side business with some of his friends who were state and divisional officers. He said: 'We cannot go on like this. Why don't you do some work for us?' His father was outraged. He threw everything off the table and shouted at Than Dai to leave the house. 'When I think about it now,' Than Dai said, 'my words were insulting to him, because all the time he restrained himself and kept his dignity. He could stand by himself without being involved in any government service.'

Than Dai's father refused to attend government-sponsored activities and celebrations, and would not allow his children to attend either. Than Dai and his siblings were often in trouble at school, because they could not participate in school-organized 'voluntary labour' activities or commemorations of Independence Day and Union Day. Than Dai's house was very near the town hall, so whenever the party officials held meetings or celebrations, Than Dai's father locked the gate to their house and denied entrance to any BSPP members. 'At that time,' Than Dai said, 'most people in Burma had to join the BSPP, even if they didn't like it. Cadres had a lot of opportunities. Some of those township cadres were my father's pupils and his friends. They could come to our home any time to visit or pay their respects to my parents, but whenever there was a celebration and they came to attend, he would never allow them to come in his house.' Although Than Dai's parents' friends often wanted to leave their bicycles and other things at their house for safe-keeping, Than Dai's father refused. During the summer holidays, however, Than Dai's house was filled with dissident teachers and former political prisoners. Most were also poor, but as they sipped tea and snacked on tea leaf salad, they found pleasure in each other's company.

When Than Dai was in eighth standard (aged fourteen or fifteen), he competed in the 'Outstanding Student' contest. He was chosen as the second best in his school, so his teachers prepared him to enter the next level of competition. Than Dai remembers his father telling him to go ahead and try, but he wouldn't be chosen because of Than Dai's father's political history. 'He was right,' Than Dai said. 'I could answer the questions, but I didn't get it. Since that time I never competed in that competition again. But I was always first or second in my class.' I asked Than Dai if he had felt angry with his father at that time. But he said no, because by that age he could appreciate what his father had done. 'In school sometimes some people would say, "He is from the rebel family." They said this with admiration. We were very proud. Sons of a rebel.'

When Than Dai's younger brother passed the high school matriculation exam, he wanted to apply to the Defence Services Academy. Before 1988, many boys dreamed of becoming military officers, not only because of the material benefits but also because in school they were taught that military officers were heroes. Than Dai remarked that even though his brother had been raised in such a political family, he still 'lost the way' because of the schooling system and the prevailing social environment. When Than Dai's brother asked his father if he could attend the Defence Services Academy, his father said grimly, 'You can go, but you cannot come home.' Finally the brother decided not to apply.

After Than Dai started university classes, his father insisted that Than Dai continue to study English with him. Than Dai's friends were incredulous that on top of his course work, he had to do homework for his father. Than Dai himself was embarrassed about it. Every weekend, he had to return home to tutor his younger brother and sister and go over his homework. This was hard on Than Dai, who wanted to have time to go out with his friends. He often complained, but his father said, 'One day you will understand me. If you want to do things for other people, you have to be educated. So you have to do it even if you don't like it, because you are my son.' Than Dai said that although he didn't dare object to this explanation, he still secretly requested his mother to tell his father to ease up on him.

Than Dai's father even came to stay with him in his university dormitory from time to time. At night, he would ask Than Dai to read to him, because his eyesight was failing and the wattage of the dormitory lights was so weak. Than Dai protested saying, 'I never saw any other parents come and sleep with their sons or ask their sons to read loudly in the room.' But his father said, 'It doesn't matter. We are not disturbing others.' Than Dai begged, 'Please, no.' But his father insisted. Than Dai's friends came by to see what was going on and were amused by the scene. Than Dai was embarrassed. Only later did Than Dai come to believe that his father was right.

In June 1988, Than Dai's elder brother participated in the student movement in Rangoon. Some of his friends came to Than Dai's house to tell his parents that, unlike the other students, Than Dai's brother had not worn a bandana across his face to disguise himself. More than that, he publicly announced his name and the names of everyone in the family when everyone else was trying to hide their identities. Soon after, military intelligence agents brought Than Dai's brother back to his home town and put him in custody. Than Dai's grandmother was furious. She berated Than Dai's parents for not preventing her eldest grandson from getting involved in politics.

When the demonstrations were about to start in Than Dai's home town in August 1988, Than Dai told his father he was going to participate. His father did not forbid him, but that night he had Than Dai look at several books about past political movements in Burma and elsewhere. He also showed Than Dai photographs of people who had been tortured, and asked him, 'If you want to do politics, you may face this one day. Do you dare?'

The next day Than Dai decided he did dare. He and his friends led the first demonstration in their town, and his mother and older brother both gave speeches to the gathered crowd. Than Dai's father stayed home. When the marchers passed Than Dai's house shouting slogans, Than Dai's father came out smiling, still eating from his plate. The crowd asked Than Dai's father to join in, but he replied jokingly, 'It's not necessary for me to come. All of my family has joined with you. I am the eldest, so I have to give a chance to them.' Than Dai said everyone understood, because Than Dai's father was living under watch and everyone knew it. 'In the blacklist in our town,' Than Dai said, 'my father was first.'

Two or three days after the first demonstration, the town activists formed a strike committee and asked Than Dai's father to become a member. He did, but when the SLORC staged a coup on 18 September, he and Than Dai knew they were likely to be arrested. They and some others hid in rural villages, moving from place to place. Finally, the authorities tracked them down. Than Dai was sleeping under some toddy trees when he was awakened by an armed soldier kicking him. He was tied up, as was his father, who had been sleeping in the monastery. When the soldiers searched their bags, they confiscated a book that discussed how soldiers should treat civilians. Than Dai complained, saying, 'This book says that soldiers must pay respect to civilians.' The soldiers responded by beating him with a stick. Then father and son were tied together and taken back into town, where they had to sign an agreement saying they would not participate in politics again. They signed but, soon after, Than Dai's father and older brother were arrested together with the rest of the strike committee.

Than Dai didn't know what to do. He thought about going to the jungle to take up arms. His mother told him he could leave if he wanted to, but that he should consider carefully, because his life would never be the same if he did. She also told him that if he left, he should not come home again until the struggle was successful. She was disgusted by students who had already come back from the border and done interviews with the government press condemning the student movement.

Within a couple of months, Than Dai's father and brother were released on bail, and Than Dai and his brother decided to join up with the student army on the border. Their parents supported them. The day they were to leave, everyone in the family was overcome with sadness. They did not know when they would see each other again. Than Dai said: 'Some friends came by that day, but we dared not reveal our plan. We had to be cautious, but we kept looking at each other. The visitors were talking. My mother was cooking. We prepared some money and clothes. We had to wait for the visitors to leave and we ate lunch together, the last lunch for us. Just before we left our home, we paid respect to our parents. My parents sat on the bed inside the room, because outside some more visitors had arrived so we dared not talk loudly. My mother was not crying, but my father was. Tears ran down his glasses. My brother asked him, "Why are you crying?" My father replied, "I'm crying because I'm proud. Because my two sons will continue the revolution which I cannot afford to do at my age."'

Than Dai and his brother managed to make their way to the border and have been working with resistance groups ever since. Although they know they have the love and support of their parents, they have had to sacrifice their family connections. Already more than ten years have passed and their parents are getting old. They do not know if they will ever be reunited.

Still, Than Dai is grateful for the way he was raised. He said: 'My father was a good example. He resisted the government in the best way he could and he could keep all his family members out of the BSPP. Now I thank him very much. If we didn't have him, we could have gone the wrong way. So we thank him, and I thank my mother because she never complained about his political views and his guidance in education. And then I thank both of them because they always taught us not to exploit others, to sympathize with the poor and oppressed. Sometimes we are human beings, so we lose our focus, but at those times, I remember my parents. They faced a lot of difficulties, especially with money, but they never knelt down or betrayed their beliefs, so I love them.'

While it is clear from Than Dai's story that some of the other town residents admired his family, no one else he knew chose to live in the same way. Trying to live outside the regime's influence takes tremendous effort, particularly when everyone else is going along with the authorities. The family became fully integrated into the community only during the 1988 demonstrations, when it seemed as if democracy was within reach.

Than Dai lived in a small town in Upper Burma. Lin Htet, another young man who grew up in a political family, lived in Rangoon. Like Than Dai, Lin Htet went through difficult years as a teenager, when he still couldn't fully appreciate his father's commitment to living by different rules. Lin Htet's father was also a 1962 student activist who had become a private tuition teacher. And Lin Htet's family was always struggling for money, too, because his father charged less than the going rate so that poorer students would have a chance to attend his classes. Like Than Dai, Lin Htet sometimes resented his father's moral uprightness, because their family could not afford the nice clothes that some other kids proudly wore.

Every summer vacation, Lin Htet's parents took him and his siblings to a rural village so that they would understand the hardships of the poor. 'My father hated privileged people exploiting peasants,' Lin Htet said. 'And he didn't want us to be rich people but to be educated people.' In the village where Lin Htet and his family regularly visited, there was no school, hospital or electricity, 'no cars, only cows'. Lin Htet's father encouraged his children to ride the cows and roll around in the dust with the village children. Once Lin Htet and his siblings settled in, they enjoyed themselves, but when it came time to head for the village the next year, they resisted again. Particularly after they became teenagers, they wanted to spend their holidays hanging out with friends in the city, but Lin Htet's father insisted they return to the village so that they would understand the suffering of others.

Like Than Dai's father, Lin Htet's father did not allow the family to participate in government-sponsored activities. Lin Htet talked about how, when he was young, he wanted to go to the Armed Forces Day celebration to see the fireworks and other amusements, but his father refused to let the family go. As a teenager, Lin Htet remembers secretly fantasizing about becoming a military doctor. He thought to himself, 'I would get a lot of respect. Girls would like me. I'd look really smart.' But he knew he could never do it because of his father and his father's dissident friends. Lin Htet said they always told him and his brothers that if someone asked them what they wanted to be when they grew up, they should answer 'a revolutionary'. Such talk terrified Lin Htet's mother's relatives.

Even though Lin Htet grew up in a family that promoted anti-government resistance, his parents found it difficult to accept Lin Htet's decision to take up politics at the tender age of fifteen. After the March 1988 demonstrations broke out, Lin Htet skipped school one day to attend a secret meeting at the zoo. As some students were break-dancing to music on their tape player, others quietly conferred with an older female student who explained to them how they could work together with the university student activists by distributing pamphlets. Many of the eager young high school students, including Lin Htet, took up the cause.

When Lin Htet arrived home, his mother asked him where he had been. Afraid she might become angry, he lied and said he had come back from school. But his mother replied that Lin Htet's teacher had already come by and told her that he hadn't attended school that day. Lin Htet remembered, 'She took a broomstick and asked me again, "Where did you go?" At first she was worried I'd been smoking. So I told her I'd attended the high school student meeting.' This only made matters worse. She scolded him angrily, reminding him that his eldest brother and sisters were already in prison for their participation in the demonstrations, and that was upsetting her terribly. He ought to think of her feelings. And besides, he was far too young. She started beating him with the broomstick.

At this point, Lin Htet's father came into the room and told his wife to stop. Although Lin Htet's parents had an agreement that they would not interfere with each other's parenting, Lin Htet's father said, 'I know he's young, but we should give him the facts and let him think for himself. It's up to him whether he wants to get involved or not. But first we should explain to him in more detail about political life and family life.' Lin Htet remembers that his mother was weeping, and he felt very sorry because he missed his arrested siblings too. Every night, his mother put their photographs under her pillow and recited prayers for them. She had even gone to a fortune-teller to inquire what magical actions (*yadaya*) she could take to improve their chances for release. And now Lin Htet had become another burden for her.

His father, though, insisted on discussing the situation with Lin Htet. He told Lin Htet how harsh a political life could be and said that he didn't think Lin Htet was old enough to make an informed decision. He asked Lin Htet to think about the family, and in particular his mother and his grandmother, who had also come into the room and started crying. But given his political upbringing and the mood in his high school class, Lin Htet felt compelled to act. Throughout the 1988 demonstrations and the election campaign period, he participated in student politics. When the military intelligence imprisoned Min Ko Naing and other student activists in mid-1989, Lin Htet realized he too might be arrested. One evening he came home in the rain, and his mother greeted him at the door with the words, 'Go! Go!' Military intelligence agents had been there looking for him and were still lurking around the neighbourhood awaiting his return. He fled into the night and has not been able to return home since.

Lin Htet's mother's reaction was typical of many Burmese families who find out their children have become politically active. But the way she and her husband and Than Dai's parents raised their children was quite unusual. Most families try to insulate their children from political realities and urge them to conform. Besides worrying about their children's safety, many parents depend on their older children to take on some of the family's responsibilities. With a deteriorating economy and high inflation, many older children are expected to help pay for their younger siblings' educations and to provide financial support for their ageing parents. If children are in and out of prison, on the run, and unable to get jobs because of their political activities, how can they support their family members?

The demands of the family and the democracy movement pull politically-aware individuals in opposite directions. Some choose to stop their political activities so they can take care of their families, while others decide that they must work for their country despite their families' objections. By entering into politics, activists realize they are also potentially putting their family members at risk, as parents and siblings are sometimes harassed or denied jobs because of their activities. Many activists find wrestling with these tensions extremely painful.

For young women, the decision to participate in political activities is particularly difficult. Single women are not supposed to go out alone or even with male friends; they should be accompanied by parents, aunts or older brothers until they are married. They cannot easily stay out late at night to attend meetings or not come home to sleep. If they do go around with male colleagues or sleep elsewhere, they can be accused of being 'bad' girls. Such cultural norms make it even harder for young women than for young men to take up politics.

Shifting Values

It was not until the 1988 demonstrations, when large numbers of people joined the pro-democracy demonstrations, that ideas about activists changed. In the early stages, only university and high school students and other long-time but often socially marginalized political activists joined in. Yet when the soldiers retreated to their barracks and the government seemingly collapsed, more and more of the parents who had raised their children to go along with the system joined their sons and daughters on the streets. Mothers took an active role, cooking for hungry protesters and joining in the marches.

During this brief six-week period, values changed. When the pro-democracy forces appeared to be winning, those who were most active in organizing the strike committees gained prestige and respect in their communities. Often shunned in earlier days, older activists like Than Dai's father found themselves the centre of attention during those heady days of freedom. At the same time, hatred of the military grew dramatically as many people witnessed soldiers brutally firing on unarmed demonstrators, including children. Thus, some military men were shocked when they were suddenly ostracized even by those closest to them.

One soldier named Maung Maung, who returned to his home town in Karen State shortly after the coup, discussed the cold treatment he received from his friends and family. Ten years had passed by the time I interviewed him, but he still clearly felt upset. He remembered: 'Before the '88 demonstrations, when I took leave and met my friends and classmates, they warmly welcomed me. They were proud of my being a soldier. But after the '88 affair, when I took leave and went home, they didn't even want to speak with me.' Even his parents were unhappy with him.

Maung Maung was a member of Light Infantry Division 22, the division most responsible for the 1988 killings. But during the shootings he had been in a remote border camp, only vaguely aware of what was happening in the urban areas. When he arrived home, his father asked him accusingly, 'Do you know what Division 22 did in Rangoon?' Maung Maung said that he explained to everyone that he wasn't involved in those shootings, and that he would never shoot students even if he were ordered to. But his friends clearly didn't believe him. 'At that time I felt very sad,' Maung Maung said. 'It really affected me.'

Maung Maung maintained that he had originally joined the military because he was impressed with the Tatmadaw's image. But after the shootings, the military no longer had any dignity in the eyes of the people. He said: 'Previously people loved us and looked on us as people they could rely on. But now they look at us with disgust. Also in their eyes, now I see fear. I can't deal with that. That's why I didn't stay for my whole leave time. I had ten days, but after seven days I went back to my battalion.'

When the military refused to transfer power after the 1990 election, family attitudes changed again. Soldiers had lost much of the respect they had once had, but parents again began thinking that only officers in the military would have a guaranteed a good life. Sons were again encouraged to seek entrance into the Defence Services Academy. Moreover, the authorities' technique of making life difficult not just for activists but also their families turned many people against their activist relatives.

Kyi Kyi, a young woman who was sentenced to four years in prison for continuing underground political activities after the 1990 election, explained how her mother's treatment of her changed over time. When she first joined the movement in 1988, her mother was worried. Her husband had died several years before, so she had had to raise her children alone. But Kyi Kyi's mother gradually became more supportive, because, Kyi Kyi says, she herself had suffered so much.

While Kyi Kyi was in prison, her mother regularly brought her food, but her relatives had all turned against her. Many served in the military. When Kyi Kyi was released, none of her relatives would talk to her, even when she visited their houses. Kyi Kyi tried to resume a normal life and sought work to support her mother and siblings. Yet whenever she managed to secure a job, a military intelligence agent would show up and inform her employers about her political background. After that, the employers would be scared to keep her on and would fire her. In one instance, the cleaning girl at a company where she worked admitted to Kyi Kyi that even she had been ordered to keep a watch on her.

The military intelligence officer also often came to Kyi Kyi's home to question her or to tell her to come to his office. Kyi Kyi refused to go with him, but her family was scared and implored her to go. He used crude language with her and demanded that she tell him where she had been, whom she had met and what they talked about. This was hard enough on Kyi Kyi, but what was worse was that even her mother and her younger siblings started to blame her. She said, 'They asked me what I had done. Of course I said, "Nothing." My family thought I must be up to something to be treated this way. I became a sort of black sheep in my family.' Finally, Kyi Kyi could no longer stand the pressure and left home.

Some children have faced even more extreme forms of disapproval from their parents. One woman I interviewed who had participated in anti-government activities in the mid-1990s was publicly disowned by her parents in a newspaper announcement. Although her family got word to her beforehand that they were doing it only because of military pressure, it was still emotionally difficult for her.

Although the military's actions are meant to break up resistance among the civilian population, military families are also affected by their policies. The SPDC Secretary-1, Lt General Khin Nyunt, felt compelled to disown publicly one of his sons, Dr Ye Naing Win, when he married a Singaporean woman.[2] After all the regime's rhetoric against Daw Aung San Suu Kyi for marrying a foreigner, Lt General Khin Nyunt's son's marriage was highly embarrassing.

Split Families

While there are families that are purely anti-government or pro-military, they are rare. Almost every family has relatives in both the military and the democracy struggle. Such divisions became particularly apparent during the 1988 demonstrations when some families contained individuals who took part in the protests and others who were gunning down the marchers. Older siblings who had gone into the military officer corps and had been appreciated for regularly sending money home, became pariahs. Younger siblings who had looked up to their older brothers with admiration, now viewed them with repugnance. The realization that the enemy was part of their own family was too much for some to bear.

Such bitter feelings can be seen in the poem of a young man who journeyed to the Thai border to join the All Burma Students' Democratic Front (ABSDF). He wrote a poem about his brother, a captain in the Tatmadaw, published in the ABSDF's *Dawn Oh Wai* (Cry of the Peacock) magazine.[3]

It's About Time They See It. It's About Time They Correct It
by Bo Si (Theh Gon)

Big brother,
Don't look down on me with a sneer.
Do you dare to fight back the eyes and the smiles of the people?
Expose your knees which have knelt under the BSPP and look.
They are covered with scars.
Aren't you ashamed?
Look at my knees which didn't kneel under the BSPP.
There are no scars.

Big brother,
Are you going to remain silent, raising your forefinger and nodding,
For the good of a group of evil spirits who are crazy for power?
Don't you know that the stars on your shoulders and your salary come from
The people's blood and sweat?
Which one are you going to look at?
The stars on your shoulders or the faces of the people?

Another student named Zaw Lwin, who comes from a town in central Burma, explained how he was raised with the idea that he would become an officer; his three male cousins were all in the army or police, and his mother had encouraged him to follow the same path. But in 1988, he joined the student demonstrations. The political climate had changed, and so had his mother's perspective. For more than two years, she fed and supported him and his colleagues as they moved from the demonstrations to election campaign work.

Zaw Lwin's aunt in Rangoon was a teacher, and her son was an army officer. In 1988, she told her son that if he shot any students, he should not return home. She said the students were her pupils and she loved them. Zaw Lwin said that his cousin was so frustrated that he cried. He had graduated from the university and knew what was right and wrong, but he was thinking of his family's survival. He was already married and didn't dare challenge his superiors' orders.

Later that year, Zaw Lwin ran into this cousin at Daw Aung San Suu Kyi's compound, just after the death of her mother, Daw Khin Kyi, in December 1988. He was shocked to see his cousin in plain clothes, wearing an NLD pin and acting like an NLD sympathizer. The cousin had been sent to the compound to see who was there and report back to military intelligence. Zaw Lwin refrained from greeting his cousin, but when his cousin caught his eye, he held up his hand signalling not to approach. Another military informer saw their exchange and assumed Zaw Lwin was also an intelligence agent. As Zaw Lwin was sitting at a table, the agent leaned over and whispered, 'What does the black ribbon mean?' Zaw Lwin told him it meant mourning for Daw Khin Kyi. The man was writing notes in the margins of a magazine, and Zaw Lwin sensed he was in a dangerous situation. If the real NLD people realized that his cousin and the other man were intelligence agents, they might think he was too. He decided his only option was to leave immediately.

When he returned to his home town, Zaw Lwin told all his relatives about seeing the cousin spying on the NLD. Later, his cousin came to Zaw Lwin's home to try to make amends. The cousin had transferred from the military to the police, and arrived at Zaw Lwin's house on a new motorcycle, smoking a cigar. Zaw Lwin recalled that his family was put off by his manner, but because of his age and rank they treated him respectfully and offered him food and tea. The cousin talked openly about his frustration with the military but said he had a family to feed. He also warned Zaw Lwin to stop his involvement in the democracy movement, for his own safety. Zaw Lwin said that his mother lost her temper and told her nephew that if he didn't have the courage to resign and do what her son was doing, he need not come to visit again.

Other families, however, have tried to smooth over their political differences and maintain close family relations. When siblings end up in opposing camps, the parents try to keep politics out of family discussions and focus on keeping the family together. Siblings are often torn by their own conflicting feelings.

Such was the case with a middle-aged man named Tint Moe who was involved in a demonstration in the mid-1970s. He has continued to hold anti-government views, while one of his older brothers has risen in a career in the foreign service. Tint Moe vividly recalled that after he was released from prison, his brother wrote to him, saying, 'You are at an age when you are very idealistic, but remember that all these things will pass and remember what you owe to your parents.'

Despite their political differences, his brother continued to send him gifts from his various postings. This made it difficult for Tint Moe to hate his brother even though he resented the suggestion that he stop his political activities. But when the brothers met up at their parents' house in Rangoon after several years, the discussion quickly became heated. As they got on to politics, Tint Moe demanded, 'Should I talk to you as a brother or should I talk to you as someone who works for the Foreign Ministry?'

Even at home, Tint Moe's brother refused to let down his guard. Tint Moe's father would sometimes ask whether various rumours about the government were true or not, but Tint Moe's brother refused to say a word. Tint Moe said, 'In the BSPP days, party members would attend political rallies and they would shout the slogans, because it helped with their promotions and careers. But then they would go home and in the privacy of their own families, they would speak their thoughts. With friends they would say, "Oh, you know, I had to say that."' But Tint Moe's brother was different. As Tint Moe put it, 'He had just one face. The private face and the public face were the same.'

Yet when I asked Tint Moe if he felt that the military regime was to blame for the tensions in his relationship with his brother, he replied, 'You could say that, but I don't feel any personal animosity towards my brother. Whatever decisions he and I have made have been influenced by the stars we were born with. I could have gone into the diplomatic service. I could have become someone who speaks for the government. I still feel that he is my brother.'

Ethnic Minority Families

Non-Burman families face the same challenges that Burman families face, but also some additional ones. Because successive regimes have stressed Burman culture, Burman history and Buddhism as central to Burmese nationalism, people of other ethnic and religious backgrounds often feel marginalized. Ethnic minority languages are almost never permitted to be taught in government schools, and non-Burmans often find it hard to rise in government careers. While ethnic minority parents tend to be forthcoming with their children about the implications of their status as minorities, like Burman parents, their intention is to raise their children for success within the pre-existing political structure.

Because minorities in Burma are often discriminated against, they feel that they have to work extra hard to gain their rightful place. Indian and Chinese children who have been denied full citizenship are not allowed to attend the medical or technological institutes, for instance. Although these children were born in Burma, as were most of their parents, the military regime did not continue the parliamentary government's policy of granting automatic citizenship to long-time foreign residents. Instead, they were issued Foreign Resident Certificates, which disqualify them from entering the top universities and professions. Even travel outside their home districts is often not possible without local authorities' permission.[4] Thus, parents must prepare their children for the fact that no matter how smart they are, many careers will be closed to them, so they should seek their fortunes in business and other unrestricted professions. Parents rarely suggest fighting against these discriminatory policies, but encourage looking for ways to adapt instead.

Among the indigenous ethnic nationalities, parents also push their children to conform. A young Mon named Nai Panna told me how his parents had their children speak Mon at home but did not encourage involvement in other Mon cultural activities. He said that, in his area, few parents wanted their children to join in Mon activities, because after learning more about Mon history and the regime's repression of their culture, they were likely to volunteer for the New Mon State Party's liberation army and end up being killed by the Tatmadaw. When Nai Panna moved to Rangoon, he joined the Mon Literature and Culture group and quickly appreciated that without achieving greater political freedom, a renaissance of Mon culture was also not possible. In 1988, he did exactly what his parents had not wanted him to do: he joined the New Mon State Party.

With the emergence of ethnic-based political parties and student fronts in the 1988–90 period, many ethnic minority families also split over which groups they should join. Some of the disputes revolved around the value placed on loyalty to one's race versus a belief in the more universal ideology of democracy. In some cases it was less a disagreement over where one's loyalties lay than an issue of idealism versus pragmatism. Some believed that only by working in a united front could they ever be successful, while others were so distrustful of ethnic Burmans that they insisted separate paths must be taken.

Among siblings, there were conflicts when one joined an ethnic-based organization and another joined a broader organization. Nai Panna talked about how upset he was in 1988 when his brother joined the ABSDF instead of the New Mon State Party. Nai Panna's brother had come to the border with a Burman friend and felt that the best way forward was to work for democracy first. More than ten years later, they still did not see eye to eye.

Thus, almost all families in Burma have felt the effects of military rule directly on relations within the family. As various members have chosen different ways of responding to the ongoing political crisis, families have often been pulled apart. And whenever there is a dramatic change in the political situation, family relations are invariably shaken up as well.

Even in cases where the parents have maintained private support for the democracy movement, young activists have sometimes felt irritated at their parents for not doing more. Some activists have tried to use this frustration to urge this generation of youth to take action. As a leader of the ABSDF, Dr Naing Aung, put it, 'Our parents didn't do it, so we have to take this responsibility. If we don't do it, the next generation will face the same problem.' This has been Daw Aung San Suu Kyi's argument. People must join together and participate now, so that everybody can live in peace and security in the future. But remembering the farmer-carpenter who is worried about getting the next meal on the table for his family, it is easy to understand why people hesitate.

The fact that parents of all backgrounds usually foster conformity with the regime reflects an interesting twist on the 'Asian Values' argument which prioritizes collective well-being over individual rights. Because Burmese parents, like parents everywhere, try to protect themselves and their children from harm, there is no collective well-being but only continued fear and insecurity for everybody.

CHAPTER 6

. . . .

Communities: Going with the Flow

'In Burmese we have an expression *ye laik, nga laik,* which means "where the water flows, the fish must go". In other words, we must go with the flow.' (Daw Sabei)

§ When people in Burma meet each other for the first time, they immediately try to determine whether the other person is above or below them in status. This is primarily determined by age, but also by other factors such as wealth and place of employment. Recognition of one's own and others' relative position in society is constantly reaffirmed through the use of prefixes in front of names and different pronouns to signify 'I' and 'you'. Thus, a man or a woman would address men their father's age as *U*, or 'uncle', and women their mother's age *Daw* or 'aunt'. Similarly, in the army, younger men are encouraged to call their senior officers *ah bah*, or father/grandfather, and to call those just above them in rank *ko gyi*, or big brother. As a result, everyone knows his place and acts accordingly. This linguistic practice creates a positive feeling of social cohesiveness, because people relate to each other as if they were all part of one big family. But at the same time, individuals must generally defer to those above them, regardless of whether they are right or wrong.

Related to the use of status markers is the concept of *ah nah day*, or a desire not to impose on others. The objective is to maintain smooth relations by considering others' feelings and refraining from saying anything upsetting. In a social context, friendly relations can be easily developed, as each side tries to demonstrate good-will towards the other. The junior-ranking person in the exchange will be particularly hesitant to bring up troubling issues. In a political context, feelings of *ah nah day* can be used to justify silence and inaction. Thus, lower-level authorities are hesitant to report bad news to those above them. Moreover, when military officers make demands on individuals and communities, they know that most people will not dare to talk back. Although fear is the main reason people stay quiet, they may tell others that they felt it wasn't their place to speak up. They were too *ah nah day*. When people do speak up, military authorities react with shocked anger, telling them to remember to whom they are talking.

The regime plays on a tradition of respect for elders to insist on unquestioning obedience from lower ranking soldiers and civilians.

Obedience is a Habit

Some activists have argued that the military is habituating people into silently obeying as part of a strategy of disempowerment. Control through humiliation is often used by the regime. Political prisoners with their heads covered are frequently ordered to jump or bend down as if there were obstacles along the path when in fact there are none. In the interrogation room they are told to pretend to ride a motorcycle, including making 'vroom vroom' noises all the while.[1] Even ordinary civilians face similar kinds of humiliation. Daw Sanda explained that to impress a government minister who would be passing their town on a train, the local authorities ordered all those living on both sides of the track to repaint their houses. 'Those who didn't do it,' she said, 'had to pay fifty kyat. Those who couldn't pay were sent out on to the train track to jump like frogs.'

U Po Khin, a farmer who became a labour organizer, talked about how the military has made regular, and sometimes arbitrary, demands on citizens, so that eventually people don't even think about protesting. He gave an example of how some villagers were toyed with in Sagaing Division. The military officers said they were going to repair the road that linked the towns of Kalaymyo and Tamu. They ordered the villagers to collect stones and firewood, clear a site, and make tar. After the villagers had complied, the battalion withdrew. The tar spoiled, and all their work had been in vain. Later, the military officers came again and said this time they really were going to repair the road and made the villagers collect everything again, without any payment. The villagers were told to pile all the supplies on one side of the road. When the officers reappeared later, they ordered the villagers to move everything to the other side of the road, and then again to the first side. The villagers had to do as they were told, no matter how capricious the command.

U Po Khin explained that sometimes the demands are for money rather than labour. For instance, businessmen in Rangoon and Mandalay have no choice but to buy tickets for military-sponsored functions or to make donations to military-sponsored charities, because if they don't, they may find their business activities hindered in all kinds of ways. U Po Khin concluded that, with time, 'When one man in an army uniform stands in front of your house and says you have to pay this amount of money, the house-owner has no thought of complaining or asking, "For what?" He doesn't ask, he just gives it.' U Po Khin said that when he and his colleagues asked villagers, 'Why do you give this money? You have the right to refuse. You have the right to question,' they answered, 'Oh, they are from the government, how can I?'

U Po Khin explained that even during the Revolutionary Council period from 1962 to 1974, it was still possible to negotiate with the authorities. Villagers could refuse to pay an unreasonably high fee or ask that forced labour be put off until the dry season when farmers had more free time. But at that time, the people making the demands were local authorities in civil service uniforms. Since the 1990s, the people making the demands have been mostly military men, armed with guns.

U Po Khin's colleague, U Tun Shein, added, 'To refuse a government order, we need a gathering. If only I refuse, I will be punished, it is sure. If we can collect the people, we can refuse. If there is an organization, it will be successful. But the government knows about that. That's why they do not allow freedom of association.' With no independent unions allowed, individuals feel overwhelmed by their helplessness in the face of the powerful military organization.

Raymond Tint Way, a Burmese psychiatrist who now lives abroad, put it in psychological terms. He said, 'People have regressed under military rule. They have become more dependent. They have had to endure so much hardship that they have become "immunized" to it. They can handle and cope with it. There are positive and negative consequences: they survive, but they don't overthrow the regime. They have learned helplessness. They see no point in resisting.'

The regime has also implemented a policy of divide and rule. Individuals are not allowed to represent their communities or even their neighbours, making people feel separated and weak. U Po Khin explained: 'If I say to the soldiers, "Sir, U Tun Shein is handicapped, so I think he cannot work, so just forget him," they will say, "What is this? Who are you? Are you a politician? If you want to speak, speak for yourself. If U Tun Shein cannot work, he will say it himself."' U Po Khin believed, 'They are trying to divide person to person, not group to group any more. It's reached that stage.'

The division of Burmese society into the military who issue orders and the people who obey them is reflected in the distortion of an old military slogan. When General Aung San was still alive, he and the military leaders of the day promoted the slogan, 'The people are our mother, the people are our father.' Under the SLORC and the SPDC, this has been changed to, 'The Tatmadaw is our mother, the Tatmadaw is our father.'[2]

Likewise, whenever senior generals visit agricultural development projects, industrial enterprises or schools, they always give the managers and workers 'necessary instructions', even if they have no expertise in that area. The regime has trivialized the country's citizens by treating them as if they have no important ideas of their own. People are treated like children who must obey their elders. Moreover, since 1988 the military has encouraged people to greet them with a prayerful gesture of respect formerly reserved for kings and monks. A return of the gesture would signal mutual respect, but the gesture is not returned.

A Nation of Prisoners

As the size of the armed forces increased dramatically, new bases, camps and checkpoints were established throughout the rural and border areas. Whereas in 1988 there were 168 battalions, ten years later there were 422 battalions.[3] There is now one soldier for every one hundred citizens despite the lack of any looming external threats.

The presence of military personnel has become a daily reality for many villagers, and wherever there are military personnel in rural areas, there are always demands for forced labour. At the very least, villagers must provide firewood and water, and often cook, clean and do small repairs around the base. If the soldiers need extra cars or boats or even ox-carts for transportation, they simply requisition the villagers' vehicles. Whenever soldiers are travelling through the jungle, they take villagers as porters. The rural communities are treated as a free labour pool to be exploited by the military as needed.

By all accounts, demands for forced labour have escalated under the SLORC and SPDC in comparison with the BSPP period. During the BSPP years, the military regime used forced labour for military-related activities, but was not particularly interested in extending the country's infrastructure. The SLORC and SPDC, seeking to upgrade the transportation system and irrigation works, have initiated numerous projects, most of which have relied on forced labour. Forced labour is also used for building and maintaining battalion bases, for work on military-owned commercial businesses in remote areas, as well as for portering.[4] In some cases, the regime has begun using land-moving equipment and soldiers for large-scale road projects, but in the more remote areas, the use of forced civilian labour continues.[5] During military offensives, when the worst violations take place, women are also taken as porters and are often raped.

The exact number of people who engage in forced labour each year is difficult to pinpoint, but the International Confederation of Free Trade Unions estimated it at 800,000 in 1999, out of a population of just under fifty million.[6] The International Labor Organization (ILO) went so far as to set up a commission of inquiry to investigate forced labour allegations in Burma and concluded that the regime was inflicting 'a contemporary form of slavery' on its citizens. As a result, the ILO took the unprecedented step of banning the military regime from attending any of its meetings or receiving any funding until it stopped using forced labour.[7] Lt General Khin Nyunt reacted angrily to the expulsion, saying that in Burma villagers were happy to work for the military or to speed up development projects.[8]

In 1997, some colleagues and I interviewed a number of Burmese about the situation in Chin State and Sagaing Division, where the use of forced labour was common. For families barely making ends meet, to lose a labourer for a week at a time meant a serious loss of income. Some of the labourers became sick and some died, either of diseases like malaria or dysentery or from work-related injuries. Zaw Htun told us about his experience working on the Thazi dam in north-western Burma.[9] He and his brother took turns doing forced labour on the dam over a period of four or five months in early 1995. Zaw Htun said, 'Soldiers were guarding us. They scolded the people and even beat them. On the worksite, the soldiers were always drunk. They always tried to fool around with the girls. The people were so angry with the soldiers but they couldn't do anything. The workers had to bring along their tools and their food. They received no salary. There were also several work accidents on the construction site, but no compensation was paid.'

Many communities have disintegrated because of the demands for forced labour and taxes. Able-bodied family members have to migrate abroad to earn money which can be sent home. In numerous villages and towns within striking distance of the Thai and Indian borders, only old people and small children remain. As one young Chin migrant worker sadly told us, 'Our village [in Chin State] used to have twenty-eight houses, but now only five houses remain. All the youth fled to [India] because we could not work in our fields due to portering and heavy forced labour.'

Intra-community tensions are also exacerbated by the authorities' demands for forced labour as well as for new recruits for the army. Some people can pay off the authorities and escape forced labour while others cannot and must go in their place. When the Tatmadaw demands army recruits and there are not enough volunteers, the village headman either has to force people to go or he has to tax the villagers to pay someone to go. In some areas, headmen also have to collect monthly taxes for porter fees. Even if a headman tries to be perfectly fair, inequities are inevitable.

The army no longer rounds up Rangoon and Mandalay residents for forced labour because of the presence of tourists and foreign embassy staff. Still, city dwellers come under the household registration system like everyone else in the country. All households must possess an official form listing the residents of the house. When anyone comes to spend the night, even if the person is an aunt or grandson, the family must report this to the ward authorities. If the guest is not reported, both the guest and the house owner can be punished. Thus, even visits to relatives' houses become government affairs.

The guest-registration system added a perverse twist to visiting friends and relatives in the Thai–Burma border area in the late 1990s. When the Tatmadaw wanted porters for its operations against the Karen National Union, soldiers took guests who registered at the ward offices. In the border towns, many traders stay with acquaintances while buying and selling goods. Because they are far from home, it is difficult for them to escape arrest, let alone get word back to their families of their fate. As one man who was taken in this way, but later managed to bribe his way out, explained, 'If the soldiers say, "Let's go," they have to go along. If they don't come back, you'll just have to assume that they are dead.'

Domestic travel is also difficult in areas outside the central plains because of the numerous checkpoints along the way. Young people who might be student activists are particularly singled out for close scrutiny, unless they belong to the USDA and can show their membership cards. Even monks have to show their registration booklets before they can purchase train tickets. But former drug-dealers and armed groups who have made ceasefire agreements are given special permits which allow them to sail through checkpoints without their vehicles or passengers being checked for illegal goods. This arrangement has made some Burmese citizens resentful of the ceasefire groups.

The weight of military rule has fallen most heavily on those living in areas of armed resistance. As part of the Four Cuts policy, the Tatmadaw depopulates its operation areas so that the ethnic nationalist armies have no one to provide them with food, information, new recruits and financial support. The human and social costs are incalculable. Villagers living in distant hamlets are forcibly relocated to strategic villages along roads, usually with a battalion of Tatmadaw soldiers based nearby. They are given no compensation and often no new land to farm. In the most extreme cases, they are put into fenced relocation sites which are more like concentration camps. Food is insufficient, water often unclean, and medicine completely lacking. In the Shadaw relocation camp in Karenni State in 1996, Amnesty International reported that out of an initial population of 4,000, between 200 and 300 died from disease and malnutrition in the first year.[10]

One of the strongest resistance armies still operating in the late 1990s was the Shan State Army (Southern). Finding it difficult to flush the Shan troops out of the mountainous area where they operated, the Tatmadaw imposed the Four Cuts policy over an area covering 7,000 square miles. According to the Shan Human Rights Foundation, between 1996 and 1998, the Tatmadaw ordered over 300,000 people from 1,400 villages to leave their homes. Anyone caught returning to his or her village or field would be assumed to be contacting the Shan resistance and immediately shot. The human population was literally erased from the landscape, with communities and families dispersed in all directions. With nowhere to go and nothing to eat, many villagers hid in the forests or slept on the outskirts of towns, but secretly returned to their land to recover stored rice. On several occasions, Tatmadaw soldiers massacred groups of villagers found hunting for food near their old homes.[11]

With KNU and Karenni National Progressive Party (KNPP) soldiers continuing to fight for autonomy in the late 1990s, large areas of Karen and Karenni states suffered similar Four Cuts operations. Approximately 40,000 Karens were displaced in a 1997 Tatmadaw offensive against the KNU and 20–30,000 Karennis were forcibly relocated between 1996 and 1999.[12] In the Karen State alone, community leaders estimate that one-third of the state's population of one million are internally displaced or in exile in Thailand.

In remaining villages in the Karen hills, villagers must travel into the jungle to reach their fields, to hunt or fish, and to gather materials for repairing their houses. These villagers regularly encounter Tatmadaw and ethnic army troops and must try to maintain smooth relationships with both of them, regardless of where their sentiments lie. Cho Zin, a Burman who lived in an area where both Karen and Tatmadaw troops operated, explained, 'We have to have a good relationship with both sides. If one side comes, we have to be afraid of them. If the other side comes, we have to be afraid of them. We don't love them or hate them. We are only afraid of them.' For him and other villagers, their main priority was simply to be able to live in peace.

The regime attempts to set ethnic minority villagers against their own ethnic nationalist armies by fining, torturing or killing villagers in retaliation for the deaths of Tatmadaw soldiers killed by the ethnic armies. At the same time, the Tatmadaw soldiers try to defend themselves by laying mines around their sleeping areas and using villagers as sentries at night. During the day, villagers are forced to act as human mine-sweepers, because the ill-equipped ethnic armies rely on landmines to defend their territory. Thus, the Tatmadaw, rather than protecting the people, uses the people to protect itself.

Cho Zin, who lived near the Thai–Burma border, said that throughout 1996 people from his village had to walk in front of Tatmadaw columns, 'clearing the route with their legs'. On the day that Cho Zin was forced to go with the Tatmadaw, he and another villager stepped on mines. The other villager died on the spot. Cho Zin was lucky. Fellow villagers got him to a hospital in Thailand, his lower leg was amputated, and he survived. The Tatmadaw offered him no compensation or assistance.

After Cho Zin was well enough to get around on crutches, he staged a one-man protest against the ongoing civil war on the Thai side of the Thai–Burmese 'Friendship Bridge' which links the two countries. Thai officials at the bridge, nervous that his actions would upset their Burmese counterparts, said they sympathized with him but he would have to stop his protest.

According to Cho Zin, in the four or five villages near his own, there were over a hundred amputees. 'If you count those who died,' he said, 'there will be about three or four hundred.' Although KNU troops had laid many of the mines, Cho Zin did not want to lay the blame specifically on either side. He said, 'We think of this as due to the civil war. If there's peace, the mines are not necessary to be there any more.'

Besides the physical dismemberment of communities and individuals that has resulted from the civil war, the military has left a legacy of increased racial hatred. In Arakan State, many Buddhist Rakhine view the Muslim Rohingya population with antipathy. The regime has denied citizenship to most Rohingya, and joined with the local Rakhine population in claiming that the Rohingya are recent illegal migrants from Bangladesh. While some entered Burma after independence, there have been Muslims settled in what is now Arakan State for centuries, with many more arriving during the colonial era. The regime has played on the Buddhist Rakhine population's fears of a Muslim takeover to drive Muslims out of Arakan State (discussed further in Chapter 11) and to recruit more Rakhine into the Tatmadaw.

Along with the expansion of the military's presence throughout the country, the regime is also engaged in an alleged Burmanization programme. There have been several reports in Karen and Chin states of Burman soldiers being rewarded with money or a promotion if they marry girls from ethnic minorities. Leaders of the armed Chin National Front, formed in the late 1980s, were so outraged by this practice that they swore they would drive out any Chin girl who married a Burman soldier.

Burman officers and soldiers who are already married are encouraged to resettle their families in minority areas, and slowly other relatives and shopkeepers come to live around new army bases. This is resulting in a shifting balance in the composition of local populations and is creating the conditions for communal strife in the future. Ethnic minorities who found comfort in their dominant numbers locally now risk becoming minorities even in their own districts. This is particularly true in central Shan State where huge areas have been depopulated by Tatmadaw campaigns. The military has sold much of the land to ethnic Burmans and Chinese immigrants and investors. Meanwhile, in early 2000, thousands of Wa families were moved from a predominantly Wa area in Northern Shan State to a former Shan-dominated area in Southern Shan State. In Northern Rakhine State, the Burmese military regime has moved Rohingya populations out of many of villages, and resettled Rakhine and Burman Buddhists in their place.[13] If the Tatmadaw's control weakens, many of the forcibly relocated people will try to reclaim their land while the new settlers will resist, saying these places are now their homes.

A Climate of Fear

Community life even in central Burma has been warped by the widespread presence of military intelligence and local informers. Although it may not be true, it is commonly believed that in urban areas there is one informer for every ten houses. Thus, people do not trust each other and cannot talk freely, even in their own neighbourhoods. Likewise, everyone knows that government agents, who look and act just like everyone else, have been planted in communities with a history of political activism, such as university campuses and monasteries.

Informers are not necessarily supporters of the regime. Some provide information because they are intimidated or they need money. However, military intelligence agents, as trained members of the Tatmadaw, are more likely to believe in the importance of their work. They are fully aware that if the regime were to collapse, they would be out of a job.

A number of activists have had the painful experience of finding out that people they once trusted or closely associated with were in fact reporting on them behind their backs. U Pyone Cho, the university library club organizer in the 1960s, talked about how he felt when he learned that one of his close friends was an informer. This man had participated with U Pyone Cho in anti-government student activities, but later he was appointed to one of the military's youth committees. U Pyone Cho said, 'He got a lot of privileges just for being an informer. He was sent to Germany for training. I was quite close to him at one stage and I really regret it. I didn't know.' U Pyone Cho couldn't believe that this friend had betrayed their ideals. U Pyone Cho said, 'What he did was against the whole student movement. How could he sell himself for that?'

Htway Win, a student activist in 1988, told how one of his fellow student union members switched sides after the failed demonstrations. His family was poor, and he needed a job, so he joined the military and was assigned to intelligence work. Meanwhile, Htway Win continued to be involved in underground student organizing into the 1990s. At first Htway Win's friend warned him and his colleagues that some intelligence agents were shadowing them; later, he identified Htway Win to other authorities who had Htway Win's name but didn't know what he looked like. Htway Win was taken to one of the military intelligence's interrogation centres, where he suffered brutal torture. At one point, his former friend brought him fried noodles and apologized. Htway Win said he was very angry at the time but, after spending many months meditating in prison, he was able to forgive him.

However, Htway Win himself came under suspicion when he was released much earlier than the three colleagues arrested with him. The parents of the other three assumed that Htway Win must have become an informer or a member of military intelligence, otherwise he wouldn't have been let out before the others. According to Htway Win and other former political prisoners, this was one of the regime's tactics. The authorities tried to sow doubts among groups that were formerly cohesive, so that they would no longer want to work together. Distrust is also created by some activists and ordinary individuals who label their rivals as intelligence agents or informers in order to reduce their popularity.

Suspicion has thus become the primary lens through which others are viewed. For the politically-minded, such a climate makes organizing extremely difficult. No one knows whom they can or cannot trust, so activists find it hard to expand their organizations or activities beyond a small group of sure friends. But even non-activists have to worry. With such a system in place, informers can report people against whom they have personal grudges.

U Pyone Cho talked about one time when he and a friend had gone to lay a wreath at the old student union site. Someone from the intelligence took their photograph. 'This picture got back to our ward,' U Pyone Cho said. 'And we heard later that the local MI was asked what action should be taken. The local MI was a woman, and she sort of liked me, but she hated the other guy. So that guy was kicked out of the university.'

Even when relaxing, people feel the need to maintain their guard. Burmese love to go to teashops and have long discussions with friends. These discussions often hit on political topics, but when the conversation becomes heated, the participants often catch themselves. They warily scan the faces of the other customers trying to guess whether any might be intelligence agents or informers, and then try to move the conversation back to lighter themes.

So many people in Burma talk of living in silence and talking in whispers. As one writer put it, 'We have no mouths, only ears.' This should be understood in the active sense. It is an effort to keep thoughts to yourself and to stop words from spilling out. Without realizing it, people serve as instruments of the regime each time they decide not to talk. One of Daw Aung San Suu Kyi's goals has been to try to break through this silence by making the open discussion of politics a normal activity.

Viewing the world as a hostile place also relates to long-held spiritual beliefs. The continued worship of *nats*, capricious spirits demanding appeasement for often unintentional slights, still colours the worldview of many Burmese today. One person I talked to compared the military intelligence to *nats*, always keeping you under their surveillance. He said that you have to respect, fear and appease them, because otherwise they may just show up and make life very uncomfortable for you.

Still, there are many instances of solidarity between local authorities and citizens. Some activists told of ward authorities who would warn them in advance about house searches, giving them time to hide any incriminating books or documents. Others believe they were able to escape arrest because local authorities, who were also their friends, did not search for them as thoroughly as they might have. One person even told of the local police secretly releasing a political prisoner for a few hours so that he could celebrate a holiday with his family. To some extent the regime must rely on these local authorities, who tend to be much more sympathetic to their neighbours' activities. But as the regime continues to increase the size of its army, it can replace more of the local civilian authorities with military men assigned to districts far from their homes. Such soldiers can usually be counted on to enforce policies more strictly.

Because the military regime has lasted so long, and people generally feel that to resist is foolish and dangerous, the community itself begins to sanction those who go against the regime. People who dare to rock the boat, even if they are admired, are seen as possible threats to the rest of the community. Most worrying, the authorities may interpret neighbours' contact with that person as indicating that they are also against the state. At the same time, activists' actions threaten the rationalizations to which the rest of the community clings. To use a phrase of Czech playwright and politician Vaclav Havel, they force others to confront that they are 'living within a lie'.[14] Most people tell themselves that resistance is impossible and useless, while certain individuals are insisting that resistance is a moral necessity. This challenges people's sense of integrity, despite the fact that they may feel they are doing the best they can for their families by keeping their heads down. Thus, during times of greater repression, communities tend to push away those who are targeted by the state.[15] This is illustrated in the stories of two political activists' wives who remained in Burma after their husbands fled to neighbouring countries to escape arrest. In both cases, the authorities hoped to isolate the women and their families as well as to cause emotional distress to their husbands in exile.

A slight, shy woman, Daw Sanda was scared to tell me her story. Speaking in a barely audible voice, she talked of the alienation she experienced in the village where her husband had once been so popular. Groups of up to ten officials would suddenly arrive at her house late at night to interrogate her about any contact she might have had with her husband. The interrogators were intimidating and, as a result of these visits, her heart would begin pounding at the slightest noise.

Worse than the interrogations was the fact that her neighbours and former friends ostracized her, afraid of being accused of having contact with 'an enemy of the state'. She explained that she had stopped going to their houses, because she knew they didn't want her to come. She said, 'When I walked through the village, I could see people looking at me from a distance. In my heart I kept saying to myself *democracy ya aung gyosa ba* [keep striving for democracy], to keep my spirits up.'

Although she knew that these friends had voted for her husband in 1990, they no longer dared to have contact with her. When I asked her if she was angry at them for abandoning her, at first she answered, 'No, I understand them,' but later she admitted to feeling bitter. When I asked, 'If there is democracy one day, will you become close to them again?' she said she would socialize with them, but there would be no feeling in her heart.

Another woman, Daw Khin Khin Yi, told of her experience after her husband, a member of the group of NLD parliamentarians who wanted to set up a parallel government, fled in 1991. Like Daw Sanda, she was routinely confronted by large groups of officials arriving at odd times to interrogate her. In addition, there were always two military intelligence watching her from their tables at the restaurant facing her house. The MI tried to isolate her family by going to her friends' houses and telling them not to visit her.

A few months after her husband's escape, she was arrested. Unable to come up with a charge against her, the military intelligence accused her of stealing a bicycle and imprisoned her. After two months of late-night interrogations she was released and returned home. Then some officials glued a poster with photographs of her husband and another NLD MP-elect on the house and in public places. The posters claimed the men were wanted criminals who had run away.

Shortly thereafter, the authorities informed her that she could no longer stay in her house, because they were going to sell it and her husband's adjacent office unless she gave them 250,000 kyat (the equivalent of several years' salary). She would have to have a friend make a formal offer to get the house back for her. She said she didn't have the money and wouldn't do it anyway. So she abandoned the house and decided to move with her children to a larger town in the district, but she found it difficult to secure accommodation because people were nervous about associating with her. Finally, she found an old man who supported the democracy movement and agreed to rent to her on the condition that she take responsibility if there were any trouble. Every week she had to sign in with the ward authorities that she wouldn't leave town. Although she said that the local authorities respected her and treated her decently, she had to continue to sign in for three years.

Her children also faced difficulties at school. While most of the teachers and students rallied around her daughter and sons, some were afraid. All students had to sign a form stating that they would participate in USDA functions, but her children refused. Fortunately, some teachers tried to protect them by concealing this information. On Armed Forces Day and Independence Day, the authorities demanded that her daughter give garlands to army personnel, but she wouldn't do it. They tried to force demonstrations of allegiance, even at local sporting events. At last, her children were overcome with frustration, and her daughter sank into a deep depression.

One day the township chairman came to Daw Khin Khin Yi and said that if she agreed to sign divorce papers, she would be permitted to engage in the lucrative business of selling forest products. She spurned his offer, but the authorities continued to harass the family, trying to break them down.

As in Daw Sanda's case, many of her former friends avoided the family. Daw Khin Khin Yi recalls, 'They wouldn't even meet my eyes in the street.'

But there were others who helped and encouraged her even though the SLORC threatened them. Ironically, it was the strangers who were her cell-mates during the two months she was incarcerated who really reached out to her. When she was first thrown into the room of female prisoners, most of whom were sex-workers, they suspected she was a brothel owner. She explained that actually she was a housewife, but her husband was an NLD parliamentarian who had had to flee. As they got to know her better, they sympathized with her, shared their food with her, and helped her with the manual labour she was ordered to perform. For one week, the guards forced her to sleep in the dankest corner of the cell where ants and mosquitoes made their homes. She was given no mat or blanket. Her cell-mates eased her discomfort by crushing up tobacco leaves and spreading them on the ground to keep the insects away. Her children didn't know where she was, so her fellow prisoners tried to send news to her family through their own relatives. This was an act of extraordinary kindness. Prisoners were only allowed to meet their relatives for five minutes, and instead of talking about themselves, the prisoners spent their visits persuading their relatives to go and meet Daw Khin Khin Yi's family.

There were people in the community who tried to help Daw Khin Khin Yi's family, but many others, worried about endangering their own families, stayed away. For those who are attempting to break through the lies, it is not the repression by the authorities that is so painful, for that is expected; it is the lack of support from neighbours, friends and sometimes even family members that makes it so difficult for activists to maintain their morale.

Min Zin, a student activist who spent several years in hiding in the 1990s, talked about the strain of living in other people's houses, where inevitably some members of the household felt that the family was taking an undue risk by sheltering him. Determined to stay in Rangoon so he could continue to network with other activists, he eluded arrest for eight years by moving from house to house. But, he said, 'politics is not twenty-four hours. Twenty-four hours is social relations.' The stress was constant.

Unable to go out, he would spend almost all his time upstairs in the house, listening to foreign radio broadcasts, reading and writing. To get exercise, he would walk back and forth on a diagonal in his cramped room. Some nights, a fellow activist would come by to see him. But if relatives or other guests came to stay, as they often did, Min Zin had to be especially careful. Family members would secretly bring him his food, and they would leave him with a chamber pot since he could not go to the bathroom. He could only take a shower if the guests went out or after they had gone to sleep, and no friends could visit him.

During the rare occasions when Min Zin's friends took him out, he said he would stay out almost the whole night. Remembering that time, he said, 'I would go to Inya Lake and sit on a bench and sometimes cry, with three or four friends with me. Because at that time, 1992-3-4, politics was so discouraging. There was no hope for us. People seemed to be happy to go shopping, go to the market, go to SLORC-sponsored ceremonies, the boat-rowing competitions, the marathon, trade fairs. On TV we always saw these scenes.' He said he believed that people only appeared to be happy with the SLORC, but that he couldn't bear it.

In the meantime, he learned that his father and his younger brother were arrested, and his family was finding it difficult to make ends meet. His older brothers opened a shop near their house, but military intelligence personnel regularly came by and threatened them. Min Zin's mother was frequently taken for questioning. All of this weighed on Min Zin's conscience.

Sometimes household searches would be conducted by local authorities and he would have to hide for hours at a time. Sometimes a friend would come in the middle of the night saying that someone who knew where Min Zin was had been arrested. He would have to move immediately. 'I couldn't expect anything,' Min Zin said. 'Life felt so meaningless.'

Later, Min Zin spent periods of time in meditation centres. He said that he found it much easier to cope with the tensions of hiding after that because he could find peace in his religious practice. Finally, in 1997, a friend of his was arrested and admitted his whereabouts, and the intelligence agents were close on his heels. He decided that his only choice was to leave the country.

Amazingly, there continue to be committed individuals like Min Zin who refuse to give up their political activities despite their fear and the tremendous personal toll. Most eventually end up either in prison or in exile. They realize that they cannot make a change happen unless there is widespread participation. Likewise, the regime recognizes that it can forestall broader engagement by isolating those who dare to live in ways that challenge the regime's legitimacy.

The Threat of Independent Groups

Under General Ne Win's one-party system, state-sponsored organizations encroached on community life much more than at any time in the past. Farmers were exhorted to join the government's farmers' organization and workers were pushed into government-controlled workers' organizations. Those who did not join the BSPP were almost never considered for prestigious awards such as 'Outstanding Student', 'Outstanding Worker', or even 'Model Red Cross Volunteer'.

In the BSPP period, the regime also sought to enforce conformity over dress and behaviour. Citizens were expected to wear Burmese *longyis* rather than western trousers, and long hair for men was strongly condemned. Local authorities even took it upon themselves to arrest teenaged couples found kissing, calling their parents to the local government office and forcing the young lovers to marry on the spot. Although such pressures loosened in the 1990s, with the children of the military elite as eager as everyone else to experiment with international styles, independent organizations continued to be viewed with suspicion. Still, some groups attempted to run social associations outside military control.

In 1995, a group of Burmese businesswomen started an organization called the Myanmar Women's Entrepreneurial Association (MWEA). The association was eventually allowed to register with the Home Ministry, but only after its members had all signed pledges that they would not become involved in political activities. The association became quite active in the business community, and even planned to erect a new office building in central Rangoon. A few days before holding a celebration to mark its first anniversary, one of Lt General Khin Nyunt's staff called the association and demanded tickets for several SLORC officials. He also informed them that they must allow Lt General Khin Nyunt to give the keynote address. Following the event, Lt General Khin Nyunt's speech was quoted at length in the newspapers.

The USDA also went after the association, demanding that MWEA members join the USDA and give contributions. A conflict erupted in the women's organization. Some argued that members should be able to decide individually whether or not they would join the USDA rather than having the whole association sucked in. But others thought it would be better for the MWEA to cooperate with the USDA in order to avoid trouble. Since then the MWEA has been perceived as being more closely associated with the regime. In the words of one observer, the organization was 'SLORCed'.

In another instance in the mid-1990s, a former 1988 activist named Ye Naing worked together with some friends to start a social welfare association in a medium-sized town in central Burma. He had grown up in a rough area and started using drugs when he was thirteen. But when he was a tenth-standard student (aged sixteen) in 1988, he gave up drinking and drugs so that people in the democracy movement would respect him. In the mid-1990s, he started trying to reform other young alcoholics and drug-addicts in his quarter by applying positive peer pressure.

After being praised by some of the neighbourhood elders for his good work, he went on to organize other students to help repair the local monastery. Although he was a Muslim, he decided that, as a Burmese citizen, he should be willing to do anything that would be good for his society. He had no money to give, but he volunteered his labour and gathered other young people to work with him.

At the same time, he formed a small organization to assist with funerals and other social events, especially for the needy. Usually people have to hire coffin bearers and buy them alcohol, because the task is considered a distasteful one. But poor people cannot afford this, so Ye Naing's group offered to carry coffins for no charge. If a couple eloped and needed money for their wedding ceremony, Ye Naing's group would give them a small interest-free loan.

Ye Naing told his group that they should help anyone who was poor or being taken advantage of. According to Ye Naing, 'The ward authorities and the local USDA chapter felt insulted when we got involved in these kinds of cases, because they felt we were doing their job.' Also, he said, the authorities were suspicious of his group because of the recognition it was gaining in the community and because he was a former student activist. In 1996, when student demonstrations broke out in Rangoon and threatened to spread to other towns, Ye Naing learned that the authorities were planning to use the occasion to arrest his group. They all ran away, but Ye Naing said that some missed home and went back. They were imprisoned.

Although some private religious-oriented organizations and university social and cultural clubs have continued to exist, the regime considers all dynamic organizations to have the potential to rally people in opposition to the government. Thus, most have been crushed or absorbed, leaving people who want to do something good for their communities with few options. They must either try to work from within a government-controlled organization or do what they can quietly, as single individuals or very small groups.

Corruption

While the regime often views private efforts to improve the community as suspicious, corruption is widely tolerated at all levels. With salaries of only $10 a month (calculated at the unofficial exchange rate in early 2000), the generals could not afford to be transparent in their financial dealings. Their comfortable lifestyles were dependent on generous compensation for granting business licences, trade privileges and promotions. Business people often did not bribe the generals directly, but went through the wives, grown children or personal assistants. Bringing a tin of English biscuits was reportedly one favoured way to sweeten a deal, if the second layer of biscuits was replaced with stacks of crisp banknotes. Likewise, when the children of senior generals marry, business associates often give them extravagant gifts, including new cars.

Those without high enough connections could run into serious trouble if they did not pay off the leading generals. In 1996, a car importer learned this the hard way. Four companies were granted licences to import cars, and three of them had close links to senior generals. The other importer was less well connected, but he was managing to bring in small shipments of cars without any serious problems, so he decided to expand. When he went to collect his latest shipment of cars at the port in 1996, he learned that all 140 had been confiscated. The reason given was that some of the models had been updated and weren't exactly the same as those listed on the original permission request. All his appeals to the Customs department were in vain. He was told that military intelligence had taken over the case. Later he found out that the cars had all been sold at low prices to senior military officers, who could either keep them or resell them for their actual price and pocket a handsome profit. Distraught, the importer wrote a letter to Lt General Khin Nyunt suggesting that if the military routinely confiscated legitimate companies' goods, no one would want to do business in Burma any more. Military intelligence accused him of writing the letter at the request of anti-regime politicians. In fact, he had had no contact with the pro-democracy movement and was interested only in making money, but his safety was in jeopardy, so he decided it was best to leave the country.

High-ranking generals and officials frequently take advantage of their positions for personal financial gain, but even among ordinary communities, few try to enforce social norms of making an honest living despite most people's desire for a moral order. This is partly because the salaries of lower-level civil servants and military personnel were so low throughout the 1980s and 1990s that they could survive only by engaging in some sort of side business, which is often technically illegal.[16] Although the salaries of civil servants and military personnel were raised significantly in April 2000, inflation also increased rapidly, eroding the value of the salary hikes.

Throughout the 1990s, impoverished teachers made ends meet by opening private tuition courses after school which students had to attend, and pay for, in order to pass their exams. Township officials demanded bribes for routine assistance, and military men of all ranks stole petrol meant for military use and sold it on the black market.[17] Such behaviour became acceptable in most communities, because parents had responsibilities to provide for their families, and they certainly couldn't do so on a government salary alone. Those who were honest and refused to engage in corrupt activities were often perceived as stupid and, in some cases, irresponsible, because they could not properly take care of their families.

While the government kept salaries low, probably because of a lack of money, and prioritized military expenditures, the regime reaped other benefits. People were so busy hustling to survive that they had no time for politics. More important, because so many soldiers and civil servants engaged in corruption and illegal activities, they were also implicated in the evil that the system produced. The whole notion of legality was turned upside down, because many activities which would be perfectly acceptable under other forms of government were treated as illegal, while other activities which most would agree are wrong were openly tolerated.

Particularly in the BSPP period, virtually all petty trade with neighbouring countries was illegal but, without it, people could not have survived because so few goods were actually produced in Burma or legally allowed to be imported. What was produced was often of poor quality, in part because state factory workers would sell some of their allotted materials and buy cheaper ones instead, pocketing the difference. In other instances, they used less of the materials than appropriate and sold the surplus. Thus, many people were involved in the business of buying goods in neighbouring countries and bringing them back in for sale. Ko Than, whose his father was a Customs officer in a town on the black market trade route, often witnessed this kind of illegal activity. He said, 'I saw some government servants doing smuggling, because they didn't have enough money to survive. I even saw high school teachers and middle school teachers smuggling things.'

Ordinary people also tried to make ends meet by working as carriers of black market goods. Ko Than talked about seeing women on trains who were caught trying to smuggle rolls of cotton cloth. After putting one roll of cloth in their bags, they would wrap as many rolls as possible around their torso and limbs, transforming themselves from the thin women that they were into fat women who could barely move. When the women were caught, they cried and begged the officers to give them their goods back. Ko Than sympathized with them. He said, 'If these Customs officers really wanted to suppress or crack down on these things, they could go to the ship or to the big boss behind these carriers, but they didn't dare to touch them because they were already paid or bribed by them, so these women were the victims.' Today, such small-scale illegal border trade continues as the regime frequently shuts border gates to punish neighbouring countries for their policies towards Burma or to try to reduce the amount of foreign exchange leaving the country.

Of course corruption exists in every country and it is typically the smallest links in the chain who are arrested. But in Burma, corruption permeates almost every aspect of people's lives. Even hospital stays can require bribes to the staff to make sure a patient is well cared for.[18] Everyone finds themselves in situations where they need to use 'tea money' or connections to accomplish basic tasks, and in many cases it is members of their own communities who are making these demands on them.

Ne Myo, the farmer-carpenter from Mon State, talked about how it was illegal to repair one's own house without permission. He said, 'We have to save our money for days and months to repair an ordinary house if part of it falls down. Just to repair the place that deteriorated.' It was not the repair costs that were so expensive, but the bribes that needed to be paid. Ne Myo said, 'While I'm repairing my house, people from the city development council will come. They'll tell me to stop. They'll ask, "With whose permission are you doing this? Don't you understand? Do you want to be arrested?"' Then

Ne Myo would have to go to the government office and the person in charge would yell at him, saying without permission he had no right to repair his house. In fact, asking for permission was useless, Ne Myo said. 'But, if I pay him 1,500 or 2,000 kyat in "tea money", that's it. I don't even need to get a paper that says "Permission".'

Although some civil servants refuse to accept gifts in return for services, many feel they need to in order to support their families and in some cases to pay for their own promotions. With advancement often being determined by loyalty and bribes rather than ability, there is little incentive to be honest. Moreover, when low-level civil servants compare the small amounts they take with what so many senior military officers are receiving, they feel justified. If and when there is a political change in Burma, many Burmese think that the most difficult problem to handle will be the restoration of a moral order. Stealing government goods, giving and taking bribes, and lying have become a way of life. In such an atmosphere where almost everyone is participating in illegal activities, it is hard to talk about good guys and bad guys.

Finally, as the military regime has insisted that it is safeguarding Burmese society and traditions, many Burmese feel confused about what is good or bad in their culture. They are infuriated by the way the regime treats them, yet the regime is always stressing the importance of maintaining Burmese culture. They believe in the goodness of Burmese traditions, and yet the entire culture seems to have been tainted by how it has been used by the regime for its own ends. People even begin to wonder if the regime itself isn't a product of their culture. Because of the totalitarian nature of the state's intrusion into virtually every aspect of people's lives, it becomes increasingly difficult to identify spaces, ideas and traditions that aren't swallowed up or twisted by the regime.

9. Praying at a pagoda, Mandalay

10. Tatmadaw soldiers being trucked through Rangoon

11. Eking out a living in rural Burma, near Mandalay Hill

12. A Tatmadaw signboard, central Mandalay

CHAPTER 7

. . . .

The Military: A Life Sentence

'Prisoners get released, but for us soldiers, there is no hope ... We will be forced to work until the day we die.' (Ex-sergeant Maung Maung)

§ The regime has engaged in extensive propaganda work to promote the idea that the Tatmadaw should play a pre-eminent role in the country's political life, despite its loss of face in the 1988 demonstrations and the 1990 election. Through its military training programmes, the state media, the school curriculum and USDA activities, the Tatmadaw leaders have sought to convince soldiers and civilians alike that the military is the only institution which can and does serve the country.

First, the regime has tried to whitewash the military's actions in the 1988–90 period. The regime has downplayed the shooting of unarmed civilians in 1988 and instead emphasized the violent actions of some of the demonstrators, asserting that it was acting only to restore order in a chaotic situation.[1] The regime now also claims that the 1990 elections were not held to elect a new parliament but merely to elect some of the delegates for the National Convention. It also argues that too much time has passed for the 1990 election results still to be valid.

Second, Tatmadaw leaders have continued to stress the armed forces' essential role in holding the country together. From the regime's perspective, the military played the most significant part in the independence movement and has quelled the civil wars raging through the country ever since. Many top officers worry that without a strong army to check the power of ethnic armed organizations, the country would collapse. This sentiment is repeated in regular proclamations on the front page of state-controlled newspapers: 'The Tatmadaw has been sacrificing much of its blood and sweat to prevent disintegration of the union.'

Many new recruits and civilians are sympathetic to this point of view. Few realize that part of the problem lies in the regime's refusal to allow self-determination for the ethnic nationalities. The more the regime tries to assimilate the ethnic nationalities, the more the ethnic nationalities feel they must establish separate political entities in order to maintain their own cultures and identities. Moreover, few people in central Burma understand the extent to which the Tatmadaw has exacerbated tensions in minority areas. For instance, military authorities in some of the remote areas have torn down churches and mosques and forced Christians and Muslims to work on the construction of Buddhist pagodas and monasteries. Most people living in the cities and villages of central Burma are not aware of such incidents.

Third, the Tatmadaw is proud of the role it has played in modernizing the country. Under the BSPP regime, very little was done to develop the country's infrastructure and, in many places, roads actually deteriorated. However, the SLORC and the SPDC regimes have built numerous new bridges, roads and rail links, as well as dams and agricultural works. With the improvement of the transportation infrastructure, and especially the building of bridges over rivers that once had to be crossed by ferry, travel to many areas has become much more convenient. Although Daw Aung San Suu Kyi stated in one of her people's forums that such work was the ordinary work of any government, many in the military feel the regime deserves credit for doing so much to advance the country.[2] As a headline in the *New Light of Myanmar* put it, 'Progress Made in Nation-building Projects at Present Many Times Greater Than in Periods When the Country Received Foreign Assistance'.[3]

Nevertheless, the military regime has not been able to bring about significant economic growth and its heavy-handed way of handling issues has led even many soldiers to conclude that the army should stick to the battlefield and allow civilians to manage the country's political and economic affairs. But any soldiers who dared to express such views would end up in prison and, with few other job opportunities available, most decide it is best to keep quiet and continue to follow orders.

Military officers tend to be more committed to continued military rule than ordinary soldiers. Having been encouraged to believe that they have a higher status than ordinary people, many come to see themselves as deserving the special treatment they receive. Military officers benefit from much sought-after privileges such as access to hospitals that actually have medicine and opportunities to buy luxury goods from abroad at greatly reduced prices. During the BSPP period, when bicycles and oxcarts were still the primary mode of transportation, captains and majors were given Mazda T2000s; colonels received Mazda jeeps; and officers above the rank of colonel were provided with Mazda 323s. In the 1990s, high-ranking military officers received Audis produced in China.[4]

Still, people do not necessarily associate a military career with full-fledged support for military rule. Like being a civil servant, being in the military (as an officer) is a job that gives Burmese citizens the best chance for social advancement and financial rewards. Before 1988, many thought of the army as an honourable career, having never seen how the Tatmadaw treated civilians in the country's remote 'black' areas. Since 1988, people no longer romanticize the Tatmadaw, but many parents view getting their children into the officer class as the best way for them to succeed and for the family to be protected. Many people believe that as long as the regime appears to be in firm control, it is better to work with it than against it.

From the regime's perspective, expanding the Tatmadaw is essential to maintaining its authority. According to one inside source, the SLORC calculated that since there were 50,000 insurgents, the Tatmadaw should have ten times as many troops, or 500,000, in order to have the upper hand in negotiations. In other words, might, rather than right, will decide the political situation. Moreover, professionalism is not as important as sheer numbers. Thus, the military increases its ranks by not letting enlisted men resign, taking in orphans at young ages, and setting recruitment quotas for villages. Migrant labourers who were arrested in Thailand and sent back to the Burma border in the late 1990s were sometimes held by Burmese authorities and told to choose between becoming a soldier or porter. While both were potential death sentences, most decided that they were better off with a gun in their hands.

Reasons for Joining

Whether or not they agree with the military's involvement in the country's political affairs, there are plenty of rural people who join the army voluntarily.[5] Foot soldiers generally join because they have no other economic opportunities. Poorly educated, from impoverished families, and often escaping from problems at home, the army is their only refuge. As one Burmese put it, 'After training, they have a gun and they have some authority. They like that.' In practical terms, it is much better to be a military man than a civilian. It is humiliating to have to live in silence and fear; by becoming military officers, or even just soldiers, men can, to a certain extent, 'empower' themselves.

It is even easier to find recruits for officer training, particularly when there are few stable job opportunities in the private sector. Moreover, military officers are considered eligible marriage prospects, because, as one young man put it, 'They can spend a lot of money. Their status is really different from ordinary people.'

The greatest heroes in Burma's history are military men. Most venerated are the imperialist kings who made Burmese kingdoms some of the most powerful in South East Asia. In modern history, General Aung San and the Thirty Comrades are revered for their daring in slipping off to Japan for military training and then fighting for Burma's independence. Ordinary soldiers and officers alike are drawn to these images.

Although financing the ever-expanding army has become more and more difficult, some officers have used their positions to enrich themselves. After General Ne Win's coup, many educated military men, particularly in the technical corps, retired or went abroad. As in the civilian sector, those who stayed were underpaid and increasingly resorted to theft and corruption. Ko Doe, who worked in the student security force during the 1988 demonstrations, talked about how the military changed over the years. He came from a strong military family; both his grandfather and father had made their careers in military service. In the early years after independence, he said, all soldiers were volunteers, but they had to meet strict physical criteria to be accepted, so those who made it were proud. Ko Doe's older relatives who had been in the military told him that even if soldiers joined for different reasons, by the end of their training, they all shared the same objective: to work for the country.

After 1970, when soldiers saw their standard of living declining, their priorities changed. Rather than focusing on learning new skills so they could contribute more, many concentrated on making money. Usually this meant stealing military supplies and selling them outside the base. Meanwhile, with all large companies nationalized, more civilians enrolled in officer training schools so that they could obtain positions of influence.

A former soldier confirmed this, saying that, after 1974, senior officers began using soldiers for their own economic interests. Particularly in the rural areas, soldiers were forced to work on senior officers' plantations and for their various commercial ventures including logging, brick-making and other labour-intensive enterprises. After 1988, such abuses increased, with officers even stealing the rations meant for frontline soldiers and selling them on the black market.[6] In the late 1990s, the battalions were told that the central command would no longer be providing rations for them, and they would have to support themselves. In many cases this meant confiscating villagers' farmland or forcing villagers to bring them food.

Without sufficient rations or clothing, living conditions for ordinary soldiers stationed in the countryside are extremely difficult.[7] Kyaw Win, a soldier who grew up in a rural area and served in the Shan and Karen states from 1981 to 1989, recalled angrily: 'We were not fed well. If we got to eat *ngapi* [fish paste], it was rotten. There was sand in the rice. The officers told us to get along with the villagers. But we had nothing to eat. And so we ate the vegetables that the villagers had planted. We didn't have the money to buy and eat them. So if they didn't give them to us, we would go and steal them at night.'

He also talked about how much the soldiers drank. Many were depressed and their salaries were insufficient to purchase anything of value, so they just bought alcohol. Members of soldiers' families also had to find paying jobs. According to a long-time resident in the Chinese border town of Ruili, a significant percentage of the many sex-workers operating there in the 1990s were from Burmese army families who couldn't make ends meet.

New recruits often do not realize what they are getting into. Kyaw Win joined when he was fifteen, because of a fight with his parents. They had sent him to stay in town with his grandparents so he could attend school for a few years, but when they asked him to return home and work on the farm, he ran away. He said, 'I joined the army because I didn't have a place to stay. There were forty people in my group. All of them had fought with their parents or fought with their brothers or sisters or uncles. I didn't meet anyone who admired the army. Not in my group. At that time, how should I put it? I was blind and deaf. I wasn't curious either. If I had money, I would go out and drink. If I didn't have money, I would sleep. I lived just like that.'

Back at the battalion headquarters in town, the soldiers lived more comfortably, but they were often forced to work like servants for their officers' families. Many resented having to clean their superiors' houses, wash their clothes and do other chores, all of which were outside their official duties. Kyaw Win said some officers treated soldiers well at the frontlines because they were scared, but back at the battalion headquarters they became arrogant and demanding.

In addition, permission for leave was rarely granted. According to Kyaw Win, in his battalion only fifteen to twenty people out of 800 were allowed leave during the one-month rest periods after six months at the frontlines. Kyaw Win said that if you did not send a bribe along with your application for leave, you would be automatically rejected.

Moreover, it was almost impossible to resign. Like other soldiers I interviewed, Kyaw Win was unable to leave, even after ten years of service. He had joined when he was fifteen, but when he turned twenty-six and thought about resigning, his superior officers refused to consider it, arguing he could still serve for many more years. Kyaw Win said, 'If you submit your resignation letter often, you will be given a promotion. Then, since you have a bar [epaulette] on your shoulder, you will become proud and you won't leave any more. You can get another bar in six months. And so you carry out your duty. After having two bars, you will become fed up. It'll be harder for you to get a third bar. But if you submit your resignation quite often, they'll give you another bar. They won't let you leave. They'll tell you, "You're still young. Don't leave yet." So when soldiers want to leave, what they have to do is to bribe people from the hospital to hospitalize them. They have to tell them, "Help me quit. I've gone crazy. I can't see. I can't hear."' Only if a specialist signs such a declaration can a youngish soldier retire.

The Danger of Expressing an Opinion

Ex-sergeant Maung Maung referred to life in the military as worse than a prison sentence. He talked about how his unit had had to work for several days on the rubber plantation of his divisional commander's daughter. When the daughter married, the family sold the plantation for a large sum of money, but the soldiers were not even provided with extra food when doing this work, let alone given any monetary compensation. 'That's why we constantly said to each other that we had been charged with life imprisonment with hard labour,' he said. 'We have no days free from that.'

Interestingly, Maung Maung is Karen and grew up in Pa-an, the capital of Karen State. He said he joined the Tatmadaw because he was inspired by what he read at school about the important role the armed forces had played during Burma's independence struggle. He said that although he was often distrusted and discriminated against in the army because he was Karen, this didn't bother him too much. What did upset him, though, was how the officers abused their power. 'In the military, there is great discrimination among the ranks,' he said. 'The officers treat us as having much less value than themselves. They eat good food. But when the soldiers get sick, they don't even check up on them. They have no sympathy.'

Even when senior officers do ask about the well-being of the lower ranks, it is better not to tell the truth. Maung Maung learned this the hard way. On one occasion when the chief tactical commander came through on an inspection, he asked the troops if they had any complaints. Maung Maung said that they had water difficulties. The chief tactical commander promised to look into it but, after he left, Maung Maung's commanding officer summoned him and some of his men and angrily told them to solve the water problem themselves by digging a well. Maung Maung said, 'Later, when any senior officer asked us if there were any problems, we kept quiet. We didn't dare to say anything. We realized that this is what "expressing your opinion" really means: you should keep your mouth shut.'

Maung Maung said he joined the army not to reach a certain rank or make a certain amount of money; fighting was what he was interested in. He wanted to be a good soldier on whom people could rely. 'But actually,' he said, 'now I'm not a good soldier for all the people, but only a good soldier for a handful of people. I cannot protect the people. I am only protecting my high-ranking officers.'

In his last post, Maung Maung's relationship with his Burmese company commander was not good. They were based out of a Karen village, and the wife of the headman told Maung Maung in Karen that she was worried about her two teenaged daughters. The captain would often get drunk and stay late into the night at her house chatting up her daughters. She said her daughters had studying to do and the captain's behaviour was inappropriate in a socially conservative Karen village. She asked Maung Maung to tell his captain to stop visiting. Maung Maung explained to her that he couldn't say this to the captain because he was an officer and Maung Maung was only a sergeant. He suggested that she send her daughters to stay at another relative's house. So the next day, she sent them to stay with her niece.

That afternoon, the captain summoned Maung Maung and ordered him to get his platoon ready. Claiming there were enemy movements about forty-five minutes away, he told Maung Maung to march over there immediately and radio back about the situation. Maung Maung did as he was told, but when he arrived at the named location, there were no enemy troops to be found. Still, his captain ordered him to stay there over night. The area was a brown area and there were only twenty-eight soldiers in the platoon. It was not safe for them to stay. They could be easily overpowered by KNU troops operating in the area.

Maung Maung protested, but the captain told him to obey and turned off his radio. At first Maung Maung didn't know what to do. To disobey an order was a serious offence, but to stay could mean risking their lives. He called his troops and informed them of what the company commander had said. Then he said that they would return to the base. 'Whether I get fired or punished, I don't care,' he said. 'I don't want you to all die here.'

After reaching the camp, the company commander summoned him, grabbed him by the shirt, and shouted, 'You didn't obey my order!' Soon after, Maung Maung found out that his captain had sent him on the mission to punish him for encouraging the headman's daughters to move. That night, the captain got drunk and barged into the room where the headman's daughters were staying.

The headman's wife ran to Maung Maung and asked him to help, but Maung Maung had no authority to stop his superior. Still, he accompanied the headman's wife to her relative's house and heard the girls shouting fearfully to their mother. He pulled out his gun, put it on automatic fire, and shot over the house. The captain burst out of the house and shot at Maung Maung three times with his pistol, but Maung Maung managed to run back to his platoon without injury.

The captain followed him, drunk and swearing that he would take action against him the next morning. Maung Maung replied, 'If you take action against me, I will tell the senior officer, that you, a captain, went into the girls' room.' This only made the captain more angry. Soon after, Maung Maung had to run away to escape being imprisoned. At the time of our interview, he was a migrant worker in Thailand.[8]

Maung Maung explained that although there were only two officers per company, they were able to control the troops by relying on divide and rule tactics. If the sergeants united with the soldiers against the officers, the officers wouldn't be able to act so abusively, so they used rewards and punishments to split the lower ranks. Those who went against their commanders were sent off on dangerous missions while those who were submissive were allowed to stay in safe locations. Maung Maung said that he explained to his soldiers how they were being manipulated, and they understood. But some wanted promotions badly enough that they went along with the officers' tactics anyway.

Maung Maung had served in the army for eleven years. 'If the military were good,' he said, 'there wouldn't be any reason for me to come over to Thailand. I still haven't completely lost my desire to be a soldier. But it's not that I want to hold a gun without reason. I want to sacrifice for the country.' He decided that serving merely to support senior officers was pointless, particularly since the senior officers had so little concern for their soldiers. 'I feel that if I continued staying in the military, there would be no one left in the army who was as stupid as me,' Maung Maung said. 'If I were killed, it would be meaningless.'

Although officers live much better than their soldiers, their lives are not free of problems either. Until early 2000, their salaries were also ridiculously inadequate, so they had to take on other work or steal and sell things on the black market to survive. Moreover, their positions are never certain and, like the ordinary soldiers, they must curry favour with their superiors in order to ensure promotion.

One doctor who served with the military for three years talked about the fear he found among the officers and their wives. He said, 'Not only were the captains and majors afraid of their superiors, but their wives were also afraid of the superiors' wives.' He knew one officer who was the personal assistant to the regional commander and lived in the same compound as his commander. His wife worked as a school teacher, but when she came home at night, she had to go over and grind the *thanaka* (traditional Burmese facial powder) for the commander's wife, as if she were her personal servant.

At the highest levels, General Ne Win controlled his men by rewarding their talent with promotions, until they became potential threats to his own power. At that point, they were sidelined into unimportant jobs, retired early, or even thrown in prison on charges of corruption or other offences. General Ne Win and the top SLORC and SPDC generals have used the military intelligence to gather information on the weaknesses of other generals, so that they could be blackmailed into loyalty, or sacked if necessary.

Thus, it is not surprising that even among officers there has been dissatisfaction with military rule. If the military were purely a professional army under a democratic government, demands for blind loyalty to senior officers and instances of abuse of power might not be such critical problems.[9] Colonel Soe Thein, who resigned in 1983, explained, 'I'm a pure soldier. I don't like the military playing in politics. Our main duty is to protect the country and the people.' He said that, even before 1988, many other officers did not like the army's involvement in politics, but they dared not talk about it: 'The majority were just pretending to like it.' He explained, 'I had no university education. There would be no outside job for me, so I couldn't get out.'

Low educational achievement among military men means not only that they cannot find other jobs, but also that their vision for a different kind of political system is limited. The doctor who served with the military recalled, 'The problem was the high-ranking commanders were mostly uneducated. They had to go out on two field operations a year, with each one lasting four months. And even during the four months in town, they were often out accompanying superiors on visits. So they didn't have a chance to read. They saw little more than the villages. Until they reach the tactical commander [colonel] level this is their life. The only other source of information for them was BBC and VOA, if they listened, which few did.'

Thus, it is not surprising that Colonel Soe Thein, like his colleagues, did not challenge the military's strategy for dealing with the armed ethnic minority groups. Although he says now that he felt the Four Cuts strategy, which targeted civilian populations, was not right, he never thought that the regime should try to negotiate with the ethnic nationalists. He said, 'Sometimes I disagreed with the Four Cuts, because it made a lot of trouble for the ethnic people. But how could I go against an order? I had to do it.' Moreover, he explained that, at that time, he and his colleagues thought federalism meant anarchy. 'We didn't think about a political solution to the problem, only fighting.' When he came to Karen-controlled territory to work with the pro-democracy groups after 1988, he changed his thinking. He said, 'Now I realize we must give autonomy to ethnic groups, but I don't agree with independent states.' Since most of the ethnic leaders are calling for federalism rather than full independence, he believes a negotiated solution is possible.

1988–90

A desire for a return to civilian rule gnawed at the consciences of many, though certainly not all, people in the Tatmadaw and, in 1988, a number of military personnel joined the demonstrators on the streets. Most came from the better-educated corps based in and near Rangoon. One who joined was a young Rakhine, Khaing Aung Soe, who had been working in the supply department of the air force for three years. He and his friends were also enrolled in correspondence courses through the Workers' College and were sympathetic to the university students' demands. Starting in March 1988, they had begun secretly collecting money for anti-government activities at Rangoon University.

When the demonstrations started in August, they at first stayed in their barracks at Mingaladon outside Rangoon, but cheered on truckloads of people heading into the city. Then on 9 September 1988, Khaing Aung Soe and a group of his friends left the barracks and joined the Rangoon University students. Khaing Aung Soe said, 'We went in full uniforms but with no guns. We arrived in the student compound and had a kind of press conference in the evening.' There were about 450 of them, including a female sergeant. The students arranged for them to stay at Thayet Daw monastery, where the monks were very supportive of the movement.

'During 1988,' Khaing Aung Soe said, 'we didn't think we'd win just by these demonstrations. We left some people in the main base to collect guns if necessary. We also made contacts with people in the Navy and Army. On the 17th, some students seized ammunition from the Trade Ministry and kept it in the monastery so they would be ready to fight the soldiers.' On the morning of September 19th, the day after the coup, the abbot of the monastery grew increasingly nervous and insisted that all the democracy soldiers leave that day.

Khaing Aung Soe recalled: 'We took the guns and hid in civilian houses. We moved every day, but after a couple of days, people were afraid and changed to civilian clothes, stored all the ammunition in monasteries and spread out. We didn't want to go back to the barracks without democracy, so six others and I made our way out to the border where we joined one of the pro-democracy armies.'

He said that a number of the officers he knew also supported the democracy movement. Some went out on the streets in civilian clothes without informing their superiors, while others encouraged those who went out but were afraid to leave the bases themselves. Khaing Aung Soe remembers his commander telling him and others, 'I won't stop you or support you if you join the demonstrations. You have to decide by yourself. But we must try to get democracy.' Before the coup, he sent a message to the monastery where all the air force defectors were staying and asked them to come back to the base. Khaing Aung Soe said that friends of his who returned to the base were imprisoned for six months and expelled from the military. His commander was forced to resign.

Many more soldiers were loyal to the regime, and followed orders to shoot the civilian demonstrators. However, at least some troops from other battalions were upset with their comrades. According to one soldier at the time, 'None of the battalions could stand the sight of Division 22,' the light infantry division that gunned down the most demonstrators in 1988. Still, it is likely that most of them would have done the same thing had they been sent to Rangoon.

During and after the election campaign period, the SLORC fired military personnel and civil servants who had actively supported the demonstrations, and reorganized its troops. The regime tried to weaken support for Daw Aung San Suu Kyi by calling her a traitor to the Burman race for marrying a westerner. In newspaper editorials and in propaganda speeches she was termed a prostitute and other shockingly derogatory epithets. Whipping up nationalist fervor, the regime achieved a measure of success with these attacks, particularly in the military. After thinking it through, though, some later changed their minds.

Maung Maung recalled that, after the coup, Brigadier General Tin Hla gave a speech to his battalion. He said, 'Aung San Suu Kyi is the wife of a foreigner. Do you want to be ruled by a woman who is the wife of a foreigner?' At first, Maung Maung said, he and others felt angry. They definitely did not want to be ruled by someone who was virtually a foreigner because of her marriage. Later, he said, he reconsidered it and discussed it with the soldiers under him. 'In Burma's history,' Maung Maung told them, 'King Thibaw was taken to India by the British. His housemate was an Indian and his gardener was an Indian. At that time, King Thibaw's relatives got married to whoever was close to them [Indians]. It's the same for the daughter of General Aung San. After the assassination of General Aung San, U Ne Win sent her abroad and she grew up abroad. Who else could she marry besides a foreigner? She didn't do anything wrong.'

The regime also told the soldiers that Daw Aung San Suu Kyi and the NLD wanted to break up the army. Even lower ranks who disliked their officers took serious offence at this for, despite the problems in the military, they were proud to be soldiers. But those who had a chance to hear Daw Aung San Suu Kyi speak in person began to doubt the regime's claims.

Another former sergeant, Nyi Nyi, who had worked at the army's weapons' production factory in Rangoon in the 1980s believes, 'It's impossible that the NLD would split the army.' He and some of his military friends had attended one of Daw Aung San Suu Kyi's campaign speeches in Rangoon in 1989. He remembers Daw Aung San Suu Kyi explaining that the Tatmadaw was founded by her father and that she herself was born in the military and grew up among soldiers. She said that she would never divide the military and the people. Nyi Nyi said, 'Some soldiers – I met four or five – cried when she said that. It really affected them.'

Nyi Nyi said he realized that his superiors were worried that the soldiers might vote for the NLD in the 1990 election, so they were trying to create a rift between the military personnel and Daw Aung San Suu Kyi. Since 1993, he said, the military has tried to channel the soldiers' interests into the USDA, which has organized mass rallies to denounce Daw Aung San Suu Kyi and the NLD.

Both sergeants claimed that they represented many of their peers in the army when they said that they supported Daw Aung San Suu Kyi and wanted the military to return to the barracks. But they didn't want to join the NLD themselves. Instead, they were hoping for the emergence of a visionary leader within the military whom they could follow. In the words of Nyi Nyi, 'The soldiers' perception of politics is that this country should be free from military rule and become a democracy as soon as possible. But it is impossible for them to make a demonstration within the military.' He thought that for people to leave the military, there must first be someone or some organization that could provide support and capable leadership. He said, 'If some military leaders appear who side with the people, then followers will emerge. We're hoping for that. If there is no leader who sides with the people, it is impossible for people in the military to break away even though they wish to do so.'

Given the fact that Maung Maung and Nyi Nyi had to flee and are now living outside Burma, they may be overstating the support of soldiers inside Burma for democracy. But they still love the army and see themselves as army men, so they are perhaps not too far off the mark. Many soldiers joined protesters in the 1988 demonstrations, and the number of military votes for the NLD in the 1990 election confirm dissatisfaction with military rule inside the military itself. Soldiers' increasingly acute economic problems, their inability to resign and the rough treatment they have suffered from their officers have soured them against the regime.

Brutality and Desertion

According to all accounts, brutality within the military has increased since 1988. This is most likely because the economic situation has continued to decline and the current military regime has no real ideology beyond enforcing national unity. Moreover, officers are generally not punished for treating their soldiers or civilians badly; they are punished only for disloyalty to their higher-ups.

As a result, a cycle of violence has developed, particularly in the remote areas, with officers treating their soldiers brutally and military men taking out their aggression on civilians. While few soldiers will admit the more unsavoury things they have done, they will discuss the abuses committed by others in the army. Ex-sergeant Maung Maung talked about how so many civilian porters died because of ill-treatment by military officers. 'But,' he said, 'we were given orders to march on, so I had to keep going ahead without looking back at them.' Reflecting on how upset he would feel if members of his own family were taken as porters, he said, 'Those officers didn't treat the porters even as cows or animals. If the porters died, they just left their bodies there. At the very least, they should cover the corpse with leaves.'

Villagers also have plenty of their own stories. A Karen village elder who fled to Thailand after the Tatmadaw's military offensive against the KNU in

1997 explained that two mentally-retarded women from his village were captured by the soldiers and gang-raped every night for ten nights. During the day, they had to work as porters. One of the women was ordered by the troops to go to the villagers who had escaped over the border into Thailand and order them to return. She went, but she warned the girls she met not to go back, telling them what had happened to her.[10]

Amnesty International and Human Rights Watch, along with several human rights groups based in Thailand and India, have documented thousands of accounts of torture, rape and other abuses.[11] Many soldiers may not want to terrorize local populations but they feel compelled to obey orders, believing that their own security is dependent on such behaviour, or they take advantage of unarmed civilians to release their own pent-up anger.

While some soldiers are still swayed by the argument that the military is needed to unify the country and wipe out insurgents, others have been dismayed by the regime's respectful treatment of Khun Sa, one of the world's top heroin traffickers in the 1980s and 1990s and the former head of the Mong Tai Army in Shan State. In the past, the government-controlled press always referred to him in derogatory terms, but after he cut a deal with the regime in January 1996, he was officially called 'U Khun Sa' and given a home in Rangoon.

One former soldier who talked with the army captains he met in Karen State in late 1998, said that they and their troops were not satisfied with the regime's handling of Khun Sa. 'When Khun Sa was making opium,' he said, 'these captains had to go and fight Khun Sa. Now since they announced on the front page of the newspaper, "May U Khun Sa live longer than a hundred years," the captains started to swear at the SPDC and Khin Nyunt and Than Shwe. They said, "When we had to fight Khun Sa, many of us died. They treat us like we're nothing."'

Since the mid-1990s, it has become possible to divide the military into three broad groups according to their feelings about whether the military should return to the barracks or continue to rule the country. Those below the rank of captain are generally dissatisfied with military rule, middle-ranking officers are sitting on the fence, and the generals are fully committed to continued military rule, if for no other reason than to preserve their privileges and to ensure they do not end up sentenced to prison or worse.

Although it is impossible to know the number of soldiers who have run away, desertion has become a problem for the army.[12] The numbers would probably be greater if soldiers had a safe haven to which they could flee. The regime tries to scare people into staying by telling them that if they are caught inside the country they will be sent to prison or executed, and if they try to escape across one of the borders, they will be killed by insurgents.[13] In 1997, a group of Tatmadaw deserters who made their way into India and joined with the Burmese pro-democracy groups there were later deported back to Burma by the Indian government.[14] Deserters who make it to Thailand generally hide their identities and work as migrant labourers, but few migrant labourers have work permits, so they can be sent back to Burma at any time. Despite the risks, four members of Maung Maung's battalion fled to Thailand within seven months of his desertion.

Aware of the fact that support for military rule within the army is not that strong, the regime has attempted to strengthen the loyalty of its forces by recruiting family members of current military personnel. With parents, brothers or uncles in the military service, a soldier would be reluctant to engage in anti-government activities, both because of family pressure as well as worries that his relatives would be adversely affected. Orphaned boys are particularly desired by the Tatmadaw, because they belong to no one and have no other allegiances.[15] The army is their only family and the barracks their only home. The military has set up special schools to train these children; once they are teenagers, they are sent into the army.

I met one such boy on a train in Shan State in 1996. Only about six years old, his parents had died and he was being taken by a group of soldiers back to their battalion headquarters. They had shaved his head and put him in an army uniform which was several sizes too big, but for the moment he was happy to be receiving so much attention.

Boys from ethnic minority areas are also brought into the armed forces through *Ye Nyunt* (Greatest Bravery) schools, where ethnic minority children receive room and board and a free education. These junior high schools are usually located on battalion bases. The students do chores around the base, and are given basic military training as well as regular classes. Parents from mountain villages often do not realize that their sons will be expected to become soldiers afterwards, wanting only for them to have a chance to learn Burmese and obtain an education. After a couple of years of schooling, the students usually have little choice but to join the military.[16]

The Rise of the Military Intelligence

The role of the military intelligence has expanded along with the increase in the size of the army. In 1999, there were as many as twenty-seven military intelligence battalions located throughout the country, as well as the head-quarters in Rangoon.[17] In the 1990s, intelligence personnel reportedly received training from China, Singapore and possibly Israel.[18] Intelligence officers are assigned not only to monitoring civilians but also to closer surveillance of the troops, whose loyalty is less certain than in the past.[19] According to one former soldier, after the military-backed NUP lost the 1990 election and it became clear that many soldiers had voted for the NLD, SLORC leaders were nervous about their troops' loyalty. To prevent a movement from developing within the armed forces, troops were moved around, the composition of battalions rearranged and counter-intelligence personnel sent to the units.

Tensions between the intelligence agents and the ordinary soldiers often run high, because the military intelligence personnel tend to have a much better standard of living than the soldiers of their rank. They generally receive more bribes and rarely have to risk their lives. According to former sergeant Maung Maung, the intelligence personnel he knew made up most of their reports and often pinned the blame for problems on soldiers they did not like.

The military intelligence recruits from the infantrymen, reportedly preferring intelligent individuals from poor families or families with military backgrounds. Unlike ordinary soldiers, intelligence personnel have a chance to go abroad as spies, if only to neighbouring countries. They generally enjoy easier lives than their peers in the infantry, and they are treated better by their superiors than ordinary soldiers are.

The military intelligence agents have more invested in the maintenance of military rule than others in the armed forces. Intelligence men have been placed in numerous civilian branches such as Customs, Immigration and the police. Were military rule to collapse, they would lose everything. As Colonel Soe Thein put it, 'The MI are the most loyal in the army. They don't care about anyone except their bosses.'

Of greater concern is the intelligence division's creation of a policy-making think tank, called the Office of Strategic Studies (OSS), in 1994. Under the direction of Lt General Khin Nyunt, the OSS develops domestic and foreign policies and writes speeches for the junta's public spokesmen. It has rapidly become the nerve centre of the regime.[20] Its members even direct archaeological digs and research into the earliest evidence of human occupation in Burma, claiming in 1998 that humans may have originated in Burma.[21] Seeking to institutionalize their power, Lt General Khin Nyunt and his intelligence colleagues have expanded their reach both geographically and vertically, delving into virtually every sphere of cultural and political life.

All branches of the armed forces, including the intelligence units, have increased their technological capabilities, but the military intelligence has also focused on upgrading its political sophistication. According to one highly-placed official, the regime recognizes that Burma's military rulers made mistakes in the past, but believes they deserve a chance to correct those mistakes now. Thus, the OSS is trying to recruit intellectuals and give them a certain degree of freedom, so that the regime has more ideas to work with.

The military intelligence still also carries out its traditional functions of interrogating and torturing political dissidents to obtain information and break their spirits. With soldiers using force to achieve pacification and intelligence agents relying on torture to extract information, a population of brutalized bodies will long serve as a reminder of the violence that has been committed. Who will be held responsible for all of this? Should individual agents and soldiers be blamed or only their leaders? Many Burmese say when things change they will not seek revenge; they want to put this nightmare period behind them and move on. But fear of punishment is certainly one of the reasons why the regime has been reluctant to transfer power.

CHAPTER 8

. . . .

Prison: 'Life University'

Insein is the name of a large prison
outside Rangoon

§ Many people in Burma do not become active in politics primarily because of their well-founded fear of being tortured and sent to prison. Since the mid-1990s, sentences for political activists accused of even the most trivial offences have typically ranged from seven to fifteen years.[1] Those who have led or organized protests receive even longer prison terms. On 7 June 1996, the military regime announced Decree 5/96, 'The Protection of the Stable, Peaceful, and Systematic Transfer of State Responsibility and the Successful Implementation of National Convention Tasks, Free from Disruption and Opposition'. According to this decree, anyone caught publicly airing views or issuing statements critical of the regime can be sentenced to up to twenty years in prison.[2]

Since domestic political opposition revived following Daw Aung San Suu Kyi's release from house arrest, members of parliament-elect from 1990 and other active NLD and ethnic political party members have been targeted by the authorities. In recent years, the regime has often held NLD party members under prolonged detention in order to wear them down so they would resign.

In 1998, when the NLD called for the 1990 Parliament to be convened within sixty days, 700 NLD members were detained, including 194 elected members of parliament.[3]

Student activists who have continued to organize demonstrations, maintain contact with the NLD, or distribute leaflets have also been treated harshly.[4] Monks who have pressed for political dialogue or protested against the regime's actions regarding religious affairs have also been incarcerated. The regime now gives much more lengthy prison sentences than in the past in order to intimidate people into staying away from politics.

Conditions in Burmese prisons are extremely difficult with insufficient food, medicine and bathing water frequently leading to debilitating health conditions and the premature deaths of many. A group of former political prisoners has documented the deaths in custody of forty-eight political prisoners between 1988 to 1999.[5] Those who are particularly charismatic or dare to lead strikes inside prison are left in solitary confinement for months or, in the case of student activist Min Ko Naing, years at a time. HIV is also spreading in Burma's prisons, in part, say former prisoners, because hospital needles are reused without being sterilized.[6] According to the political prisoners I interviewed, drug-addicts are often allowed to work in the hospitals, giving injections to themselves and other prisoners.

There are over forty prisons in Burma, but detainees are also often temporarily held at police stations, military barracks and interrogation centres.[7] Most political prisoners end up at one of the dozen larger facilities, and are frequently incarcerated in the same rooms as criminals. Political prisoners arrested in the Rangoon area are sent to Insein prison, which is located just outside Rangoon, and many are eventually transferred to prisons upcountry where conditions are often worse and family visits more difficult to arrange. During the 1990s, Burmese prisons held between 1,000 and 2,000 political prisoners at any given time, as released prisoners were replaced by newly-arrested activists and political party members.[8]

Before arriving at prison, political prisoners must pass through one of the country's twenty interrogation centres where one intelligence officer told an activist, 'You will be squeezed to the last drop like sugar cane in a juice press.' *The Human Rights Yearbook* for 1997–98, compiled by the Human Rights Documentation Unit of the exiled National Coalition Government of the Union of Burma, describes the techniques used in interrogation centres as including:

> beatings rigorous enough to cause permanent injury; shackling of the legs or arms; burning victims with cigarettes; applying electric shocks to the victims' genitals, finger tips, toes, ear lobes, and elsewhere; suffocation; stabbing; rubbing of salt and chemicals in open wounds; forcing victims to stand in unusual

and uncomfortable positions for extended periods of time, including 'riding the motorcycle,' which entails standing with arms outstretched and legs bent, and the 'helicopter,' in which the victim is suspended by the wrists or feet from a ceiling fixture and then spun around; deprivation of light and sleep; denial of medicine, food, exercise, and water for washing; employing the 'iron rod' in which iron or bamboo rods are rolled up and down the shins until the skin is lacerated; ordering solitary confinement with extremely small and unsanitary cells for prolonged periods, and using psychological torture including threats of death and rape.[9]

Political prisoners are kept at interrogation centres for periods of a few days up to a few months before being transferred to prison.[10]

Once in prison, political prisoners are treated like common criminals, are often beaten, and can be called out for further interrogation at any time. In the early days of the Ne Win regime, political prisoners were sometimes treated with more respect than criminals, but this is no longer the case. Although criminals are more likely to be sent to the frontlines as porters and to labour camps to work in quarries and build roads, some political prisoners have also faced these punishments. According to Amnesty International and other human rights organizations, hundreds of labour camp prisoners have died from untreated injuries and illnesses, malnutrition and ill-treatment.[11]

While political activists are in prison, the military intelligence and prison authorities try to destroy their morale, so that after they are released they will not participate in resistance activities again. In Myingyan prison, for instance, political prisoners were ordered to spend hours catching flies, shining the iron cell doors, and 'polishing' the bare ground in their cells with the base of a small bottle.[12] Long periods in isolation cells are also used to demoralize political prisoners. If political prisoners do not literally go mad or become numb from being repeatedly degraded in various ways, they may resort to informing on their comrades in return for special privileges which make life in prison bearable. For those who are trying to maintain their commitment, it is disheartening to see fellow prisoners deteriorate psychologically or give up their political ideals for material comforts.

Still, prison is a place where people have a chance to think and analyse issues deeply and intimate bonds are formed. While the entire country, and even the military itself, has been compared to a prison, for some, experiences in Burma's actual prison system can be mentally liberating. Despite the miserable living conditions, people of different views are able to engage in lengthy debates together, a chance they rarely have outside prison. This chapter explores how political prisoners try to create a community, maintain their morale and improve themselves, and looks at what happens to them after they are released.

Torture and Maintaining Morale

U Hla Aye, a poet who was imprisoned in the BSPP period for anti-government activities, found the mental tortures at the interrogation centre as painful as the physical tortures. When he was interrogated in the heat of the summer, he was stripped naked, covered in salt and beaten. He and other colleagues were also forced to stand barefoot on heated iron sheets to burn the soles of their feet. Most horrible were the electric shocks. He explained, 'They did it to our genitals so that we became disfigured.'

Besides the pain, the authorities used humiliation. U Hla Aye said: 'The authorities were acting under the belief that there are no political prisoners. Everyone is a criminal. That's the simplest form of torture in prison.' In the interrogation room, he and others were forced to pretend they were riding aeroplanes and motorcycles, making all the accompanying noises as if they were small children. The intelligence also tried to depress him and other political prisoners by telling them their wives had taken other lovers or that their mothers were about to die.

Once he passed through the interrogation centre, he was sent for trial. Rather than being held in a courtroom, the trial was conducted at the entrance of the prison, with the judge reading out his sentence according to the instructions given by military intelligence personnel. Then he was taken into the prison, where, he says, the military intelligence 'instructed the prison wardens to break our spirits'.

While U Hla Aye was held at Insein prison, he was frequently summoned for further interrogations. In order to make prisoners talk, they would be left naked for several days in a tiny cell full of faeces and maggots. U Hla Aye managed to keep himself together during his experiences in this cell, but some of his colleagues suffered mental breakdowns.

Political prisoners are often transferred to far-away prisons, making it difficult or impossible for their families to visit and bring them food. U Hla Aye was moved to Thayawaddy prison, a three-hour drive from Rangoon. He recalled: 'Some families in Rangoon didn't know that we'd been moved to Thayawaddy prison. They inquired in many different ways and found out only later. It was just to create more difficulties for living and eating. It is a form of torture intended to make groups of political prisoners become fed up with politics.'

Although family members were allowed to send food parcels to political prisoners, part of the food was usually taken by the prison authorities. U Hla Aye remembers that some of his cell-mates who had been in prison before didn't even try to fight the situation. They simply told their families to divide the food into separate packages, with half for the prison wardens and half for themselves. Some prison wardens even went to prisoners' cells just after visitors had left. U Hla Aye said: 'They came with their dinner plate to ask for food. If you gave it to them willingly, you could have a quick extra cup [of water] on top of the five that you were allowed for bathing.'

The desire for communication is so strong that prisoners are willing to risk punishment in order to create a connection with other prisoners. U Hla Aye recalled that even if prisoners were put in solitary confinement, they would try to communicate with those in neighbouring cells by knocking on the walls. At the very least, they tried to learn each other's names and why they were there, even though they knew they would be severely beaten if they were caught.

Obtaining news from outside is also important to political prisoners who are eager to keep abreast of current events. U Hla Aye said families and friends were sometimes able to send information in by wrapping food in pieces of newspaper. If someone was taken to the court, he would try to get news from his family there. Upon returning to his cell, he would pass on what he had learned to other prisoners.

When I asked how people maintained their political convictions under these circumstances, U Hla Aye said, 'Each person has his own way of doing it. Some say to themselves, "I will never betray my work and my beliefs. I will never become a traitor." There were also some who tried to control themselves with the social spirit that told them not to betray each other. Some turned to religion. Some turned to their hobbies.'

U Hla Aye tried to comfort himself by composing poems. He said, 'Only five minutes a day when we emptied our toilet pots did we get to touch the earth with our feet. In those free times we tried to analyse ourselves. While analysing the life that we had been through, we tried to compose poems from the feelings and the experiences that we had had and the things that touched our hearts.'

After U Hla Aye was released, he was eager to convey the bitterness of his prison experience and the thirst he had felt for freedom, but he could not publish such poems in Burma. Poets and writers with anti-government backgrounds find that their work on even the most innocent subjects comes under intense scrutiny by the censorship board.

Life University

Tun Way had just graduated from high school when he was imprisoned in 1975. For him, prison really was his university, and he treated it as such. A high school senior from a rural area, he was a good student and his teachers regularly called on him to contribute articles to the school bulletin board. After witnessing the military's repression of the workers' strike in Rangoon in 1974, he eagerly helped to make posters and banners for the one-year anniversary demonstration in 1975. On 11 June 1975, he was arrested along with many others at Shwedagon Pagoda, where the strike committee had set up its headquarters. He was taken to an interrogation centre, and the torture began.

'I realized how brutally the authorities torture during interrogations,' Tun Way said. 'Even if we sincerely did not know the answer, the authorities thought we were lying and used more brutal methods of torture.' Tun Way said that the interrogators often alternated styles, treating him nicely and using persuasion and then beating him up without asking him anything particularly important. Fighting the exhaustion was also difficult. Tun Way remembered, 'When the interrogators went out of the room, we tried to lean against the wall and take a nap because we were so sleepy after two or three days of non-stop interrogation. When they came back into the room and saw that we were leaning against the wall and sleeping, they kicked us all over with their military boots.'

After ten days, Tun Way and about fifty other prisoners were sent to a building in the Criminal Investigation Department's compound near Insein prison. There they were told to sit on the floor, beneath three military officers from the army, navy and air force. A military officer told them they were in a military tribunal and read out the charges against them, including threatening the state, violating the Insurgency Act, misusing public property and stealing.

During the demonstrations, students had burned coffins with the names of Ne Win and San Yu, a senior military general at the time, written on the side. Tun Way remembered: 'We had requested the coffins from one man as a donation, but he was called as a witness during our trial. The officer asked him whether the students had taken the coffins by force. He said yes, so we were charged for robbing coffins from that man.'

Tun Way tried to come to terms with his imprisonment by telling himself that change never comes without sacrifice. While in prison he could do little to bring about change, but at least he could study. Despite the constant bouts of skin diseases and other ailments, he and his university student cell-mates held frequent discussions on the political history of the country and why resistance was necessary.

For much of the time, Tun Way was held in a large cell with fifty other people, including politicians and lawyers. Although they were not allowed to read or write in prison, some of the prisoners secretly managed to obtain articles from foreign magazines. In Tun Way's cell, one of the older prisoners translated articles on foreign politics from *Time* magazine and explained them to the other inmates. Another gave a contextual analysis of the events presented in the articles. 'Then free discussion followed,' said Tun Way. 'All had the right to speak, discuss and give different opinions.'

Tun Way was exposed to a variety of views through these discussions and revelled in the diversity. He also began to study English and modern Burmese poetry and to develop his talents as a poet. As time went on, he and his fellow inmates began to put together magazines in their cells. With no pens or pencils permitted, Tun Way and his friends had their visitors hide ink refills in food packages. They created makeshift pens by encasing the refills in two thin strips from their sleeping mats, held together with a rubber band. Tun Way became a member of the editorial group and collected articles from other inmates. Because they could only write at night, when they were not being watched, it took over a month to finish producing one issue. Once the publication was complete, prisoners would take turns reading it, secretly passing it from cell to cell.

Tun Way and his cell-mates also organized ceremonies to mark the anniversaries of political strikes. Sometimes they held a hunger strike and spent the day in silence. On other occasions they sang political songs. Around the new year, they chanted *thangyat*, anti-government songs written for the occasion.

Tun Way found prison a good place to develop his intellect and create deep bonds of friendship with people from all over the country. Having to share food, blankets and secrets for four or five years, he and some of his cell-mates became closer than siblings. But, he said, some prisoners could not endure the difficulties of prison life and resorted to informing on fellow inmates in return for a blanket or some small privilege. 'The privilege would be quite small,' he said, 'but these people were happy to have it under such harsh living conditions.'

For Tun Way, family visits were especially emotional. He was overjoyed when a family member visited, because he could get food and obtain news about the rest of his family and friends. Prison visits were always on Sundays, so Saturday night, everyone would be happy and excited. On Sunday mornings, prisoners were called out in small groups for the brief visits with their relatives.

During the early days of his imprisonment, Tun Way and other prisoners were forced to wear their prison uniforms to their meetings with visitors. Tun Way recalled: 'It made the visitors, especially our parents, upset and sorrowful. Due to the torture we faced and the lack of sufficient food in prison, my parents could not recognize me in my prison uniform. As soon as they recognized me, my mother started crying. Within the very short five-minute meeting, she could not speak a word; she just kept crying.' Later, the prison authorities allowed the prisoners to wear civilian clothes during the visits. Tun Way, like other prisoners, borrowed a shirt, *longyi* and slippers from other prisoners. When he returned to his cell, he passed the set of nice clothes to someone else to wear. Tun Way said: 'We wanted to make ourselves look as good as possible. Some even wore a jacket to look better.'

Being thrown in prison at such a young age, Tun Way matured quickly. He recalled: 'Prison was like a university of life. In real universities, you have to spend four academic years to be a graduate. But for me I spent four years at life university.' Tun Way realized that he needed to develop his knowledge while in prison, because after his release he would not be allowed to enroll in a formal educational institution. Moreover, he would not be treated like an ordinary person. He said: 'People who are just released from prison are always one step behind and different from normal people. So it is important to study and learn, as well as to be confident.'

After his release, Tun Way became a poet, and in 1988 he joined the pro-democracy demonstrations. Now living outside Burma, his poems are often featured on Burmese-language radio broadcasts from abroad.

Feelings of Guilt

Many prisoners feel guilty about the trouble they have caused their families by taking up politics. Often they are the primary wage-earners. If they are students, they may have dashed their families' hopes for their futures and even negatively affected their parents' and siblings' job opportunities. Once a member of the household is arrested, the whole family comes under increased surveillance and sometimes harassment. Some political prisoners feel so guilty that they encourage their wives or girlfriends to break up with them so that their lives will not also be destroyed. One political prisoner who felt this way wrote a song about it and sang it for me when I interviewed him several years later.

> *Released Maiden*
>
> A miserable wild night in a storm,
> without a chance to meet a sunbeam.
> There is still turbulent, heavy rain everywhere.
> It is time for us to part.
> Take this white scarf, darling,
> as my gift to keep you company.
> And tie up your loose hair with it.
>
> Please try to comprehend
> the meaning of my gift, a white scarf.
> And encourage yourself
> to pass through the sea of life.
> Don't worry for me.
> My white scarf will help you
> to tie up your loose hair.
> Feel free and leave tenderly from my shore.
>
> Feel free darling,
> Feel free darling,
> Leave tenderly from my shore.[13]

During his many years in prison, this man's girlfriend did end up going her own way. Although he is now free and living in Burma, everyone who gets close to him knows they may be putting themselves at risk.

Female Prisoners

In the 1990s, there were more female political prisoners than ever before, as many young women took active roles in the 1988 demonstrations and the election campaign and then continued underground, organizing activities despite their parents' objections. Particularly difficult for younger female prisoners is the humiliation of being told by their interrogators that they are loose girls who are surely sleeping around with male colleagues.

One young woman, Kyi Kyi, had been a university student in 1988 and had participated enthusiastically in the 1990 election campaign. She spent a year in a rural area going from door to door explaining to villagers and townspeople what the BSPP had done wrong and what the NLD planned to do for the country. She returned to Rangoon at the time of the elections, but, after the junta ignored the election results, she continued working with a student group that was writing and distributing pamphlets about the political situation. In 1991, she was arrested. When she told me her story in 1998, her eyes were still bright, but there was a weariness about her that reflected what she had been through.

After her arrest, she was taken to an interrogation centre. She was not beaten, but the intelligence personnel taunted her and suggested she had had affairs with her male colleagues. She said: 'For example, if I had gone to a meeting with a group of male friends, they would say something like, "You have the audacity to go with all these men when you're the only girl? Your pluck is very commendable."' Her interrogators referred to her as *kaung ma*, a derogatory term for a woman. They said, 'Hey *kaung ma*, we're asking you nicely because we don't want to get physical. So you better just answer. You want us to beat you, don't you? That's the only way you would talk. You're so cunning. You think so highly of yourself. Who do you think you are?'

When they asked her if she would continue to be involved in politics if they let her go, Kyi Kyi said she wasn't doing politics. She was involved in the students' movement and would continue to be. With that, a heavy object was slammed down next to her. Wearing a blindfold, she was told, 'What do you think that was? That was a gun. I can kill you right now if I want to.'

Only letting her rest for brief intervals between long periods of interrogation, the intelligence agents also tried to play her against other detainees. Kyi Kyi remembered: 'They would say, "That *kaung ma* is revealing everything about you. Why do you keep covering for her?" And they would say the same thing about me to another person.'

Although Kyi Kyi says she did not confess the names of her colleagues or their activities, in most cases, prisoners cannot resist the torture inflicted on them and do confess. After they have been broken, prisoners are sometimes brought into a room with sacks over their heads and made to confess everything again, without knowing that their colleagues are sitting in front of them. The political prisoners were depressed by such confessions, and some had difficulty keeping up their morale. But once in prison, fellow inmates tried to encourage each other so that they could survive.

When Kyi Kyi first arrived in prison, she said she was so afraid that she did not have the courage to look around. Exhausted from the days of interrogation, she slept almost constantly. Finally, other inmates urged her to get up and eat or her health would deteriorate. Sleeping on the cold cement floor, she, like others, soon developed high blood pressure. She had trouble eating the prison food, but other prisoners shared their food from home with her, helping her to keep her spirits up.

For Kyi Kyi, developing empathy and warmth towards other prisoners, political and criminal, was an important part of her prison experience. She explained how she became close to other prisoners after talking to them about their lives. 'Those charged with murder told me why they felt they had to kill and the injustice done to them,' she said. 'The prostitutes too described their experiences to me. Their lives were absolutely pitiful. When we asked them why they decided to become prostitutes, the main reason was that they didn't know how to make a living any other way. For some, their lives were destroyed. They didn't have any money and their parents too were helpless. They were uneducated. They said to us: "How else could we make a living? We don't how to do anything."' Kyi Kyi said that the sex-workers and some of the other female criminal prisoners hoped that one day the activists could bring about changes that would make their lives better. For that reason, they sometimes helped the political prisoners.

Still, Kyi Kyi found it hard to overcome the physical difficulties of prison life. At one point, she was housed in a building which was divided into ten cells, all of which were infested with mice and rats. At night, the inmates would awaken to rats biting their hands and feet, and, even when they were eating, the mice would sometimes steal their food. Finally the authorities agreed to renovate the building because of the threat of plague. The prisoners were moved to another building where they met up with other political prisoners and began doing physical exercises together. Accusing the women of engaging in military training, the prison authorities sent them back to their former cells before the walls were dry. The chemical vapors were overwhelming, causing many of the prisoners to become ill.

Kyi Kyi and her cell-mates were allowed to walk outside for only fifteen minutes a day, and they could use only two or three cups of water per day for showering. Kyi Kyi recalled: 'As for washing clothes, we [political prisoners] had to use second-hand water already used by those who had given bribes. This was a kind of torture. They didn't severely limit water because it was expensive. It was done on purpose.' Like the male prisoners, female prisoners were not allowed any pens, pencils or books, even about religion. But Kyi Kyi crafted writing implements to write poetry, and she and her cell-mates often sang at night to pass the time. On the anniversaries of important days, the female political prisoners would wear white, make little wreaths out of twigs and flowers, and float them in the prison drainage ditch. Although the prisoners had to do this surreptitiously, Kyi Kyi said, they experienced a feeling of gratification at being able to make the secret gesture.

A couple of times a month, the female prisoners gathered together to share their food, discuss politics and analyse each other's behaviour. During Kyi Kyi's first two years of imprisonment, she was housed with about fifty female political prisoners in one common area, and they would break into groups of seven or eight for the sessions. Later, when there were fewer political prisoners, Kyi Kyi said they held the discussions more often. Although the female political prisoners generally tried to live within the prison rules, some criminal prisoners invented complaints and reported on them to the authorities. Their numbers reduced, the political prisoners were less able to stand up to abusive guards. Thus, Kyi Kyi recalled, 'people were becoming increasingly depressed and tensions were building. So these discussions were necessary as a means to boost morale and encourage each other.'

As time went on, Kyi Kyi herself struggled with the emotional difficulties of prison life. She began to smoke and isolated herself from others. She was disillusioned by some of the other political prisoners who had turned on their comrades and she began to lose faith in the movement. But when she stared out of the window and saw the child prostitutes lined up for their meals, she said her determination to continue the struggle returned. She recalled: 'The girls were only about thirteen or fourteen years old and wearing little skirts. I felt the utmost pity for them.' She also observed hunched-over old women who had been arrested for selling snacks on the street without a permit. Seeing such people imprisoned made her angry, an emotion that helped her maintain her commitment during the last three years of her imprisonment.

After Kyi Kyi's release, as described in Chapter 5, she continued to be hounded by military intelligence and even her family became increasingly suspicious of her.

Covert Assistance

Moe Aye was arrested in 1990. Like Kyi Kyi, he had been involved in the 1990 election campaign and continued to work with politically active student groups when the election results were not honoured. After being tortured in an interrogation centre for two months, he was sent to Insein prison. There he and his colleagues, with the secret help of some prison authorities, were able to set up elaborate systems for studying.[14]

At first, he said, the political activists were divided by their ideologies, but eventually they were able to overcome these differences and accept that, regardless of which organization they originally came from, they now belonged to only one category, that of political prisoners. Incarcerated with Buddhist monks as well as Protestant pastors who had been part of a failed Karen insurrection in the Irrawaddy delta in 1991, the student prisoners had a chance to study Buddhism and Christianity. Drawing on their collective talents, the prisoners also set up study groups for English, Burmese history and even Japanese. All the studying had to be done covertly, for if they were caught, they would be severely punished and sometimes put in isolation cells.[15] But the prisoners were not deterred. They created sheets out of plastic bags used to deliver food and wrote on those with pointed implements. By holding the piece of plastic up to the light, the scratches could be read.

Moe Aye lived in a row of cell blocks with four political prisoners in each cell. During bathing time, one person would forfeit his bath to hurry to the cell of an older political prisoner who would write out five or ten English vocabulary words with translations in Burmese. After a couple of months, the student prisoners moved on to grammar. If they didn't understand what was written, the next day one would use his bathing time to get an explanation. Then the lessons would be sent on to the next cell. Moe Aye recalled: 'For over one year, we studied by plastic. After that, we knew how to approach the warden.'

Moe Aye and several of the other inmates came up with a plan to sell the coffee mix and milk powder their families gave them in return for study materials. They started off by asking the warden to bring them an issue of *Time* magazine, which could be purchased on Pansodan Road in central Rangoon. Although the magazine cost only 50 kyat, the prisoners offered to pay the warden 250 kyat for smuggling the magazine in. The warden agreed and secretly carried in a few folded-up pages at a time. It took twenty days to get the whole magazine.

Moe Aye wanted to translate the articles into Burmese for others to read, but it was too difficult to do on plastic. So he and his friends collected more coffee and milk powder and paid the equivalent of 100 kyat to the warden in return for bringing in a 20-kyat notebook, page by page, and a pencil. Then Moe Aye began translating, selecting in particular articles about regional politics as well as essays and opinion pieces. Although Moe Aye knew more English than his cell-mates, he was not fluent. Thus, they decided they needed a dictionary and began saving their milk powder for that as well. Moe Aye recalled: 'All students were trying very hard to study English. If the SLORC gave the right to study, it would be very good. But as you know, they never gave that right. They sent us to prison because they wanted to close our eyes and our ears.'

In 1992, Moe Aye and his friends managed to get information about the American presidential election from a recently released friend who obtained newsletters and election materials from the American embassy. Having known only Burmese elections, they wanted to learn how the American system worked. Although they weren't sure how Democrats and Republicans differed, Moe Aye said they were hopeful that whoever won would support the democratic movement in Burma.

Moe Aye and his friends also developed a knocking system for communicating from cell to cell during times when the prisoners were ordered to remain silent. Because the Burmese alphabet has many more letters and vowels than English, they decided to use English. One tap equalled A, two taps equalled B, and so on. To decode a sentence from the next cell, one person would count the number of taps while another would translate the numbers into letters and words. The usefulness of this communication system only increased the prisoners' desire to study English.

Moe Aye explained how during one less restrictive period, political discussions were held almost every night in his block of cells. To come up with the discussion topic, one person per cell would forgo his bath to consult with the inmates in the other cells. By the time all of the cells had been let out in turn for their baths, the inmates would have agreed on a specific topic. In the afternoons, cell-mates would quietly discuss the topic in their cells. Late at night, after the guards had retired, one spokesman per cell would state his cell-mates' views on the topic. Each cell would take a turn. If intelligence personnel showed up to carry out a surprise check, a code would be knocked from wall to wall, and everyone would fall silent. The prisoners knew that if the authorities found out about such talks, the instigators would be punished and transferred to another part of the prison.

During these dialogues, sometimes older politicians would challenge the younger inmates' interpretations of historical events. The younger inmates had gained their knowledge from books written by the BSPP and did not know what had really happened, for instance, during the 1974–75 workers' strikes. Some of the prisoners were old communists, and the younger prisoners would request them to tell of their experiences with the Communist Party in the jungle. On those nights, everyone would listen quietly as one of the elder men shared his recollections.

Moe Aye said, during the less tense periods he and his friends were so busy studying English and politics that they were almost happy. 'Sometimes,' he said, 'we forgot our mothers and our family.' But whenever there was a crackdown and no one could talk or study, it was not so easy. Moe Aye said: 'On those nights we asked each other, "Hey, don't you remember your mother?" And others would answer wistfully, "Yes, I remember my mother."'

Moe Aye explained that some of the prison authorities shared the students' frustrations with military rule but, like others in Burma, they did not dare to openly express their discontent for fear of losing their jobs. As a half-measure, a few tried to help the political prisoners in small ways.

In one case, the prisoners banded together to demand the right to read the newspaper, threatening a hunger strike if their demand was not granted. One of the senior prison authorities became worried and called some of the prisoners to his office. He said: 'Please understand my situation. I can do nothing. I understand you, because my son and daughter are students. If you want the newspaper, please request it of the MI office.' But the intelligence personnel refused the request, telling the prisoners that if they initiated a hunger strike, they would be beaten.

Later, that senior prison officer often walked by the student prisoners' cells chewing betel nut. The first time he offered betel nut to the prisoners, they didn't know what to say, because it was not allowed in prison. But then Moe Aye thought he was trying to convey something, so he accepted the offer. When the prison officer handed over the betel nut, it was wrapped in a page of newspaper. Likewise, as soon as Daw Aung San Suu Kyi was released from house arrest, a sympathetic prison warden gleefully brought the news to Moe Aye and his cell-mates. In other instances, some of the usually tight-lipped wardens came to the political prisoners' cells when they were drunk to complain about the military regime.

Most of the prison authorities were not particularly interested in human rights, but some were angry with the regime because they had been passed over for promotion. Like other civil servants, they resented having to serve under retired military officers who were less educated than themselves. Moe Aye said he and his colleagues tried to convince such wardens that their situation would not improve until democracy was achieved.

Release

Once political prisoners are released, their lives are never the same. They and their family members are followed, treated with suspicion and hassled. In some cases, former political prisoners' families even turn against them. Although they have been freed from physical confinement, they often find themselves socially isolated.

Moe Aye talked about how lonely he felt after his release. As the only person from his village to have served a long prison sentence, he was the subject of intense gossip. He had to report to the MI regularly, and he couldn't meet his old friends because he was under surveillance. Although his family said to him in private that they were proud of him, in public they told everyone that he was bad and they couldn't control him.

Moe Aye recalled how difficult it was to reintegrate into his family. His first night home, his mother was so happy to see him that she had made many kinds of curry to celebrate. But he said he couldn't eat. 'I at once remembered my friends in prison, and I wanted to pack up the food and send it to them. For over one month I couldn't eat very well.'

The local military intelligence agents warned Moe Aye to stay away from all political groups, and especially from the township NLD. He agreed to comply, but the agents had their informers checking on him constantly. This worried his mother. When he went to a hospital in another town for medical treatment, an intelligence agent there approached him and demanded to know why he had come without reporting to the MI officer in his township first. Moe Aye told him that he had only been ordered to stay away from the NLD and going to the hospital had nothing to do with politics. The intelligence officer let him go, but Moe Aye found the experience upsetting. The tension increased during the December 1996 student demonstrations in Rangoon. Three policemen posted themselves outside his house and kept a constant watch on him. Although the policemen were friends of his, Moe Aye realized he could be rearrested at any time, and the stress was taking a toll on his mother.

Min Thein, another student who spent four years in prison in the early 1990s, faced similar problems. After his release, his friends were reluctant to sit and talk to him in a teashop, and some even tried to persuade him to give up politics. When he visited his friends' houses, their parents treated him coldly. They were worried that Min Thein might try to recruit their children for anti-government activities.

Some former political prisoners wash their hands of politics and look for jobs in the private sector. Others try to contribute to society through teaching or writing. Both Min Thein and Moe Aye decided they had to leave Burma. Finding refuge in the political offices of the exile movement, Moe Aye wrote several articles about social and political conditions in Burma for English- and Burmese-language publications. He then went on to work for the Democratic Voice of Burma radio station. Min Thein joined up with former colleagues now living in a border area and continued to maintain secret contact with activist friends inside the country.

While young political prisoners try to make the best of 'life university', some students outside prison have also sought to create their own educational programmes. As we shall see in the next chapter, those who are not satisfied with the formal education system turn to former political prisoners and anti-government intellectuals to develop a course of study that supports their political objectives.

CHAPTER 9

. . . .

Education: Floating Books and Bathroom Tracts

'Education gives you confidence in yourself and strength to make decisions. The more people are uneducated, the more you can keep them down.' (A Burmese educator)

§ In the late 1940s and 1950s, Burma boasted one of the highest literacy rates in Asia and an expanding educational system. It has been devastating for educated parents to see their children growing up far less knowledgeable than they. The military regime has placed a low priority on education for several reasons. First, they fear that the more people are educated, the more likely they are to mount serious challenges to military rule. Second, the top generals are not highly educated themselves, and often resent better-educated people. And third, with limited funds at hand, they have funnelled resources into expanding and equipping the army rather than the schools. Only 4 per cent of the national budget is spent on education while over 40 per cent goes to the military.[1]

While the number of schools and primary teachers has increased, schools are generally run down and lacking even the most basic equipment. So little money is provided that many schools levy an annual tax on students, along with various other fees throughout the year (such as table, water pot and maintenance fees), to keep the school running.[2] There are rarely enough textbooks available, so students who do not receive books in the classroom must buy photocopied versions, at a much higher price, on the black market. On top of this, parents must purchase uniforms for their children. Many families cannot afford all these expenses, and their children end up spending little or no time in school.

According to UNICEF's 1995 report *Children and Women in Myanmar*, 39 per cent of children in Burma never attend primary school, and 34 per cent who start school drop out between kindergarten and fifth standard (age nine). Only 27 per cent of all children in the country finish primary school.[3] Particularly in rural areas, parents often need their children to help them with farm work and household chores, including taking care of younger siblings.

Many parents feel that a few years of education will not help their children get a job anyway.

For those who do attend school, poverty and malnutrition also affect their performance. A primary school teacher in Karen State in the 1970s and 1980s talked about how the parents of one of his students told him to punish their son if he did not behave in class. In fact, the child had a hard time concentrating, because, as the teacher found out, his parents were unable to feed him before he came to school in the morning. The child was too hungry to pay attention.

The Curriculum

Every government uses its education system to try to inculcate certain attitudes in the minds of the country's youth. In Burma, successive military regimes have asserted central control over the development of the curriculum, with Lt General Khin Nyunt, the military intelligence chief, serving as the head of the National Education Committee. Government textbooks, reinforcing the regime's propaganda in the state-controlled media, stress the honour of the military and the necessity of continued military rule to maintain the country's political stability.

In primary and secondary education, teachers and even headmasters have no input in curriculum development and can not deviate from the textbooks in their teaching. As one headmaster put it: 'The curriculum was really a top-down process. It was worked out only from the top and then proscribed. So we had nothing to do or discuss or criticize. We just had to follow it.'

In the mid-1960s, General Ne Win ordered that English no longer be used as a medium of instruction. English was linked to colonial rule, and true nationalists were supposed to speak in Burmese only. Many educated parents, who spoke beautiful English from their days in school, were anguished by this policy. They realized that Burma was a small country and fluency in English was essential to integrating with the global economy and outside ideological currents. Nevertheless, many high school and university students absorbed the government's propaganda and mocked friends who used English in conversation. It was not until 1979, when General Ne Win's daughter failed her entrance exam into a British medical school because of her poor English, that teaching in English was reinstated.[4] Still, English teaching in Burma today is greatly inferior to what it was in the past, because so few fluent teachers remain.

Rewriting history has been a key project for the regime. Since Daw Aung San Suu Kyi's rise in political importance in 1988, for instance, the military people in charge of textbook production have downplayed the role of General Aung San and focused instead on the need for military leadership to hold the country together. General Aung San was a military leader but he later resigned in order to enter democratic politics as a civilian. In the past, the regime emphasized General Aung San's role as founder of the army, but Daw Aung San Suu Kyi has argued that General Aung San never intended for the army to oppress the Burmese people. Thus, the textbooks now talk much less about General Aung San and more about the importance of national unity and solidarity.

U Kyaw Moe, a former high school teacher, worries about the implications of the government's educational policies on students. He realizes that they will grow up thinking that their teachers have taught them 'the facts', when in fact they are being given large doses of propaganda. He said, 'The government would like to govern the country for a long, long time, so they have changed the ideology of the students little by little, step by step, very systematically.' He found teaching history and economics the most difficult, because the gap between the textbooks and reality was so wide.

Another teacher in the Burma Socialist Programme Party period (1974–88) who felt the same explained how the textbooks extolled the productivity of the country's great factories, but in fact most factories at the time were not operating. 'There were no raw materials,' he said. 'All the clerks and labourers were sitting on the floor reading books or talking about rumours.'

Nevertheless, this teacher, who lived in a rural town and was too young to have experienced democratic rule, did not have any ideas about how to change the educational system. 'We had only one system that we knew,' he said. 'If we had had a chance to see books about other systems, about which education system is good, we could have compared. But we had no books.'

Ethnic minority teachers have particularly suffered, because they are forced to teach a curriculum which almost completely excludes their histories and cultures. Divergent perspectives on pre-colonial Burman kings' history of conquest are not included, giving the impression that ethnic tensions in Burma resulted only from British colonial policies.

Although ethnic minority languages are theoretically allowed to be taught at the early primary school level, implementation of the policy has been fraught with obstacles. According to a Karen headmaster who promoted the Karen curriculum, the Karen textbooks were submitted for approval in 1967, but they were not actually printed until the 1980s. Whenever he asked in Rangoon about the delays, he was told there was not enough paper. After the textbooks were finally printed, no new teachers were provided to teach Karen. If the teachers on staff could not read and write Karen already, they were unable to instruct their students. Such policies are perhaps not surprising, because it is in the regime's interest that fluency in other languages be gradually eliminated and minority populations become assimilated into the Burman majority population. In this way, there will be less basis for minority claims against the state's unifying projects.

The military regime is doing what it can to impress its ideology on the population through the educational system and the media. It hopes to erase any thoughts conflicting with its own proscribed version of history and politics. In the BSPP days as well as now, high school and university teachers have had to attend training and refresher courses in which they are taught military drills, techniques for monitoring students, and political ideology. Such courses are used to weed out or dampen the spirits of independent-minded teachers and to instruct them in how to inculcate the regime's propaganda.[5]

U Kyaw Moe attended such a three-month course in the early 1970s before becoming a high school teacher. He said the instructors taught them how to control their students and how to 'renew' their ideology. He said: 'They said ideology is renewable, so your students' ideology only depends on you, the teachers. If your students get bad ideas, it is because of you, so you must think of the students as clean toys which you can form as you like.'

When I asked U Kyaw Moe how he felt about this, he said, 'There was a great storm in my heart and in my mind. But what could I do at that time? I had a family. So I tried to get great endurance and I sat very quietly.' But several years later, during the election period, he joined the NLD and offered an alternative education, at least to certain students. 'I had my own tuition classes in my house,' U Kyaw Moe said. 'I taught them very openly because I selected the students who would like to attend my tuition classes. I took great care to select them. They were members of the NLD, the same party as me, and I was their leader in the party.' He says that in his private classes, he and his students spent far more time discussing politics than lessons. But in school he didn't dare to deviate from the curriculum. If he were arrested, he feared his family would not be able to make ends meet.

In the government's school system, learning consists of rote memorization, and exams call for the exact repetition of the teachers' or textbooks' words, with no room for critical thinking. This teaching method is regarded as normal and parallels a common learning style for young students in the monasteries, where monks order small boys to memorize Buddhist texts.[6] Rote memorization is the usual teaching method throughout Asia, including in democratic Thailand and Japan, although this is beginning to change. But in Burma the effect is perhaps more damaging, because it reinforces submission to all authority, a message students are getting in virtually every dimension of their lives.

U Kyaw Moe, who now lives abroad, said: 'It is very hard for westerners to understand, but in Burma, there is no retort to elders or teachers. They must obey everything in front of the teacher or their parents.' Even if the teacher makes a mistake, the student has no right to correct the teacher. While students may grumble behind their elders' backs, they do not learn how to make logical arguments or how to understand the complicated nature of many issues for which there is no single right answer.

U Kyaw Moe thought that, in theory, the Educational Ministry could shift to a more open teaching style, because some Burmese educators have been abroad to study other educational techniques. But he said it was not in the regime's interest. If students and teachers are permitted to discuss issues freely, the students will be far less likely to accept the regime's propaganda.

Buying Good Grades

Corruption has been another factor which has lessened the value of the in-school educational experience. For the past twenty years, teachers' salaries have been so low that they have had to look for supplemental sources of income to make ends meet. Some run small businesses, such as selling snacks to students, but many survive by offering private tuition. They do not teach the full lessons during regular school hours so students must attend the extra classes after school. Although this is illegal, the authorities generally turn a blind eye, because they understand that the teachers cannot survive otherwise. In other cases, school authorities sell goods at inflated prices to students during school hours, which students often feel obliged to buy.

In 1995, a twelve-year-old student described such a situation in a letter to his aunt who lived outside the country. His headmaster, U Ba Pe, was trying to make some quick money before retiring. Nwe Nwe, his sister, could not resist the pressure, although the letter-writer, Moe Aung, did.

> Dear Auntie,
>
> How are you? I am praying that you are well. This evening I feel like writing, so I'm writing you ...
>
> U Ba Pe is not good. He is forcing students to buy calendars worth about 20 kyat for 45 kyat. Nwe Nwe is scared of her teacher so she bought one. But I didn't buy it because it is not worth it. My class teacher loves me, so he didn't say anything about my not buying one.
>
> They are also selling shoulder bags at inflated prices. They take a profit of about 75 kyat per bag. There are 5,000 total. The teachers had to go sell the bags in Rangoon. It's pitiful, isn't it. The truth is that the teachers have a duty to make the students excel in their education and to improve their morality. They are being ordered to do things which have nothing to do with teaching activities.
>
> I can't say that U Ba Pe is a bad person. He is about to retire, so it's his last chance to take advantage of his position. He'll easily get at least 300,000 kyat.
>
> I'm going to go to sleep. Good-bye.
>
> Moe Aung

Another way for high school teachers to make money is on the grading of the matriculation exam, the defining moment in a student's life. Entrance to college is decided solely by a student's score in the exam. In many instances, matriculation exams are marked up for students whose parents have given large cash donations to the teachers responsible for doing the marking. One former tutor who checked exams told of the examiners putting blue ink fillers into red pens so that they could change the answers on certain students' exam papers. Then they would use another red pen to mark the score.

Big money can also be made by selling the exam questions in advance. The result is not only the degradation of the education system, but also the introduction of greater inequalities in opportunities for further education. Poorer students are much less likely to make it into the universities, because they can afford neither all the private tuition classes nor the bribes for higher scores.

Since 1991, the same has been true at the university level. Many lecturers do their real teaching in private tuition classes and sell their exam questions for large sums of money. Even medical students must attend tuition classes. As one university professor in the mid-1990s explained: 'My salary was 1,250 kyat [about $4 in the late 1990s] but the monthly fee for the car that took my daughters to and from school was one thousand. So university professors teach poorly in class, so the students must go to their private tuition classes.'

Many university students come from elite families and can afford tutoring charges and bribes to get their exam scores raised, but others cannot. Taking a cynical view, student activist Moe Thee Zun explained how he and his friends tried to equalize the differences in the mid-1980s. They encouraged poor students to copy during the examinations.

In the 1990s, university lecturers were reportedly being encouraged to put easy questions on the exams and even sometimes overlook copying in order to appease students whose frustrations with the educational system and economic problems could otherwise be channelled into political protests.[7] Needless to say, the idea of actually learning something in the classroom has been largely lost in all of this.

University Life

Under successive military regimes, the primary focus in the development of the university system has been the containment of student activism rather than the improvement of the quality of education. The demonstrations that sparked the nationwide protests in 1988 originated on university campuses in Rangoon, where students from different universities could easily link up and mobilize the local population. Since 1988, the military regime has tried to prevent this from happening again by moving students from campuses in central Rangoon to sparsely populated areas outside the city and by expanding the number of regional colleges.

The expansion of regional colleges is theoretically positive in that it should mean wider access to higher education and lower costs, because more students could live at home while attending classes. The problem is that the regional colleges tend to be so under-funded and under-equipped that the quality of education is greatly inferior to what is available for students in Rangoon.

The regime also encourages students to enroll in distance education programmes, in which they come to the campus only once or twice a week. This is convenient for students who need to work to support themselves, and, because the distance education classes continued during the university closures, many students shifted to this programme. However, the quality of education is not as high as the regular courses. From the regime's perspective, though, there is a benefit. The students in distance education do not have much of an opportunity to develop friendships and associations that could lead them into political activity.

Even those students who study full-time on campuses in Rangoon generally get little out of the formal teaching. Students have to spend time in political ideology courses, and university curriculums must be approved by military censors, limiting the fields of inquiry, particularly in the humanities and social sciences. Moreover, many of the best teachers have gone abroad, where they can earn a decent income and teach more freely.

Since 1964, students have been assigned their courses according to the scores on their matriculation exams, regardless of whether or not they have any interest in the subject. The regime decides how many students should enter each subject, but despite the fact that there are almost no jobs in certain fields, students continue to be assigned to subjects like physics and zoology. As a result, many families feel that a university education is useless unless their children are accepted into courses which guarantee jobs, such as medicine, engineering or international relations.[8]

As in primary and secondary school, education in the university is also based on repetition rather than developing analytical skills. A university graduate explained: 'Even at the university level it is just rote memorization. You either get the information from the textbook or go to class and get it from the teacher, but there is no need to go to class.' In his four years at Rangoon University, he never once went into the library. Even those who do visit the library are not allowed to take out books unrelated to their subject.

Students who try to be conscientious about their studies often find it pointless. Aung Zin, a medical student, talked about his experience in preventative and social medicine the mid-1980s. The class had to carry out health education programmes in nearby communities, and Aung Zin was sent to Mingaladon village, near the airport. He was expected to take care of three or four households, giving health education and treating minor illnesses. The idea was that after recommendations had been made, particularly about diet and sanitation, the families' health would improve. The students were expected to make follow-up visits to ensure this happened, but Aung Zin says he was the only one in the class who actually visited the villagers again. Everyone else made up their reports.

Aung Zin wanted to help the families. He found that in one of his assigned houses, the ventilation was poor, the latrine was not very clean, and there were two TB patients. He suggested that the TB patients get treatment at a hospital or clinic, but they said they were poor and could not afford the six-month treatment. Even if they went to the public hospital, they would have to pay for all the medicine themselves. Since Aung Zin was given no medicine by his department, he could do little for them. Soon he realized that his visits were making the family feel embarrassed and uncomfortable. According to Burmese tradition, when a visitor comes, the host must offer some coffee, tea or snacks. Since the family had little money, they could not afford to give Aung Zin anything, and they also couldn't show him any improvement because they could not pay for treatment. 'Later,' Aung Zin said, 'I gave up and made up reports like everyone else.'

Rather than preparing for classes, professors and lecturers must spend a good chunk of their time patrolling the campuses for students engaging in political activities. When universities were open in the mid-1990s, most professors had to patrol three times a week, and on anniversary days of political events (i.e. 7 July, 13 March), professors were compelled to skip their classes if they conflicted with their patrol duty.

One woman who taught at Rangoon University in the mid-1990s explained how each professor had to take responsibility for the behaviour of several assigned students. Because the authorities practised a policy of 'guilt by association', meaning professors could be blamed for the political activities of their students, she told her students to stay out of politics. 'If you get involved,' she told them, 'we'll both be in trouble.' She said she didn't feel good about saying this, because as an educator, her real duty was supposed to be teaching, not policing. But the authorities hoped to take advantage of the students' respect for their teachers to keep them in line. Nevertheless, this professor and many of her friends refused to follow through on the regulation that their assigned students sign in at their offices every morning. She gave the students the sign-in sheets and told them to handle it by themselves.

The extent of the authorities' nervousness is apparent in another example. A university professor in Rangoon who had to teach English to a class of several hundred students in the early 1990s was ordered to hold on to the microphone at all times, even when writing on the chalk board. The authorities were concerned that a student might jump on stage and use the microphone to make a political speech.

Control is the primary concern for the military regime. Without a current student or staff identification card, it is impossible to enter most university campuses. The campus is like a fort, with locked gates and guards at the entrances. This means that students who have graduated cannot come back and visit on campus, nor can the general public use the universities' facilities. The main reason is to prevent alumni and other activists from stirring up the students. Surveillance is carried out by military intelligence agents and informers, with student activists claiming they often take the guise of gardeners, cleaners and other university employees.

Over the years, successive military regimes have not hesitated to close down the universities for extended periods whenever political unrest broke out. Between 1962 and 1999, universities have been shut down thirteen times, from periods of a month up to more than three years.[9] Between 1988 and 2000, the universities were closed more than they were open. Classes were cancelled from June 1988 to May 1991, from December 1991 to May 1992, and from December 1996 to July 2000. Besides the military institutes, only some of the masters' degree programmes in Rangoon and the smaller technical colleges, generally located far from Rangoon, have continued classes. The medical institutes reopened in February 1999.

When the main universities were reopened after a three-year closure from 1988 to 1991, one-year courses were shortened to four months in order to get the students out as quickly as possible. Although the regime understands that the country will not be competitive without an educated workforce, its first priority is to prevent anti-government demonstrations from erupting. For that reason, some student activists argue, drug and alcohol use on campus was widely tolerated. Alcoholic and drugged students have little interest in politics. While students engaged in even minor anti-government activities are quickly ferreted out, some students I interviewed complained that heroin was being sold out of dormitory rooms on campus.

In the meantime, the regime worked to upgrade the educational qualifications of its own people. After 1988, the military established separate military medical and technology institutes which never shut down. In the future it is likely that those who attend military institutes or the four-year Defence Services Academy will be far better educated than ordinary civilians. Most students in these institutes come from military and civil servants' families, and all must have 'clear' backgrounds, meaning no history of anti-government activism in the family.

The military has also sent a few individuals abroad for higher studies, with the understanding that they would come back and work for the regime. For instance, trusted lecturers from the History Department were sent out in the mid-1980s to study international relations curriculums and to draw up a new curriculum to train future foreign affairs staff. According to an international relations graduate, this came about after General Ne Win travelled abroad and realized that the quality of his foreign affairs staff was far inferior to that of other countries. In the 1990s, the military intelligence also sent a student abroad for graduate studies in political science. This in itself is a good indicator of the long-term investment the regime is making in order to maintain leadership.

As noted earlier, in the BSPP period, government leaders often talked about *lu gaung, lu daw*, meaning a good, or loyal, person is better than a clever one. At that time, members of the military generally had low levels of education. Today, however, the military is seeking to raise the educational achievements of its own members while holding the civilian population's education hostage to political quiescence. With more resources going to the military institutes, the regime is in effect creating a two-tier system where the best quality education is available only to those who work for the military.

Study Groups and Floating Books

Unable to rework the existing education system, some students have taken their educations into their own hands. Students have sought out private tutors and created secret study groups as they have searched for an understanding of what is wrong with their country and how to go about changing it.

The idea of developing an alternative education in Burma has its roots in the colonial period. During the 1920 student strike against the Rangoon University Act, older students tutored younger students at the strike centres, and this led to the formation of National Schools, where the primary language of instruction was Burmese rather than English, and Burmese subjects were emphasized. Later, the young Aung San and other friends set up a communist study group to read political literature and make plans about how to achieve independence. Many other students and intellectuals in the colonial period also looked to foreign literature for clues as to how to overthrow colonial rule. Since General Ne Win's takeover in 1962, a small number of students have turned to private libraries, study groups and private teachers in order to study political developments in other countries and to learn more about resistance movements in Burma's past.

In the BSPP period, a number of anti-government intellectuals who were not allowed to work in the government school system, or chose not to, became full-time private tuition teachers. From time to time, they selected students who demonstrated intelligence and an interest in politics and tried to develop both their understanding of politics and history and their sense of responsibility to the community. Often their training included physical exercise, to develop discipline, or social work, to promote altruism.

Mi Mi, a plucky female student who walked out alone to argue with the authorities during a tense student demonstration in the late 1990s, had studied with such a private teacher when the universities were still closed between

1988 and 1991. Her teacher had been a student activist in 1974, and he believed in the importance of discipline as well as intellectual rigour. Mi Mi and his other students had to go for morning runs at four o'clock, with lessons beginning at nine. They spent the whole day reading and listening to his lectures about the history of Burma.

Htun Htun, a reflective young man, studied from another charismatic dissident in the early 1980s. A former communist, the tutor invited interested high-school-age students to his house where he would lend them leftist-inspired novels and books on history and social analysis. Htun Htun started visiting the teacher when he was about fifteen and often spent the whole day there, cooking, eating and talking with his teacher and other students. The teacher sought to correct the students' understanding of their country's past as they had learned it in their school textbooks. He talked often about the independence struggle, emphasizing that it was not just the army, as the textbooks would have everyone believe, which had made independence possible. Political organizations and ordinary civilians had also played essential roles. By portraying the people as essentially passive, the regime was trying to make people believe that it was natural that the army should lead and the people should follow.

The tutor also insisted that his students spend a significant amount of their time doing social work, especially at the local monastery. Every holy day, his students were expected to circle the town with gongs, alms bowls and a Buddha image collecting contributions for the monastery. Although the authorities knew this teacher was a dissident, he was also well respected in the community for his promotion of religious and social welfare activities.

After Htun Htun was arrested briefly in March 1988, he said, 'My teacher was so happy I was arrested that he was jumping up and down.' Htun Htun explained: 'Teachers want their students to become activists.' And indeed many students who have undergone such self-initiated educational programmes do. Htun Htun has continued to work for the democracy movement, although he had to move to the Thai–Burma border to escape long-term imprisonment. Meanwhile, during the 1988 pro-democracy uprising and the election campaign, Htun Htun's teacher became so involved that he sold virtually all his possessions to support the movement. Later he ended up in prison, leaving his family penniless.

Forming student-led study groups is another way inquisitive high school and university students have sought to expand their knowledge and challenge their intellects. While ordinary Burmese readers find pleasure in romance novels and thrillers, politically inspired students seek out the literature of oppression and resistance, political theory and the biographies of freedom-fighters such as Nelson Mandela.

Some intellectuals have private libraries in their homes which are the sources of books for young readers. Moe Thee Zun, the 1988 activist, began his political education in the personal library of a committed BSPP member. This man's library consisted mostly of BSPP books on history, economics and ideology, but it was there that Moe Thee Zun developed a passion for reading. When he was in junior high school, he began visiting another house in his neighbourhood where a Rangoon University lecturer lived. During school holidays, Moe Thee Zun would spend the entire day reading at her house. On the weekends, many people visited this house, including former political prisoners, teachers and song-writers. As the adults sat together discussing books and politics, Moe Thee Zun would quietly listen.

Soon, he and his friend, who took the name Min Ko Naing in 1988, began penning poems and short stories at their school. Teachers asked them to write things for the school's wall magazines and literature room, and they both produced short pieces and collected other students' articles and poems. Moe Thee Zun remembers: 'These were only about social issues, love stories, childish ideas maybe, but at that time we thought of ourselves as very mature.'

Around 1980, Moe Thee Zun formed a study group with some older students, and he began leading a Tuesday and Saturday literature discussion in his ward. 'The group's purpose,' he said, 'was to use literature to educate people about the political situation and motivate them to consider taking action.' The study groups provided students with an opportunity to question and discuss rather than merely listen and repeat. Much of what they read were the translations of great works by Tolstoy, Chekhov, Dostoyevsky, Camus, Sartre, Hemingway and Steinbeck. Because it was difficult to find these books, they took turns reading them. They also tried to obtain copies of *Time* and *Newsweek*, assigning one person to obtain back issues from the embassies. One member of the group would translate the articles into Burmese because most members were not fluent in English.

In 1986, the literature discussion groups expanded to several towns, and they were able to collect a number of books. The way the system worked was that no one could own a book permanently. Once a person had read it, he or she would write a short comment and the name of his or her home town in the back and pass it on to another member. In this way, books travelled all over Burma. Sometimes a book would return to the original owner six months or a year later. Moe Thee Zun remembers the excitement he felt when one of the books he had sent off months before was returned to him. 'My book was running through Burma,' he said, 'floating through our network.' For those who had developed political ideas, knowing they had similarly-minded peers in other parts of the country was very important. They often felt isolated among their own school-mates, most of whom thought it pointless to question military control.

Moreover, most parents did not want their children to become politicized, and teenagers who did begin independent political studies usually had to hide their activities from their parents. Aung Zin, for instance, had been a model high school student who had written award-winning essays extolling the virtues of BSPP rule. His parents were thrilled when he was accepted at medical school and expected him to join the civil service as a doctor. Once at the university, however, his interests changed. Rather than read his textbooks, he set himself a goal of reading one hundred key books in political science, literature and philosophy within a year. He did not inform his parents about how he was spending his time but, as a result of his reading, his ideas about his country's political situation shifted dramatically. He participated in the 1988 student demonstrations, escaped to the Thai–Burma border, and has held a high position in one of the pro-democracy groups based there ever since.

Teashops and Bathrooms

Despite successive regimes' attempts to keep politics out of the classroom, daring students find ways to carry out underground political education activities in their schools and universities. Those who have studied politics on their own attempt to disseminate information to others in order to motivate them to participate in any anti-government activities that might take place. Secret student groups write and distribute magazines on university campuses, with the goal of inspiring other students to recognize injustice. Such magazines contain fiction, poetry and other articles which have not been censored, and circulate among interested students.

Ethnic minority groups also organize government-recognized literature and culture committees on campus which produce annual magazines and calendars. While some members of these groups are interested only in social and cultural activities, the committees are also key recruiting grounds for ethnic minority political activists. Several ethnic minority university students who joined armed ethnic nationalist groups after the 1988 demonstrations had been active in university literature and culture committees, where they had become increasingly frustrated with the regime's restrictions on the teaching of their languages and histories.

Teashops on and near university campuses are favourite gathering places for students, whether to discuss romance or politics. Many students arrive at their universities knowing little or nothing about the anti-government protests that took place in Rangoon. More politically-aware students take it upon themselves to educate less aware friends through their discussions in teashops and dormitory rooms.

Min Zaw, the university student whose mother made him become a monk in 1988, told me that for two years he never went to the classroom. 'My classroom was the teashop,' he said. 'We read poems and talked about what we should do, because at that time, we were all upset with the government.'

Bathrooms have also been the site of alternative education and even of minor political action. Many former students talked about learning of the destruction of the student union building in 1962 from pamphlets posted in the university bathroom stalls. Such pamphlets have also called for students to mark the anniversary each July by wearing black, which a varying number of students continue to do each year.

Bathrooms were a much-used site for political activity in schools in 1988, because they afforded anonymity to those who wanted to promote political messages. When the universities were closed in March and then again in late June 1988, high schools and primary schools remained open. University students encouraged high school students to organize their class-mates and many eagerly did so. Teachers found it increasingly difficult to teach as schools buzzed with furtive political activities.

One former student remembers that during the weeks before the nation-wide demonstrations in August 1988, the bathroom at his school was full of political posters and cartoons. At lunchtime, he recalls, the teachers would be waiting at the entrance to the bathrooms, but they hesitated to go in, because everyone inside was shouting. Locking themselves in the stalls, where no one could see them, the boys shouted slogans to their class-mates outside. Those students who really had to use the toilets were out of luck.

Teachers warned their students to stop their political activities, but most did not record the perpetrators' names as they were ordered to. According to several high school student organizers, teachers were often torn between support for what the students were doing and fear that they would get fired if they allowed the students to continue. One school student in Rangoon who often wrote political slogans on the blackboard before the teacher arrived said his teacher begged her class not to do such things. She told her students, 'You should pity me. I'll lose my job.' But he said that when he went to his teachers privately to ask for money for the movement, many contributed.

A high school student from a town near Mandalay recalled that his female teachers sympathized with the protesting students but cried and said, 'Please stay quietly. You are very young and even though you are so smart, democracy will not come soon.' However, some teachers did eventually become involved in the pro-democracy demonstrations. Even just seeing their teachers clapping in support of student speeches led some more cautious students to join in.

Another way that young activists in Rangoon tried to educate students in the early 1990s was by handing out pamphlets to students on their way to school in the morning. However, students caught with pamphlets were some-times arrested and severely interrogated until they revealed who had given them the pamphlets. Student activist Lin Htet and his colleagues devised a method of protecting both the distributors and the recipients. Folding five pamphlets very tightly together, they stapled an instruction sheet on top saying: You can pass this on, you can use these slogans for demonstrations at your school, or you can stick this on a wall.

The activists then made maps with all the school locations and the main routes people walked to each one. On the prescribed day, the activists would fan out in groups of two and walk towards the students who were coming to school. The university students would hand packets to the school students, telling them to give the packet to another class-mate. The recipient would look for a name on the top, see the instructions and then start opening it, but because of the tight packaging, by the time it was open, the distributor would be gone. The recipient would not have had time to notice the distributor's face, so even if the recipient were arrested, he or she would not be severely punished, because the package had been unwittingly received.

'But then,' Lin Htet said, 'the SLORC announced a new regulation that it was illegal to receive notes on the way to school. So the activists had to adapt. They used pretty university girls to do the distribution. The high school guys couldn't resist.'

Male students sometimes had the opposite problem when giving pamphlets to female students. One male activist remembered: 'The female students were very shy and afraid it was a love letter.' Many boys in Burma declare their love by putting a letter in a girl's book-bag on her way home from school, so the activists had to reassure the girls that they weren't giving them love letters but pamphlets which they could read and pass on to friends.

Other techniques which students used to distribute pamphlets included leaving a stack on top of a bus, so that when it pulled out, the pamphlets would scatter in all directions and could be picked up by curious bystanders. Lin Htet and his friends also relied on what they called the 'Shelley method', named after the Romantic poet, Percy Bysshe Shelley. In the early 1800s, Shelley sent out pamphlets promoting atheism to academics and clerics around Oxford. Burmese students in Rangoon also sent pamphlets by post, selecting addresses from the telephone book, which Lin Htet referred to as 'the activist's best friend'. Sometimes the military intelligence, who read the mail selectively, caught the pamphlets, but the students tried to ensure that at least some got through by using several different kinds of envelopes.

Lin Htet told how in 1995, a group of students translated an article from *Reader's Digest* and put it into one of the university magazines. The story was about four political prisoners and it included addresses to write to in order to demand their release. Lin Htet said that his group of student activists decided to do something similar. 'We made pamphlets with questions about student issues: "Are you satisfied with the education system? Do you want to change it? Check the boxes 'yes' or 'no' and send it back to this address." This was for more active participation than just reading a pamphlet. They needed to act a bit. It got a good response, so then we adapted it to the NLD. We sent out another questionnaire saying, "If you still support the NLD, check this box and send it to BBC, VOA, and the NLD."'

Before 1988, most pamphlets and political literature were 'printed' individually, using a fluorescent tube. The original was set face up in a wooden tray with a blank piece of paper over it. Then the tube was rolled across the paper and the copy removed. Each copy had to be done separately. The originals were either written by hand or typed. Since 1988, some activists have had access to computers, printers and Xerox machines, although ordinary copy-shops do not dare to make copies of anti-government literature. Faxing is also extremely difficult, because it is illegal to use a fax machine not registered with the government, and fax transmissions can be monitored by the military intelligence's surveillance equipment.

The students' political discussions at teashops and the writing and distribution of pamphlets may seem like trivial activities in the face of a determined military regime, but because of the key role that students have played in political movements in the past, the authorities treat those distributing even the most rudimentary political literature harshly. The generals understand that if people do not have concrete ideas about how to change Burma and are lacking leaders and organizations to spearhead a movement, they will remain quiescent. However, if a group of committed individuals can develop a vocabulary to describe the country's problems, propose alternatives and organize themselves into effective networks, they may be able to mobilize the general population. Many of the student leaders in the 1988 demonstrations had previously been members of study groups or had worked with private tutors from dissident backgrounds, and some had been involved in writing and distributing political literature before the demonstrations broke out.

Thus, it is perhaps not surprising that students describe the distribution of political manifestos as more dangerous than carrying heroin. As one student explained, you only need to distribute a package of heroin once and you will obtain a large sum of money. If you are arrested, you still have a chance to bribe your way out, and even if you can't, the sentence is not long. But for pamphlets, you not only do not receive any money but you usually have to use your own money for transportation and production costs. You have to distribute pamphlets many times to have any effect, and, if you are arrested, you will be sentenced for several years, with no chance of bribing your way out.

Although many students do not directly involve themselves in political activities, they are sometimes willing to help out their activist friends. Ma Aye Aye, who was a high school student activist in the 1990s, explained: 'I have some friends who are interested in politics but they are not permitted to get involved by their parents. And some of them are totally uninterested in it. But they helped my work for the sake of friendship.' For instance, when she asked them to join her in wearing the *pinni*, a traditional cotton jacket regularly worn by NLD members, on National Day, they did so. When she wanted to stick anti-government stickers on a wall at school, her friends would help by watching to see if there were any teachers nearby. When she needed money for political activities, and tried to raise funds by selling fun-fair tickets, her friends would buy as many tickets as they could afford. 'And in later years,' she said, 'when the situation was worse and it was unsafe for me to handle pamphlets, I could hide them at the houses of friends who had never been involved in politics.'

Particularly when the democracy movement seems to have little hope of succeeding, high school students, like everyone else, have appeared apathetic. Ma Aye Aye said: 'Some high school students are only interested in gaining good marks in the SPDC's exam-oriented education system. Some are lured by cigarettes and alcohol and spoiled while still young.' Needless to say, the activist student is a rare breed, but when protests break out, other students often join in, whether out of loyalty to friends or a desire to participate in making history.

Radio and Other Educational Sources

Few people besides students and intellectuals read political books or magazines. However, a much broader audience tunes into Burmese radio broadcasts from foreign-based stations. Listening to the British Broadcasting Corporation (BBC) and the Voice of America (VOA) became particularly popular during 1988, when the foreign stations gave full accounts of the demonstrations and killings. In the 1990s, two new stations attracted attention: the Democratic Voice of Burma (DVB), set up by pro-democracy activists in Norway, and the Burmese section of Radio Free Asia (RFA), based in the United States. Both focus almost exclusively on political, economic and educational issues in Burma.

In the mornings and evenings, people of various backgrounds can be found at home hovering near the radio listening to the broadcasts of at least one of these stations. Through the radio, Burmese have found out about the successful political transition in South Africa, the collapse of Indonesian dictator Suharto's regime, and East Timor's determined struggle for independence. Many Burmese recognize that other countries are progressing while they are falling farther and farther behind. While Burmese cherish their cultural and religious traditions, they are distressed by their inability to enjoy the political and economic freedoms that so many people in the world now take for granted. Tourists may be delighted by Burma's quaintness and slower pace of life, but when Burmese travel abroad, even as migrant workers to border areas in neighbouring countries, they become painfully aware of how far Burma lags behind other countries. Many long for even the most basic services such as piped water systems, regular electricity and reasonably well-equipped schools and hospitals.

The radio opens a window to the wider world, and provides hard-to-get news about what is really happening in their own country and what kinds of policies foreign governments are developing with relation to Burma. For instance, city-dwellers can find out about the effect of the Tatmadaw's military campaigns on ethnic minority villagers in remote areas, and they can hear the speeches of ethnic minority political leaders based along Burma's borders. They can listen to excerpts from Daw Aung San Suu Kyi's addresses to international forums, and they can become informed about actions taken by international organizations such as the United Nations to promote a resolution of Burma's political crisis. Likewise, the ethnic minority language broadcasts of the Democratic Voice of Burma have provided news, techniques of non-violent resistance and cultural programmes to people who are not fluent in Burmese. The ethnic nationalities appreciate these broadcasts, because their languages are never spoken on the state-controlled radio stations.

Radio broadcasts have also been linked to political actions. The most dramatic example was the BBC's broadcast of an interview with a student in July 1988. The student announced that student activists were calling for a nationwide strike on 8/8/88, and the radio broadcast served as the primary vehicle for spreading the message.[10] As a result, tens of thousands of people came out on the streets throughout the country. Ten years later, in 1998, students in exile broadcast plans for a 'yellow campaign' inside Burma. People who backed Daw Aung San Suu Kyi and her call for convening the Parliament elected in 1990 were requested to wear yellow clothing. The news spread from radio listeners to others by word of mouth and, on the appointed days, vendors in many markets arrived at their stalls clad in yellow blouses or yellow *longyis*. People who wanted to show their support but did not dare wear yellow outfits, sported yellow clips in their hair or a yellow pen in their shirt pockets.

Foreign radio broadcasts have provided the most accessible means to obtaining non-regime perspectives on politics and society, but the military has done all it can to discourage listening. In the 1990s, soldiers were forbidden to listen to foreign broadcasts, and civilians caught tuning in have been threatened with prison sentences.[11] In December 1999, a seventy-year-old tea-shop owner in Kachin State was sentenced to two years' imprisonment for having his radio tuned to a Voice of America broadcast.[12] Thus, some people are reluctant to listen to foreign broadcasts, and those who do listen tend to do so in the privacy of their own homes, with the volume low and their doors and windows shut.

The regime's most effective tool against those who would listen to radio broadcasts seems to be the threat of arrest. However, it has occasionally jammed radio broadcasts, including those of the BBC, and it maintains some leverage over Burmese broadcasters abroad who still hold Burmese passports and hope to make visits back to Burma.[13] Nevertheless, listenership tends to wax and wane according to political conditions within the country. Whenever there are anti-government protests or increased activity by Daw Aung San Suu Kyi and the National League for Democracy, more people tune in. When the regime seems fully in control and political change but a dream, fewer people bother to listen.

As we shall see in the next chapter, many Burmese film-makers, writers, musicians and artists have also tried to open the eyes of their fellow citizens. Other avenues for expanding knowledge through foreign media include the Asia editions of *Time* and *Newsweek* magazines, which are allowed in the country, although any articles relating to Burma or the trials of former dictators in other Asian countries are ripped out. Satellite TVs, which feature CNN and BBC broadcasts, are also available to the rich and to employees working at hotels catering to foreigners.

While access to the internet has made it possible for Burmese activists outside the country to organize and share news about Burma, inside the country the internet is still largely off-limits. Only a few Burmese government officials, NGO members and businessmen with ties to the regime have even had access to e-mail, with periodic disruptions. Users are not allowed to download *The BurmaNet News* or any other sources of information that might be critical of the regime. In 1996, the regime issued a decree stating that anyone caught with an unauthorized modem could be sentenced to from seven to fifteen years in prison.[14]

The intellectually starved in Rangoon have turned to the United States Information Service and the British Council libraries in Rangoon. Books on international politics and democracy as well as on a wide range of subjects of general interest can be read there or borrowed. Both also have English-language learning materials, which students can use to improve their English, whether to apply for a job in an international company or to be able to read more widely, since so little is translated into Burmese. These libraries also sponsor talks and short courses and show occasional broadcasts of international news programmes. Those outside Rangoon have no access to such facilities. They must make do with radio broadcasts, floating books and their imaginations.

13. A Rangoon teashop, a favourite hangout for students and intelligence agents

14. Remnants of free expression: secondhand books on sale, Rangoon

15. Remembering the good old days, Mandalay

16. Karen villagers fleeing a Tatmadaw offensive and seeking refuge in Thailand, 1997

. . . .

CHAPTER 10

The Artistic Community: In the Dark, Every Cat is Black

'We have no true pleasure because we cannot share our thoughts.'
(A poet, Rangoon)

§ Artists, writers, poets, film-makers and musicians provide social commentary, express the deepest feelings of the people, and serve as creative forces
which can inspire and motivate. Since the mid-1960s, however, their ability to
communicate openly has been severely curtailed. During General Ne Win's
rule, they were primarily controlled by the censorship board, but, since 1988,
successive military regimes have used both the carrot and the stick, bestowing
on them awards and cell-phones while also threatening them with oblivion, to
keep them in line.

Censorship

As early as August 1962, the Revolutionary Council promulgated the
Printers' and Publishers' Registration Act, which said that all printers and
publishers must register with the Ministry of Information and provide copies
of every published book. Before a book could be distributed, the Press Scrutiny
Board had to OK it. In some cases entire books were banned and the whole
print-run had to be thrown away. Magazine publishers were frequently ordered
to delete certain paragraphs or even whole articles, so the publisher would
have to go through every single issue inking over the section or ripping out
the pertinent pages.[1] Magazine buyers would thus be aware of the hand of
the censors when their magazine suddenly skipped from page 25 to 28 or
when there was a black square over a section of text. In the late 1990s, the
regime decided to hide the work of the censors by requiring magazine editors
to rewrite sections that were deemed inadmissible, so that the readers would
never know that the magazine had tried to get across a more provocative
point.

The effect of these practices is that authors and editors are under severe
pressure to self-censor. Publishers don't want to risk financial loss by having

their books printed and then rejected. Likewise, magazine editors try to avoid being subjected to extra scrutiny and delays because of articles which push the limits. Thus printers and publishers prefer to work with writers who do not challenge the boundaries.

Maung Tha Ya is one writer who refused to compromise. After 1988 he wrote short stories which alluded to the killings of pro-democracy demonstrators. As a result, his work has been banned ever since.[2] Some writers give in and write only about non-controversial topics, some focus on doing translations instead, and some stop writing altogether. Still, there are writers who are committed to the idea that they should act as the moral conscience of the nation, and they try to convey their messages through the use of metaphors and symbols. As Anna Allott has described in *Inked Over, Ripped Out*, such writers are confronted with a dilemma: if their metaphors are too obvious, the censors will catch them; if they are too obscure, not only the censors, but also the readers will miss the point.[3] Sometimes the opposite happens, and readers impute meanings to the text that the author did not intend, or at least that s/he publicly denies.

Besides the censorship, all publications must include the regime's propaganda slogans on the first page. Under the SLORC and SPDC regimes, this meant the 'Three National Causes': namely, 'non-disintegration of the union, non-disintegration of national solidarity, and consolidation of sovereignty'. Thus, even when reading a book or magazine in their own homes, people feel the presence of the state intruding.

Like writers, film-makers are also subject to a thorough censorship process. First, a film-maker must submit approximately twenty pages detailing the storyline and scene descriptions to the censorship board. The board includes more than a dozen members from different departments, including forestry, agriculture, trade and military intelligence. If its members see anything they perceive as possibly anti-regime, they demand an explanation or simply stop the project. U Sein, a well-known film-maker in the 1980s, explained: 'If there was a scene with a tree on a mountain, for instance, they might interpret this as against the regime. They might be suspicious about why the tree was situated on top of the mountain.' In addition, the Forestry Department representative would be called on to check that the forest was going to be properly represented.

If the storyline is approved, the film-maker is issued permission to buy a certain amount of film. Because the film has to be imported, U Sein said, the regime rations its distribution to limit the amount of foreign exchange leaving the country. Thus, film-makers are typically only given 25,000–30,000 feet of film to produce a 10,000-foot feature film. Usually, film-makers shoot 100,000 feet or more for a feature film, but in Burma, film-makers have to make do with far less. Because they can shoot only two or at most three cuts of a scene, the quality of the films is often uneven. Film-makers are also hampered by poor equipment. U Sein recalled: 'Most of the cameras I used were older than me, and I was forty at the time.'

By the time a film-maker receives his film, as much as a year may have passed. U Sein said: 'At first, you feel very enthusiastic about your story, but after waiting a year, you lose the feeling, your mood is gone, and your ideas have changed. But you have to go through with it, or the financier will kill you.'

In the 1990s, many film-makers got around these restrictions by producing their films on videotape, which could be freely purchased. But no matter how the film has been made, before it can be released, it must be presented to the censorship board. This is usually the worst time for film-makers, because the censors can challenge the film on any number of grounds. Even if the film has no anti-government overtones, the censors may try to find fault with it in order to extract bribes from the producer. Censorship board jobs are coveted because gifts of whisky and cash are virtually guaranteed in return for agreeing to sign off on a film.

In addition, U Sein, like other film-makers, came under fire for criticisms he considered absurd. For instance, there was a rule that film-makers should promote traditional culture whenever possible in their films. U Sein agreed with this rule, so in one film he included a scene with a mother singing a nursery rhyme to her newborn baby. He placed toys around the room, including a traditional set of small puppets, comprised of two court officials, one prince, one princess, Zaw Gyi (a legendary wizard), and a horse. But the censors told him that the puppets represented *nats* (spirits) and had no place in the movie.

When U Sein protested to the army censor that he was merely trying to promote traditional culture, the censor told him to write a letter of appeal. However, the appeal was rejected because Zaw Gyi, the wizard, was among the puppets. Since the regime was a socialist one, wizards were not allowed. U Sein appealed again, pointing out that the Burmese national dance troupe routinely performed the Zaw Gyi dance around the world. He was told that the dance fell under the Culture Department while his film came under the Information Department, and their policies were not the same. Still, he was informed he could get a letter of recommendation from the Culture Department and resubmit his appeal. He did so, but this time, he was accused of expressing metaphorically that the regime was merely a set of puppets. After wasting six months on this, he gave up and cut the scene. In this case, the problem was that none of the censors wanted to risk trouble with their superiors and therefore no one dared to stand up for him. U Sein was known to hold anti-government views, so his work came under greater scrutiny than other less politicized film-makers, but still the unpredictability of the process was a burden on everyone.

In some cases, U Sein intentionally tried to create films which could be interpreted as imparting a political message. He made one film about two insurgents, one poor and one rich, who decide to stop fighting and go home. Before they can escape, the poor man is seriously injured. He survives only thanks to the ministrations of his friend. Later, the rich friend invites the poor man and his family to come and live in his compound. After paying for the poor man's son's education, he insists that the boy work for him in his sawmill. Although the boy has other plans, he and his parents feel that they owe it to the rich man to do as he asks. Then the rich man makes a much more serious request. He asks the boy to save his family's name by marrying a female relative who is pregnant out of wedlock. After much anguished discussion, the boy and his parents finally agree. However, some time after the wedding, the girl admits to her husband that the rich man raped her. When the rich man makes yet another outrageous demand, the boy and his family lose control and go after him. A bloodbath ensues, and everyone dies, except for the young woman's newborn baby.

Soon after the film reached the censorship board, the authorities called U Sein in and demanded to know whom each of the characters really represented. They told him they suspected the rich man symbolized the military, the poor man and his family stood for the people, and the baby represented the students. The military may have saved the country during the independence period, but the demands it was now making on the people were unacceptable and were causing unnecessary tragedy and suffering. U Sein admitted that the film could be interpreted in that way, but that it could also refer to the problems that arose when married couples or family members took advantage of debts of gratitude to make excessive demands.

Despite the fact that U Sein never mentioned the government in his film, he was almost arrested. In the end, he was allowed to distribute the film, but only after changing the title and the ending. In the revised conclusion, most of the characters are not killed, implying that the rich man's actions do not have widespread negative connotations.

Still, U Sein said, audiences easily grasped the real meaning of the film because they invariably related what they saw on the screen to their current suffering. Moreover, the scandal surrounding the film made it extremely popular, and elaborate descriptions of the real ending spread around the country. As U Sein recalled delightedly: 'The audiences had imaginations, so they participated in completing the film.'

In Burma, people grow up reading between the lines. This helps film-makers, writers and poets who cannot criticize the regime directly. At the same time, film-makers may not always intend a political message, but the audience naturally relates the film's content to the national mood. As U Sein put it: 'The government was the common villain, so you couldn't avoid it.'

U Sein saw himself as particularly unlucky in this regard. He explained: 'Burmese believe that the position of the planets when you are born influences your fate. I have been born into a situation where people can easily read my hidden meanings. Sometimes I only have one or two messages, but people interpret it ten ways of their own. The military intelligence overhear these interpretations in teashops, so it made it difficult for me.'

Film-makers also had to contend with censors who came to think of themselves as art critics. One of U Sein's films was about a psychopath who killed six people. The censors had no problem with the content but decided the film would be even more thrilling if the psychopath killed nine people. Ordered to add three killings, U Sein was even given more film, a rarity. U Sein felt that six killings was sufficient, but he had to do as they demanded. Commenting about the censors' intervention in his and others' work he said: 'They thought they had the right to decide this. These foolish things piled up, and we almost went crazy.'

From time to time, U Sein agreed to direct government propaganda films with storylines written by the regime. He said he didn't mind doing anti-drug and anti-smuggling films, and in return he was viewed with less suspicion by the authorities. Similarly, actors and actresses who agree to work in government propaganda films find their chances of winning Academy Awards vastly improved while those who decline are passed over. A well-known actor, Kyaw Thu, refused to participate in a propaganda film in 1993. In 1994, he did a film that received popular acclaim, and the film board wanted to give him the Academy Award. But, said a friend of his, the military interfered, so he didn't get it and neither did the film. Later, he agreed to make one film with the government. The following year he received the Academy Award, despite the fact that he reportedly felt his performance in the government film was inferior to his previous independent work.

Much of the talk in the artistic community revolves around determining what level of cooperation with the regime is acceptable. Mo Mo Myint Aung, a famous actress who has won five Academy Awards, is seen as having gone too far by many of her peers. Besides appearing in government films, she has written letters for the government newspapers declaring her support for soldiers on the frontlines. Each time a well-known person agrees to a higher level of cooperation with the regime, the community's unwritten standards of acceptable behaviour are challenged. Because the regime ties the opportunity to work and receive public recognition to outward displays of support for military rule, film-makers, writers and artists who seek to remain independent often find themselves isolated and marginalized.

The Power of Music

Like film-makers and writers, musicians also face dilemmas over where to draw the line between being able to work creatively and having to do the regime's bidding. Not only do they have to deal with the censors but, before 1990, they also had to include a certain number of 'constructive' songs on their recordings. In the 1970s and 1980s, finding places to perform and then having to dress and act conservatively were other difficulties for young singers trying to keep in step with the rock-and-roll craze that was spreading around the world.

Mun Awng, a Kachin singer from northern Burma, remembered when the Beatles became famous and 'guitar fever' spread through Burma. The government distrusted the free-spirited nature of such music, and in state-controlled newspapers, cartoonists represented bad characters as men sporting long hair, belts with peace symbols, and guitars in their laps. Mun Awng said the government called such musicians 'destroyers of tradition' and never gave them permission to perform in public venues.

Mun Awng and others resorted to playing their guitars outside girls' dormitories on university campuses. He often stayed up the whole night singing and playing music with friends, wooing female students at the same time. This custom developed out of the long tradition of village boys visiting girls' houses in the evening to chat, or walking back and forth near their houses singing or playing an instrument.

Mun Awng came from Myitkyina, the capital of Kachin State, where teenaged boys still spent their evenings milling around in front of girls' houses, hoping for their attention. He had grown up singing in the church and dreaming of Rangoon, where there were recording studios, theatres and famous songwriters. In those days, Myitkyina bordered on a war zone; the Kachin Independence Army and Tatmadaw troops frequently engaged in shootouts just outside town. Mun Awng and his family waited out the gun battles in the trench behind their kitchen.

Although Mun Awng viewed Rangoon as the best place to develop his talents, once he began attending university there, he realized that only the campuses (at night) afforded the freedom to sing what he wanted. In his final year in university, Mun Awng deliberately failed his exams so he could enjoy one last year of relative independence. But he had just recorded an album with some friends, and soon after a producer agreed to distribute it. The album was an instant hit, and Mun Awng's life as a professional musician began.

In front of the girls' dormitories, Mun Awng could sing whatever he wanted, but his recorded albums were subject to strict controls. One out of every four songs had to be *ah kyo byu thachin*, a 'constructive song'. Mun

Awng said coming up with such songs was a struggle for some bands who ended up exhorting their listeners to be careful of traffic. He and his group tried to create songs that fulfilled the requirement without being ridiculous or preachy, but the censorship of his other songs drove him crazy. He said: 'That's why I decided I didn't want to be a professional singer in Burma any longer. When you try to write something, you have to start thinking about the boundary first. It's not supposed to be like that.'

When the censors forced him to change his lyrics because they suspected a certain word had anti-government connotations, Mun Awng found it upsetting. He said: 'They don't care about the meaning of the song or the combination of the lyrics, sentence by sentence. They never consider how the artists or musicians or writers made their lines.'

One song that Mun Awng submitted to the censor board was called 'Beh lu si, lu si' or 'Line of Ogres'. The song explained that to make good music, first you have to tune the strings properly, and then you have to know the right frets and the right sound. Mun Awng remembered: 'The censors didn't like it, because they thought it meant the right person for the right job.' Mun Awng had to change most of the lyrics and record it according to the government-approved version. He said: 'Only people who could hear me singing in private could know the real lyrics.'

By 1988, Mun Awng had become famous and successful, but he was fed up with the restrictions. One day he told his producer that the next album he sang would not go through the censorship board. Mun Awng remembers: 'He looked at me like he thought I was sick.' But Mun Awng ended up doing what he said. His next album was recorded in Thailand.

When the demonstrations broke out on 8 August 1988, Mun Awng joined in. Then on the afternoon of 10 August, while he was taking a break from marching, he heard shooting and saw someone running, holding his head. Mun Awng realized the person was wounded and ran up to him. He recognized him as one of his room-mate's friends. Mun Awng said: 'He was shot in the back of his neck, and the bullet went through his cheek. We had to reach the hospital before the army reached the junction, so we had to run with that wounded person. But a lot of people helped, and the first car stopped for him.' At the hospital, Mun Awng saw many more people who had been shot by soldiers. He said that the experience changed his life. Once the military cracked down, he decided to head for the Thai border. After arriving in Karen territory, he was given a quick course in basic military training by the newly formed All Burma Students' Democratic Front and sent to a student battalion allied with the KNU.

Thrown into battle situations for which he was ill-prepared, he began to question what he was doing. He said: 'You know when I was a teenager, I said I didn't care if I died. But during the fighting, I realized, "Oh shit, I do care about dying."' Having to spend his days with a gun instead of a guitar also upset him. Finally, he said, he decided he should continue the struggle as a musician rather than as a soldier.

Convinced that the power of music could revive the spirits of democracy activists inside the country and along the border, he put together an album called *Battle for Peace*. Composed by writers inside Burma as well as by colleagues in the ABSDF, many of the songs memorialized the events of 1988. A few were marching songs for demonstrators. Others expressed hope for a new beginning.

Tapes of Mun Awng's new album were taken secretly into Burma and also played over Burmese-language radio stations broadcasting from abroad. People in Burma made their own copies of the tapes and passed them on to friends. Some of the songs became famous. Mun Awng talked about how he heard that in one town in Shan State a few of his friends would sit around at night and sing his songs on a street corner. And another friend told him that there was a group of students in Rangoon who would go to their favourite teashop late in the evening when only local people were around and play the tape there. Other students talked about how when they sang songs under girls' dormitory windows, some girls insisted that they would listen only if their suitors sang Mun Awng's songs.

The real proof of his impact came in December 1996 when student demonstrations broke out in Rangoon. As well-armed troops moved in on all the streets surrounding the junction where the students were gathered, the students kept up their spirits by singing the national anthem and three of Mun Awng's rallying songs. Those who didn't know the songs by heart read from lyric sheets that had been prepared and passed out by student activists. The English translation of one of the songs is as follows:

Peacock Messenger

Fly, fly, red fighting peacock
Fly up to the heavens.
Through the wild, dirty violent storm
Forever carrying the red flower of revolution
With immeasurable power in your wings.
We will march forward swiftly,
Towards the dawn,
To enter into a new era,
For we have faith in your strength.

Fly, fly, red fighting peacock
Fly up to the heavens.

Forever carrying the red flower of revolution

Our time has arrived, we'll establish a new system.
By the strength of the peacock,
We'll restore human rights
For the sake of our people.
To remake history, to surely change for the better,
The peacock messengers are flying in unison.

Mun Awng later saw a videotape of the demonstration, which had been made by a westerner who had been present. Watching a whole new generation of students empowered by his songs, he was amazed. 'It's incredible,' he said. 'I can't describe it. I think I was right.'

Other frustrated singers who are not as politically-minded as Mun Awng have also left the country. I met a Burmese rock band playing at a hotel in China. They explained that they had left because it was so difficult for them to make a living in Burma. If they wanted to play a concert, they would have to do it under a government banner such as the army or the government-affiliated Myanmar Maternal Child and Welfare Association. The concert promoter would have to pay the government organization first. Because it was not legal to perform in the nightclubs that had sprung up since 1988, performers had to hand over a share of the profits to the police or a local authority. Whenever there were any problems, the government would shut down the clubs, so their work was unstable. And few people had enough money to pay for nightclubs or concert tickets anyway.

Because instruments were so expensive and music lessons were beyond their budgets, they were unable to develop their skills inside the country. While rich kids could buy video lessons and even go abroad to study music, ordinary people had no access to such opportunities. In China, the lead singer of the Burmese rock band said, not only could they make money, but they felt much more free. Still, they hoped that one day they could go back. And when I asked them to play something for me, they chose 'Ah May Ein', 'Mother's Home', a song of nostalgia and longing.

Like Mun Awng, the military regime has realized the power of music to influence people, and in the mid-1990s has made more concerted efforts to use music to build support for the regime. An article in the *New Light of Myanmar* on 23 February 1998 announced:

The second group of thirty-four film stars and vocalists led by Captain Zaw Win Naing of the Ministry of Defence have left here by special Tatmadaw flight for Kengtung this morning to entertain Tatmadawmen building the Kengtung–Mongphyat–Tachilek road for ensuring secure and smooth transportation ... They were seen off at the Yangon [Rangoon] International Airport by Director of Public Relations and Psychological Warfare Colonel Khin Aung Myint and officials of the Directorate of Defence Services Intelligence.[4]

The regime has also persuaded famous singers to perform propaganda songs in return for special privileges. Sai Hti Hsaing, a Shan singer who entertained the 1988 pro-democracy demonstrators with progressive songs, now sings what the regime wishes and has been provided with a house and car in return. Idolized by teenagers, Zaw Win Htut long resisted singing propaganda songs but in 1994 he was banned from performing in public. Seeing his career disintegrating, he agreed to work with the regime in order to be able to perform again. The result was 'Maha', a song extolling the government and the vast lands it controls. Because of its catchy tune, 'Maha' became an instant hit. Zaw Win Htut lost the support of some of his more political fans, but even democracy supporters found themselves unconsciously humming along with his new song.

By encouraging or intimidating popular singers to work with them, the regime both improves its ability to reach a wider audience with its message and also discourages the discontented from taking action. When students see their favourite stars belting out propaganda songs, they lose confidence in their own abilities to resist the generals.

The regime no longer actively discourages rock-and-roll and heavy metal, although it still places restrictions on musicians' attire and forbids them from dancing on stage.[5] By claiming that it is safeguarding traditional Burmese culture against decadent western influences, the regime has garnered a certain amount of respect among the older generation. But among the younger generation, there is a strong desire to be current with international trends. They feel that the regime is holding them back, and that popular culture is yet another arena where the Burmese lag far behind the rest of the world.

In the mid-1990s, the junta realized that it must make some accommodation in order to try to win the support of the new generation. It now allows some modest forms of western dress on TV programmes, and in 1995, it started a new TV station, Myawaddy TV, featuring contemporary music videos and movies. Myawaddy TV does its own recording and editing, using the talent of local stars under the direction of military intelligence personnel. News is presented in brief sound-bites, interspersed with entertainment programmes. The point is to reach audiences who refuse to watch Myanmar TV, the other government channel, which broadcasts stern-looking government appointees reading out lengthy government news reports in a monotone, footage of army officers attending meetings and visiting monasteries, and marching songs. In fact, the quality of television programming is so bad that people watch mostly for the advertisements, considered the only creative moments on television.

Although the generals have claimed the moral high ground in affirming their commitment to traditional values, the pro-democracy movement in exile has tried to subvert the regime by using a traditional form of chanting, *thangyat*, to critique the military's policies. *Thangyat* are performed during the new year festivities in April, with new lyrics being set to standardized chant rhythms each year. Such songs provide a vehicle for the expression of popular dissatisfaction with government officials and abuses of authority and have been performed since the pre-colonial period. The military regime has forbidden independent performances of *thangyat* in the country, but students who fled to the Indian border after 1988 have produced annual tapes addressing the regime's policies on forced labour, tourism, narcotics, AIDS and other issues. The tapes have been surreptitiously sent into the country and frequently played over foreign-based Burmese-language radio broadcasts.[6]

'Mad' Art

Like films, music and literature, art can be used to agitate people, so the art world has been another arena for the battle between the military regime and independent thinkers. In 1988, art students played a key role in making banners, logos and designs for the pro-democracy demonstrations and the independent newspapers and magazines that sprang up. The military subsequently put an end to this by permanently closing the fine arts club at Rangoon University. None of the main universities offers courses in painting, so students interested in art must study at one of the two three-year art academies, neither of which requires passing a high school matriculation exam, at the University of Culture founded in the mid-1990s, or with private teachers.

Commercial art galleries can be found in Rangoon and Mandalay, but public exhibitions come under government scrutiny. Before exhibitions can even be announced, the organizer must submit a detailed written description of each of the paintings to the Information Ministry. Then, before the exhibition opens, the authorities come to do a final inspection. If any painting is considered anti-regime, it is not only taken down but the painting itself is also stamped 'censored'.

Under the BSPP, modern art was considered too subversive to be taught at the country's two art academies. The Culture Ministry instead urged the teachers and students to channel their creativity into forms of art which could be used to promote state-sponsored ideals. Sitt Nyein Aye, a student at the Mandalay Art Academy in the 1970s, remembered, 'The BSPP people came to the school and said, "Art for politics' sake, not art for art's sake".' The students were told that to explore abstract ideas in art was selfish. If the work couldn't be readily understood by farmers and workers (and, one supposes, the censors) it shouldn't be done.

When Sitt Nyein Aye saw examples of modern art for the first time at a book fair sponsored by the United States Information Service, he was stunned. He said, 'I was angry because I never knew about these before.' After looking at the books, he and another class-mate began secretly to study modern art with two artists outside the academy. They had to hide their work from the headmaster and many of the teachers and students who derided modern art as 'mad art'.

Still, his teachers were aware of his extracurricular activities. As a result, he said, he was denied the school's top prize despite his superior talent. Sitt Nyein Aye was crestfallen. The prize-winner was sent to Europe for further studies, something he could never afford on his own. Moreover, Sitt Nyein Aye had wanted to take the prize back to his family and the monks at his village monastery to show that their confidence in him had been justified.

Sitt Nyein Aye came from a small village of only sixty houses. There were no educated people in the village, and his young life was spent mostly in the monastery. The few students who wanted to continue their education beyond primary school had to move to town. Sitt Nyein Aye's parents were farmers with no extra money for education. He was able to attend high school only because of financial support from the monks at his village monastery. After graduating without the prize, Sitt Nyein Aye was too upset to go back home. Instead, he made a life for himself on the streets, sketching and selling his work to passers-by. Although poor and often hungry, Sitt Nyein Aye found pleasure in remaining true to his ideals. He said: 'I didn't do any commercial work at that time. I wanted to create. I lived only for this.'

In school, Sitt Nyein Aye had been hampered by his instructors' rigidity as well as by lack of supplies. 'Ten people had to share one water-colour cake,' he recalled. 'Oil paints were rationed out equally by colour in tiny amounts. You couldn't get more. Sometimes we needed a lot of black and only a little white, but we couldn't do anything.' When painting on the streets, there were no restrictions.

Once or twice a week, he would take his sketches to his teachers for their comments. At the time, they had no idea that he was homeless. They were happy to teach him because he was clearly so devoted to developing his abilities. And they instructed him not only in the skills of painting but also in the finer points of Buddhist philosophy. Encouraging him to deepen his thinking about all aspects of life, these teachers provided him with the kind of holistic education that informed traditional teaching relationships but was so lacking in the formal curriculum.

As his art developed, so did his political awareness. He wrote an article entitled 'In the Dark, Every Cat is Black', which attacked the regime for killing people's creativity and forcing them into the same mould. He said: 'They hate educated people, so they oppress all people who can rule or create or invent.' What saddened him and his teachers was that the regime made it so difficult for talented older artists to hand over their knowledge to the younger generation. Instead, artists felt that they had to hide their skills and their work.

Sitt Nyein Aye is an exception, and after a few years even he began to think about his responsibilities to his parents and siblings. He decided that he had to take up commercial work to earn a decent living. But his political leanings got the better of him. Asked to design a small calendar for junior college students, he included a sketch of the Rangoon University student union building, which had been blown up by the Ne Win regime in 1962. For that, he spent two months in custody.

After his release, he threw himself into apolitical work. Soon, his studio was inundated with orders. Previously, all signboards were done with coloured letters on a white background. But Sitt Nyein Aye revolutionized commercial art in Upper Burma by incorporating a wide variety of colours, textures and designs developed from his study of modern art. Even the authorities were drawn to his work. He designed a new badge for the military and did small projects for military intelligence personnel. Although he achieved success, Sitt Nyein Aye said he still wasn't happy. He claimed: 'I had the exact opposite problem as before. I had a lot of money, and a lot of materials, but no time to paint my own things. So I thought, "Success is like a prison".'

Still, he used the money he made to bring a measure of prosperity to his village. Besides donating money and clothes, he purchased goats and cows for villagers to raise. He also opened a small art course every summer, bringing children to Mandalay to study with him. By 1988, he was beginning to move away from his commercial business in order to focus again on more creative work. But then the demonstrations broke out, and he set up an independent newspaper under the auspices of an activist monks' association. The day after the coup, he fled with a group of students to the India border, where he has invested his talents in producing artwork for the resistance groups' offices and publications.

Since Sitt Nyein Aye left the country, Burmese artists' interest in contemporary forms of art has grown. But the fact that modern art by its nature takes a defiant attitude towards tradition and control makes it an obvious area of concern for the regime. And artists, because of their powerful ability to convey emotions and immortalize historical events in single images, have been subject to constant surveillance.

Public Talks

Still popular in Burma is the tradition of writers giving public talks, or *haw byo bwe*. Especially in the winter months when farmers have more free time, writers travel around the country visiting literary friends and speaking to the public. These events are much anticipated by rural audiences, who are eager to hear the writers' reflections on society and the issues of the day. The talks often contain implicit commentaries on the political situation, but they are also usually full of humour and word-plays, giving writers a chance to display their wit.

In the 1988–90 period, writers had an opportunity to speak more freely than they had been able to under the BSPP regime. A number of talks were organized throughout the country. At one such event in 1990, a well-known writer got the audience laughing when he gave examples of how he saw everything upside down.[7] After describing recent crashes of jumbo jets around the world in which hundreds of people had died, he insisted that other countries should follow Burma's example and only purchase small planes. Then when they crashed, only a few people would die.

He also recalled his response to a report in one of the government-controlled newspapers stating that the government's department of heavy industry had produced 300,000 spoons and forks. He asked, 'If the department of heavy industry produced 300,000 spoons and forks, what did the department of light industry produce?'

After the military's refusal to transfer power after the 1990 election, writers had had to rein themselves in again. Speaking permits were more difficult to get. The country's supply of paper at subsidized prices was tightly controlled, and there was no underground press to speak of, except for the occasional magazines produced by university students. Economic subjects could be written about somewhat more openly in some of the new magazines that emerged in the 1990s, but only in their informal get-togethers could writers continue to talk freely. Still today, groups of poets and writers meet weekly at certain teashops to discuss literature and current events, and some privately circulate more political poems and cartoons among their close colleagues.

Despite the sense of powerlessness many writers now feel, some have tried to infuse new ideas into society, even if the presentation is not great literature. In the BSPP period and even in the parliamentary era, social realism was the most prominent literary trend. Writers portrayed the hardships people were suffering, with the implication that only a different kind of government (often communist rather than democratic) could bring relief. While the writers captured people's emotions, few offered any concrete solutions. As one writer put it: 'If they had talked about what they wanted to do, they would have gotten into trouble.'

In the 1990s, a number of writers felt that they must do more for their readers. It is in this context that articles focusing on self-improvement took off in literary circles. Translations of American advice books such as *The Seven Habits of Highly Effective People* by Stephen R. Covey sold rapidly, while editors of serious journals featured 'overcome all odds' stories translated from *Reader's Digest*. One of the main proponents of this school of thought was a writer and public speaker named U Aung Thinn. He advocated focusing on individual development, setting goals and using willpower to achieve results.

Tapes of his motivational talks were extremely popular and sold well throughout the country.

Such ideas were criticized by more radical students who saw them as a move away from broader political objectives and towards personal, and often materialistic, ends. Indeed, because the goals to which the self-help proponents were dedicated were not explicitly political, the regime allowed them to speak fairly openly. From the standpoint of the regime, if these techniques are used to encourage people to further their personal careers as businessmen, for instance, all the better.

Some proponents of the self-actualization school have argued that the restoration of democracy in Burma requires the development of a democratic culture, and a democratic culture depends on the widespread cultivation of management techniques, reasoning skills and self-reliance. The regime, on the other hand, has promoted the idea that its leaders alone know what is best for society. Because the top authorities are sincerely working for the country, no one has the right to challenge their policies. This has led to a kind of numbness on the part of the general population. According to one writer who supports the self-actualization literature: 'We need to fight our passivity.' Many of the proponents of western motivational techniques hope that by following concrete steps, people will gain confidence in their ability to think and act. As one well-educated woman put it: 'Fear has deprived a lot of people of their reasoning power.'

Some social critics have tried to get around the censors and also encourage people to refine their analytical skills by presenting an ideal type, and then have the readers do the work of comparing conditions in Burma with the model presented in the article. For instance, they might write about the characteristics of a health care system that has worked well somewhere else. The readers must then contrast that system with the current system in Burma and consider what changes need to be made. Such an approach parallels the attempts of the National League for Democracy and other groups to educate people about what a just society ought to look like by applying traditional Buddhist criteria for good governance. Thus, intellectuals have looked both outside Burma and back into Burma's past for ideas and examples with which to reveal the weaknesses of the current regime.

Finally, while support for greater cultural openness can often be linked to a confrontational attitude towards military rule, advocating the preservation of traditional culture does not necessarily overlap with support for the regime. For instance, Daw Ahmar, a well-respected writer and dissident, is also a strong proponent of the maintenance of traditional Burmese culture. In a series of articles reproduced in a book entitled *Ah May Shay Sagaa*, she deplored the growing numbers of Burmese girls dressing in western skirts and pants and the replacement of polite salutations which denote status differences with casual western terms. She was upset to hear small children departing from guests' houses calling out a brief 'bye-bye' to the adults instead of using longer Burmese phrases which express gratitude and humility.[8] For many older Burmese, enjoying the beauty and richness of the Burmese language and culture provides one of the few simple pleasures in an otherwise difficult political and economic environment.

CHAPTER II

Religion and Magic: Disappearing Jewels and Poltergeists

'A monk cannot tell authorities about people's problems. If he does, the authorities will consider that monk to be their enemy.' (A monk, Mandalay)

§ While many Burmese seek solace and community through their spiritual practices, the regime also penetrates the religious sphere in many ways. The ruling generals are constantly demonstrating their own piety through lavish donations to monks and monasteries in a bid to shore up their moral authority. At the same time, the regime feels it must keep monks under surveillance, because the country's spiritual leaders are the main alternative voices of authority, and they have frequently intervened in the country's political crises. Because so many people in Burma are deeply religious, the use of religion for political ends can be effective in both positive and negative ways. The regime can bring people together in support of important Buddhist activities, but it can also take advantage of religious fervor to fan violence against practitioners of other religions.

Buddhism and Politics

The primary duties of Buddhist monks towards lay people are to instruct them in the philosophy and practice of Buddhism and to accept appropriate donations from them, so that lay people have a chance to make merit. Although frowned on by conservative monks, many monks also engage in fortune-telling, astrology and the giving of protective charms and incantations to lay people. They themselves may firmly believe in the efficacy of such practices, and they want to help their supporters, whose main concerns are with their daily lives rather than with seeking enlightenment.

At critical points in Burma's history, monks have felt compelled to venture further into the realm of worldly affairs and take up politics. In the early 1900s, monks played a leading role in organizing protests against the colonial government, particularly because they felt their religion had been insulted. In the decades since General Ne Win took over, the lay community has often looked to the monks for leadership in their struggle against unjust governance.

U Nandiya, a strict, middle-aged monk from Mandalay, put monks' participation in political affairs into a philosophical and historical perspective. He had become a novice monk when he was young and decided he liked monastic life, so he became ordained as a full monk at twenty and has been in the monastery ever since. In his opinion, everyone must accept the suffering that all humans face; namely, desire, sickness, ageing and death. But suffering from injustice is not natural and should be eradicated. He explained: 'If you have a headache and take aspirin, the headache will be reduced, but if you think this is your fate, then the headache isn't reduced. Also, everyone in Burma knows we need a good government and political system so that we can have a good life. So we must work for this. The Buddha never talked about fate, so we shouldn't get too confused with our fortunes. We should focus on work, knowledge, and effort.'

U Nandiya gave an example from the Buddha's life to reinforce his point. He said that during the Buddha's lifetime, the Buddha himself tried to solve social conflicts, such as a dispute over water distribution between Bihar and a neighbouring state. There are also plenty of examples from Burma's own past. 'During the Pagan dynasty,' he said, 'monks were also active for the people. King Narapatisithu [AD 1173–1210] forced people to build pagodas. He forced them to cut trees and bake bricks. So one of the Buddhist monks suggested to the king that he shouldn't force people to do this kind of work. But the king ignored him. The monk said, "I won't stay in this kind of kingdom, because you have no justice."'

According to U Nandiya, what contemporary Burmese monks hate most is the regime's forcible collection of money, including for religious purposes. Such donations should be purely voluntary, he said. The monks also disagree with the use of forced labour and feel unhappy that people's lives are made so difficult by all of the military government's demands. Thus, in 1988, the monks participated in the pro-democracy demonstrations. U Nandiya explained how the monks from his monastery joined with students from a branch college of Mandalay University. He said: 'The monks hid students and politicians in monasteries because they had enough food and places to sleep there, and the monks could protect them from arrest. And people are always coming and going for religious affairs, so it was a good cover for activists to meet with their contacts.'

In 1988, the monks took over the administration of Mandalay and many surrounding villages. People from outlying districts ventured into the city to ask the monks to come out and administer their areas until peace was restored. Several groups of monks did so. The monks also set up a rotation system to handle security and administrative duties in the various quarters of Mandalay.

In many cases, the monks became informal judges, solving people's disputes. Because the population of monks in Mandalay is large and well-respected, they were able to maintain a certain degree of order in the city.

U Nandiya remembered one case when some demonstrators arrested an army captain with a pistol and brought him to the monks' headquarters. After the monks asked him about his battalion number, his duties and his home town, they gave him a travel pass and told him to go home or back to his base. Without the monks' authorization, the captain could have been killed by the demonstrators.

When I asked U Nandiya if Buddhist monks stood for the people, he replied, 'Buddhist monks stand for justice.' But on the subject of the slingshot fights during the 1990 religious boycott, he admitted that the monks had gone too far. 'It was not appropriate to do this,' he said. 'It broke Buddhist discipline. But most who participated were very young. People supported it because they hated the military so much, but didn't dare to fight by themselves.'

Besides their concern for the suffering of the lay community, monks have also been directly affected by military rule. Ill-conceived economic policies and heavy taxation of villagers in remote areas have made it difficult for villagers to provide adequate support for the monks. In Mandalay, many impoverished Burmese have sold their homes to Chinese immigrants and moved to the outskirts of town, leaving monks in the city centre with no one to feed them.

Not surprisingly, successive military regimes have promoted monks who support them or who adhere to the belief that monks should not participate in political activities. Student activists, on the other hand, have tried to encourage and work with monks who feel compelled to fight against injustice. Monks realize that they risk debasing the monkhood as an institution by plunging into the dirty world of politics, but they also risk being seen as irrelevant if they remain indifferent to the suffering of the people who bring them their daily sustenance.

Among the Buddhist population as a whole, there are mixed feelings about whether or not monks should participate in politics. At the same time, many Burmese are influenced by the belief that suffering in this life is a result of bad deeds in the past, so one might as well just accept the political situation as inevitable. When the time for change comes, it will happen by itself. Particularly in times of intense repression, such thinking tends to predominate. Individuals focus more on personal efforts to improve their chances for a better next life through praying, adhering to Buddhist discipline and making religious donations.

The temple represents an important space in society, and one that is generally perceived as belonging outside military control. Time spent in religious establishments often provides a respite from personal and political tensions outside. Meditation, in particular, has played an interesting role. When on the run, just released from prison or feeling stressed from the dangers of their political work, some activists have turned to monasteries and meditation centres as sanctuaries where they can regain peace of mind. Meditation has led more than a few out of their political lives and into a focus on spiritual development. Others have used the sense of calmness and stability obtained from meditating to help them ward off depression and continue their political work.

As much as the regime realizes that people do not want to see armed soldiers in the monasteries, the generals feel that they must keep the monks under surveillance. The regime is well aware that most political uprisings in the past have been led by students or monks or a combination of the two. The students are bold and committed, but they lack authority. The monks, on the other hand, have moral authority among the people, as well as an organizational structure that allows them to mobilize quickly and widely. Thus, the junta has developed a two-pronged strategy to prevent citizens and monks from coalescing into a powerful anti-government force. First, they have tried to limit the influence of the monks, particularly in their role as advocates of the people. And second, they have used combinations of rewards, gifts, surveillance and intimidation to make monks hesitant to defy the regime.

Before the military took over, monks say that they were often able to intervene if certain authorities were treating people unjustly. But now the army refuses to honour this role. Villagers and townspeople still complain to monks about their sufferings, such as having to do forced labour or pay monthly porter fees, but they know the monks cannot persuade the authorities to stop such abuses. There have even been instances of military commanders telling abbots to call on people to build feeder roads so that it will appear as if the work is a religious donation rather than forced labour. One of the few material ways that monks can help their local populations is by donating part of the food they have received to the very poor. Such gestures alleviate their hunger temporarily but do not address why they are hungry.

Perhaps not surprisingly, abbots and senior monks have, by and large, been more willing to go along with the regime while younger monks have been more sympathetic to the democracy movement. Senior monks have far wider responsibilities, such as maintaining their monasteries and taking responsibility for the monks underneath them, whereas the young monks, like students, are freer and more motivated by their zeal for justice.

Although monks are supposed to live simple lives with only a few necessary possessions, many have found it hard to reject the luxuries offered by generals and other benefactors. Lavish gifts to senior monks include TVs, VCRs and fancy cars, all of which are technically prohibited by the monks' code of discipline. The junta has also built special hospitals solely for monks, with equipment and treatment far superior to that found in public hospitals.

The regime particularly rewards supportive monks with large donations and religious titles. Meant to be bestowed on those who show a superior mastery of Buddhist doctrine, the titles instead often go to monks who are loyal to the regime. In some cases, they are given to senior monks whose loyalty may be in doubt, but whom the regime hopes to co-opt. Even if the monk himself continues to view the regime with distaste, others may see him as tainted by having accepted the title.

Successive military regimes have also secretly placed intelligence agents in the monasteries, so if any monks are discussing politics or meeting with political activists, their activities will be reported. The planted monks can also urge other monks to stay out of politics. In some cases, military authorities have tried to obtain representation on monastery committees as well so that they could keep an eye on the goings-on at the monasteries. One Mandalayan who was a member of a monastery committee in the BSPP period explained that, in Mandalay, the BSPP authorities often tried to get their own men elected to the monastery committees, but the temple supporters generally resisted.

U Nandiya described some of the other methods successive regimes have used to rein in the country's approximately 300,000 monks. They abolished religious associations outside the government's control and, through the state-controlled media, defamed respected monks who took anti-regime stands. 'For instance,' U Nandiya said, 'they publish "news" that the monk has drunk liquor or slept with a woman. They don't bother with ordinary monks, even if they are doing bad things.' At the same time, the senior generals look for loyal monks to promote to leadership positions on the state-controlled supreme council of monks. Such monks can be counted on to discipline younger monks. U Nandiya said: 'The SLORC is using some monks who don't have enough knowledge of worldly affairs. They believe that the SLORC is doing great work for the Buddhist religion because they are always building new monasteries.'

In Burma there has always been a tension between the belief that every government is bad and best avoided and the idea that the government is the defender of the Buddhist faith. As noted earlier, the legitimacy of kings in Burma and throughout South East Asia rested in part on their fulfilling their duties as religious patrons. Recognizing that there is still credibility to be gained from such activities, the SLORC and the SPDC have invested much of their time in the restoration of pagodas and the presentation of donations to monks.

In April 1999, the military regime oversaw the completion of the restoration of the Shwedagon Pagoda, the most revered pagoda in the country. By initiating a large-scale restoration, the generals sought to win the respect of the people and to establish further their right to rule. The political significance of the event can be seen by the fact that they even released some NLD members from prison for two days to be able to attend the restoration ceremony.

While many civil servants and others were ordered to make donations of cash and labour for the restoration project, few resented it. They are intensely attached to this stunning pagoda which symbolizes the spiritual soul of the nation. In addition, they believe their donations will help them achieve a higher status in their next lives, leading them closer to their ultimate goal of nirvana. The pagoda is believed to contain eight hairs of the Buddha which were brought to what was then a Mon kingdom by two merchant-disciples of the Buddha. Over the centuries, the pagoda has been expanded and restored several times. According to the regime's figures, by the end of March 1999, the call for donations had brought in 94 lbs of gold, the equivalent of $2 million in cash, and nearly 68,000 pieces of jewellery, which could be broken up and used to decorate the bejewelled umbrella at the top of the pagoda.[1]

In 1996, the military regime negotiated a lease with the Chinese government to have a tooth relic of the Buddha flown from China to Burma for a few months. Many people in Burma were grateful to the regime for arranging this, because they believe that the tooth relic has tremendous power and significance. The junta also oversaw the construction of tooth relic pagodas in Rangoon and Mandalay to house a replica of the tooth relic, imbued through a ritual with the potency of the original.

Still, many people realize that the regime has tried to use its highly publicized religious activities to gain political legitimacy. One common joke in Burma is that a disgruntled customer complains to the shop where he bought his TV, 'This is supposed to be a multi-colour TV but all I ever see is green and yellow.' The meaning: the news on government-controlled TV consists largely of military personnel, in their green uniforms, giving donations to monks, in their yellow robes.

The Disappearing Jewels

Despite the authorities' apparent devotion to Buddhism, there have been several reports of military men engaged in the plunder of Buddha images and old pagodas. When pagodas are built, the patrons and well-wishers place gems and other valuables in a sealed treasury located under the centre of the pagoda. The landscape of Upper Burma is dotted with old pagodas which have fallen into disrepair. These pagodas have become prime hunting grounds for fortune-seekers in green uniforms. In one case in Sagaing Division, villagers were forced to dig up the treasury under military orders. When they reached the treasury, the soldiers ordered them to leave the area. According to one of the villagers, the soldiers then cordoned off the pagoda, removed the valuables, and took them away.[2]

A much more dramatic incident took place in Mandalay in 1997 when one of the most sacred Buddha images in Burma was mysteriously damaged. After King Bodawpaya conquered Arakan in 1784, he had had the huge bronze Mahamuni Buddha image split into pieces and brought up to a site just outside Mandalay where it was reconstructed and housed in a new temple. This image, which has become the symbol of Arakanese national identity, was revered by Arakanese, Mon and Burmans alike for centuries. It was also believed to contain a precious stone in its navel which would give miraculous powers to its possessor.

In 1996, some Mandalay authorities insisted that it was time for a renovation. During the renovation, a mysterious hole appeared in the belly of the statue, where the gem was thought to be located. As senior monks began to investigate the case, rumours quickly spread that one of the two monks who possessed a key to the building had been forced by a military officer to open the building at night. As a result, a senior monk called monks from all the major monasteries in Mandalay to a meeting to discuss the issue. During the course of the all-day meeting, in which answers about what had happened were not forthcoming, a monk and another man suddenly came into the room to announce that a Muslim man had raped a Buddhist girl.[3]

Some of the already frustrated monks decided to take action, and headed to the Muslim man's house, which they ransacked, and went on to damage a nearby mosque. As the news spread, a frenzy of attacks on mosques broke out in Mandalay and other cities. Over the next few days, monks could be seen wielding long sticks and desecrating mosques, often while riot police passively watched the scene from a distance. There were also several reports of people seeing monks with walkie-talkies under their robes, and a few had very shiny heads indicating they had just been shaved. In other words, it was widely believed that military men dressed as monks were involved, although many real monks did most of the damage. In the meantime, the hype surrounding the damage done to the Mahamuni image was forgotten, and its belly was patched up. Later, it turned out that the girl had not been raped after all. As for the precious stone, no one knows if it really was in the stomach of the Buddha, and whether or not the thieves managed to extract it.[4]

The Mahamuni incident occurred just before the annual monks' exams were scheduled to take place. Rather than provide a gathering place where the monks could discuss taking action against the regime, the military postponed the exams. When the exams were finally held a year later, the monks had to pair off and be responsible for each other. If one monk were to engage in anti-government activities, the other one would also be in trouble. As they have done in other communities, the authorities imposed a policy of communal punishment for the acts of individuals in order to reduce the possibility of unrest.

Monks and the NLD

In late September 1996, the SLORC sought to punish NLD members for their political defiance by issuing a decree forbidding NLD members from becoming ordained as monks. Monks were also told to be wary of NLD members frequenting monasteries, because the NLD was supposedly trying to encourage monks to join the anti-government movement. Lt General Myo Nyunt, the then Minister of Religious of Affairs, claimed: 'Although [the NLD members] are Buddhists, they are unaware of the sin of dividing the monks.'[5] This order contravened Buddhist doctrine and was generally ignored by monks. However, it can be seen as an attempt to reverse the 1990 monks' boycott against the military, when monks refused to accept offerings from or carry out ceremonies for members of the military and their families. The aims seem to have been to put a distance between the monks and the NLD, to demoralize NLD members, and perhaps to turn ordinary citizens against the NLD for purportedly politicizing the monkhood.

In the meantime, supporters of Daw Aung San Suu Kyi often put her photograph on their Buddhist altars in their homes, signifying their respect for her and their wish that she be protected by higher powers so that she could continue to lead the struggle on their behalf. The NLD has not directly encouraged monks to come out on its side but, as noted earlier, the leaders of the NLD have routinely drawn on Buddhist teachings to explain their political points, and ordinary people have tried to ascertain the political sympathies of venerated monks.

Stories about Daw Aung San Suu Kyi's and Lt General Khin Nyunt's visits to the Thamanya abbot indicate the extent to which people are looking to the monks to support their political ideals, even if only symbolically. A devout, elderly monk from the Pa'o ethnic minority group, U Vinaya, set up a monastery on Thamanya hill twenty miles outside Pa'an, the capital of Karen State, in 1980. Over the years, U Vinaya has built up a large following that now spans the entire country. A vegetarian, he is famous for his strict practice, and people believe that he has magical powers. If they are blessed by him, their businesses will be successful, they will pass their exams and their other wishes will be fulfilled. On weekends, up to 3,000 people come to see him, including large numbers of businessmen and students from Rangoon.

The Thamanya abbot also generously allowed Karen villagers fleeing from the civil war between the Tatmadaw and the KNU to build huts on monastery land around the foot of the mountain. In 1996, there were several thousand Karen villagers living there, free from the food and labour demands of both the Tatmadaw and the KNU. Some of the villagers farmed, but many worked at the monastery preparing enormous amounts of food for the endless stream of visitors.

The Thamanya abbot has never talked openly about politics, but he is certainly perceived as a possible threat by the military government because of his ability to attract people. Members of the military regime, including Lt General Khin Nyunt, have visited him. And so has Daw Aung San Suu Kyi. In her first trip outside Rangoon after she was released from house arrest in 1995, she headed directly to Karen State to pay her respects to the Thamanya abbot. During her visit, a picture was taken of her sitting at his feet. This picture was later copied, laminated and widely distributed by supporters of Daw Aung San Suu Kyi, who took it to signify the abbot's tacit support for her and the democracy movement. To this the abbot has merely said that anyone can have their picture taken with him.

When I was travelling in Burma in 1996, I heard several apocryphal stories comparing Daw Aung San Suu Kyi's and Lt General Khin Nyunt's visits to the monastery. One version claimed that when Daw Aung San Suu Kyi arrived at the foot of the long stairway up to the monastery, the abbot came down to welcome her. But when Lt General Khin Nyunt arrived, the abbot did not descend. The abbot invited Daw Aung San Suu Kyi to visit again, but he did not extend the same invitation to Lt General Khin Nyunt. When Lt General Khin Nyunt tried to give the abbot a van, he refused the gift saying, 'Monks don't need vans. Take it back.' In another variation, it was said that when Lt General Khin Nyunt got in his car to leave, it wouldn't start. He had to go back up to the abbot, who told him that only after he had got rid of his anger would the car start. Probably not one of these details is true, but they reflect people's desires for a different reality.

The military regime courted the Thamanya abbot for two reasons. Besides wanting to rein him in, they also hoped to garner more support from the Burmese populace by showing respect to a monk whom the people adore. The regime encouraged the abbot to move to Rangoon, where they could have more contact with him. He rejected the offer, saying he was perfectly happy where he was. However, his refusal to move should not necessarily be seen as a snub against the regime. He was over eighty years old and had developed a close relationship with the people in his area.

Still, the regime kept a close eye on him. Although guns are not supposed to be brought into any monastery, on the day I visited, armed Tatmadaw soldiers were patrolling the nearby primary school sponsored by the monastery. When I asked why there needed to be armed soldiers at a school award ceremony during daylight hours, I was told that it was for the children's security. I couldn't help but wonder if it had more to do with demonstrating that, ultimately, this territory was under the regime's rather than the abbot's control.

In late 1999, the junta was caught off balance by the publicized demands of two venerated monks, U Zawtipala, the abbot of Kyakhatwaing monastery in Pegu, and U Kundalabiwuntha of Mahaghandharon monastery in Mandalay. Issuing separate appeals to both the regime and the NLD, the senior monks urged them to work together for national reconciliation. U Zawtipala, who had never been involved in politics, even offered to act as a mediator in talks between the NLD and the regime. He asked both sides to be flexible but also suggested that the government should not go against the will of the people.[6] While the NLD issued a statement declaring that the party was willing to accept the abbots' guidance, the regime suggested that the senior monks had been used by its political opponents. In a written response to the appeals, the regime insisted that 'The National League for Democracy should be willing to adopt a more realistic and flexible policy.'[7] The generals ignored the call for dialogue.

Repression of Christians

Besides cultivating loyal Buddhist monks, the regime has sought to win the support of the majority Burmans by encouraging the promotion of Buddhism among non-Buddhist peoples. Throughout military rule, foreigners have been able to come to Burma to study Vipassana meditation at monasteries and meditation centres. This is a source of pride for Burmese citizens, who generally view Burmese Buddhism as the most pure form of Buddhism being practised today. With regard to the ethnic minorities in Burma, many Burman Buddhists share the military regime's perception that if the ethnic minorities 'became' Buddhists, it would be beneficial for them, and there would be fewer separatist demands. Christians are still often seen as having supported British colonial rule, and find it difficult to rise to high-ranking positions in government service, particularly in the army.

Ethnic minority Christians, who comprise perhaps 10 per cent of the country's population, have been particularly targeted since the 1988 coup. Although Christians in the cities and towns in central Burma have not faced physical persecution, they have been harassed in various ways. Endless delays in approving building permits for new religious structures are common, and there have been cases of newly-built churches being pulled down even after the proper permit was obtained. Church leaders wanting to attend Christian conferences abroad find it difficult to get passports. The authorities in the Ministry of Religious Affairs even battled the Myanmar Council of Churches over terminology and graduation attire.

A member of the Myanmar Christian Council, which represents twelve Protestant denominations, explained some of the challenges they faced in the mid-1990s. Lt General Myo Nyunt, the Minister of Religious Affairs at the time, informed the council that they could no longer use the word *thoukdan kyan* for 'Proverbs', even though it had been used since the first translation of the Bible into Burmese more than one hundred years ago. Lt General Myo Nyunt did not want them to use this word because Buddhists used it in their doctrinal texts. The council member explained: 'Not long after, the Christians invited [Lt] General Myo Nyunt to a Christmas Eve dinner in Rangoon. He gave a long speech which had been written for him and included quotes from the Bible, including sections from Proverbs. Then the MCC elders wrote a letter to the government saying that since [Lt] General Myo Nyunt himself had used the word *thoukdan kyan* for Proverbs, why can't we? So then the Ministry of Religious Affairs dropped the issue.'

The council member also talked about how, in 1995, the SLORC sent a letter to the Myanmar Christian Council saying that secular colleges use caps and gowns at their graduation ceremonies, so divinity colleges would have to choose some other form of attire. He said that the MCC wrote back explaining that since medieval days in Europe, when colleges were religious institutions, gowns had been used. Secular institutions had only come later. After that, the Ministry of Religious Affairs dropped the issue.

Christian communities in remote areas, especially where armed anti-government forces operate, have faced much harsher pressure. In particular, Christians in Karen and Karenni states on the eastern border and in Chin State and Sagaing Division on the western border have seen their churches burned down, their pastors arrested and Tatmadaw soldiers disrupt services. One Chin pastor explained: 'On Sundays we can't have a full service, because they take porters that day, too. They refuse to make an exception. Sometimes they also take porters during the church service. We can't do anything. Sometimes we intercede on behalf of villagers. We say, "Let that man be a porter two days from now." But they never listen. They always say, "These are orders from above." They never understand the villagers.'

In the remote Naga hills, some parents in the late 1990s allowed their children to accompany authorities to what they were told were lowland secular schools, only to find out later that their children had been sent to Buddhist monasteries and made into novice monks.

Particularly in Chin State, the regime was upset by an evangelical Chin group's plans to convert all Chin to Christianity by the year 2000, as part of an international Christian campaign. In response, the authorities tried to lure Christians into becoming Buddhists by offering them exemption from forced labour as well as food allowances or money.[8] Another Chin pastor told about a Christian village of two hundred houses in Tamu township, Chin State, where the authorities went even further. He said: 'The military came and offered rice and money to those who converted to Buddhism. Some were also given buffaloes and land for cultivating rice. Fifty houses converted. One man who converted was then appointed by the military as the headman.'

Such activities on the part of the regime are also aimed at creating splits among the ethnic minority communities, thus weakening their resistance to state control. As with artists and writers, conflicts develop within religious communities over what degree of cooperation is acceptable and who has gone too far. People within the community begin to view each other with suspicion, and bonds of trust are broken down. However, to some extent the Christian community has been able to counter these pressures and maintain its vitality by putting much of its energy into group activities.

Similar to the Buddhist community, there has been an ongoing debate in the Christian community about whether the current sorry state of affairs is 'God's will' or demands action. Those pastors and church members who attribute current suffering to God's will believe that they are being punished, usually because of moral laxity in the community. For them, more disciplined behaviour and more fervent prayer are the keys to a better future. Other Christians reject this position as too passive and insist that God rewards only those who act. But because action usually means coming into confrontation with hostile authorities, following through requires strong commitment.

The Christians are a minority population, so they have been reluctant to take an active role in politics in the heartland of Burma, although church leaders in predominantly Christian ethnic minority areas have in some cases been more outspoken. Among the armed ethnic nationalist groups where Christians are in the majority, many members have viewed their struggles as necessary not only to protect their ethnic rights but also their religion. In central Burma, the Christian community has focused on redressing social problems and encouraging personal development, somewhat along the lines of the self-actualization writers. Pastors, church staff and motivated church members have worked together to organize English classes, youth leadership courses, drug rehabilitation programmes, and summer conferences which bring together people from all over the country. These activities have to some degree provided an alternative arena for the development of ideas and skills and have helped to create mutual understanding among people from different ethnic groups.

Foreign missionaries have been banned from living in Burma since the mid-1960s, but foreign church officials have continued to visit Burma, and Burmese Christians sometimes manage to make their way to conferences and religious institutions outside the country. As a result, they have been able to appeal for some financial assistance from abroad and to learn about the role of the Christian community in political movements and development pro-grammes in other countries. Such links with the outside world have also made them feel less isolated. Some young Buddhists have observed with interest the successes of the Christians' social programmes, and Burmese Buddhist activists in exile have looked to more socially engaged forms of Buddhism, such as exist in Thailand, for inspiration.

Exploitation of Muslims

Like the Christian community, the Muslim community is well aware of its minority status and has tried to maintain a low profile in Burma. The largest concentration of Muslims is in Arakan State. Smaller Muslim populations are scattered throughout the cities, towns and rural areas of Burma, and mostly consist of the descendants of farmers, clerks and traders who came during the colonial period. The Muslim community provides some social services, such as a large free clinic in Rangoon, but generally stays out of the political arena. However, there are several Muslims in the NLD, who clearly hope that a democratic government would stop much of the discrimination they have experienced under military rule.

Feelings of antagonism towards the Muslim population lurk just beneath the surface of more than a few Burmese. This is due in part to British encouragement of Indian immigration, which resulted in Bengalis and Indians quickly obtaining wealth and prominent positions. Perhaps most upsetting to Burmese Buddhists is the idea of Muslim men marrying Burman women and converting them to Islam. Throughout military rule in Burma, successive regimes have used the spectre of a Muslim takeover to whip up nationalist sentiments. In particular, when anti-regime tensions are running high, incidents of intolerable behaviour by Muslims always seem to pop up and are used to channel anger into communal conflicts.

For instance, in July 1988, pamphlets supposedly written by Muslims encouraging fellow Muslims to marry Burmese women suddenly appeared in Taunggyi and other towns where anti-military feelings were growing after the student demonstrations in Rangoon. As expected, Muslim–Buddhist conflicts broke out, and the shops and homes of Muslims were attacked and looted. Such pamphlets have shown up several times in Burma over the past ten years, including in October 1996 in Rangoon, when pamphlets appeared saying in part:

Burmese Citizens – Beware!

The Muslims living in Burma are attempting to expand their religion while destroying Buddhism in Burma by using the following ways:
1) Land: All the land in the country shall be owned by the Muslims.
2) Money: To organize Buddhists to become Muslims using the power of money.
3) Women: To organize Buddhist women to get married with Muslims using money and other ways.
4) Doctrine: To preach Muslim doctrine in every place.
5) State power: After successfully using these above methods and [the] majority of the people become Muslim, to take state power.[9]

Although many people now realize that these pamphlets are intended to incite unrest, some people still fall for them every time, and the damage done leaves an indelible mark.[10]

In other cases, the military has sought to drive Muslims out of Burma. During the 1997 Tatmadaw offensive against the Karen National Union, soldiers looted and destroyed the mosques in many of the towns and villages which the KNU had previously controlled.[11] One Muslim man was getting water from a well in front of a mosque in his village when Tatmadaw soldiers came out of the mosque ripping up the Koran. He said, 'They threw the pieces of the Koran on the street. When the Muslim women on the street saw this, they cried and felt such pain. The SLORC soldiers said, "Don't cry! This is not a Muslim country. This is a Buddhist country! Go away!"'[12] In other cases Muslims were killed. As a result of the campaign to clear the area of Muslims, hundreds of Muslims fled with Karen villagers across the border into Thailand.

The Muslim Rohingya community in northern Arakan State has been particularly targeted. A heavy-handed Tatmadaw operation in the area drove 200,000 Rohingyas into Bangladesh in 1978, and although many later returned, a Tatmadaw-orchestrated forced relocation programme in 1991 sent 250,000 Rohingyas over the border again.[13] Eight years later, tens of thousands were still in Bangladesh, refusing to go home because the military regime would not agree to accept them as citizens and would not guarantee their protection.[14] Among local Buddhist Rakhines, the Burmese population in general, and even the opposition groups, there is little apparent sympathy for their plight. The regime has been able to play off different populations against each other, and although those opposed to military rule know that they must be unified, they have often fallen victim to their own fears and prejudices.

As much as the junta has promoted the Buddhist religion, even ethnic minority Buddhists are dissatisfied by the regime's explicitly Burman version of Buddhism. Mon and Shan monks have faced difficulties in distributing literature in their own languages, and in some cases they have been prohibited from taking Buddhist exams in their own languages. Shan people were furious when SLORC authorities took over the funeral arrangements for a famous Shan monk who died in Hsipaw in the mid-1990s. The entire ceremony was Burmanized, from the design of the structure holding the coffin to the way he was cremated. Likewise, when the regime restored a famous Shan temple in Hsipaw, the Shan-style roof was replaced with a Burmese-style one. Thus, the regime has attempted to impose a homogeneous culture that is both Buddhist and Burman, and while this policy has offended many, from members of other religions to members of other ethnic nationalities, they have found it difficult to unite in opposition.[15]

Fortune-telling and Sympathetic Magic

While Buddhism preaches the importance of realizing the impermanence of all living things, many Burmese are attached to beliefs in the power of spirits and magic to affect their present lives. Even the most devout Burmese Buddhists do not necessarily deny the existence of spirits, but insist that whether they exist or not is irrelevant in the larger quest for enlightenment. Thus, the brother and sister spirits whose shrine is on Mount Popa (described in Chapter 1) continue to be propitiated in return for protection. Some of the most devoted followers are military generals and especially their wives. This is because the pattern of those in power removing potential rivals continues, and generals vying for the top slots are in the most precarious positions of all. In 1996–97, for example, there were two attempted assassinations against SLORC Secretary-2, Lt General Tin Oo. In the second instance, a letter bomb was delivered to his house, but his daughter opened it instead and was killed by the explosion. Despite the regime's well-developed skills at routing out underground activists, this crime was never solved. Most believe it was perpetrated by rivals within the regime.

The popularity of fortune-telling tends to wax and wane in Burma in relation to the economic situation. In periods of stability and prosperity, fortune-tellers are consulted less, whereas in times of insecurity and stress, more people turn to fortune-tellers for help. Ever since 1988, interest has reportedly increased.

Numerous books and magazines are devoted to fortune-telling and astrology, partly because it is difficult to write legally about much else, but also because people are devouring them. Besides including stories of magical occurrences and special powers, they feature in-depth coverage of horoscopes and antidotes to the troubles that might befall the readers. The simplicity of the techniques for cheating fate helps people to feel they are doing something concrete to assert control over their lives, despite living in conditions where in fact they are often pawns in someone else's game. During the 1988 demonstrations, for instance, one mother had her sons eat bowls of *mohingha*, a fish and noodle soup often served at funerals. This was her own brand of cheating fate. She reasoned that if they ate the funeral food before joining the demonstrations, they would not be killed.

The SLORC and SPDC also apparently tried to thwart the rise of Daw Aung San Suu Kyi through astrological means. According to one person working with the Education Ministry, in 1996 the regime reportedly changed the rules for the beauty contests held at annual school sports competitions. The officials were told to eliminate any girls whose astrological charts predicted strong leadership potential, because this was associated with Daw Aung San Suu Kyi assuming power.

In March 1999, an apocryphal story about Lt General Khin Nyunt's test to predict Burma's political future was whispered from person to person in Rangoon. It went like this:

> As rain fell during the recent full-moon day of the hottest and driest month of the Burmese calendar, a story about Khin Nyunt started spreading. According to this story, Khin Nyunt climbed up to the top part of the Shwedagon Pagoda at 4.00 a.m. He placed a lion made of mud and a peacock made of wax at the top part of the pagoda, and vowed that the peacock should dissolve and the lion get harder as a sign that he will continue to rule the country. On the other hand, if Daw Aung San Suu Kyi were going to rule the country, the lion would dissolve and the peacock would get harder. Many people thought the peacock would dissolve as the weather was very hot. But unexpectedly, it started raining around 11.00 a.m., and it lasted until the evening. Finally, the figure of the lion dissolved, while the peacock became harder.[16]

This story is probably not true, but it wouldn't surprise people in Burma if the generals were to engage in such actions. As noted earlier, General Ne Win frequently turned to magic to strengthen his hold on power. In this case, the tale is likely to be part of a 'whispering campaign', where one side tries to derail the other by the use of rumours, a technique frequently used by both the military regime and the opposition. With facts always hard to come by, stories such as this spread quickly and serve to raise the morale of the beleaguered opposition.

Numerology and choosing auspicious dates have been subjects of intense concern for the military regime and pro-democracy activists alike. According to one fortune-teller who takes his job quite seriously: 'The military officers think that it is better to act by calculating things according to astrology than doing things haphazardly. I also think that way. Compared to doing things when you want to do them, it's better to do things after a careful calculation and choosing the right time.' He strongly believed that the NLD could compete with the regime only by doing the same. 'In order to be successful in holding their meetings, and doing organizing trips, they may use astrology,' he said. 'If they have to face their enemy the SPDC, [they should calculate] what day and what time will be advantageous for them.' Although he thought that Daw Aung San Suu Kyi herself did not consult astrologers, he was sure that others in the NLD did. He certainly hoped so, for he felt that if the NLD picked astrologically appropriate days for its important events, this could help them.

Moreover, he recommended that Daw Aung San Suu Kyi should stay away from the number 8, which is not a lucky number. He said that the chances of success on an eight date are very low, only about 20 per cent. Instead she should counter the regime with 9 or 12. One prominent student activist said that a couple of fortune-tellers had also warned his group not to hold events or put out statements on an eight date. Thus, if a political anniversary fell on an eight, his group dated its statement the day before or the day after.

In consultation with astrologers, first General Ne Win and later the SLORC chose 9 as their lucky number. Nine is also the special number of the *nats*, and thus is strongly associated with power. As a result, the regime issued currency notes in denominations of 45 kyats and 90 kyats, which at least can be credited with keeping the population's math skills up. The SLORC staged its coup on 18 September, with September being the ninth month, and the 18th also representing a nine, because 1+8=9.

Likewise, the SLORC sought to guarantee that the National Convention would work in its favour by carefully putting delegates into groupings whose total numbers equalled nine. There were eighty-one NLD members plus eighteen other elected representatives from various parties. Each of these added up equals 9, and the two numbers added together (81 + 18) equal 99, which if added again equals 18, and 1 + 8 = 9. Then there were 603 appointed representatives, 6+0+3 = 9. The total number of delegates was 702, which again equals 9.

This was pointed out to me by a citizen-sleuth who revelled in uncovering the regime's magical activities. He also showed me the 1-kyat notes issued by the SLORC, which appear to have a series of four 8s inside the numeral 1, which, when turned sideways, resembles a chair. A chair is often used to symbolize ruling power. The meaning, he said, was that the regime had overcome the pro-democracy movement. Whether or not the regime really intended this is not the key issue. The point is that people are reading meanings into everything around them, and that the psychological battle for political ascendancy is as important as the physical struggle.

Many citizens believe that because the generals are engaging in extensive *yadaya chae* (cheating fate) activities, they can prolong their rule.[17] Thus, fighting them is likely to be futile. Some astrologers have even suggested that the reason Burma has suffered so long under military rule is partly due to the date selected for independence. U Nu's astrologers chose 4.20 a.m. on 4 January 1948. According to the fortune-teller above, the astrologers knew this wasn't a particularly auspicious day, but rather than delay independence another month, they had to select the least bad day in January. The problem was that the planet of Mars was ascendant during January, and Mars symbolizes the military and fighting. Thus, the rise of the military in political life was partly determined by choosing this particular date for independence. Again, whether or not this is accurate, it is a story which has relevance for people in Burma and influences their actions.

By the same token, many people are willing to support the idea that if they pick the right date, an overthrow is still possible. The exile community, and some former 1988 activists inside Burma, tried to promote the idea of organizing another mass movement to commence on '9/9/99', 9 September 1999, numerologically an extremely auspicious date. However, the military regime was well prepared and posted military personnel in all public areas where people might gather. Up to 500 activists, monks and NLD members were arrested or detained in the six weeks preceding 9/9/99. A few small protests broke out but were quickly dispersed.[18]

Spirits of the Dead

As hard as the regime tries to control the living, it must also confront the dead. In 1996, the SLORC ordered the digging up of Kyandaw cemetery, a large cemetery on a prime piece of land between the town centre and Rangoon University. This cemetery contained the graves of people from different faiths, and surviving family members were extremely upset about having to move the remains of their ancestors to a distant cemetery outside the city. For many, the financial burden was also a significant factor, because they had to pay for the digging up of the grave, transportation charges, and then a reburial fee at the new site. For others, their religious beliefs forbade the exhumation. The reason for the move was that the authorities wanted to sell the land for a large sum of money. The buyer was rumoured to be the recently rehabilitated drug lord of north-eastern Burma, Khun Sa.[19]

Two years later, in June 1998, strange occurrences were reported at Myinegone junction, not far from the cemetery. Myinegone was also where, on 21 June 1988, up to seventy students and twenty policemen were killed during an anti-government demonstration. Suddenly, on the tenth anniversary, a poltergeist was reported at the location. Plates and cups were said to have risen off tables in a teashop, and televisions were levitating and smashing into each other in a nearby appliance store. One person even reported turning on a TV and seeing an image of blood. It was believed that the spirits of those killed in 1988 were coming back to haunt the regime.

Dismayed by this attack from an unexpected quarter, the Rangoon divisional commander hurried to the scene where he read out an announcement telling the spirits that they had been released from their duties on earth and could move on. Such announcements are customarily read at funerals in Burma. People in the area held their own ceremonies, inviting monks to come and recite chants to drive away the spirits. While one such ceremony was taking place, it was said that donated juice bottles started moving and smashed into each other. Police and soldiers were sent to block off the area and disperse a huge crowd. In the state-sponsored *Kyemon* newspaper, an editorial accused political groups of spreading false rumours about poltergeists to stir up trouble.[20]

After a few days the situation calmed down, and the regime was able to breathe more easily again. However, it is exactly this kind of incident which reminds the military that their hold on power is always tenuous and challenges will continue to appear, if not in the form of direct confrontations then through unexpected and even bizarre occurrences. For, ultimately, the battle to shift the balance of power in Burma is a psychological one. When the supporters of democracy feel that powerful forces are aligned with them, they may shake off their fear and act, but because the psychic aspects play such a key role, nobody can predict when.

CHAPTER 12

The Internationalization of Burma's Politics

§ The international community's various dealings with Burma have been as politicized and complex as Burma's internal dynamics. After 1988, both the regime and the pro-democracy movement looked abroad for support and legitimacy. The regime sought military aid, foreign investment and membership in regional groupings, while Daw Aung San Suu Kyi urged the international community to do more to bring about a resolution of Burma's political crisis. Several kinds of international actors have interacted with Burmese political forces, including foreign governments and international political bodies, foreign companies, international NGOs and UN agencies, and the media. This chapter considers some of the debates which have arisen around foreign involvement in Burma.

Foreign Governments' Relations with Burma

While the military regime, the pro-democracy groups and the ethnic nationalist organizations looked to other governments for support, foreign governments adopted policies towards Burma which reflected a mix of self-interest, pragmatism and moral imperatives. Thus, in the mid-1960s and 1970s, China strongly supported the Communist Party of Burma, but in the 1990s, the Beijing government became the regime's strongest ally. In the 1990s, the United States was Daw Aung San Suu Kyi and the pro-democracy movement's most vocal backer; although some agencies and representatives within the US government were advocating closer relations with the military regime. Meanwhile, neighbouring countries like Thailand and India alternately engaged the regime, the pro-democracy groups and ethnic nationalist organizations, as they tried to manage the impact of Burma's political crises on their own countries.

After the 1988 coup, Burma's military junta was ostracized by most governments, with many initially refusing to recognize the SLORC. However, the generals in Rangoon were able to turn to China for critical military support. Between 1990 and 1997, China furnished as much as 3 billion dollars' worth of military equipment to the Tatmadaw.[1] Besides fighter aircraft, tanks and artillery, China sold Burma radar, signals intelligence equipment and electronic warfare equipment.[2] The Chinese armed forces also provided training for Burma's army, air force and navy. Although some of the Chinese equipment was of poor quality and malfunctioned, the Tatmadaw was able to boost its capacity significantly.

China assisted Burma's military in return for access to intelligence information. China was eager to keep an eye on India's military activities as well as to monitor shipping in the Indian Ocean and through the Straits of Malacca.[3] China also looked to Burma as a market for Chinese goods and an important trade route to the Indian subcontinent and the Indian Ocean. As a result, the Chinese invested in the development of ports, roads, bridges, dams and factories in Burma.[4] Chinese consumer goods flooded Burma's markets, and as opportunities for making money expanded, the presence of Chinese in central Mandalay, the traditional centre of Burmese culture, grew rapidly. In 1999, some estimates put the Chinese population of the city as high as 30 per cent, with most being recent immigrants.[5]

China was also an important ally for Burma in international forums such as the United Nations, because it too opposed foreign demands to improve domestic human rights records. Nevertheless, by the late 1990s, the Beijing government was increasingly concerned about the burgeoning drug trade in southern China. With most heroin addicts sharing needles, HIV/AIDS infections spread in tandem. In *War in the Blood*, Chris Beyrer stated that 80 per cent of China's HIV infections were in Yunnan, where Burmese heroin was readily available.[6] Although the heroin was coming from Burma, the regime said it could not control the ceasefire groups producing and trafficking the drugs.

As much as the generals in Rangoon relied on support from China, they recognized that such dependence was dangerous and did not sit well with the domestic population. As a result, the regime also sought to improve ties with other governments in the region who were eager to contain China's spreading influence. Thus in the 1990s, Singapore supplied Burma's military with weapons, ammunition, training, and probably the communications equipment that enabled the regime to increase its monitoring capabilities over phone, fax and data transmissions.[7] Singapore also became one of Burma's largest foreign investors, with most of its money channelled into the development of the tourism industry.

Before Suharto's fall in 1998, Indonesia was also an important supporter of Burma's generals. The SLORC and SPDC regimes looked to Indonesia as a model of how a military-backed government could maintain control at home while also developing good relations with international financial institutions and foreign governments. In addition, the Suharto regime pushed for Burma's entry into the Association of South East Asian Nations (ASEAN), the primary political and economic grouping in the region.

Until the mid-1990s, successive military regimes in Burma had had no interest in joining ASEAN. But with membership promising to lead to increased investment and a degree of protection from western condemnation over its refusal to democratize, the SLORC began to lobby for inclusion. Although some ASEAN nations expressed concern about Burma's pariah status, they were eager to lessen China's influence over Burma. Likewise, some members opposed the West's confrontational stance towards Burma and believed they could have greater success in persuading the regime to act more moderately through a policy of political and economic engagement.

Despite Daw Aung San Suu Kyi and some western governments' calls for ASEAN not to grant Burma full membership, ASEAN accepted Burma in 1997. As a result, ASEAN relations with the European Union (EU) were affected, because the EU refused to allow Burma to participate fully in annual EU–ASEAN meetings until the Burmese regime showed improvements in human rights and made political concessions.[8] In the late 1990s, this resulted in a number of joint meetings being postponed and much time spent on negotiations for how to include Burma in joint meetings without according them the same status as other participants. At the May 1999 joint meeting, a compromise was reached in which Burmese representatives could attend meetings held in South East Asia but not speak. Burmese delegates were not able to participate in any joint meetings held in Europe because of the EU's visa ban on regime officials.

ASEAN members hoped that by granting Burma membership in the association, the generals would lessen repression at home. However, Burma's generals did not change their policies. With the collapse of military rule in Indonesia, Thailand and the Philippines called for a rethinking of ASEAN's commitment to non-interference in its members' affairs. At the ASEAN meeting in Manila in July 1998, Thai Foreign Minister Surin Pitsuwan proposed a new policy of 'flexible engagement', meaning that ASEAN should be able to have frank discussions about domestic issues which have implications for other countries in the association.[9] The Philippines' Foreign Minister, Domingo Siazon, publicly urged the junta and the opposition to begin a political dialogue without preconditions.[10] It was just before this meeting that Daw Aung San Suu Kyi was stopped at a roadblock outside Rangoon when she attempted to make a trip by car to the Irrawaddy delta to visit party members. Refusing to turn back, she spent several days camped at the roadblock, reflecting the extent to which her movements were being restricted by the regime. The

Burmese regime, however, reminded fellow ASEAN members of ASEAN's long held policy of non-interference in its members' domestic concerns. Other members of ASEAN did not approve the proposed 'flexible engagement' policy, and the Asian economic crisis led ASEAN member countries to focus more on their problems at home than on regional policy issues.

Meanwhile, Burma's military regime sought to play up its membership in ASEAN. Burma's generals tried to portray themselves as part of a solid group of Asian partners standing in opposition to the West. In Lt General Khin Nyunt's opening speech at an ASEAN trade ministers' meeting in Rangoon on 1 May 2000, he stated that during the Asian financial crisis, doomsayers in the West had attacked Asian values and expressed doubts about the future of ASEAN, but they had been proven wrong. Myanmar itself, he said, provided a good example of a country that was turning around economically.[11] In smaller ways as well, the regime touted its ASEAN connection. The regime had a song written to commemorate its inclusion in the association, and the generals even named their website, at www.myanmar.com, the Myanmar-ASEAN website.

With long borders abutting Burma, the Thai and Indian governments felt compelled to nurture their relationships with the often unpredictable Burmese military. Very little of the Thai–Burma border had been jointly demarcated, with the actual location of the borderline in dispute in several areas. Meanwhile, businessmen from Thailand and India, as in other South East Asian countries, were also eager to take advantage of trade and investment opportunities in resource-rich Burma, where wages were low and relatively few commodities were being produced.

In the past, the Thai military quietly supported the armed ethnic nationalist groups controlling virtually all of the Burmese side of the Thai–Burma border. This was part of a Cold War strategy to maintain a buffer zone which would make it more difficult for communists from China, Burma and Thailand to link up. But as the communist threat faded, and, in the 1990s, the opposition groups began losing ground to the far larger and better-equipped Tatmadaw, the Thai military changed course. Taking a pragmatic view, and also lured by logging, fishing and other investment opportunities in Burma, Thailand's generals began to improve relations with the Burmese junta. They cooperated in pressuring the ethnic nationalist armies to make ceasefire agreements with the Rangoon regime. As a result, the New Mon State Party, which depended on access to Thailand for supplies, came under particular pressure and finally agreed to a ceasefire in 1995.

As Thailand's trade and foreign investments in Burma grew, Thai civilian governments also had to balance a concern about the regime's repressive behaviour, which often resulted in refugee flows into Thailand, and the Thai business community's calls for better relations with the military regime. Such conflicts were apparent in the Thai government's handling of the Burmese embassy takeover in Bangkok in October 1999 and its reaction to the Burmese regime's subsequent unilateral closure of the Thai–Burma border. The Burmese hostage-takers told the media that they had undertaken such a drastic action only to refocus the world's attention on Burma and to demand a political dialogue between the military regime and the NLD. With regard to the hostage-takers, Thai Interior Minister Sanan Kachornprasart told the press: 'We don't consider them to be terrorists. They are student activists who fight for democracy.'[12]

From the Thai government's perspective, their handling of the situation was commendable. No one had been killed or injured, and it was all resolved quickly. But the generals in Rangoon were outraged that the hostage-takers had been viewed sympathetically and had escaped arrest. The regime promptly revoked all Thai fishing concessions in Burmese waters and shut the border to trade. Thai businessmen demanded that the Thai government do something. Soon after, the Thai government put pressure on all Burmese political activists living in Thailand to register with the United Nations High Commission for Refugees and to agree to be resettled in a third country as soon as possible. Then they began trying to deport as many of the estimated 700,000 to one million illegal Burmese migrant workers as they could catch. On 23 November 1999, the Thai Foreign Minister flew to Rangoon to smooth relations with Burmese officials. The next day, the Burmese regime reopened the border to trade.

Likewise, the Burmese regime stopped construction on the Mae Sot–Myawaddy 'Friendship Bridge' linking Thailand and Burma for almost two years in the late 1990s until it exacted concessions from the Thai government.[13] It sought more pressure on the KNU and Burmese dissidents operating out of Thailand. Even though the full cost of the bridge construction was borne by the Thais, the regime assumed it could count on Thai businessmen to pressure the Thai government to do whatever was necessary to keep the construction on track.

Of course, by delaying such projects, the regime sacrificed much-needed income too, but eliminating its political opposition, rather than improving the economy, was the regime's top priority. Thus from 1995 to 1998, the Tatmadaw did nothing to stop, and in some cases actually participated in, Democratic Karen Buddhist Army (DKBA) attacks on refugee camps in Thailand.[14] The DKBA, a group which broke away from the Karen National Union in early 1995, was fostered by the Tatmadaw in order to counter the KNU. The Tatmadaw perceived the refugee camps as strongholds for the KNU, because many families with members in the KNU lived there. The Tatmadaw also wanted to see the refugee camps closed down, because their existence served as evidence that Burma was not as peaceful as the regime claimed. By burning down the refugee camps, the refugees would feel that they were no worse off in Burma than in Thailand, so they might as well go home. Moreover, the Thais might feel that the best way to eliminate the border incursions would be to repatriate the refugees. The policy worked to a certain degree. Some refugees went back and Thai military units repatriated a few groups of refugees. Other refugees were moved to camps farther away from the border where they would be safer from attack.

Within the Thai government, there were often multiple Burma policies, with the Ministry of Foreign Affairs sometimes taking a different line from the Royal Thai Army, and each Thai military division and border patrol police unit crafting its own policy with regard to the Tatmadaw and opposition forces operating along various sections of the border. In the late 1990s, as much as civilians in the Thai government were sympathetic to the pro-democracy movement, they generally tried to engage Burma's military regime as well. The generals in Rangoon, however, appeared unmoved and were angered that their opposition continued to have access to Thailand. In a symbolic gesture apparently meant to warn Thailand of the strength of the Tatmadaw, the regime erected statues of one of Burma's great empire-building kings, Bayinnaung, at two border points with Thailand. In the mid-1500s, King Bayinnaung invaded Thai territory (then known as Siam), conquering the capital and bringing back loot and war captives. The message of these statues appeared to be, 'Don't think we couldn't do it again'.

As in Thailand, in the mid- and late 1990s, the Indian government both encouraged Burma's opposition and made deals with the regime. Worried about China's activities in Burma, India sought to improve ties with the junta in the hope of limiting China's influence.[15] At the same time, much of north-eastern India bordering Burma continued to be wracked by civil war, with armed ethnic minority separatists demanding an end to Indian rule in their states.[16] India tried to end the civil war both by improving the economies of the north-eastern states and by weakening the strength of the separatist armies. Working with the junta, India sought to liberalize cross-border trade and to persuade the regime to stop allowing armed militants from north-eastern India to hide out in Burma.

Because members of armed Chin, Kuki and Naga fronts fighting against the Tatmadaw had also taken refuge in north-eastern India, the Burmese military had an incentive to cooperate with the Indian government. In 1995, the Burmese and Indian military jointly carried out Operation Golden Bird to capture insurgents along both sides of the border. However, the Tatmadaw abruptly called off the operation when the Indian government awarded the prestigious Jawaharlal Nehru Peace Award to Daw Aung San Suu Kyi.[17] There was widespread sympathy for the Burmese pro-democracy movement in India and in particular for Daw Aung San Suu Kyi, who spent several years in Delhi when her mother was the Burmese ambassador to India. In May 1998, Daw Aung San Suu Kyi and the NLD called for the regime to allow the Parliament elected in 1990 to meet. Three months later, seventy-five members of India's Parliament signed a petition supporting the NLD's call.

Burma's generals insisted that no other countries had the right to interfere in their domestic affairs, but they were unwilling to admit the extent to which their policy decisions had serious implications for their neighbours. The refugee crisis is just one example. Although most of the funding for the refugees' food and medicine was provided by outside sources, Burma's neighbouring countries, especially impoverished Bangladesh, still suffered a heavy burden. Not only did they have to provide security, but the local population was also often resentful of the refugees' presence. In many cases the refugee populations also contributed to deforestation as they scoured the terrain near their camps for firewood and housing materials.

The failure or inability of the regime to eradicate drug production has had particularly profound consequences for Burma's neighbours. Addiction to Burmese heroin expanded rapidly in the Indian border state of Manipur, which developed one of the highest rates of HIV infection in India. In 1999, the Thai Development Research Institute estimated that 214,000 Thais were addicted to heroin and 257,000 Thais, including large numbers of high school students, were addicted to amphetamines.[18] The pills, like heroin, were primarily being produced by the United Wa State Army in north-eastern Burma and smuggled across the border. Thai officials estimated that 600 million amphetamine pills produced in Burma would enter Thailand in 2000 alone.[19] With the Burmese military regime saying it could not stop drug-trafficking into Thailand, Thai army officials and civilian authorities became increasingly irritated. They knew they could not bring the trafficking under control without Rangoon's co-operation.

Other diseases were not stopped by national borders either. Although Thailand had wiped out elephantiasis, a severely disfiguring affliction, Burmese refugees and migrant workers inadvertently reintroduced the disease. Malaria and tuberculosis were brought back into Thailand in the same way. To make sure that drug-resistant strains of these two potentially fatal diseases do not develop along their common border, Thailand and Burma must coordinate their treatment and prevention policies. But with ties between the two countries often strained, even health meetings have been subject to cancellation.[20]

Burma's more aggressive foreign policy marks a departure from the past. In the parliamentary period, Prime Minister U Nu adopted a non-aligned policy in order to keep Burma out of the Cold War battlefield. Under General Ne Win, Burma was closed off from virtually all foreign investment and participated in few multinational associations. But in the 1990s, Burma's generals recognized the value of Burma's geo-strategic position and attempted to use it to their advantage.

For instance, the regime developed closer relations with the Pakistani military. Having already sold weapons to the Tatmadaw in 1999, the Pakistani military proposed setting up an air base in north-western Burma, not far from the Indian border.[21] With relations between India and Pakistan, both nuclear powers, always unstable, and China supporting Pakistan in order to undermine India, the Burmese regime was entering dangerous waters. But the generals were apparently confident that they could take advantage of the conflicts between China, India and Pakistan to obtain a degree of military and political support from all three. Experienced at playing off different groups against each other at home, the junta attempted a similar strategy in its foreign policy.

In the 1990s, the United States government took the most hard-line stance against Burma's generals. It made it clear that it would block any proposed World Bank or IMF loans to Burma until there was measurable progress towards democracy. In May 1997, the US Congress passed a sanctions bill that forbade any new investment by American companies in Burma. The United States also imposed a visa ban on top SLORC officials and their family members. After the SLORC's crackdown in 1988, the United States had refused to post an ambassador to Rangoon, and throughout the 1990s, a lower-ranking chargé d'affaires ran the American embassy. The United States took the high ground on Burma in part because it could afford to. The American government perceived no direct national security threats in Burma and, except for Unocal, American companies had invested little in the country.

Nevertheless, within the US government there were differences of opinion on how to deal with Burma. Some congressmen and State Department officials opposed the imposition of sanctions on US businesses. At the same time, in the mid- and late 1990s, the Drug Enforcement Agency (DEA) called for increased counter-narcotics assistance to Burma. The DEA argued that the regime was making progress on drug arrests and only by working with the regime could drug production be reduced. However, in its 1999 report on narcotics in Burma, the US State Department wrote:

> While there were cases of interdiction and arrests of members of some cease-fire groups for narcotics trafficking, the GOB [government of Burma] has been unwilling or unable to take on the most powerful groups directly. Cease-fire agreements with insurgent ethnic groups dependent on the narcotics trade involve an implicit tolerance of continued involvement in narcotics for varying periods of time.[22]

At the same time, even if generals in Rangoon were not directly involved in the drug trade, Burmese military officers at the local level were profiting from

240 · *Living Silence*

the drug business through taxing the farmers, the owners of heroin refineries and the traffickers.[23] And a number of the country's major investments in infrastructure projects and hotels were made by drug kingpins permitted to launder their money and establish legal businesses, often in the form of joint ventures with military-owned holding companies.[24]

In 1996, the regime negotiated a surrender deal with Khun Sa, an armed opposition leader and drug warlord long wanted in the United States on heroin-trafficking charges. The regime in Rangoon refused to extradite him despite the US government's offer of a $2 million reward. Instead, he was allowed to move to Rangoon, to make property and transportation investments, and to build two casinos near the Thai border. He was also believed to have continued his involvement in the drug business.[25] Although the regime sought favourable publicity with its increased drug busts in the late 1990s, the economy was in a state of collapse. The regime could not afford to eliminate the money generated from drug-trafficking and was not ready to take on the heavily armed groups involved in the drug trade.

Like many other countries, members of the EU were also concerned about drug production and political repression in Burma. However, within the EU, different countries adopted different positions on how to deal with Burma. The French and German governments were opposed to economic sanctions, while by early 2000 the British government was taking a harder line, including encouraging Premier Oil to withdraw from Burma. The EU as a whole adopted a visa ban against top Burmese officials and their supporters in 1996 and, in 2000, announced it would publish the list of names of people banned and freeze their assets. It also placed an export ban on equipment 'that might be used for internal repression or terrorism', although it promised to send a mission to Rangoon to discuss increased humanitarian aid to Burma as well.[26]

Canada took measures to indicate its frustration with the regime in August 1997, when it withdrew Burma's preferential tariff eligibility and instituted a policy of discouraging Canadian businesses from investing in Burma. Canada suspended bilateral aid to Burma in 1988, but in 1999 it decided to break its no-contact policy with the regime in order to cooperate on drug issues.

The Australian government was also critical of political repression in Burma but, in 1999, it attempted a different tack. It began consulting with the regime on the possibility of setting up an internal human rights commission and providing human rights training for the police. Daw Aung San Suu Kyi, however, expressed little faith in the project, comparing it to 'asking the fox to look after the chicken'.[27]

Throughout the mid- and late 1990s, western embassy officials, particularly American and British, maintained regular contact with Daw Aung San Suu Kyi and top NLD leaders and sent representatives to NLD functions. ASEAN embassy staff, on the other hand, generally refrained from attending NLD events, not wanting to irritate the regime. Meanwhile, Japan took a position between western and ASEAN governments on Burma, trying to persuade the regime to change its ways by offering the promise of bilateral aid. Japan called for the regime to take specific actions such as making progress towards democratization and reopening the country's universities. The Japanese government let the regime know that if such actions were taken, Japan would be able to provide much-needed development assistance.

Although Daw Aung San Suu Kyi's release appears to have been related to Japanese diplomatic efforts, the generals did not hesitate to reimpose restrictions on her movements once she became a threat to them. Meanwhile, recognizing the importance of Japanese support, Daw Aung San Suu Kyi tried to reach out to the Japanese public through a weekly column for the *Mainichi* newspaper in 1995 and 1996. Entitled 'Letters from Burma', it described the leading members, activities and policies of the NLD and the kinds of repression her party and ordinary people face under the military regime.[28] Nevertheless, the business community in Japan lobbied hard for improved relations with Burma's generals. Eager to gain a foothold, even if the economy in Burma did not improve in the short term, Japanese businesses urged the Japanese government to resume overseas development assistance to Burma in order to smooth the way for future Japanese investment.[29] The Japanese government, while eager to see democracy restored, also worried that if it did not maintain influence with the military regime, China would monopolize political and economic access to Burma.

International bodies have likewise had to consider whether isolating or engaging the regime in Rangoon would be more likely to facilitate change. The United Nations attempted a variety of approaches. It appointed a special rapporteur to document human rights abuses in Burma and passed annual resolutions highly critical of the regime's policies of repression. The resolutions called for the regime to begin a dialogue with Daw Aung San Suu Kyi and the pro-democracy movement as well as with the ethnic nationalities, but went unheeded. The UN also appointed special envoys to try to persuade the regime to negotiate with its opposition. In 1998, the United Nations' Secretariat sent a high-level representative to Rangoon to float the idea of providing $1 billion worth of World Bank aid to Burma if the regime would enter into a dialogue with the NLD.[30] This idea had come out of a meeting held in Chilston, England, in 1998, which included several ambassadors and high-level officials from countries concerned about Burma. But the generals said no. In March 2000, representatives of several Asian and western governments met in Seoul to reconsider their options. Opinions continued to be divided over whether isolation or engagement was more likely to bring the regime to the negotiating table. With China still willing to support the regime and other countries pursuing mixed policies, the regime apparently did not feel unduly threatened.

Corporations, the Media and International Campaigns

Corporations investing in Burma in the 1990s came under harsh criticism from Daw Aung San Suu Kyi. Following her release from house arrest, she argued that any investments made under the military regime, when the economy was not really open to all, would benefit only the generals. Foreign companies, however, claimed that their activities could contribute to the country's economic development, bring about a rise in the standard of living, and perhaps ultimately lead to political changes. Given Burma's rampant poverty and unemployment, many Burmese were eager for any jobs regardless of the political implications. Yet, to be successful, foreign businesses operating in Burma had to have good connections with the generals. Many established joint-ventures with military-owned companies.

In at least two cases, the Tatmadaw purportedly used forced labour and committed other abuses in connection to foreign investment projects: the Yadana gas pipeline constructed by Total and Unocal and the Yetagun pipeline, in which Premier Oil had a significant interest. In May 2000, the head of Premier Oil admitted that isolated instances of human rights and environmental abuses had taken place in the area where the Yetagun pipeline was constructed.[31] In the United States, two lawsuits were filed against Unocal and its two top executives for the company's investment in the Yadana pipeline. The lawsuits argued that Unocal must take responsibility for the Tatmadaw's reported confiscation of villagers' land without compensation and the Tatmadaw's alleged use of forced labour to construct military outposts and access roads along the pipeline route. Unocal originally claimed that it had no evidence such abuses occurred since the contract was signed, but documents which were surrendered during the trial indicated otherwise. Nevertheless, the judge ruled that Unocal could not be held responsible.

By early 2000, foreign investment in Burma had declined precipitously, due to sanctions, the Asian economic crisis, the lack of the rule of law, and the regime's own mismanagement of the economy, which made it difficult for foreign companies to earn a profit. The regime continued to blame Daw Aung San Suu Kyi for the country's poor economic performance, arguing it was her call for sanctions that was resulting in fewer jobs for the Burmese people. However, in its 1999 report, the World Bank, while agreeing that sanctions had played a role in limiting investment, also blamed the regime for not carrying out necessary reforms and asserted that the regime's economic policies had disproportionately affected Burma's poor.[32]

Both the military regime and Daw Aung San Suu Kyi were well aware of the importance of the international media in publicizing their respective points of view abroad. The military regime initially allowed most foreign journalists to meet with Daw Aung San Suu Kyi after she was released from house arrest. But when the media's interest in Daw Aung San Suu Kyi failed to die down, the generals began restricting access. Soon the regime was, for the most part, only granting journalist visas to those it hoped would write stories which portrayed the regime in a favourable light. In several instances, journalists had to agree that they would not visit Daw Aung San Suu Kyi. Some freelance journalists got around such restrictions by entering Burma on tourist visas, although in many cases, they were found out and barred from entering the country again. While there were several Burmese stringers in Rangoon working for foreign news agencies, they came under severe pressure not to report on stories that would reflect badly on the regime. Meanwhile ordinary Burmese citizens and political party members put themselves at great risk if they talked to the international press. In 1997, Daw San San, an NLD MP-elect, was sentenced to twenty-five years in prison for giving an interview to the BBC in which she was critical of the military regime.

The regime frequently cut Daw Aung San Suu Kyi's telephone line, making it nearly impossible for her to conduct phone interviews with journalists outside Burma. Daw Aung San Suu Kyi tried to maintain contact with the international community through producing periodic videotaped addresses which were secretly taken out and played at conferences and events abroad. For instance, she provided a videotaped keynote address for the 1995 NGO Forum on Women in Beijing, and she sent out addresses for the fiftieth anniversary of the Universal Declaration of Human Rights in December 1998, and for the 1999 Hague Appeal for Peace Conference. Despite the restrictions placed on her and her party, Daw Aung San Suu Kyi was able to make Burma much more of an issue for foreign governments than it had ever been in the past.

In 1997 and 1998, representatives of the military regime worked with two US consulting firms, Jefferson Waterman International and Bain and Associates, to improve their image abroad. The firms sought to get stories favourable to the regime placed in the press and helped organize journalists' visits to Burma to see the regime's achievements.[33] The focus was on repealing sanctions and repudiating the regime's image as a 'narco-state'. As part of this campaign, in April 1998, the regime helicoptered a select group of journalists and embassy personnel to the headquarters of various ceasefire groups in northern Burma, where the leaders and village headmen pledged their commitment to eradicating drug cultivation.

The generals in Rangoon benefited from the fact that the international media generally focused only on stories about individuals with international profiles. Thus, while they reported anything that happened to Daw Aung San Suu Kyi, because she was a well-known figure abroad, they did not usually give much coverage to anyone else in the pro-democracy movement. Even other key members in the NLD and ethnic minority political parties received little media coverage and so could be harassed or arrested without an international outcry. Similarly, the annual dry season attacks on ethnic nationalist armies, which frequently resulted in the forced relocation of thousands of civilians, went virtually unreported. Journalists could not obtain access and as one journalist told me, those offensives were so common in Burma that they were not news.

Because events in Burma were not of pressing concern to most people in the rest of the world, Burmese and foreign activists periodically felt the need to resort to dramatic gestures to raise international awareness. The embassy takeover and plane hijacking by young Burmese men are two extreme examples, but foreigners also sought to focus world concern on Burma by getting themselves arrested. A group of foreign activists entered Rangoon on tourist visas to pass out pamphlets on the tenth anniversary of the 1988 uprising. The pamphlets, which stated, '8-8-88 – don't forget – don't give up', were handed out to hundreds of curious Burmese at monasteries and marketplaces in Rangoon. While they hoped to encourage the Burmese by demonstrating their solidarity, the foreign activists also knew they were likely to be arrested. The eighteen, including six Americans, three Thais, three Malaysians, three Indonesians, two Filipinos and an Australian, were held for six days before being sentenced to five years' imprisonment with hard labour. Then, the sentences were commuted and they were deported. When they returned to Bangkok, they were greeted by throngs of journalists and their story was picked up around the world.[34] Similarly, James Mawdsley made three trips into Burma in which he was arrested for distributing anti-government literature and in at least one case, entering without a visa. In August 1999, he was sentenced to seventeen years in prison and served fourteen months before being released in October 2000. James Mawdsley described his activities as part of a campaign to highlight the regime's human rights abuses, and his case also received extensive press coverage.

Meanwhile, the National Coalition Government of the Union of Burma (NCGUB) in exile and Burmese students and democracy supporters outside Burma sought to promote their country's cause, often in conjunction with local activists. They pressured multinational corporations to withdraw their investments and tried to increase governmental support for the pro-democracy movement. Relying heavily on e-mail and the internet to network and distribute information, the US-based Free Burma Coalition expanded to over one hundred chapters in 1996.[35] Pepsi, Levi-Strauss and Heinekin and several other companies pulled out of Burma, in part because of activists' pressure. Other companies withdrew or reduced investments because of the Asian economic crisis and difficulties of working with the regime.

As a result of the Free Burma movement's efforts, selective purchasing laws, preventing the purchase of goods from all companies doing business in Burma, were passed in twenty-five American cities, counties and the state of

Massachusetts between 1995 and 2000. After the US Supreme Court struck down the selective purchasing laws in 2000, Free Burma groups switched to divestment campaigns.

Responding to Daw Aung San Suu Kyi's call for a tourist boycott of the regime-sponsored 'Visit Myanmar Year' in 1996–97, the Free Burma movement launched a worldwide campaign to stop travel agencies from offering package tours to Burma and to urge tourists to stay away. The campaign significantly reduced tourist arrivals, embarrassing the military regime. The generals had launched Visit Myanmar Year not only to make money but also to increase the regime's legitimacy at home and abroad.[36]

Meanwhile, the Burmese border-based resistance organizations, which included elected parliamentarians, NLD members, former student activists and ethnic nationalists, served as conduits for information in and out of the country. Besides trying to get reports about human rights abuses and political developments out to the international community, members of the border-based organizations also worked to get news about global standards on human rights and strategies for resistance into the country. Operating out of cramped offices in border towns and capital cities in Burma's neighbouring countries, Burmese and ethnic minority activists were able to participate in developing international campaigns and to cultivate links with student, professional and religious groups willing to assist them. Through lobbying trips to the United Nations and foreign capitals and speeches at international human rights conferences, they informed a wider audience about the crisis in Burma and broadened their own political understandings.

It should be noted that the armed struggles of the student activists and the ethnic nationalists were far less successful. Of the 10,000 students who originally came to Burma's borders after 1988, only about one thousand remained in early 2000. The students were no match for the Tatmadaw, and many died, returned home or resettled abroad. Likewise, many of the armed ethnic organizations, which had been fighting Rangoon governments for decades, found that they could no longer compete with the Tatmadaw and agreed to ceasefire deals, hoping to continue to press for their political agendas through a dialogue with the Burmese generals.

Political and Humanitarian Assistance

In a September 1999 statement distributed abroad, Daw Aung San Suu Kyi pointedly told the international community: 'What we need now is more than just talk. We need concrete action.'[37] As of mid-2000, neither the UN nor foreign governments which follow Burma closely had seriously contemplated the use of force to unseat the regime. Besides alternately attempting to isolate or engage the regime, various governments and international organizations offered financial support to non-violent activists abroad, humanitarian support to refugees, and some development assistance inside Burma.

Several western governments and foundations provided funding to non-violent Burmese activists and journalists in exile, with the hope that they could strengthen the pro-democracy movement inside the country through increasing people's access to information.[38] For example, two radio stations, the Democratic Voice of Burma, based in Oslo, and Radio Free Asia's Burmese section, based in Washington DC, received financial support. Several opposition newspapers, in Burmese and ethnic minority languages, were funded for the same reason, although their distribution was necessarily limited because anyone caught with them could be imprisoned. Meanwhile, foreign governments and foundations sought to strengthen the capacity of the exile movement and to increase solidarity between the ethnic nationalities and the pro-democracy activists, for instance by sponsoring constitutional seminars for the groups to draft a provisional constitution for the country. Foreign funders also provided computers, fax machines and internet access to numerous organizations in exile so that they could distribute information and communicate more easily with each other. Burmese activists abroad have often found it difficult to project the image of a united front, because pro-democracy activists and representatives of the various ethnic nationalist organizations are opposing the regime for different reasons and tend to be most concerned with their own organizations' specific interests.

Because the regime limits opportunities for instruction in indigenous languages other than Burmese, education in their own languages has been a priority for many of the ethnic nationalities. The New Mon State Party's education department worked with foreign organizations to develop a new primary school curriculum in Mon and to introduce a new approach to teaching. In the 1990s, the NMSP's education department ran 300 schools in its area going up to the high school level. Through its dialogues with international educators, the education department decided it wanted to move away from rote memorization and towards more student-centred learning. To encourage more creativity and analytical thinking in the classroom, all the Mon teachers were retrained. In the years after the NMSP concluded a ceasefire agreement with the SLORC in 1995, the education department found it more difficult to maintain its schools because of reduced financial support from the NMSP and frequent pressure by military authorities to replace the Mon schools with government-controlled schools. Nevertheless, the schools continued to operate throughout the late 1990s.

Foreign governments and private relief organizations also provided humanitarian assistance for the hundreds of thousands of Burmese refugees who fled to neighbouring countries during the 1990s. Two hundred and fifty thousand Rohingyas from Burma were housed in refugee camps in Bangladesh between

1991 and 1995, although most were eventually repatriated under a controversial United Nations-sponsored programme. In 1998, the United States Committee for Refugees put the Burmese refugee population at 53,000 in Bangladesh, 140,000 in Thailand, and 40,000 in India.[39] Most of these people received some assistance in the form of food, housing materials and medical care, and there was basic support for schools in the camps. As of 1998, there were an estimated 500,000 to one million displaced people in Burma, mostly in the Karen, Karenni and Shan States. While some relief groups tried to get food and medicine to them, most were scattered in the jungle and extremely difficult to reach.

At the same time, UN organizations and the approximately one dozen expatriate non-governmental organizations sought to provide assistance to needy populations within Burma.[40] In a major policy shift in the mid-1990s, the regime began allowing foreign organizations to set up programmes inside Burma, particularly in the fields of health, education and income generation. With poor sanitation, malnutrition, preventable diseases and high risks of HIV infection leading to unnecessary illness and death for many Burmese, foreign agencies sought to alleviate some of these problems.

However, Daw Aung San Suu Kyi asked that any organization working in Burma consult not only with the regime but also with the NLD. She was also concerned about the fact that expatriate organizations could not operate independently but generally had to work in conjunction with government ministries or government-organized 'non-governmental' organizations. Meanwhile, the regime made it clear that it did not want international NGOs to meet with Daw Aung San Suu Kyi. As in many countries in the world with repressive governments, international NGOs had to make difficult decisions about how and if their assistance could be effective and what kinds of compromises they would and would not be willing to make.

The expatriate organizations were able to carry out a number of beneficial activities in the country in the fields of health, early education and income generation, and introduced a new vocabulary of grassroots development and local empowerment. Nevertheless, in some cases the generals also tried to ensure that they directly profited. For instance, some expatriate organizations were told they had to hand over vehicles to military officers in return for being able to continue their programmes. And the regime often sought to channel assistance towards organizations working to support its own political objectives. For instance, a UNDP household survey which was given to the government's statistical office was then farmed out to members of the USDA to administer.[41] In 1996, two international organizations financed a health-related publication put out by the Myanmar Maternal and Child Welfare Association (MMCWA). Besides health news, the funded issues also ended up including MMCWA speeches criticizing 'internal destructionists', in other words, the NLD.[42] Such actions made it difficult for international NGOs who wanted to continue to help ordinary citizens but could not stop the authorities from interfering or politicizing their assistance. It should be noted that various NGOs and UN agencies handled these challenges in different ways. In addition, some NGOs found progressive and dedicated people within government ministries and government-controlled organizations with whom they could work more easily.

International NGOs resisting the regime's restrictions or seeking to consult with NLD members had to risk being forced to discontinue their programmes. A number of Burmese pro-democracy representatives abroad argued that international NGOs should not be in Burma under such circumstances, particularly since if the regime did not have to support health care and education itself, it could divert more money into repressing the population. Whether the regime felt that it no longer had to contribute as much because the NGOs were there is unclear, but according to the 1999 World Bank report, state funding for both primary education and health care declined steadily in the 1990s.[43] Nevertheless, the international organizations operating in Burma argued that given the terrible health and education problems in Burma, not to intervene would be unconscionable. Some also pointed out that having an international presence in the country was important in and of itself, because of the witnessing role international NGOs could play and the dialogues they could initiate with people in and out of the government.

Interestingly, the International Committee of the Red Cross (ICRC), which pulled out of Burma in 1995 because the regime would not allow ICRC representatives to visit political detainees, returned to Burma in 1999. While it initially faced opposition from many pro-democracy supporters, it was later praised by NLD leaders for managing to obtain access to over 1,500 prisoners in numerous prisons and government 'guesthouses'. In 1999 and early 2000, the ICRC met with a member of the NLD once a month, and while sticking to its core conditions, it also found ways to negotiate with the generals.[44]

What, then, has been the effect of international involvement on Burmese people's lives? As of late 2000, various international initiatives had reinforced the regime's pariah status but they had not succeeded in bringing the regime to the negotiating table. People still lived without the rule of law or the rights to speak and gather freely. Meanwhile, a limited degree of economic openness and foreign investment meant more opportunities, particularly for those with connections to the regime. But with a high inflation rate and continued economic stagnation in most sectors, many Burmese found themselves barely able to survive.

Ardent democracy supporters generally welcomed the sanctions and tourist boycott, because they made the democracy activists feel that they had crucial support abroad. Nevertheless, there were also businessmen and former democracy activists who believed more economic engagement could lead to greater political openness. Less politically-engaged people, particularly in rural areas, had little understanding of the international initiatives and their impact. And some democracy supporters sought to take advantage of new jobs created by foreign investment or the tourist industry, so they could better support their families, but also enjoyed meeting foreign visitors and explaining the country's problems to them. Similarly, many individuals willingly participated in programmes established by international NGOs, in order to learn new skills, improve their health and derive comfort from the fact that someone cared about their welfare.

Still, without a fundamental change in the way the government operated, more broad and lasting improvements were difficult to imagine. Because of the regime's unwillingness to share power, decentralize decision-making, or introduce the necessary measures to reform the economy, it was unable either to resolve the country's political crises or lift the standard of living of the majority of the population. Were a democratic government in place in Burma, it is likely that many of these issues could be dealt with more forthrightly, although eradicating the drug problem, peacefully resolving ethnic minority political rights, and creating a prosperous, well-educated society will take years of dedicated effort.

CHAPTER 13

Conclusion: A Different Burma

§ Successive military regimes in Burma have managed to hang on to power by using a combination of repression, intimidation, financial incentives and propaganda. Those who would oppose the generals, be they students, monks, elected members of Parliament or ethnic nationalists, face harassment at best, and prison sentences, torture and death at worst. Thus, even though people may complain bitterly about military rule in private, they are reluctant to take action. Moreover, as much as the regime would like to obtain wholehearted support from the population, it is not necessary. All that is needed is for people not to resist.

The SLORC and SPDC regimes have balanced the threat of violence with financial inducements to neutralize their opponents. They have offered business opportunities to elected MPs who agree to resign and to the leaders of armed ethnic groups who make ceasefire agreements. They have provided generous donations to monks who do not question military rule, and they reward movie stars and musicians who advocate the regime's policies through their work. Furthermore, they have tried to redirect anger about deteriorating economic conditions away from themselves and towards those who have advocated sanctions and other punitive measures.

The generals have also relied on propaganda to keep their opposition divided. Capitalizing on lingering resentment over the British policy of privileging non-Burmans, they have been fairly successful in arguing for a strong, centralized state with a unified culture. Many of Burma's majority Buddhist citizens and monks have supported the idea of Burma as a Buddhist nation. As a result, it has often been difficult for the ethnic nationalists and pro-democracy activists to link their struggles.

The depth of opposition to military rule became clear during the 1988 pro-democracy demonstrations and the 1990 election. But the generals ignored their citizens' and the international community's appeals for a political transition. It seems that the more the regime feels cornered, the more defensive it becomes. And yet when it feels that its control is secure, it sees no need to compromise with its opponents. Thus, if the NLD or the students do nothing, they are ignored, but when they take action in order to spur the junta to make concessions, they are brutally punished. Likewise, the ethnic nationalists have found that no matter how they struggle for their political rights, through party politics, the National Convention, or armed resistance, the regime has sought to disregard or delay considering their demands whenever possible.

If large numbers of Burmese people were to engage in non-violent resistance activities, and if the Burmese pro-democracy groups and the ethnic nationalist organizations could adopt a shared programme of action, it is possible that the regime would find itself in a position where it had to make compromises. But since 1990, the generals have managed to isolate political activists and sow enough fear into the general population that people generally police themselves. Moreover, the generals have been able to limit contact between ethnic political leaders and pro-democracy leaders inside the country.

Whenever repression intensifies, many people in Burma become cynical about the possibility of effecting change and turn to fatalistic interpretations of their situation. Still, the idea of a different future is kept alive through the determined struggle of Daw Aung San Suu Kyi, U Tin Oo and numerous other committed NLD and ethnic political party members, through student demonstrations and monks' calls for dialogue, through writers, film-makers, and artists who manage to convey anti-government sentiments despite the censors, and through news of political change in other former dictatorships.

Where is Burma's Ramos?

For a political transition to occur in Burma, it is likely that there will need to be a convergence of three factors: unified domestic political pressure, international pressure and a powerful group in the military which throws in its lot with the democratic movement. Either the senior generals need to see that it is in their interest to negotiate with the NLD and ethnic representatives, or an influential military faction must break away from the ruling junta. It should be understood that a split in the military would not necessarily have to revolve around a desire by some generals to restore democracy but could begin as a rivalry for power. Such a scenario would also require a catalyst, perhaps in the form of an economic breakdown, the death of a powerful leader or a growing populist movement.

In South Africa, international pressure and widespread domestic resistance set the pre-conditions for a political transformation. But it was not until De Klerk agreed to negotiate with Mandela and to dismantle apartheid that change was possible. The South African economy was deteriorating because of sanctions and boycotts, and De Klerk felt that continued intransigence would only lead the country to ruin.[1]

The Philippines offers another model where two powerful generals split away from Marcos, but not because they were committed to democracy.[2] Former Defence Minister Juan Ponce Enrile and General Fidel Ramos were angry about not obtaining the promotions they had hoped for. Meanwhile, Marcos' overspending and economic mismanagement had severely weakened the economy. At the same time, a people power movement backed by the Catholic Church had formed around Corazon Aquino, the wife of slain political leader Benigno Aquino and the real winner of the February 1986 presidential election. As the situation became more unstable, Enrile and Ramos saw their chance. They set up a rebel headquarters at Camp Aguinaldo in Manila. When it became clear that the forces loyal to Marcos were going to attack, civilian demonstrators surrounded the base to protect the Enrile–Ramos faction, putting nuns in front. Many soldiers defected to the Enrile–Ramos camp, and others refused to shoot the nuns and the civilian protesters. Representatives of the US government told Marcos they would fly him out of Manila, and he complied, although he originally assumed he was only being airlifted to his home province. Instead he was taken to Hawaii.

Although Enrile and Ramos originally intended to take power for themselves, not to restore democracy, they had to work with Corazon Aquino and the democracy movement. And she, realizing the need to placate the army, agreed to share power with them. In the first three years of her administration, disgruntled groups in the military made several coup attempts against the fledgling democratic government. But Aquino managed to hang on, convincing Ramos in the process of the importance of maintaining a democratic system. After her term of office was over, General Ramos was elected to succeed her, and the military gradually came to accept democratic rule.

In Burma, the economy has also been severely weakened, a pro-democracy movement emerged in the late 1980s, and there has been a fair amount of international pressure on the regime to negotiate. But so far Rangoon's generals have refused to budge, and no De Klerk or Ramos has emerged. Perhaps this is partly because international pressure has not been strong enough, and the regime has been able to rely heavily on China. Perhaps, too, it is because the regime feels it has successfully been able to dismantle and silence its opposition. In the Philippines and South Africa, some public opposition in the form of legal organizations and an alternative press were tolerated, but in Burma, the pro-democracy movement has had virtually no legal channels for organizing and disseminating its views, and even the smallest anti-regime actions are harshly punished.

Even if the regime were to agree to negotiate, determining how to handle sensitive ethnic minority issues could also be difficult. While the armed ethnic nationalist organizations desperately want peace and recognize the need for a dialogue between the generals and representatives of the pro-democracy movement, most also believe that ethnic issues must not be sidelined. But who would represent the ethnic minorities? Would leaders of armed organizations or leaders of ethnic political parties sit at the table? And which ethnic representatives would be acceptable to all ethnic groups? Ethnic leaders have been thinking about these issues and seeking to identify individuals who might be able to speak on behalf of all the groups, but they have not been able to hold any kind of conference to discuss such matters openly.

Still, many of Burma's ethnic leaders developed greater trust in Daw Aung San Suu Kyi as she sought to include ethnic political leaders in the CRPP, invited them to NLD events, and addressed some of their concerns in her speeches. It is possible that the ethnic political organizations would be willing to allow Daw Aung San Suu Kyi to meet with the regime first, with the understanding that ethnic demands would have to be resolved in conjunction with the establishment of a new political system. It is also possible that all parties might agree to an interim government in which power would be shared among representatives of the military, the pro-democracy groups and ethnic minority leaders. Such an arrangement could provide time for a new constitution to be written and for the ethnic nationalities' political status to be worked out. With an independent media and the chance for political leaders to address the public freely, a climate more tolerant of decentralization and pluralism could emerge in Burma.

The Restoration of Civil Society

For a political transition to succeed in Burma, democratic practices need to be inculcated and the division of political power must be resolved in a way in which most people feel satisfied. After centuries under the absolutist rule of kings and decades under repressive military generals, people in Burma today have little experience with democratic norms. Even members of the pro-democracy movement find it difficult to develop the openness and tolerance required of a democratic culture. As student activist Min Zin wrote in an article in *The Irrawaddy* news journal: 'The idea that democracy is a way of life that you must practice in your daily life, in your organization, and in your community is pretty far removed from our practice, attitude, and behavior.'[3]

Rigid thinking, hierarchical power structures and a culture of mistrust have characterized not only the military regime but, in many cases, the opposition groups as well. In many political organizations operating inside Burma and in the border areas, more value is often placed on being a strong-willed leader than a team player. Lower-ranking members are told to take orders, not ask questions. And constructive criticism is frequently interpreted as a challenge rather than a contribution. Burmese activists can find it difficult to evaluate different ideas because they have had no exposure to critical

254 · *Living Silence*

thinking. They have never been taught to weigh both the positive and the negative aspects of various policies.

Still, there is hope. Many activists operating outside Burma have become more sophisticated in their thinking. Likewise, a number of Burmese studying and working abroad have learned the importance of working cooperatively and tolerating different views. In the future, it is to be hoped that some of these exiled Burmese will return home and contribute their newly-acquired skills and perspectives to rebuilding the country. Inside Burma, Daw Aung San Suu Kyi and some other NLD leaders, intellectuals and students have sought to encourage debate and dialogue and have emphasized the importance of learning from other countries' experiences.

Although the regime has often said that western-style democracy is not appropriate for Burma, many of the core values enshrined in a democratic system are also deeply rooted in Buddhism. Buddhist ideology is fundamentally broad-minded, and it insists on a detached attitude towards the world. Each person must make his or her own way towards enlightenment, and this must be done by recognizing that everything to which we cling is ultimately impermanent. If such tenets were applied to political and social relations, racial prejudices and ideological inflexibility should ideally find little support.

At the same time, Buddhist philosophy insists that individuals use their powers of reasoning to make informed decisions. As General Aung San wrote in 1935 in an essay entitled 'Burma and Buddhism', the Buddha told his followers not to believe anything merely because it was written in a religious book, often repeated or stated by people in positions of authority. Beliefs and ideas, he said, must be tested by observation and analysis, be reasonable and beneficial to all. Concerned that Burmese were slipping into a pattern of passive acceptance, General Aung San stated: 'It is therefore the bounden duty of every true Burman to revive the spirit of criticism, inherent in Buddhism, and apply it to every problem affecting Burma.'[4]

Resolving the ethnic nationalities' demands will require compromises by both Burmans and the various other indigenous nationalities. First and foremost, Burmans need to accept that this problem will not just go away. Concessions must be made for peace to be maintained. There must be a willingness to redistribute power so that majority rule does not mean that the ethnic minorities will always be in a disadvantaged position. This could mean devolving more political power to the state or local level and perhaps creating two houses of Parliament, in which representation by population and ethnicity are balanced. Some have also suggested redrawing the political map. Currently, there are seven states and seven divisions. One idea is to consolidate the seven divisions, which contain majority-Burman populations and cover about half of Burma's territory, into one Burman state, with equal rights to the seven other ethnic minority states. However, this may not be viable considering that the Burman population is much larger than any of the other nationalities' populations, and the geographical dispersion of Burmans is vast. Some of the ethnic nationalists have also called for the ethnic minority states to have the right to secede at any time, a proposition which most Burman politicians are understandably reluctant to accept. However, there will at least have to be strong guarantees in the constitution which give the ethnic nationalities confidence that their political authority will not be eroded over time.

A further problem is the presence of populations of smaller ethnic groups within the ethnic minority states. For instance, the Was in Shan State are seeking some degree of political autonomy, as are the Lahus in Shan State. In resolving the distribution of power between the central government and the states and within the states, much needs to be considered, including control over resources, language policies, educational policies and political representation.

Moreover, the various ethnic nationalities espouse different political views and thus cannot be treated as a homogeneous group. Some of the armed nationalist organizations have promoted nationalism at the expense of pluralism in order to galvanize support among local populations. In civil war areas, some ethnic nationalist organizers routinely dismissed all Burmans as 'the enemy'. Although ethnic resistance groups such as the KNU, KIO and NMSP did take in large numbers of Burmese students and politicians, the mistrust has still not been eradicated. Some of the smaller resistance organizations operating in mixed ethnic regions, have, however, advocated equality, tolerance and freedom of religion. The small Karenni State Nationalities People's Liberation Front (KNPLF), for instance, includes Buddhist Shan, Christian and animist Kayah, Kayan and Karen members. A female captain doing health work and community organizing for the KNPLF told me if there were democracy in Burma, she would be happy to work for people anywhere in the country; it didn't have to be only in the KNPLF area.

Finally, people from ethnic minority backgrounds who live in Rangoon, Mandalay and other towns and villages in central Burma have different perspectives from those living in remote areas. Already integrated with the majority population, they are often most concerned with religious, cultural and educational rights and eradicating prejudice. Many of the educated ethnic minorities in the heartland of Burma have been upset by the authoritarianism that has characterized some of the armed ethnic organizations. Although they may strongly support the protection of ethnic minority rights, they are eager to see democracy restored. Of course there is also a large population of people of mixed ethnic backgrounds who defy simple categorization but who generally would like to see far less emphasis on the issue of race.

Another issue that is sure to be challenging is what to do about all the individuals who committed serious abuses under military rule. How should those who have raped, tortured and killed civilians be dealt with? One course of action would be to establish a truth and reconciliation commission, similar to that in South Africa, with or without the right to prosecute. Whatever decision is made, it is most likely to affect not only the Tatmadaw but also members of resistance armies who committed human rights abuses.

Were Burma to achieve a transitional government or full democracy, what would the country be like? Initially, there could well be political violence, communal tensions and continued corruption, but at least people would be able to speak and write freely and would no longer fear being conscripted as porters or forced labourers. It would be a time of exuberant hopes and thoughtful reflection but, if the experiences of other newly-democratizing countries are of any relevance, it is likely that the political culture would change too slowly for some while the material culture would change too quickly for others. Improving the standard of living would be the key issue for most people, and preventing the emergence of wide gaps in income levels would be likely to prove particularly challenging. In many ways, Burma would probably become less distinctively Burmese as it integrated into the global economy, but Burmese would also presumably feel more confident about their status within the international community. There would be an explosion of newspapers, magazines, art shows, theatre and film-making, with debates raging about how best to develop the country, how to reassess social and cultural practices, and how to reconfigure political and economic relations. Universities, markets and teashops would be teeming with people comparing experiences and sharing ideas. In short, Burma would no longer be a place of silence.

Notes

Introduction

1. 'Daw' is a term of respect for an older woman. In Burma, people call Aung San Suu Kyi, 'Daw Aung San Suu Kyi' or, if they are close to her, 'Daw Suu'. I have also used 'U', a term of respect for an older man, where appropriate.

2. Kay Merrill, 'Burma Looks Set to Reject the Lessons of History', *Jane's Intelligence Review*, 1 August 1999.

3. David Brunnstrom, 'Myanmar Embassy Gunmen Villains then Heroes', *Reuters*, 3 October 1999.

4. 'Suu Kyi Party Condemns Thai Hostage Drama', *Agence France Presse*, 28 January 2000.

5. Quoted in 'Yangon to the UN: Thanks, But...', *Far Eastern Economic Review*, 25 December 1998.

1. Historical Legacies

1. S. J. Tambiah, 'The Gallactic Polity: The Structure of Traditional Kingdoms in Southeast Asia', *Annals of the New York Academy of Sciences*, No. 293 (July 1977), pp. 69–97.

2. For instance, Victor Lieberman, *Burmese Administrative Cycles: Anarchy and Conquest, c.1580–1760* (Princeton, NJ: Princeton University Press, 1984), p. 98, describes how King Thalun resettled Mons, Shans, Siamese, Laos, Indians and Arakanese in the agricultural areas around his capital.

3. E. R. Leach, 'The Frontiers of "Burma"', *Comparative Studies in Society and History*, Vol. 3, No. 1 (October 1960), pp. 49–68.

4. Father Vincenzo Sangermano, *The Burmese Empire a Hundred Years Ago* (Bangkok: White Orchid Press, 1985 [1st edn 1833]), pp. 73–4, describes the capriciousness of many kings who had rivals and subjects killed at the slightest suspicion.

5. See R. C. Temple, *The Thirty-Seven Nats* (London: W. Griggs, 1906) for different versions of this tale and further information on the role of *nats*.

6. See David I. Steinberg, *Burma: A Socialist Nation of Southeast Asia* (Boulder, CO: Westview Press, 1982), pp. 24–34, for a fuller discussion of Britain's motives.

7. See Chapter 3 of Thongchai Winichakul's *Siam Mapped: A History of the Geo-Body of a Nation* (Honolulu: University of Hawaii Press, 1994).

8. Chao-Tzang Yawnghwe, 'The Burman Military: Holding the Country Together?', in J. Silverstein (ed.), *Independent Burma at Forty Years: Six Assessments* (Ithaca, NY: Cornell University Southeast Asia Program, 1989), pp. 86–7.

9. See Dr San C. Po, *Burma and the Karens* (London: Elliot Stock, 1928) for a Karen assessment of the impact of Christianity and education on the Karens.

10. Maung Maung Pye, *Burma in the Crucible* (Rangoon: Khittaya Publishing House, 1951), pp. 15–16.

11. U Maung Maung, *From Sangha to Laity: Nationalist Movements of Burma: 1920–1940* (Australian National University Monograph on South Asia No. 4, 1980), Chs 8–10.

12. Maurce Collis, *Trials in Burma* (Bangkok: Ava Books, 1996 [1938]) discusses the social aspects of discrimination; J. S. Furnivall, *Colonial Policy and Practice* (London: Cambridge University Press, 1948), discusses the economic policies that encouraged racial divisions.

13. The Karenni State was recognized as separate from Burma during the colonial period, although it was eventually ruled like the other frontier areas. After the British had taken control of lower Burma in the mid-1850s, the British and King Mindon had signed an agreement recognizing the Karenni territory's independence in order to maintain a buffer between the British and Mindon's kingdom.

14. See Maung Maung, *Burma's Constitution* (The Hague: Martinus Nijhoff, 1959).

15. See Kin Oung, *Who Killed Aung San?* (Bangkok: White Lotus, 1996) for more details.

16. For an account of this period from a civil servant of Indian heritage see Balwant Singh, *Independence and Democracy in Burma, 1945–1952: The Turbulent Years* (Ann Arbor, MI: University of Michigan Center for South and Southeast Asian Studies, 1993).

17. Yawnghwe, 'The Burman Military', pp. 92–4.

18. See Manning Nash, *The Golden Road to Modernity: Village Life in Contemporary Burma* (Chicago, IL: University of Chicago Press, 1965), p. 322.

19. For more information on U Nu's policies in the 1950s, see Hugh Tinker, *The Union of Burma* (London: Oxford University Press, 1957), Chs 4–12.

20. Nash, *Golden Road to Modernity*, pp. 280–1.

21. Mary Callahan, *The Origins of Military Rule in Burma*. PhD Dissertation (Ithaca, NY: Cornell University, 1996), Chs 8 and 9.

22. Ibid., pp. 468–80. Callahan also refers to a paper presented at the annual commanding officers' conference in 1958 questioning the appropriateness of democratic rule for Burma.

23. See ibid., pp. 480–1; U Thaung, *A Journalist, a General and an Army in Burma* (Bangkok: White Lotus, 1995), pp. 38–41.

24. Steinberg, *Burma*, pp. 70–1.

25. Ba Maw, *Breakthrough in Burma, Memoirs of a Revolution, 1939–1946* (New Haven, CT: Yale University Press, 1968), p. 196.

2. The Ne Win Years, 1962–88

1. Bertil Lintner, *Outrage: Burma's Struggle for Democracy* (Bangkok: White Lotus, 1990) p. 39.

2. David Steinberg, *Burma: A Socialist Nation of Southeast Asia* (Boulder, CO: Westview Press, 1982), p. 79; David Steinberg, 'The Union Solidarity Development Association', *Burma Debate*, January/February 1997.

3. John F. Cady, *The United States and Burma* (Cambridge, MA: Harvard University Press, 1976), p. 248.

4. Steinberg, *Burma*, p. 79.

5. Josef Silverstein, 'Burmese Student Politics in a Changing Society', *Daedalus*, Vol. 97, No. 1 (1968), p. 291.

6. Josef Silverstein quoted in Lintner, *Outrage*, pp. 43–4; interview with a Burmese journalist.

7. Interviews with Chins whose family members were imprisoned, and see Pu Lian Uk, 'No Room for the Chin in Burman Monopolized Politics', *Burma Debate*, December 1994/January 1995, p. 30.

8. R. H. Taylor, 'Elections in Burma/Myanmar: For Whom and Why?', in R. H. Taylor (ed.), *The Politics of Elections in Southeast Asia* (Cambridge: Cambridge University Press, 1996), p. 175.

9. Lintner, *Outrage*, p. 59.

10. Mya Maung, *Totalitarianism in Burma: Prospects for Economic Development* (New York: Paragon House, 1992), p. 25.

11. Cady, *The United States and Burma*, p. 253.

12. Ibid., p. 254.

13. Information on the 1969–78 protests from U Tint Zaw, a former Rangoon University professor, U Aung Saw Oo, a long-time political activist, and other activists who were involved.

14. See Andrew Selth, *Death of a Hero: The U Thant Disturbances in Burma, December 1974* (Brisbane: Griffith University Centre for the Study of Australian–Asian Relations, April 1989), for a full account.

15. Ibid., p. 15.

16. Ibid., p. 23.

17. See Bertil Lintner, *Burma in Revolt: Opium and Insurgency Since 1948* (Boulder, CO: Westview Press, 1994), Ch. 7; Martin Smith, *Burma: Insurgency and the Politics of Ethnicity* (London: Zed Books, 1999), Chs 13 and 15.

18. See Lintner, *Burma in Revolt*, pp. 209–11; Smith, *Burma*, Ch. 14.

19. Smith, *Burma*, pp. 259–60.

3. Breaking the Silence, 1988–90

1. See Bertil Lintner, *Outrage: Burma's Struggle for Democracy* (Bangkok: White Lotus, 1990) for a full account of the 1988 demonstrations.

2. For a translation of one of Aung Gyi's letters, see *Asiaweek*, 8 July 1988. Excerpts from another letter were printed in *Asiaweek* on 12 August 1988.

3. Lintner, *Outrage*, pp. 80–1.

4. In South East Asia, men can enter and leave the monkhood at will. In Burma, Buddhist men generally enter the monkhood once as young boys and again when they have reached the age of about twenty. Most stay only for a week or a few months, although some choose to become monks for life.

5. Lintner, *Outrage*, pp. 94–103.

6. This figure has been widely cited but never verified.

7. The British Library has a collection of nearly one hundred unofficial publications from this period. See Anna J. Allott, *Inked Over, Ripped Out: Burmese Storytellers and the Censors* (Chiang Mai, Thailand: Silkworm Books, 1994), p. 15.

8. *Asiaweek*, 9 September 1988.

9. *Asiaweek*, 2 September 1988.

10. According to Bertil Lintner, *Burma in Revolt: Opium and Insurgency Since 1948* (Boulder, CO: Westview Press, 1994), p. 294, not only did the leadership of the CPB not authorize participation in the uprising but the majority of the troops (mainly Was) did not even know an uprising was happening.

11. 'Going Back to Work, Sullenly', *Asiaweek*, 14 October 1988.

12. The ten ethical rules are: generosity, morality, self-sacrifice, integrity, kindness, austerity, non-anger, non-violence, patience and harmony. For a more complete description see Aung San Suu Kyi, *Freedom from Fear and Other Writings* (London: Penguin Books, 1991), pp. 170–3.

13. A student activist told me how he and his colleagues had been given leaflets to distribute with pictures of Daw Aung San Suu Kyi's head attached to a nude body, but they had destroyed them in disgust. He said the authorities assumed that some student groups would be happy to distribute them because of their disagreements with Daw Aung San Suu Kyi over participation in the election.

14. 'Bar the Name, Much the Same', *Asiaweek*, 23 June 1989.

15. 'Anniversaries of Anger', *Asiaweek*, 7 July 1989.

16. 'Heading for a Showdown', *Asiaweek*, 14 July 1989.

17. Michael Aris, 'Introduction,' in Aung San Suu Kyi, *Freedom from Fear*, p. xxi.

18. For a description of events at Daw Aung San Suu Kyi's compound on the day of her arrest, see 'Truth Will Come One Day', *Burma Debate*, August/September 1995, p. 11.

19. Interview with Daw San Kyaw Zaw, 29 November 1998.

20. Lintner, *Burma in Revolt*, p. 304.

21. This figure was given in an Amnesty International report cited in Lintner, *Burma in Revolt*, p. 377. He says others put the number even higher.

22. Robert Taylor, *The State in Burma* (London: C. Hurst, 1996), p. 177.

23. See 'Burma's Cheated Voters', Letters to the Editor, *Asiaweek*, 10 August 1990.

24. See All Burma Students' Democratic Front, *To Stand and Be Counted: The Suppression of Burma's Members of Parliament* (Bangkok, June 1998), p. 20, for the full statistics.

25. 'The Ides of September', *Asiaweek*, 14 September 1990.

26. Lintner, *Burma in Revolt*, pp. 311–12.

4. Military Rule Continues

1. This English translation of the questionnaire was provided by Dr U Ne Oo in Australia.

2. Anthony Davis and Bruce Hawke, 'Burma: the Country that Won't Kick the Habit', *Jane's Intelligence Review*, 1 March 1998.

3. *International Narcotics Control Strategy Report* (Washington, DC: US Department of State, March 1996).

4. Kei Nemoto, 'The Japanese Perspective', *Burma Debate*, August/September 1995, pp. 23–4.

5. I did not attend this event but subsequently watched a videotape of the performance.

6. See 'Human Rights Watch/Asia Condemns Sentencing of NLD Supporters', *Human Rights Watch/Asia*, Press Release, 20 March 1996.

7. Human Rights Watch/Asia reported the arrest of three men in Mandalay for distributing videos of the People's Forum. 'Human Rights Watch/Asia Condemns New Arrests of NLD Supporters', *Human Rights Watch/Asia*, Press Release, 11 January 1996.

8. Daw Aung San Suu Kyi's weekend talk, 16 March 1996 (translation from a tape of the talk).

9. *New Light of Myanmar*, 12 November 1996 (posted on the internet).

10. A full list of Lt General Khin Nyunt's titles was compiled by *The Irrawaddy* and posted on the maykha listserver by David Arnott on 28 May 1999.

11. The USDA was modelled on General Suharto's mass party, Golkar, in Indonesia. See David I. Steinberg, 'The Union Solidarity Development Association', *Burma Debate*, January/February 1997.

12. 'All Must Keep Vigil and Prevent Negatively-oriented Destructive and Subservient Traitors from Intruding into Educational Realm and Using Students in Bids to Gain Political Power', *New Light of Myanmar*, 11 December 1996.

13. 'Notification No. 6', *Committee Representing the People's Parliament*, 9 February 1999.

14. '183 Parliament Representatives Remain Valid in Myanmar', *Xinhua*, 18 October 1999.

15. Craig Skehan, 'Junta Cut Off Aris' Last Words', *Bangkok Post*, 31 March 1999.

16. The Karenni State Nationalities People's Liberation Front, the Shan State Nationalities People's Liberation Organization and the Kayan New Land Party issued a joint statement, and the New Mon State Party and the Shan State Army issued individual statements. See *The BurmaNet News*, No. 1104, 25–27 September 1998, for more information on the military regime's reaction and statements by some groups against the CRPP.

5. Families: Fostering Conformity

1. Burma Socialist Programme Party, *Facts About Burma* (Rangoon: December 1983), pp. 236–42.

2. 'Burmese General, Wife Disown Son', *The Nation*, 26 February 1998. Lt General Khin Nyunt was quoted as saying Ye Naing Win was disowned 'for his inexcusable deed'.

3. Published in the All Burma Students' Democratic Front's *Dawn Oh Wai* (Cry of the Peacock) magazine in 1989. Translated by T.

4. While long-time Indian residents have suffered under this system, migrant Chinese with a bit of money have found ways to purchase citizenship papers. See Dermot Tatlow, 'China's Shadow', *Asiaweek*, 28 May 1999.

6. Communities: Going with the Flow

1. See All Burma Students' Democratic Front, *Tortured Voices: Personal Accounts of Burma's Interrogation Centres* (Thailand: self-published, July 1998).

2. Written in huge letters on an elevated water tank at the Defence Services Academy in Maymyo, Shan State, among other places.

3. Maung Aung Myoe, *Building the Tatmadaw: The Organisational Development of the Armed Forces in Myanmar, 1948–98* (Canberra: Strategic and Defence Studies Centre, Australian National University, 1998), p. 52.

4. Karen Human Rights Group, *Summary of Forced Labor in Burma*, KHRG No. 97–S1 (7 August 1997).

5. US Department of Labor, *Report on Labor Practices in Burma* (Washington, DC: Bureau of International Affairs, September 1998).

6. 'Forced Labour in Burma', ICFTU Online Press Release, 7 May 1999.

7. International Labor Organization, *Resolution on Burma* (Geneva: ILO, 1999).

8. 'Myanmar Lashes West for ILO Expulsion', *Associated Press*, 17 June 1999.

9. Images Asia, Karen Human Rights Group and the Open Society Institute's Burma Project, *All Quiet on the Western Front? The Situation in Chin State and Sagaing Division, Burma* (Thailand: January 1998).

10. Amnesty International, *Myanmar Aftermath: Three Years of Dislocation in the Kayah State* (June 1999).

11. Shan Human Rights Foundation, *Dispossessed: Forced Relocation and Extrajudicial Killings in Shan State* (Thailand: April 1998).

12. Amnesty International, *Myanmar: The Kayin (Karen) State Militarization and Human Rights* (June 1999) and *Myanmar Aftermath: Three Years of Dislocation in the Kayah State* (June 1999).

13. See Curt Lambrecht, 'The Return of the Rohingya Refugees to Burma: Voluntary Repatriation or Refoulement?', *US Committee for Refugees*, March 1995; 'More Buddhist Settlements', *Arakan Rohingya National Organization News Journal*, Vol. 2, No. 2 (February 2000).

14. Vaclav Havel, 'The Power of the Powerless', in *Living in Truth* (London: Faber and Faber, 1987).

15. See Khin Myo Chit, 'Dandruff in my Halo' in *Burma Debate*, Spring 1999, for her comments about the isolation faced by activists and their families. For instance, 'Once a man is taken into detention, his family might as well put a cross on their door like people of medieval Europe did when they were stricken with the Black Death.'

16. See 'In Rangoon: Civil Servants and Cemeteries', *Burma Issues*, Vol. 9, No. 1 (February 1999).

17. Civil servants and taxi drivers are provided with rations of petrol at subsidized prices, but the rations are insufficient. The prices on the black market are often much higher.

18. See Martin Smith, *Fatal Silence? Freedom of Expression and the Right to Health in Burma* (London: Article 19, July 1996), pp. 21–2.

7. The Military: A Life Sentence

1. See Lt Col. Hla Min's statement, entitled, 'Development During the Period the Military Government Assumed State Responsibilities', posted on the www.myanmar.com website as of 11 November 1999. He states that some western governments and media wrongly depicted the movement as a peaceful demonstration for democracy.

2. See the English translation of Daw Aung San Suu Kyi's remarks on 11 February 1996, in *Burma Debate*, January/February 1997, pp. 21–2.

3. *New Light of Myanmar*, 6 June 1996.

4. Communication, 3 August 1999.

5. See Images Asia, *'No Childhood at All': A Report about Child Soldiers in Burma* (Thailand: 1996), for similar accounts of why young boys join the army.

6. See Karen Human Rights Group, *Interviews with SLORC Army Deserters* (Thailand: 18 May 1996).

7. See Images Asia, *'No Childhood at All'*.

8. For accounts of soldiers raping female villagers see NCGUB Human Rights Documentation Unit, *Human Rights Year Book 1997–8: Burma* (Bangkok, July 1998), pp. 352–62.

9. Even former Brigadier-General Aung Gyi, who worked closely with General Ne Win in 1962, complained to Radio Free Asia in an interview about the problems of corruption and nepotism among the top military officers. See Aung Zaw, 'Driving Tatmadaw's Top Brass Mad', *The Nation*, 20 September 1998.

10. Images Asia and BurmaNet, *Nowhere to Go: A Report on the 1997 SLORC Offensive Against Duplaya District (KNU Sixth Brigade), Karen State, Burma* (Thailand: April 1997), p. 28.

11. Other groups documenting human rights abuses include the All Burma Students' Democratic Front, the Arakan Rohingya National Organization, the Chin Human Rights Organization, the Karen Human Rights Group, the Karen Information Center, the Human Rights Foundation of Monland, the Human Rights Documentation Unit of the National Coalition Government of the Union of Burma, the Shan Human Rights Foundation, the Shan Herald Agency for News, Burma Issues, the Burmese Relief Centre, and Images Asia. Excerpts from their reports are often posted in *The BurmaNet News*, at www.burmanet.org.

12. Some deserters have said that officers do not remove their names from the ranks for some time, because the officers can collect the deserters' salaries. See Federated Trade Unions of Burma, *Situation of the SLORC Soldiers*, 2 May 1998 (posted in *The BurmaNet News*).

13. See 'Better the Devil You Don't Know', *The Irrawaddy*, July 1999, pp. 20–1.

14. Soe Myint, 'India and Burma: Working on their Relationship', *The Irrawaddy*, March 1999, p. 22.

15. See Andrew Selth, *Transforming the Tatmadaw: The Burmese Armed Forces Since 1988* (Canberra: Australian National University Strategic and Defence Studies Centre, 1996), p. 50.

16. Images Asia, Karen Human Rights Group, and the Open Society Institute's Burma Project, *All Quiet on the Western Front? The Situation in Chin State and Sagaing Division, Burma* (Thailand: January 1998), pp. 52–3.

17. 'Job Program Said Benefiting Burmese Spies', *Phuchatkan* (a Thai newspaper), 10 June 1999. The English translation was posted in *The BurmaNet News* on 16 June 1999.

18. Andrew Selth, *Burma's Intelligence Apparatus* (Canberra: Australian National University Strategic and Defence Studies Centre, June 1997), p. 23.

19. See Selth, *Burma's Intelligence Apparatus*, p. 28.

20. Bertil Lintner, 'Velvet Glove', *Far Eastern Economic Review*, 7 May 1998.

21. See Gustaaf Houtman, *Mental Culture in Burmese Crisis Politics: Aung San Suu Kyi and the National League for Democracy* (Tokyo: Tokyo University of Foreign Studies, Institute for the Study of Languages and Cultures of Asia and Africa, 1999), pp. 142–7.

8. Prison: 'Life University'

1. See All Burma Students' Democratic Front, *To Stand and be Counted: The Suppression of Burma's Members of Parliament* (Bangkok: June 1998) for a list of NLD MPs and party members who have been detained and imprisoned.

2. See the NCGUB Human Rights Documentation Unit, *Human Rights Yearbook 1997–8: Burma* (Bangkok: July 1998), p. 109.

3. 'Burma', in Human Rights Watch/Asia, *Human Rights Watch World Report 1999* (Human Rights Watch, 1999).

4. See Amnesty International, *Myanmar: Imprisonment of Students* (Amnesty International, April 1997).

5. Communication from a group of former political prisoners, June 1999.

6. See Win Naing Oo, *Cries from Insein* (Bangkok: All Burma Students' Democratic Front, 1996), p. 25.

7. According to the *Far Eastern Economic Review*'s Intelligence section (3 June 1999), there are forty-eight prisons and more than 900 gaols in Burma.

8. See Amnesty International and Human Rights Watch annual reports on Burma.

9. NCGUB Human Rights Documentation Unit, *Human Rights Yearbook 1997–8: Burma*, p. 290.

10. See All Burma Students' Democratic Front, *Tortured Voices: Personal Accounts of Burma's Interrogation Centres* (Bangkok: July 1998), for more information about interrogation centres.

11. See Amnesty International, *Myanmar: Conditions in Prisons and Labor Camps* (22 September 1995).

12. Assistance Association for Political Prisoners, *A Report on the Situation of Political Prisoners Detained in Burma* (Thailand: 1 April 2000).

13. Translated by ATN.

14. The information provided here comes from interviews with Moe Aye. He has also discussed aspects of his prison experience in his self-published book, *Ten Years On: The Life and Views of a Burmese Student Political Prisoner* (Bangkok: 1999).

15. In 1995, twenty-two political prisoners were given extra sentences after a raid of their cells turned up printed materials such as *Time* and *Newsweek* magazine articles, transcripts of foreign radio broadcasts, short stories and poems, and pro-democracy literature. Some were tortured and placed in tiny dog cells for their 'crime'. See All Burma Students' Democratic Front, *Pleading Not Guilty in Insein* (Bangkok: February 1997).

9. Education: Floating Books and Bathroom Tracts

1. Win Htein, 'Learning in Limbo', in *The Irrawaddy*, May 1999, p. 20.

2. See Karen Human Rights Group, *Interviews on the School Situation*, KHRG No. 96-16 (Thailand: 10 May 1996).

3. UNICEF, *Children and Women in Myanmar: A Situation Analysis* (Rangoon: 1995), pp. 33–4.

4. Bertil Lintner, *Outrage: Burma's Struggle for Democracy* (Bangkok: White Lotus, 1990), p. 62.

5. See Karen Human Rights Group, *The Situation of Children in Burma* (Thailand: 1 May 1996).

6. Monks at higher levels do engage in serious discussion of Buddhist philosophy, but for young children who attend monastery classes for only a few years, most of the learning is based on memorization.

7. 'While Schools are Closed', *Burma Issues*, Vol. 7, No. 9 (September 1997); Communication, 3 August 1999.

8. This policy was originally introduced in order to fill the need for more trained graduates in the sciences and technical fields. See Josef Silverstein, 'Burmese Student Politics in a Changing Society', *Daedalus*, Vol. 97, No. 1 (Winter 1968), p. 287.

9. Communication from Aung Saw Oo, June 1999. Universities were shut down in 1962, 1963, 1969, 1970, 1974 (twice), 1975, 1976, 1987, 1988 (twice), 1991 and 1996.

10. Lintner, *Outrage*, p. 91.

11. See Karen Human Rights Group, *Interviews with SLORC Army Deserters*, KHRG No. 96-19 (Thailand: 18 May 1996), p. 3; Win Htein, 'Time to Change the Tatmadaw's Image', *Mizzima News Group* (posted on *The BurmaNet News* on 26 March 2000).

12. NLD Statement No. 21 (2/00) cited in the transcript of Daw Aung San Suu Kyi's videotaped message to the 56th Session of the UN Commission on Human Rights, 5 April 2000.

13. In 1996, VOA transferred the Burmese services director after she began extensively covering the regime's activities and limiting air time for her staff's reports on pro-democracy activities.

14. Matthew Pennington, 'Fearing Free Speech Pandora's Box, Myanmar's Rulers Block Internet', *AP*, 18 April 2000.

10. The Artistic Community: In the Dark, Every Cat is Black

1. For a history of the development of censorship in Burma see Anna J. Allott, *Inked Over, Ripped Out: Burmese Storytellers and the Censors* (Chiang Mai: Silkworm Books, 1994).

2. See David Brunnstrom, 'Military Rule in Myanmar – A Writer's Tale', *Reuters*, 25 August 1999.

3. Allott, *Inked Over, Ripped Out*, p. 31.

4. 'Film stars, vocalists to entertain Tatamadawmen building roads in Kengtung', *New Light of Myanmar*, 23 February 1998.

5. See 'Regulations for Entertainers', *New Light of Myanmar*, 25 February 1995

(translated and reprinted in *Burma Debate*, November/December 1995, p. 34) for a list of what male and female performers can and cannot wear on stage.

6. The tapes have been produced by the Committee for. Non-violent Action in Burma (CNAB), based in New Delhi. The Democratic Voice of Burma and Radio Free Asia have broadcast their songs.

7. Videotape of the 1990 Writers' Forum.

8. Ludu Daw Ahmar, *Ah May Shay Sagaa* (Rangoon: Tet Lan Sabay, August 1997).

11. Religion and Magic: Disappearing Jewels and Poltergeists

1. Patrick McDowell, 'Grand Pagoda being Restored', *AP*, 19 July 1999.

2. Images Asia, Karen Human Rights Group, and the Open Society Institute's Burma Project, *All Quiet on the Western Front? The Situation in Chin State and Sagaing Division, Burma* (Thailand, January 1998), pp. 42–3.

3. These details were provided in a confidential report written in early May 1997. A videotape of this monks' meeting and the damage done to the Mahamuni image was later circulated outside Burma.

4. See 'Burmese Monks Protest Innocence', *The Nation*, 28 March 1997; Aung Zaw, 'Rangoon Plays the Muslim Card', *The Nation*, 28 March 1997; and 'Eyewitness Recalls Recent Unrest in Burma', *The Nation*, 5 April 1997, for more details.

5. 'Minister Says Opposition Trying to "Divide the Monks"', BBC Radio (translated from a Burmese-language Radio Myanmar broadcast), 29 September 1996.

6. 'Senior Monk Appeals to Burmese Ruling Council, Opposition to Hold Peace Talks', BBC Radio, 4 November 2000. Note: this is a translation of the DVB's Burmese-language broadcast on the subject on 2 November 1999.

7. See Min Zin, 'Taking the Lead: The Need for a Peace Movement in Burma', *The Irrawaddy*, February 2000, pp. 14–15.

8. See 'Religious Persecution', *Chin Human Rights Organization* (India: February 1997).

9. Images Asia, *Report on the Situation for Muslims in Burma* (Thailand: May 1997), Appendix.

10. Such pamphlets were also reportedly distributed through local authorities in several towns in Shan State in June 1996 and led to attacks on Muslim shops in Kalaw. Communication, June 1996.

11. See Images Asia and BurmaNet, *Nowhere to Go: A Report on the 1997 SLORC Offensive Against Duplaya District (KNU Sixth Brigade) Karen State, Burma* (Thailand: April 1997), pp. 8–17.

12. Ibid., p. 11.

13. See Amnesty International, *Union of Myanmar (Burma): Human Rights Violations Against Muslims in the Rakhine (Arakan) State* (May 1992).

14. See Amnesty International, *Myanmar/Bangladesh: Rohingyas – The Search for Safety* (September 1997).

15. See Gustaaf Houtman, *Mental Culture in Burmese Crisis Politics: Aung San Suu Kyi and the National League for Democracy*, Study of Languages and Cultures of Asia and Africa Monograph Series No. 33 (Tokyo University of Foreign Studies, 1999), Ch. 5, for what he calls the regime's 'myanmafication' project.

16. Communication from a border source who received the information from Rangoon, April 1999.

17. See Aung Zaw, 'Shwedagon and the Generals', *The Irrawaddy*, May 1999.

18. See Aung Hla Tun, 'Yangon Braces, but Quiet on "Four Nines Day"', *Reuters*, 9 September 1999.

19. See Ma Hnin Hlaing Oo, 'In Booming Rangoon, There's No Rest for the Dead', *The Nation*, 31 January 1997; 'Burmese Dead are Obstacle to Modernization', *Reuters*, 3 February 1997.

20. Maung Hmat Gyauk, *Kyemon* Newspaper (Rangoon), June 1998 (note: my copy of the article is undated).

12. The Internationalization of Burma's Politics

1. Desmond Ball, *Burma's Military Secrets: Signals Intelligence from the Second World War to Civil War and Cyber Warfare* (Bangkok: White Lotus Press, 1998), pp. 219–29.

2. Ibid., p. 219; Anthony Davis, 'Burma Casts Wary Eye on China', *Jane's Intelligence Review*, 1 June 1999.

3. Ball, *Burma's Military Secrets*, p. 224.

4. Dermot Tatlow, 'China's Shadow', *Asiaweek*, 28 May 1999.

5. Ibid.

6. Chris Beyrer, *War in the Blood: Sex, Politics and AIDS in Southeast Asia* (London: Zed Books, 1998), p. 107.

7. William Ashton, 'Burma Receives Advances from its Silent Suitors in Singapore', *Jane's Intelligence Review*, 1 March 1998.

8. 'EU Firm on Burmese Stand at ASEAN Meet', *The Nation*, 27 May 1999.

9. Kavi Chongkittavorn, 'ASEAN Needs "Flexible Engagement"', *The Nation*, 20 July 1998.

10. 'Siazon Calls for Open Dialogue in Myanmar', *Straits Times*, 26 July 1998.

11. Stephen Collinson, 'Asean Trade Ministers Open Meeting in Myanmar', *AFP*, 1 May 2000.

12. David Brunnstrom, 'Myanmar Embassy Gunmen Villains then Heroes', *Reuters*, 3 October 1999.

13. See 'Irate Villagers Threaten Protest Over Stoppage of Work on Moei River Bridge', *The Nation*, 13 June 1995; Yindee Lertcharoenchok, 'One Bridge, Two Different Views', *The Nation*, 15 August 1997.

14. 'Us Condemns Burma for Role in Camp Attacks', *The Nation*, 1 February 1997; Yindee Lertcharoenchok, 'Karen Refugees under Threat of Further Attacks from Burma', *The Nation*, 6 February 1997.

15. Soe Myint, 'India and Burma: Working on their Relationship', *The Irrawaddy*, March 1999.

16. Some of the armed ethnic minority organizations operating on both sides of the India–Burma border, such as the Naga National Council, received arms and training from China. See Martin Smith, *Burma: Insurgency and the Politics of Ethnicity* (London: Zed Books, 1999), p. 252.

17. Teena Gill, 'Myanmarese Defections Shock Junta, Indian Government', *Indian*

Express (New Delhi), 5 October 1999; Images Asia, Karen Human Rights Group and the Open Society Institute's Burma Project, *All Quiet on the Western Front? The Situation in Chin State and Sagaing Division, Burma* (Thailand, January 1998), pp. 6–7.

18. Shawn W. Crispin and Bertil Lintner, 'Drug Tide Strains Ties', *Far Eastern Economic Review*, 9 September 1999.

19. 'Burmese Troops "Live off the Land"', *Far Eastern Economic Review*, 18 May 2000.

20. Aphaluck Bhatiasevi, 'Rangoon Postpones Meeting on Health', *Bangkok Post*, 27 October 1999.

21. Atul Aneja, 'Pakistan Plans Air Base in Myanmar?' in *Asian Age* (New Delhi), 28 October 1999.

22. Bureau for International Narcotics and Law Enforcement Affairs, US Department of State, *International Narcotics Control Strategy Report, 1999* (Washington, DC: March 2000).

23. Bruce Hawke, 'Narcotics – Burma's Military Implicated', *Jane's Intelligence Review*, 1 October 1998; François Casanier, 'A Narco-Dictatorship in Progress', *Burma Debate*, March/April 1996.

24 Anthony Davis and Bruce Hawke, 'Burma: the Country that Won't Kick the Habit', *Jane's Intelligence Review*, 1 March 1998.

25. Ibid.

26. 'Myanmar Slams EU over Sanctions', *AFP*, 11 April 2000.

27. 'Australian FM Calls for Change in Myanmar', *AFP*, 16 November 1999.

28. These articles were compiled into a volume: Aung San Suu Kyi, *Letters from Burma* (London: Penguin Books, 1997).

29. William Barnes, 'Activists Fearful of Japanese Investment', *South China Morning Post*, 1 December 1999.

30. 'Yangon to the UN: Thanks, But...' *Far Eastern Economic Review*, 25 December 1998.

31. Terry Macalister, 'Premier Oil Admits Abuses in Burma', *Guardian*, 16 May 2000.

32. Thomas Crampton, 'Burma's Debt is Pushing Economy to the Brink – the World Bank Warns', *International Herald Tribune*, 15 November 1999.

33. R. Jeffrey Smith, 'Burma's Image Problem is a Moneymaker for U.S. Lobbyists', *Washington Post*, 24 February 1998.

34. 'Foreign Activists Go on Trial,' *South China Morning Post*, 14 August 1998; 'US Students Head Home after Burma Expulsion', *The Nation*, 17 August, 1998.

35. The Free Burma Coalition and other Burma activist groups abroad set up mailing lists and websites to distribute information and develop strategies. See www.freeburma.org.

36. See Christina Fink, 'Visit Myanmar Year: Tourism in Burma', in Jill Forshee, with Sandra Cate and Christina Fink (eds), *Converging Interests: Traders, Travelers, and Tourists in Southeast Asia* (Berkeley: International and Area Studies, UC Berkeley, 1999).

37. Reprinted in *Asian Age* (Delhi), 9 September 1999.

38. Some of the larger foundations and organizations which have provided support are the Danish Burma Committee, the Friedrich Naumann Foundation, the International Republican Institute, the Jesuit Refugee Service, the Kim Dae Jung Foundation, the National Endowment for Democracy, the Netherlands Organization for Inter-

national Development Cooperation, the Norwegian Burma Council, the Olaf Palme International Center, and the Soros Foundation's Open Society Institute.

39. United States Committee for Refugees, *Burma Country Report 1998* (Washington, DC: 1998).

40. Organizations working in Burma include the Adventist Development and Relief Agency, Association François Xavier Bagnoud, CARE, Médecins du Monde, Médecins sans Frontières, Save the Children, World Concern, World Vision, UNICEF, United Nations Development Programme and the World Health Organization.

41. 'Cash for USDA members participating in Household Expenditure Survey', *The New Light of Myanmar*, 30 March 1996.

42. See the 1996 MMCWA publications (in Burmese). The sponsors' names are listed on the back page.

43. See Crampton, 'Burma's Debt …'.

44. 'Moving Forward', *Asiaweek*, 22 April 2000.

13. Conclusion: A Different Burma

1. See, for instance, James Barber, *South Africa in the Twentieth Century: A Political History – In Search of a Nation State* (Oxford: Blackwell, 1999).

2. See Mark R. Thompson, *The Anti-Marcos Struggle: Personalistic Rule and Democratic Transition in the Philippines* (New Haven, CT: Yale University Press, 1995).

3. Min Zin, 'Spiritual Revolution', *The Irrawaddy*, Vol. 7, No. 2 (February 1999), p. 18.

4. Aung San, 'Burma and Buddhism', *The World of Books*, Vol. XXI (April 1935); reprinted in Mya Han, *General Aung San's Literary Handiwork* (Rangoon: University Historical Research Department, 1998), pp. 61–2.

Bibliography

Note: There are no surnames in Burmese, so I have listed Burmese names alphabetically according to the first letter of the first word of their names. Some authors have used 'U' in front of their names in their publications. In such cases, I have listed them under U.

Books and Academic Articles

All Burma Students Democratic Front (1997) *Pleading Not Guilty in Insein* (Bangkok: self-published).

— (1998) *To Stand and be Counted: The Suppression of Burma's Members of Parliament* (Bangkok: self-published).

Allott, Anna J. (1994) *Inked Over, Ripped Out: Burmese Storytellers and the Censors* (Chiang Mai, Thailand: Silkworm Books).

Aung San Suu Kyi (1991) *Freedom from Fear and Other Writings*, ed. Michael Aris (London: Penguin Books).

Aung-Thwin, Michael (1985) *Pagan: The Origins of Modern Burma* (Honolulu: University of Hawaii Press).

Ball, Desmond (1998) *Burma's Military Secrets: Signals Intelligence from the Second World War to Civil War and Cyber Warfare* (Bangkok: White Lotus Press).

Barber, James (1999) *South Africa in the Twentieth Century: A Political History – In Search of a Nation State* (Oxford: Blackwell Publishers).

Beyrer, Chris (1998) *War in the Blood: Sex, Politics and AIDS in Southeast Asia* (London: Zed Books).

Burma Center Netherlands and Transnational Institute (eds) (1999) *Strengthening Civil Society in Burma: Possibilities and Dilemmas for International NGOs* (Chiang Mai, Thailand: Silkworm Books).

Burma Socialist Programme Party (1983) *Facts about Burma* (Rangoon: BSPP).

Cady, John F. (1958) *A History of Modern Burma* (Ithaca, NY: Cornell University Press).

— (1976) *The United States and Burma.* (Cambridge, MA: Harvard University Press).

Callahan, Mary (1996) *The Origins of Military Rule in Burma*, PhD Dissertation (Ithaca, NY: Cornell University).

Carey, Peter (ed). (1997) *Burma: The Challenge of Change in a Divided Society* (London: Macmillan).

Clements, Alan and Leslie Kean (1994) *Burma's Revolution of the Spirit: The Struggle for Democratic Freedom and Dignity* (Bangkok: White Orchid Press).

Donkers, Jan and Minka Nijhuis (eds) (1996) *Burma Behind the Mask* (Amsterdam: Burma Centrum Netherlands).

Fink, Christina (1999) 'Visit Myanmar Year: Tourism in Burma', in Jill Forshee, with Sandra Cate and Christina Fink (eds), *Converging Interests: Traders, Travelers, and Tourists in Southeast Asia* (Berkeley, CA: International and Area Studies, UC Berkeley), pp. 85–107.

Furnivall, J. S. (1956) *Colonial Policy and Practice* (New York: New York University Press).

Havel, Vaclav (1987) *Living in Truth*, ed. Jan Vladislav (London: Faber and Faber).

Houtman, Gustaaf (1999) *Mental Culture in Burmese Crisis Politics: Aung San Suu Kyi and the National League for Democracy*, Study of Languages and Cultures of Asia and Africa Monograph Series No. 33 (Tokyo: Tokyo University of Foreign Studies, Institute for the Study of Languages and Cultures of Asia and Africa).

Kin Oung (1996) *Who Killed Aung San?* (Bangkok: White Lotus).

Koenig, William J. (1990) *The Burmese Polity, 1782–1819: Politics, Adminstration and Social Organization in the Early Konbaung Period* (Ann Arbor: University of Michigan, Papers on Southeast Asia).

Leach, E. (1960) 'The Frontiers of Burma', *Comparative Studies in Society and History*, Vol 3, No. 1, pp. 315–35.

Lehman, F. K. (1967) 'Ethnic Categories in Burma and the Theory of Social Systems', in Peter Kundstadter (ed.), *Southeast Asian Tribes, Minorities, and Nations* (Princeton, NJ: Princeton University Press) pp. 93–124.

Lieberman, Victor B. (1984) *Burmese Administrative Cycles: Anarchy and Conquest, c. 1580–1760* (Princeton, NJ: Princeton University Press).

Lintner, Bertil (1994) *Burma in Revolt: Opium and Insurgency Since 1948* (Boulder, CO: Westview Press).

— (1990) *Outrage: Burma's Struggle for Democracy* (Bangkok: White Lotus).

Ludu Daw Ahmar (1997) *Ah May Shay Sagaa* (Rangoon: Tet Lan Sabay).

Maung Aung Myoe (1998) *Building the Tatmadaw: The Organisational Development of the Armed Forces in Myanmar, 1948–98* (Canberra: Strategic and Defence Studies Centre, Australian National University).

Maung Maung (1959) *Burma's Constitution* (The Hague: Martinus Nijhoff).

Maung Maung Gyi (1983) *Burmese Political Values: The Socio-Political Roots of Authoritarianism* (New York: Praeger).

Maung Maung Pye (1951) *Burma in the Crucible* (Rangoon: Khittaya Publishing House).

Mi Mi Khaing (1943) *Burmese Family* (Bloomington: Indiana University Press).

Mya Han (1998) *General Aung San's Literary Handiwork* (Rangoon: University Historical Research Department; sections in Burmese and English).

Mya Maung (1992) *Totalitarianism in Burma: Prospects for Economic Development* (New York: Paragon House).

Nash, Manning (1965) *The Golden Road to Modernity: Village Life in Contemporary Burma* (Chicago, IL: University of Chicago Press).

Rotberg, Robert I. (ed). (1997) *Burma: Prospects for Political and Economic Reconstruction* (Cambridge, MA: World Peace Foundation).

San C. Po, Dr (1928) *Burma and the Karens* (London: Elliot Stock).

Sangermano, Father Vincenzo (1985) *The Burmese Empire a Hundred Years Ago* (Bangkok: White Orchid Press; 1st edn, 1833).

Selth, Andrew (1993) *Death of a Hero: The U Thant Disturbances in Burma, December 1974*, Australia–Asia Paper No. 49 (Brisbane: Griffith University Centre for the Study of Australia–Asia Relations).

— (1996) *Transforming the Tatmadaw: The Burmese Armed Forces Since 1988* (Canberra: Australian National University Strategic and Defence Studies Centre).

— (1997) *Burma's Intelligence Apparatus* (Canberra: Australian National University Strategic and Defence Studies Centre).

Shway Yoe (1963) *The Burman: His Life and His Notions* (New York: W.W. Norton).

Silverstein, Josef (1977)(1968) 'Burmese Student Politics in a Changing Society', *Daedalus*, Vol. 97, No. 1, pp. 274–92.

— *Burma: Military Rule and the Politics of Stagnation* (Ithaca, NY: Cornell University Press).

— (ed.) (1989) *Independent Burma at Forty Years: Six Assessments* (Ithaca, NY: Cornell University Southeast Asia Program).

Smith, Martin (1999) *Burma: Insurgency and the Politics of Ethnicity* (London: Zed Books; 1st edn, 1991).

— (1993) *Ethnic Groups in Burma: Development, Democracy and Human Rights* (London: Anti-Slavery International).

— (1993) *Fatal Silence? Freedom of Expression and the Right to Health in Burma* (London: Article 19).

— (1991) *State of Fear: Censorship in Burma (Myanmar)* (London: Article 19).

Spiro, Melford E. (1967) *Burmese Supernaturalism* (Philadelphia: Prentice-Hall).

Steinberg, David I. (1982) *Burma: A Socialist Nation of Southeast Asia* (Boulder, CO: Westview Press).

— (1997) 'The Union Solidarity Development Association', *Burma Debate*, Vol. 4, No. 1.

Tambiah, S. J. (1977) 'The Gallactic Polity: The Structure of Traditional Kingdoms in Southeast Asia', *Annals of the New York Academy of Sciences*, No. 293, pp. 69–97.

Taylor, Robert (1987) *The State in Burma* (London: C. Hurst).

— (1996) 'Elections in Burma/Myanmar: For Whom and Why?', in R. H. Taylor (ed.), *The Politics of Elections in Southeast Asia* (Cambridge: Cambridge University Press).

Temple, R. C. (1906) *The Thirty Seven Nats* (London: W. Griggs).

Than Tun (1988) *Essays on the History and Buddhism of Burma* (Arran, Scotland: Kiscadale Publications).

Thompson, Mark R. (1995) *The Anti-Marcos Struggle: Personalistic Rule and Democratic Transition in the Philippines* (New Haven, CT: Yale University Press).

Thongchai Winichakul (1994) *Siam Mapped: A History of the Geo-Body of a Nation* (Honolulu: University of Hawaii Press).

Tinker, Hugh (1957) *The Union of Burma* (London: Oxford University Press).

U Maung Maung (1980) *From Sangha to Laity: Nationalist Movements of Burma: 1920–1940*, Monograph on South Asia No. 4 (Canberra: Australian National University).

Venkateswaran, K. S. (1996) *Burma: Beyond the Law* (London: Article 19).

Vum Son (1987) *Zo History: With an Introduction to Zo Culture, Economy, Religion and Their Status as an Ethnic Minority in India, Burma and Bangladesh* (Self-published).

Yawnghwe, Chao-Tzang (1989) 'The Burman Military: Holding the Country Together?' in J. Silverstein (ed.), *Independent Burma at Forty Years: Six Assessments* (Ithaca, NY: Cornell Southeast Asia Program).

Personal Accounts

All Burma Students' Democratic Front (1998) *Tortured Voices: Personal Accounts of Burma's Interrogation Centres* (Bangkok: self-published).

Aung San Suu Kyi (1997) *Letters from Burma* (London: Penguin Books).

— (1997) *The Voice of Hope: Conversations with Alan Clements, with contributions by U Kyi Maung and U Tin Oo* (London: Penguin Books).

Aye Saung (1989) *Burman in the Back Row* (Hong Kong: Asia 2000 Ltd).

Ba Maw (1968) *Breakthrough in Burma, Memoirs of a Revolution, 1939–1946* (New Haven, CT: Yale University Press).

Collis, Maurice (1943) *The Land of the Great Image: Being Experiences of Friar Manrique in Arakan* (New York: New Directions Books).

— (1996) *Trials in Burma* (Bangkok: Ava Publishing House; 1st edn, 1938).

Falla, Jonathan (1991) *True Love and Bartholomew: Rebels on the Burmese Border* (Cambridge: Cambridge University Press).

Lintner, Bertil (1996) *Land of Jade: A Journey from India through Northern Burma to China* (Bangkok: White Orchid Press; 1st English edn, 1990).

Mirante, Edith (1993) *Burmese Looking Glass: A Human Rights Adventure and a Jungle Revolution* (New York: Grove Press).

Moe Aye (1999) *Ten Years On: The Life and Views of a Burmese Student Political Prisoner* (Bangkok: self-published).

Sargent, Inge (1994) *Twilight over Burma: My Life as a Shan Princess* (Honolulu: University of Hawaii Press).

Singh, Balwant (1993) *Independence and Democracy in Burma, 1945–1952: The Turbulent Years* (Ann Arbor, MI: University of Michigan Center for South and Southeast Asian Studies).

Smith Dun, General (1980) *Memoirs of the Four-Foot Colonel*, Data Paper No. 113, Southeast Asia Program, Department of Asian Studies (Ithaca, NY: Cornell University Press).

U Nu (1975) *Saturday's Son* (New Haven, CT: Yale University Press).

U Thaung (1995) *A Journalist, a General and an Army in Burma* (Bangkok: White Lotus).

Win Naing Oo (1996) *Cries from Insein* (Bangkok: All Burma Students' Democratic Front).

Yawnghwe, Chao-Tzang (1987) *The Shan of Burma: Memoirs of an Exile* (Singapore: Institute of Southeast Asian Studies).

Literature

Khin Myo Chit (1969) *The 13 Carat Diamond and Other Stories* (Rangoon: Sarpay Lawka Book House).

Ludu U Hla (1993) *The Caged Ones*, trans. Sein Tu (Bangkok: White Orchid Press; 1st English edn, 1986).

Ma Ma Lay (1991) *Not Out of Hate*, trans. Margaret Aung-Thwin, ed. William H. Frederick (Athens, OH: Ohio University Center for International Studies).

Maung Htin (1998) *Nga Ba*, trans. Maw Thi Ri (New Delhi: Irrawaddy Publications).

Mya Than Tint (1996) *On the Road to Mandalay: Tales of Ordinary People.* trans. Ohnmar Khin and Sein Kyaw Hlaing (Bangkok: White Orchid Press).

Orwell, George (1934) *Burmese Days* (New York: Harcourt Brace).

Reports

Images Asia (1996) *'No Childhood At All': A Report about Child Soldiers in Burma* (Thailand: May).

— (1997) *Report on the Situation for Muslims in Burma* (Thailand: May).

Images Asia and BurmaNet (1997) *Nowhere to Go: A Report on the 1997 SLORC Offensive Against Duplaya District (KNU Sixth Brigade) Karen State Burma* (Thailand: April).

Images Asia, Karen Human Rights Group and the Open Society Institute's Burma Project (1998) *All Quiet on the Western Front? The Situation in Chin State and Sagaing Division, Burma* (Thailand: January).

International Labor Organization (1999) *Resolution on Burma* (Geneva: ILO).

Shan Human Rights Foundation (1998) *Dispossessed: Forced Relocation and Extrajudicial Killings in Shan State* (Thailand: April).

UNICEF (1995) *Children and Women in Myanmar: A Situation Analysis* (Rangoon: UNICEF).

United States Committee for Refugees (1998) *Burma Country Report 1998* (Washington, DC: US Committee for Refugees).

United States Department of Labor, Bureau of International Affairs (1998) *Report on Labor Practices in Burma* (Washington, DC: US Department of Labor).

United States Embassy, Rangoon (1997) *Foreign Economic Trends Report* (Rangoon: US Embassy).

Also numerous reports by the following organizations

Amnesty International
Chin Human Rights Organization
Burma yearbooks of the Human Rights Documentation Unit of the NCGUB
Human Rights Foundation of Monland
Human Rights Watch/Asia
Karen Human Rights Group

Magazines

Asiaweek
Burma Debate (produced by the Soros Foundation's Open Society Institute)
Burma Issues (produced by Burma Issues in Thailand)
Irrawaddy (produced by the Irrawaddy Publishing Group in Thailand)
Far Eastern Economic Review
Jane's Intelligence Review

Websites

www.burmanet.org – the BurmaNet News

www.freeburma.org – links to many Burma-related websites, including the Free Burma Coalition and ethnic minority websites

www.myanmar.com – the military regime's website

Index

7–7–77 movement, 44

8, as lucky number, 228–9
8–8–88 movement, 54–5, 70, 77, 113, 114, 143, 146, 152, 184, 186, 191, 204, 244; commemoration of, 70; soldiers join protesters, 154

9, as lucky number, 229–30

agriculture: effects of land reform on, 32–3; productivity of, 80
'Ah May Ein' ('Mother's Home'), 205
ah nah day, concept of, 120
Ahmar, Daw, Ah May Shay Sagaa, 211
AIDS see HIV/AIDS
alcohol, used among students, 182
All Burma Federation of Students' Unions (ABFSU), 53, 56, 64
All Burma Students' Democratic Front (ABSDF), 67, 78, 115, 118, 203
Allott, Anna, 198
amnesia, collective, 101–5
Amnesty International, 125, 155, 161
amphetamines: addiction to, 238; produced in Burma, 6
Anawrahta, King, 16, 17
ancestor worship, 14
Anti-Fascist People's Freedom League (AFPFL), 21, 23, 24, 26, 32; Clean, 27, 28; constitution of, 22; Stable, 27, 28, 29
Aquino, Benigno, 252
Aquino, Corazon, 252
Arakan League for Democracy, 99; electoral gains of, 69
Arakanese, 14, 15, 17, 23, 24, 28, 127, 219
Aris, Michael, 60; death of, 98; refused a visa for Burma, 97
Armed Forces Day, 131

armed struggle, 2, 24, 28, 29, 46, 47, 49, 57, 62, 109, 245 see also ethnic nationalities, armed groups
arms purchasing, by Tatmadaw, 233
art gallery exhibitions, censorship of, 207
artistic community, 197–212; role of, in pro-democracy demonstrations, 207–9
Asian financial crisis, 235
Association of South East Asian Nations (ASEAN), 234; Burma's interest in joining, 234–5
astrology, 40–1, 201, 213, 227
Aung, Daniel, 83–5, 87
Aung Gyi, Brigadier, 27, 29, 61; letters to General Ne Win, 53–4
Aung Gyi, U, 63
Aung San, General, 21, 22, 28, 30, 41–2, 46, 56, 92, 122, 145, 153, 183; assassination of, 23, 66; 'Burma and Buddha', 254; history of, rewritten, 175–6
Aung San Suu Kyi, Daw, 1, 13, 60, 61, 62, 63, 64, 65, 71, 79, 91, 115, 118, 129, 144, 175, 176, 191, 192, 228, 240, 251, 254; addresses international community, 191, 245; arrest of, 66–7; asks organizations to consult with NLD, 247; attacked by regime, 65–6, 91, 94, 96, 153, 227, 242 (for marrying a foreigner, 114; through entertainment industry, 90); awarded Jawarharlal Nehru Peace Award, 237; awarded Nobel Peace Prize, 81; calls for resisting authorities, 104; calls for tourism boycott, 244–5; calls for convening of Parliament, 238; calls for foreign businesses to stay out of Burma, 94; calls on international community for support, 232; criticism of General Ne Win, 66; disqualified

from running in elections, 67; *Freedom from Fear*, 4; house arrest of, 66, 69; journalists not allowed to visit, 243; *Letters from Burma*, 4, 241; movements restricted by regime, 234; photo placed on Buddhist altars, 220; public talks from her front gate, 88–9; released from house arrest, 2, 78, 86–91, 159, 172, 221, 241, 242; removed from NLD central executive, 86; restricted access to, 5; soldiers prepare to shoot, 66; speech at Shwedagon pagoda, 60; support for, 100 (by some soldiers, 153; by USA, 232); telephone line cut, 243; time spent in India, 237; travel possibilities restricted, 97, 99; trusted by people, 253; *Voice of Hope*, 4

Aung Shwe, U, 85
Aung Thinn, U, 210–11
Aung Zeya, 46
Aung Zin, 180–1, 186
Australia, critical of repression in Burma, 240
autonomy, 85, 99, 151, 255
Aye Tha Aung, U, 99
Aye Win, Dr, 38

Ba Maw, Dr, 29
Ba Pe, U, 178
Bain and Associates, 243
banditry, 23
Bangladesh, refugees in, 246–7
Bar Council, criticism of BSPP, 59
bathrooms, as meeting place for students, 186–90
Bayinnaung, King, 237
Beyrer, Chris, 233
'black' areas, 38
black dress of demonstrators, 91
black market, 137, 150; for rice, 33, 35; tolls extracted from traders, 47
Bo Aung Gyaw Street Agreement No. 1, 98
Bodawpaya, King, 219
Bogyoke government, 27
Bohmu Aung, 98
books, 'floating' of, 185
bribery, 40, 99, 104, 125, 135, 136, 138, 147, 169, 189
British Broadcasting Corporation (BBC),

54, 151, 189, 190, 243; jamming of, 192
British Council, 192
British East India Company, 18
British rule, 17–21; ending of, 21; refusal of self-government, 21; resistance to, 17, 18, 20
'brown' areas, 38, 149
Buddha, 254; hair relics of, 218; Mahamuni image, 219; tooth relic of, 218
Buddhism, 13, 14, 17, 19, 23, 26, 39, 40, 41, 59, 65, 71, 144, 170, 177, 217, 224, 250, 254, 255; and politics, 213–18; British disrespect towards, 18; conversion to, 223; conversion to Islam, 225; discipline of, 215, 216; principles of, 89; projected as state religion, 28; promotion of, 222; Theravada, 16, 17
Burma: beginnings of militarization of, 26–30; British rule in, 17–21; defined as 'Least Developed Country', 50; embassy taken over in Thailand, 236; foreign policy of, 238–9; independence of, 21–6 (announced, 23); lack of fixed class structure, 15; separated from India, 21
Burma Socialist Programme Party (BSPP), 34, 35, 36–42, 51, 54, 61, 80, 101, 102, 106, 109, 115, 117, 123, 133, 137, 144, 167, 171, 176, 177, 183, 185, 186, 210, 217; membership of, 39, 79; opposition to, 42, 50, 59; party members dismissed, 45; resignations from, 58
The BurmaNet News, 6, 192
Burmanization, 69–70, 127, 226
Burmans, 14, 21, 29, 30, 39, 40, 58, 99, 117, 127, 222, 254–5; viewed as invaders, 48
Burmese language, 212
'Burmese Way to Socialism', 32

Canada, withdraws Burma's preferential tariff, 240
car importers, problem of corruption, 135–6
cars: ordered to drive on right, 41; provided to military, 144

censorship, 34, 90, 197–201, 207, 211; of art gallery exhibitions, 204; of film-makers, 198; of musicians, 202 (of dress, 206); reading between the lines, 200

Central Intelligence Agency (CIA), 78

cheating fate activities, 229

Chin National Front, 127

China, 7, 17, 24, 26, 35, 62, 205, 232, 235, 237, 239, 252; border agreement with, 27; interest in Burma as market, 233; sale of arms to Burma, 233; stops support for CPB, 47; support for military regime, 4, 241

Chinese in Burma, 18, 20, 21, 127, 215, 233; anger against, 34; attacks on, 35; leave country, 32

Chins, 14, 18, 22, 36, 39, 44, 124, 127, 223, 237

Chit Khaing, U, 79

Cho Zin, 126

Christianity, 14, 18, 28, 39, 59, 144, 170, 224, 255; plan to convert Chins, 223

Christians, repression of, 222–4

civil servants, questionnaire to, 78–80

civil society: re-emergence of, 58–60; restoration of, 253–6

civilians, die of ill-treatment by military, 154

client relations in political organizations, 64

Cold War, 238; buffer zone strategy, 235

Committee Representing the People's Parliament (CRPP), 3, 96–9, 253

Communist Party of Burma (CPB), 23, 46–7, 63, 66, 67, 78, 171, 232; collapse of, 80; Red Flag branch, 24; White Flag branch, 24, 46

confessions of prisoners, 168

cooperatives, 36; establishment of, 33; ministry of, 44

corporations, investment in Burma, 242–5

corruption, 40, 135–8, 146, 256; in education system, 178 *see also* bribery

Covey, Stephen R., *The Seven Habits of Highly Effective People*, 210

Cultural Revolution (China), 35

dams, building of, 233

Dawn Oh Wai (Cry of the Peacock) magazine, 115

Decree 5/96: 'The Protection of the Stable ... Transfer of State Responsibility ...', 159

Defence Services Academy, 101, 107

democracy, 1, 23, 241, 256; inculcation of, 253; restoration of, requirements for, 211; superficial rooting of, 30; western-style, 254 *see also* multi-party rule

Democratic Alliance of Burma, 80

Democratic Karen Buddhist Army (DKBA), 236

Democratic Party for a New Society (DPNS), 64

Democratic Students' Organization, 25

Democratic Voice of Burma (DVB), 173, 190, 191, 246

demonetization of bank notes, 50, 52

Dobama Asiayone ('We Burmans Association'), 19, 20

donations: for restoration of pagodas, 218; forcible collection of, 214; to military-sponsored charities, 121

drugs, 207, 240, 249; attempt to eradicate cultivation of, 243; films against, 201; production of, 238; trafficking of, 80, 83, 239, 240 (in China, 233)

Drugs Enforcement Agency (DEA) (USA), 239

e-mail, access to, 192

East Timor, 190

education, 24, 112, 131, 174–92, 248; buying of good grades, 178–9; by rote memorization, 177; development of curriculum, 175–8; prison as, 159–73; university life, 179–83; value placed on, 103 *see also* schools

elections, 68–9; rigging of, 97

electricity: access to, 191; shortages of, 99

elephantiasis, 238

embassy take-over, 236, 244

English: no longer used for teaching, 175; reinstated for teaching, 175; study of, 107, 164, 170–1, 192

Enrile, Juan Ponce, 252

ethnic nationalities, 21, 33, 65, 77, 80, 98, 151, 222, 224, 249, 251, 255; armed groups, 33, 41, 48, 62, 94, 125, 224, 245, 252; divided by British, 20; ethnic demands of, 4; families of, 117–19; handling of issues involving, 252, 254; political parties of, 83; rights of, 13; self-determination refused, 143; teaching of languages, 176; tensions between, 176

European Union: pressure on Burma regime, 234; concerned about drugs and repression in Burma, 240

families: activist, 105–12; in ethnic minorities, 117–19; fostering conformity, 100–19; split, 114–17
fear, cultivation of, 127–33
federalism, 36, 98, 99, 151
fertilizers, imports of, 80
fighting-peacock, image of, 56
film-makers, limited supply of film stock, 198–9
films, reading between the lines of, 200
FOC ('Free of Charge') system , 92
food shortages, 62
forced labour, 48, 78, 123–4, 161, 207, 216, 223, 242
foreign investment *see* investment, foreign
fortune-telling, 41, 227–30
Four Cuts strategy, 48, 125, 126, 151
France, 17; relations with Burma, 240
Free Burma groups, 91, 244
frontier areas, problems of, 21–2
funerals, assistance with, 134–5

General Council of Burmese Associations (GCBA), 18
Germany, relations with Burma, 240
go go trees cut down by General Ne Win, 41
God's Army, 3
government, viewed as enemy, 29, 217
guest-registration system, 124–5
guilt feelings among prisoners, 166–7
Gunness, Christopher, 54

Hague Appeal for Peace Conference, 243
Havel, Vaclav, 130; 'The Power of the Powerless', 89
health care, 180–1, 248; nationalization of, 38

Heineken, pull out of Burma, 244
heroin, 155, 189, 239, 240; addiction to (in India, 238; in Thailand, 238); refineries opened in northern Burma, 80; taxation of trade, 47; used among students, 182
hijacking of aircraft, 1–2, 7, 244
Hinduism, 59
HIV/AIDS, 207, 238, 247; epidemic of, 6; in China, 233; spread of, 160
Hla Aye, U, 162–3
Htun Htun, 184
Htway Win, 128
Human Rights Watch, 155
Human Rights Yearbook (Human Rights Documentation Unit), 160
humanitarian assistance, 245–9
hunger *see* malnutrition
hunger strikes, 19, 67, 165, 172

imports, cutting of, 33
imprisonment, 5, 25, 35, 36, 44, 78, 93, 97, 104, 111, 131, 132, 250; of comedians, 87; prisons opened, 59; statistics for political prisoners, 3
Independence Day, 87, 106, 131
independence of Burma, 21–6; date selected for, 229
India, 7, 26, 62, 232, 233, 235, 239; British rule in, 17; refugees in, 246–7; relations with Burma, 237; support for pro-democracy movement, 237
Indians in Burma, 18, 20, 21, 23; leave country, 32; encouraged by British, 225
Indonesia, 234; support for Burma regime, 233–4
inflation, 77, 136
informers, 127–8, 165, 173
international campaigns on Burma, 242–5
International Committee of the Red Cross (ICRC), not allowed to visit political detainees, 248
International Confederation of Free Trade Unions (ICFTU), 123
International Labor Organization (ILO), 123
internationalization of Burma's politics, 232–49

Internet, access to, 192
interrogation centres, 162, 170
investment, foreign, 32, 77, 91, 242–5, 248; decline of, 94, 242; encouraged, 80; openness to, 70
Inya Lake, slaughter at, 54
The Irrawaddy news journal, 253
Islam, conversion to, 225

Japan: aid conditional on political openness, 86; invasion of Burma, 21; relations with Burma, 240–1
Jefferson Waterman International, 243
jinglee sharpened arrows, 56
journalists: denied access to ethnic conflicts, 244; gaoled, 28; told not to visit Daw Aung San Suu Kyi, 243
Justice and Liberation Warriors, 2

Kachin Independence Army (KIA), 78, 202
Kachin Independence Organization (KIO), 47, 81, 255
Kachin State, creation of, 22
Kachins, 14, 18, 22, 28, 29, 48
Karen language, teaching of, 176
Karen National Union (KNU), 6, 37, 38, 47, 48, 62, 78, 124, 125, 149, 154, 220, 226, 236, 255
Karen State, creation of, 22–3
Karenni National Progressive Party (KNPP), 125
Karenni State, 24
Karenni State Nationalities People's Liberation Front (KNPLF), 47, 255
Karennis, 14, 18, 23, 27, 28, 29, 126, 247
Karens, 3, 6, 14, 18, 20, 22, 23, 29, 37, 38, 48, 58, 126, 127, 148, 151, 154, 170, 220, 247, 255; tensions with Burmans, 22, 24
Kayahs, 255
Kayw Kayw, 103–4
Khaing Aung Soe, 151–2
Khin Aung Myint, Colonel, 205
Khin Khin Yi, Daw, 131, 132
Khin Kyi, Daw, 116
Khin Nyunt, Lt General, 82, 92, 94–5, 114, 123, 134, 136, 155, 157, 175, 220, 221, 228, 235
Khun Sa, 155, 230, 240

kings of Burma, 14, 15; activity of, 16, 17; ethical rules for, 65; legitimacy of, 217; promotion of Buddhism, 19
De Klerk, F.W., 251
Ko Doe, 56–7, 146
Ko Than, 137
Kodaw Hmaing, Thakin, 44
Kukis, 237
Kundalabiwuntha, U, 222
Kyakhatwaing monastery, 221
Kyaw Ba, General, 94
Kyaw Moe, U, 176, 177–8
Kyaw Thu, 201
Kyaw Tint, 55
Kyaw Win, 146, 147
Kyaw Zaw, General, 66
Kyi Kyi, 113–14, 167–9
Kyi Maung, U, 79, 86, 88, 89, 90

Lahu National Progressive Party, 83
Lahus, 83, 85, 255
land reform, 24, 32, 35
laundering of drugs money, 240
law and order campaigns, 35
law courts, under Revolutionary Council, 39–40
Law Yone, Edward, 47
leadership, need for, 60–3
legality, concept of, reversed, 136
Leh Pyu, 'Power 54', 90
Let Ya, Bo, 29
Levi-Strauss, pulls out of Burma, 244
libraries, 192; private, 185
Light Infantry Division 22, 113, 152
Limbin, Peter, 79
Lin Htet, 110–12, 187–8
Lintner, Bertil, 4, 37
literacy, 174
longyis, wearing of, 65, 133, 165
lu gaung, lu daw, 39, 183
Lu Zaw, U, imprisonment of, 87–8
lucky numbers, 228

Ma Aye Aye, 189, 190
Ma Pyu, 102–3
Mae Sot–Myawaddy 'Friendship Bridge', 236
magic, 213–31; sympathetic, 40, 111, 227–30
Mahaghandharon monastery, 222

Mahagiri (King of the Mountain), legend of, 16, 26
malaria, 124, 238
malnutrition, 125, 175, 216, 247
Mandalay: administration taken over by monks, 214–15; religious boycott organized by monks, 71
Mandalay Institute of Technology, 93
Mandalay University, 214
Mandela, Nelson, 184, 251
Mao Zedong, 24, 46
marriage, 200
Martyr's Day, celebration of, 66
Maung Aung, 79
Maung Aye, General, 82, 94
Maung Maung Nyo, 58
Maung Maung, Dr, 57
Maung Maung, ex-sergeant, 143, 148–50, 153, 154, 156, 157
Maung Tha Ya, 198
Mawdsley, James, sentenced to imprisonment, 244
Mazda 323 cars, provided to military, 144
media, relations with Burma, 242–5
medical institutes, protests at, 52
meditation: role of, 216; Vipassana, 222
merit-making, 40, 41; monks' boycott of ceremonies, 71
Mi Mi, 183–4
Mi Mi, Daw, 39–40, 59
migration and immigration, 7, 18, 104; exodus of students to border, 62; of migrant workers, 105, 145, 149, 156, 191; of students, 93; to borders, 109 *see also* Indians in Burma *and* Chinese in Burma
military forces: brutality in, 154–5; cycle of violence in, 154; desertion from, 154–6; financing of, 145; heroes in Burma's history, 145; impossible to resign from, 147; officers (benefit from privileges, 103, 144; enrich themselves, 99, 146; political concerns of, 27; profit from drugs trade, 239); raising educational level of, 183; recruitment quotas, 145; rise in numbers of, 123; soldiers in monasteries, 216; voluntary joining by country people, 145
military intelligence (MI), 40, 56, 87, 88,

114, 116, 127, 128, 129, 131, 136, 150, 162, 172; active among students, 45; agents beaten, 57; in monasteries, 217; rise of, 156–8; trained abroad, 156
military regime, 1, 13, 77–99; beginnings of, 26–30; conformity with, 101; coup staged, 62; durability of, 4; increased numbers of soldiers, 77; low priority on education, 174; period of ascendancy, 78–82; possible punishment of, 255–6; surveillance of foreigners, 7; survival under, 7; techniques of control, 5
military service, as a life sentence, 143–58
Min Ko Naing, 51, 52, 53, 67, 111, 185
Min Thein, 173
Min Zaw, 54–5, 186–7
Min Zin, 81–2, 132–3, 253
mine-sweeping, by humans, 126
Mirante, Edith, 4
missionaries, foreign, banned from Burma, 224
Mo Mo Myint Aung, 201
modem, unauthorised, penalty for possession of, 192
Moe Aung, 178
Moe Aye, 169–73
Moe Thee Zun, 50–1, 52–3, 56, 61, 62, 67, 102, 179, 185
mohingha soup, 227
Mon Literature and Culture Group, 118
Mong Tai Army, 155
monks, 54, 55, 57, 59, 68, 89, 125, 152, 208; and the NLD, 220–2; arrest of, 44; attempts to limit influence of, 216; belief in their own supernatural powers, 60; civil disobedience of, 70; communal punishment of, 219; examinations of, 219; fortune-telling activities, 213; hospitals built for, 216; imprisonment of, 160, 170; killing of, 70; leadership role of, 45, 214, 216; method of education, 177; monasteries raided by soldiers, 71; ordered to register with government, 40; organize religious boycott, 71; protests by, 55, 59–60; reject offers of luxury gifts, 216, 221; rewarded by regime, 217, 250; surveillance of, 216
Mons, 14, 15, 17, 23, 24, 28, 118, 226

mosques, attacks on, 219, 226
multi-party rule, 52, 61
Mun Awng, 202–5; *Battle for Peace*, 204; 'Beh lu si, lu si' ('Line of Ogres'), 203; *Peacock Messenger*, 204–5
music, power of, 202–7
musicians, dress controls on, 206
Muslims, 23, 47, 59, 127, 134, 144, 219, 226; conflict with Buddhists, 54, 57; exploitation of, 225–6; in NLD, 225
Mya, General, 62
Myanmar, use of term, 5, 6, 70, 78
Myanmar Christian Council, 222, 223
Myanmar Maternal and Child Welfare Association (MMCWA), 205, 247
Myanmar National Democratic Alliance Army, 80
Myanmar TV, 206
Myanmar Women's Entrepreneurial Association (MWEA), 134
Myanmar-ASEAN website, 235
Myat Hla, U, 57, 63
Myawaddy TV, 206
Myint Aung, General, 94
Myo Nyunt, Lt General, 83, 85, 220, 222–3

Nagas, 14, 237
Nai Panna, 118
Naing Aung, Dr, 118
Nandiya, 214–15, 217
Narapatisithu, King, 214
National Coalition Government of the Union of Burma (NCGUB), 70, 160, 244
National Convention, 69, 82–6, 87, 98, 143, 229, 251
National Day, 190
National League for Democracy (NLD), 3, 45, 63, 64, 65, 66, 67, 68, 69, 70, 72, 77, 83, 85, 86, 87, 89, 90, 91, 94, 96, 97, 102, 116, 131, 132, 153, 154, 167, 173, 177, 189, 190, 192, 211, 218, 220–2, 228, 241, 243, 245, 247, 248, 251, 253, 254; calls for Parliament to be convened, 96, 160, 238; conflict with NUP, 68; electoral gains of, 1, 69, 71; imprisonment of members of, 159, 160, 230; leadership suppressed, 82; members forbidden to be ordained as

monks, 220; persecuted by regime, 88, 97; some soldiers vote for, 156; walk-out from National Convention, 87
National Unity Party (NUP), 63, 69, 156; electoral gains of, 69
nationalization, 35; of banks, 32; of health care, 38; of private schools, 34, 106; of shops, 32, 33
nats: associated with number 9, 229; censorship of, 199; cultivation of, 16, 129
Ne Myo, 104, 105, 137–8
Ne Win, General, 24, 27–8, 30, 31–49, 62, 82, 83, 95, 106, 133, 146, 150, 161, 164, 183, 197, 214, 228, 238; announces resignation, 54; gambles on a horse, 45; interest in magic, 40–1; opposition to, 43; orders English not to be used for teaching, 175; seizure of power by, 29
New Light of Myanmar, 90–1, 95, 144, 205
New Mon State Party (NMSP), 47, 62, 78, 98, 118, 235, 246, 255
newspapers, opposition, 246
NGO Forum on Women (Beijing), 243
NGOs, difficulties for, 247–9
non-violent methods of struggle, 3, 57, 78, 251
Nu, student union leader, 19
Nu, U, 23, 26, 27, 29, 34, 47, 61, 79, 238; death of, 81; pledge to make Buddhism state religion, 28
Nwe Nwe, 178
Nyi Nyi, sergeant, 153, 154

obedience, as a habit, 121–3
Office of Strategic Studies (OSS), 157
Ohn Myint, 39
one-party rule, 35, 36, 42, 53, 55, 61, 133
Open Society Institute, Burma Project, 6
Operation Golden Bird, 237
opium, taxation of trade, 47
opposition, legal, concept of, 25
Organization of Students and Youth for National Politics, 64
Ottama, U, 19

Pa'o National Organization, 81
Pa'os, 14, 47

pagodas: building of, 41, 144, 214; jewels stolen from, 218–19; restoration of, 217; Shwedagon, 1, 19, 20, 53, 228 (committee for renovation of, 95; demonstration at, 92–3; restoration of, 217–18; strike committee headquarters at, 164)

Pakistan, relations with regime, 239

Palaungs, 14, 47

Par Par Lay, U, imprisonment of, 87–8

parents, conformity of, 103, 104, 117, 186

Parliamentary Democracy Party (later People's Patriotic Party), 47

parties, formation of, encouraged, 63, 64

People's Assembly (*pyithu hluttaw*), 35

People's Forums, 88–9

People's Volunteer Organization (PVO), 24

Pepsi: boycott of, 91; pulls out of Burma, 244

petroleum, 18

Philippines, 234, 252

Phone Maw, 51; death of, 91

pinni cotton jacket, 190

Po Khin, U, 31, 121–2

poems, 115, 163, 166, 185, 187

polite salutations, decline of, 211–12

political assistance, 245–9

political ideology courses at universities, 180

political literature, printing of, 189

poltergeist, report of, 230

Popa, Mount, 16, 26

population survey conducted by regime, 36–7

porterage, forced, 48, 145, 154, 161, 216, 223

poverty, 175, 242

Premier Oil, 242; encouraged to withdraw from Burma, 240

press-ganging of civilians, 48

Printers' and Publishers' Registration Act, 197

prisons: as life university, 159–73; Coco Island, 33; communication by knocking, 163, 171; confessions of prisoners, 168; deaths in custody, 160; female prisoners, 167–9; food parcels stolen, 162–3; holding capacity of, 160; Insein, 86, 160, 162, 170; maintaining morale in, 162–3; Myingyan, 161; release of prisoners, 172–3; Thayawaddy, 162; use of isolation cells, 161 see also interrogation centres *and* torture

private associations, registration of, 34

pro-democracy movement, 1, 4, 6, 13, 46, 47, 71, 72, 78, 89, 99, 100, 112, 187, 190, 206, 229, 231, 246, 248, 250, 251, 252, 253; support for (from abroad, 232; from India, 237; from military officers, 152; from Thailand, 237; from USA, 232)

prostitution, 168; of children, 169

protective charms, 213; wearing of, 60

public talks (*haw byo bwe*), 209–12

Pyone Cho, U, 31, 128, 129; library run by, 33–4

radio: as source of education, 190–2; foreign-based, 207; jammed by regime, 192; soldiers forbidden to listen to foreign broadcasts, 191

Radio Free Asia (RFA), 190, 246

Rakhines, 127, 226

Ramos, General Fidel, 252

Rangoon, renamed Yangon, 70

Rangoon Institute of Technology, 93; protests at, 51, 91

Rangoon University, 35, 38, 152, 180, 181, 202, 207, 209; anniversary celebrations, 42–3; organization of students, 151; protests at, 42–5, 50–4, 103, 179; riot at, 31 see also student unions

rape, 67, 78, 200, 219, 256; by military, 155; of female students, 51

Readers' Digest, 188

Red Bridge incident, 51

refugees, 246–7

regional colleges, expanded, 179–80

religion, 213–31

Revolutionary Council, 31–5, 122

rice: quotas, farmers' failure to meet, 50, 68, 104; rations reduced, 43; scarcity of, 34 see also black market, in rice

roads, building of, 144, 216, 233

Rohingyas, 47, 127; driven into Bangladesh, 226; in refugee camps, 246

Sabei, Daw, 120
Sai Hti Hsaing, 206
Salai Zal Seng, 39
salaries: of civil servants, 136; of generals, 135; of soldiers, 146, 150; of teachers, 178
San Kyaw Zaw, Daw, hunger strike of, 67
San San, Daw, 243
San Yu, 164
Sanan Kachornprasart, 236
Sanda, Daw, 130, 131
sangha monks' conference, organized by government, 40
Saw, U, 23
Saw Luther, 48
Saw Maung, General, 63, 69, 82
Saw Tu, 36–8
Saya San rebellion, 20, 60
school: fees for, 104, 105; membership of youth organizations in, 101; National Schools, 183; nationalization of, 34; outstanding student competitions in, 102; primary, 175, 221 (non-attendance at, 174; teaching in Mon language, 246); private *see* nationalization, of private schools; tax levy on students, 174; *Ye Nyunt* (Greatest Bravery), 156
Sein, U, 198–201
Sein Lwin, General, 54; removed as president, 57
Sein Mya, U, 79
Sein Win, Dr, 79; escapes to border, 70
selective purchasing laws, in US, 244–5
sex-workers, 147, 168
Shan Human Rights Foundation, 125
Shan Nationalities League for Democracy, electoral gains, 69
Shan State Army (SSA), 47, 125
Shan State Nationalities' People's Liberation Organization (SNPLO), 47
Shans, 14, 22, 24, 27, 28, 29, 58, 125, 226, 247, 255
Shelley, Percy Bysshe, 188
Siazon, Domingo, 234
Si, Bo, (Theh Gon), 115
silence, of soldiers, 148
Singapore, 233
Sitt Nyein Aye, 207–9
slingshot battles, 71, 215

Smith, Martin, 4, 48
smuggling, 137
socialism, disastrous effects of policies, 77
Soe Myint, 1–2
Soe Thein, Colonel, 150–1, 157
Soe Win, Captain, 39
songs: as source of empowerment, 205; 'constructive', 202–3; writing of, 166
South Africa, end of apartheid, 251
South East Asian Peninsular Games, riot at, 42
spirits of the dead, 230–1; worship of, 14
squatters in Rangoon, 27, 28
State Law and Order Restoration Council (SLORC), 62, 63, 65, 66, 67, 70, 81, 82, 83, 84, 86, 87, 90, 95, 98, 108, 122, 123, 132, 133, 144, 145, 150, 152, 156, 171, 188, 198, 217, 220, 223, 226, 227, 229, 233, 234, 246, 250; distanced from BSPP regime, 69; infrastructure projects of, 80; orders digging up Kyandaw cemetery, 230; renamed State Peace and Development Council (SPDC), 94–9; rules by decree, 80; visa ban in USA, 239
State Peace and Development Council (SPDC), 122, 123, 144, 150, 155, 198, 217, 227, 228, 250
status markers, use of, 120
strategic villages, relocation to, 125
strikes, 62, 163, 171; called by students, 59; inside prisons, 160; of dock workers, 55; of students, in 1920, 19–20; spread via radio, 191; strike committees, 56, 108 *see also* hunger strikes
student activism and demonstrations, 2, 3, 25, 31, 33, 38, 42, 45, 46, 50, 51, 54–5, 61, 68, 71, 81, 82, 91–3, 102, 106, 108, 109, 110–11, 112, 125, 128, 132, 134, 135, 152, 167, 169, 173, 179, 181, 182, 183, 184, 190, 215, 225, 227, 236, 245, 251
student unions, 56, 59, 70, 92, 129; destruction of building at Rangoon University, 31, 187, 209; underground, 51
Students' United Front, 25
study groups, formation of, 185

Sukhumbhand Paribatra, 3
Surin Pitsuwan, 234

Tatmadaw, 28, 36, 46, 48, 58, 62, 77, 80, 81, 95, 99, 113, 115, 118, 122, 124, 125, 128, 143, 144, 145, 148, 151, 153, 154, 191, 202, 205, 221, 223, 226, 235, 236, 237, 239, 242, 245, 256; as profit-making corporation, 26; confiscation of villagers' land, 242; defamation of, an offence, 67; origins of, 26–7; recruitment into, 127 (of orphan boys, 156)
taxation, of villagers, 215
teachers, responsible for monitoring students' activities, 45, 181, 187
teak, 18
teashops, as meeting place for students, 186–90
television, 206
temple, as important space in society, 215
Thai Development Research Institute, 238
Thailand, 3, 7, 14, 33, 62, 105, 126, 149, 154, 155, 156, 203, 224, 232, 234, 235; attacks on refugee camps, 236–7; border closed by regime, 236; investment in Burma, 235; refugees in, 235, 246–7; sympathetic to pro-democracy movement, 237
thakin ('master') movement, 19
Thamanya monastery, 220, 221
Than Dai, 105–10, 112
Than Shwe, Senior General, 82, 95
thangyat songs, 165, 207
Thant, U, funeral of, 43–4
theft: of government goods, 138; of military supplies, 146
Thein San, 43
Thet Win Aung, imprisonment of, 93
Thibaw, King, 153
Thirty Comrades, 21, 29, 30, 42, 47, 52, 61, 66, 98, 145
thoukdan kyan, word no longer used, 222–3
Three National Causes, 198
Time magazine, 164, 170, 185, 192
tin, 18
Tin Hla, Brigadier General, 153
Tin Maung Oo, 44
Tin Oo, Lt General, 45, 227

Tin Oo, U, 61, 63, 64, 65, 79, 86, 88, 89, 90, 251; arrest of, 66; disqualified from running in elections, 67; removed from NLD central executive, 86
Tin Tin Nyo, 81
Tint Moe, 116–17
Tint Swe, Dr, 68
Tint Way, Raymond, 122
Tint Zaw, U, 35
torture, 5, 42, 78, 157, 159, 160–1, 162–3, 164, 169, 250, 256
Total company, 242
tourism, 190, 207, 248; call for boycott of Burma, 245; promotion of, 80
trade unions, independent, outlawed, 34
trade with foreign countries, illegal, 137
tuberculosis, 238
Tun Kyi, General, 94
Tun Shein, U, 122
Tun Way, 163–6

unemployment, 242
UNICEF report, *Children and Women in Myanmar*, 174
Union (*Pyidaungsu*) party, 28
Union Day, celebration of, 106
Union Solidarity and Development Association (USDA), 95, 101, 131, 134, 135, 143, 153, 247; membership of, 95
United Kingdom (UK), contact with Daw Aung San Suu Kyi, 240
United Nationalities League for Democracy (UNLD), 98, 99
United Nations (UN), 50, 191, 233, 245, 247
UN High Commission for Refugees, 236
UN Development Programme, household survey, 247
United States Committee for Refugees, 246
United States Information Service (USIS), 192, 207
United States of America (USA): backing for Daw Aung San Suu Kyi, 232; broadcasting from, 190; contact with Daw Aung San Suu Kyi, 240; lawsuits against Unocal, 242; stance against military regime, 239; support for Kuomintang, 24
United Wa State Army, 80, 85, 98, 238

Universal Declaration of Human Rights, 243
universities, 179–83; closure of, 43, 44, 50, 52, 53, 81, 93, 101, 182; like fortresses, 182; perceived as useless, 180; re-opened, 81, 93, 182
Unocal company, 239, 242

videotape, films produced on, 199
Vigorous Burmese Student Warriors, 3
villagers, neutrality of, 25
Visit Myanmar Year, 2455
Voice of America (VOA), 151, 189, 190, 191
vote-rigging in elections, 36–7

Was, 14, 46, 85, 127, 255
water: access to, 191; shortages of, 99
wealth, distribution of, 32
welfare state, 24, 25
western dress, 211; permitted on TV, 206
'white' areas, 38
Win Aung, U, 4
Win Htein, U, 97
Win Tin, U, 97

Wisara, U, 19
women, participation in political activities, 112
World Bank, 242, 248; aid to Burma, 241
writers, freedoms of, 210

Yan Naing, Bo, 61
Yadana pipeline, 2452
Ye Min, 51–2, 55
Ye Naing Win, Dr, 114
Ye Naing, 134–5
Yetagun pipeline, 242
Young Men's Buddhist Association (YMBA), 18
Young Men's Christian Association (YMCA), 18, 59

Zagana (comedian), 58
Zaw Gyi (wizard), 199
Zaw Htun, 124
Zaw Lwin, 115–16
Zaw Win Htut, '*Maha*', 206
Zaw Win Naing, Captain, 205
Zaw Zaw Oo, 82
Zawtipala, U, 221–2

Politics in Contemporary Asia Series

Zed Books has major lists in the fields of Economics and Development Studies, the Environment, Gender, Cultural Studies and Politics. We also publish Area Studies, including our Politics in Contemporary Asia Studies. Titles in print include:

S. M. Ali, *The Fearful State: Power, People and Internal War in South Asia* (1993)

Chris Beyrer, *War in the Blood: Sex, Politics and AIDS in Southeast Asia* (1998)

Levon Chorbajian, Patrick Donabedian and Claude Mutafian, *The Caucasian Knot: The History and Politics of Nagorno-Karabagh* (1994)

Pierre Donnet, *Tibet: Survival in Question* (1998)

Christina Fink, *Living in Silence: Burma under Military Rule* (2001)

Suzanne Goldenberg, *Pride of Small Nations: The Caucasus and Post-Soviet Disorder* (1994)

Jim Goodno, *The Philippines: Land of Broken Promises*

John Hilley, *Mahathirism, Hegemony and the New Opposition in Malaysia* (2001)

Peter Marsden, *The Taliban: War, Religion and the New Order in Afghanistan* (1998)

Ahmed Rashid, *The Resurgence of Central Asia: Islam or Nationalism?* (1994)

W. Courtland Robinson, *Terms of Refuge: The Indochinese Exodus and the International Response* (1999)

Martin Smith, *Insurgency and the Politics of Ethnicity* (revised and updated edition, 1999)

John Taylor, *East Timor: The Price of Freedom* (1999)

For full details of these and Zed's other titles, as well as our subject catalogues, please write to: The Marketing Department, Zed Books, 7 Cynthia Street, London N1 9JF, UK or e-mail: sales@zedbooks.demon.co.uk

Visit our website at: http://www.zedbooks.demon.co.uk